ACTING
FOR REAL

Drama Therapy
Process, Technique,
and Performance

Renée Emunah

Brunner/Mazel Publishers • New York

Library of Congress Cataloging-in-Publication Data

Emunah, Renée.
  Acting for real : drama therapy process, technique, and
performance / Renée Emunah.
      p.   cm.
  Includes bibliographical references and index.
  ISBN 0-87630-730-6 :
  1. Psychodrama.   I. Title.
RC489.P7E48   1994
616.89'1523—dc20   93-44042
                                                             CIP

Copyright © 1994 by Renée Emunah

Published by
BRUNNER/MAZEL, INC.
19 Union Square West
New York, New York 10003

Manufactured in the United States of America

10 9 8 7 6 5 4 3 2 1

To my clients, with whom and for whom this work developed,
and especially to those whose courageous stories lace these pages—
for all they taught me
about possibility

Contents

PART II: TECHNIQUES

PART III: PERFORMANCE
**The Story of Seven People and the Play They Created
About Their Lives**

Foreword

by Adam Blatner, M.D.

Acting for Real offers the first integrated and systematized approach to drama therapy, a field that unites theatre and psychotherapy. The author is one of the foremost pioneers in this dimension of the creative and expressive arts therapies and the director of one of the first graduate training programs for registered practitioners of drama therapy. The clinical depth of her discussion makes this book valuable to experienced practitioners as well as students.

Emunah has clearly addressed the way psychodrama interfaces with drama therapy, and since I am a psychodramatist as well as a child and adult psychiatrist, I appreciate this inclusive attitude. She shows how and why psychodrama may be conceptually and clinically integrated with drama therapy and then goes on to demonstrate some ways drama therapy complements psychodrama. Three examples: (1) Many patients are not ready to directly address the emotionally loaded issues in their real lives, and playing out related themes in imaginary roles allows for a degree of emotional distance. (2) The graded series of exercises extends the "warm-up" through many sessions and at the same time strengthens patients' egos, which helps prepare them for deeper, more direct insight-oriented work (i.e., psychodrama). (3) The working-through of the insight and catharsis achieved in a psychodrama can be facilitated by drama therapy techniques such as performance or ritual. Furthermore, the author presents the clinical rationale for using a wide range of techniques, most of which she invented and which have not been described elsewhere.

Through drama therapy, people can be helped to recapture the freshness of their early childhood's excitement and vitality, dimensions of the personality that tend to become stifled in the ordinary course of development. Indeed, many forms of psychopathology may be understood in part as representing disorders of excitement and spontaneity, problems with re-connecting with the innate flow of images, impulses, feelings, and activity that characterize the innocent exuberance of young children. This primal vitality is the equivalent of what Freud was alluding to with his concept of "primary narcissism," but the term is misleading because healthy children are not essentially aggrandizing the self in their enthusiasm, but rather the self becomes naturally strengthened in the course of feeling and being validated for enjoyments, sadnesses, angers, preferences, fears, and other experiences.

Drama re-engages these more primal modes of interacting via physical action and direct interaction with others, which contrasts with the more artificial and restrained context of traditional verbal therapy in which the patient narrates to a therapist. In addition to insight, though, participants in drama therapy, psychodrama, or indeed any of the arts therapies develop a deeper connection between the socially mediating "ego" and the more profound sources emanating from the creative unconscious, or, to be even more direct, the "soul."

Drama therapy offers an intensification of the psychotherapeutic process by introducing a wider range of methods for accessing images and affects, thus contributing to the growing need for more cost-effective types of psychiatric treatment. It can be applied in the contexts of day treatment centers, inpatient psychiatric hospital units, psychosocial rehabilitation programs, self-help groups, and so on. The author reveals a good deal of sophistication in considering the underlying psychological processes in her clients, which suggests that drama therapy should be recognized as a type of psychodynamic therapy. As such it may be integrated with other forms of individual, couple, family, and group therapies. Drama therapy can also be applied as an adjunct along with the other arts, occupational, and recreational therapies. For example, in substance abuse programs, drama therapy can help participants to discover nonintoxicating activities for experiencing pleasure and community.

Beyond the treatment of psychiatric problems, drama therapy may be applied in modified form in such settings as senior citizens' centers, for promoting vitality and the production of a kind of oral history; religious retreats, for heightening the relevance of social and spiritual issues; the schools, for promoting involvement and a more active type of learning; professional training or continuing education programs, for teaching creativity, communication, and empathy; and community education for life enhancement. Therefore, the ideas in this book will be of significant benefit not only to drama therapists, psychodramatists, creative arts therapists and other types of psychotherapists, but also to group leaders in nonclinical contexts.

In summary, *Acting for Real* delivers what its title suggests: There is great untapped wealth in the psyche, and drama offers a particularly potent and multimodal vehicle for accessing these inner resources. Patients' role repertoires are expanded in depth as well as breadth, because drama therapy cultivates spontaneity and the capacity for self-reflection. Furthermore, in helping patients to dare to relinquish those defensive patterns that have become counterproductive, it is necessary to put them in touch with a more reliable source of self-esteem, and the most natural source is the rich flow of vitality, imagination, and spontaneity which, if properly appreciated, constitutes a vibrant core of being.

Acknowledgments

This book was developed, written, and revised over a long period of time; many people played an important role—directly or indirectly—in some aspect of that journey.

In the field of drama therapy, two colleagues deserve special acknowledgment: David Read Johnson—for his exemplary work and for his thorough reading of the manuscript and insightful suggestions, and Alida Gersie—for her astute feedback and loving encouragement.

There are several other practitioner/scholars in the field whose works have also been engaging and inspiring, most notably Robert Landy, Sue Jennings, and Eleanor Irwin. In the related field of drama-in-education, the work of Richard Courtney has been highly elucidative. Psychologist Brian Bates' study of acting has been another important influence; I am also grateful for Dr. Bates' review of the manuscript and for our thought-provoking discussions.

I am indebted to Adam Blatner for encouraging me to write this book and for offering detailed comments on the manuscript. Dr. Blatner's first book had been a source of inspiration to me long before I met him in person. Our contact over the past years has been deeply enriching.

My heartfelt appreciation is extended to: Natalie Gilman, Senior Editor at Brunner/Mazel, for her efforts and enthusiasm throughout this project; Lonny Shavelson for his artfulness in actualizing the image I envisioned for the book cover; Idabelle Fosse for modeling for the cover photo; and Paul Bishop for his generous assistance.

Three former graduate students offered invaluable help: Deborah Pearl Styles and Stacey Daraio served at various stages as research assistants, and Douglas and Deborah Styles worked on the index. Current student Shefali Kumar provided some excellent last-minute assistance. Working with each one of them was a pleasure.

I also owe thanks to: Allee Blatner, William McKelvie, Verona Fonté, Stuart Kandell, Clement von Kirschenheim, Tina Stromsted, Mike Lafferty, Dean Elias, Susana Coto McKenna, John Argue, and Stuart Miller.

A number of psychiatrists, psychotherapists, administrators, and supervisors directly influenced or supported my early clinical work in the field. Ann

Nathan at Langley Porter Psychiatric Institute was a wonderful model for working with acting-out adolescents. Anne Petty and Craig Smith at Gladman Memorial Hospital Day Treatment trusted my work and their own intuition enough to be the first administrators in the Bay Area to support and integrate a drama therapy program—long before the field officially existed. Karl Knobler and Gil Lanese, subsequent directors, helped drama therapy become an even more integral part of the clinical treatment at that facility, where I worked for 14 years. Regina Scott at Pacific Medical Center's residential "lodges" was similarly facilitative; her support and our eventual friendship are deeply appreciated.

The members of my former theatre company, *Beyond Analysis,* deepened my belief in the powerful connection between theatre and healing, and will always be remembered with fondness and respect.

My mother, visual artist Helene Aylon, deserves acknowledgment not only for her careful reading of parts of the manuscript and her consistent encouragement, but more importantly for fostering from the start my own creativity as well as an aesthetic sensibility that to this day we share. I also wish to acknowledge my father—for the treasures he gave me before his untimely death; my grandmother—for her abundant nurturance; and my brother—for his steadfast brotherliness and for keeping me laughing.

My gratitude—multilayered and complex—is extended to my former partner, Christian Marouby, for sharing my life throughout most of the years in which the ideas for this book formed; the profound love and support in that relationship were the backstage to the development of my career as a drama therapist.

I am thankful to my colleagues at the California Institute of Integral Studies, especially George Kitahara Kich and Eva Leveton for their encouragement with this book and their highly valued contributions to our program. Dr. Kich and I also worked together at Westside Lodge; our long-term collaboration and friendship are irreplaceable. I am also very appreciative of the support of C.I.I.S. president, Robert McDermott; former academic dean, Jurgen Kremer; and associate provost, Paul Schwartz.

My students at the Drama Therapy Program at the California Institute of Integral Studies (and formerly at Antioch University, where the program began) always illuminate my work. Witnessing the intelligence, creativity, compassion, and enthusiasm of so many of the students and alumni of this program makes teaching a joy; this new generation of drama therapists perenially revitalizes my hope for the field.

Prologue

"I can play scenes in drama better than I can play scenes in my life," says a client of mine. I can understand both his satisfaction and his concern; it is true that the stage offers the freedom to surpass our usual limitations. But I know that my client's dramatic performances signify possibilities for real life. And sure enough, six months later, he says to me: "The way I'm acting in my life now is catching up with the way I act in drama."

One usually thinks of drama as the mirror to life, rather than the reverse. Yet clients in drama therapy often maintain that by "pretending to be in drama" they are able to do something in real life that was previously too difficult or frightening. For it is in the context of drama that they experienced, in many cases for the first time in their lives, what had seemed beyond reach in actuality. The experience is not so much one of fantasy as one of embodying an untapped part of themselves. On some level they sense, rightfully, that the character improvised in the scene has emerged from their own being. The character is contained within the self and the self *encompasses* the character; the role is now a part of themselves which can be accessed in real life.

In life, we are subject to patterns of behavior, to habitual response; we fall prey to restricted self-perceptions and the influence of others' limited expectations of us. In the world of make-believe, these constrictions do not apply. We have the freedom and the permission to do what seems to be so difficult to achieve in life—to alter behavioral and role patterns. Under the guise of play and pretend, we can—for once—act in new ways. The bit of distance from real life afforded by drama enables us to gain perspective on our real-life roles and patterns and actions, and to experiment actively with alternatives. *Drama liberates us from confinement,* be it socially or psychologically induced. The dramatic moment is one of emancipation.

Life is finite, and there are only so many experiences we can have. Time and circumstance restrict the number of roles we will play, situations we will encounter, fantasies and hopes we will realize. In dramatizations, however, as in dreams, the possibilities are infinite. Both dramatizations and dreams offer us the opportunity to have new experiences. In a 10-minute dream we can have the experience of being prisoner or princess, we can express endless rage or love toward someone in our lives, we can create a magnificent piece of music or writing—all of which are as vivid and intense as real-life experience. (In fact, when we wake up, we are often startled that "all this didn't really happen, it was *only* a dream.") Likewise, during a dramatization, our senses, minds, and bodies are involved in such a way that, for the moment, the experience is real. Dreams and drama—both of which draw upon our capacity to imagine and visualize—are two primary phenomena wherein we experience something *as though it were taking place,* whereas in fact it is not. We get the benefit of the experience, while being exempt from consequence. Our experiences are magnified, experiences that can function to broaden our perspective on life and expand who we are as human beings.

The expansion of who we are occurs because dreams (when vivid) and dramatizations (when engaged in with seriousness and integrity) become part of our life experience; like life experience, they hold the power to affect us as people. Joseph Chaikin, the well-known theatre director, phrased it this way: "In former times acting simply meant putting on a disguise. When you took off the disguise, there was the old face under it. Now it's clear that the wearing of the disguise changes the person. As he takes the disguise off, his face is changed from having worn it. The stage performance informs the life performance and is informed by it" (1984, p. 6).

The dramas we live on stage and the dramas we live during our sleep both reflect and affect our lives. There is a kind of dreaming called lucid dreaming, in which one realizes one is dreaming and helps shape the dream, while remaining fully asleep. Stephen LaBerge of Stanford University's Sleep Research Center writes in his book *Lucid Dreaming* (1985) about laboratory evidence indicating that "what happens in the inner world of dreams—and lucid dreams especially—can produce physical effects on the dreamer's brain no less real than those produced by corresponding events happening in the external world. The results of the experiments...show that the impact of certain dream behaviors on brain and body can be fully equivalent to the impact produced by corresponding actual behaviors. What we do in dreams (or leave undone) can at times affect us as profoundly as what we do (or do not do) in our waking lives" (p. 98).

The same is true of drama. There is a powerful relationship between the stage act and the life act. *Drama behaviors* also impact on brain and body. The behaviors, roles, and emotions portrayed in drama become part of one's repertoire, a repertoire that can be drawn upon in life situations. It is difficult, and rare, to respond in a new way to an old situation in life. It is not as difficult to respond in a new way to the same situation in a dramatic scene. The experience of the new response in the scene facilitates such a response in real life. Dramatic options, often discovered in a moment of spontaneity, can become life options. Dreams are "dramas reflecting our psychological state and the process of change taking place in it," writes psychologist Ernest Rossi (1985). I believe that Rossi's description of dreams as "a laboratory for experimenting with change in our psychic life" (p. 142) applies to drama as well. Of course dreams are primarily the creations of the unconscious and dramas are primarily of the conscious. Dream creations are unrestricted; no stage set is too elaborate or cumbersome. Although dramas are more practically restrictive, the fact that the performance takes place in a waking conscious state leads it to be more easily assimilated into real life. The boundary between drama and real life is a thin one; the dramatic experience is *nearly* a real-life experience. Of all the arts, drama is the closest to daily interaction.

Drama is a vehicle not only for experiencing and integrating new aspects of ourselves, but also for expressing suppressed *shadow* aspects of ourselves. Facets of our personalities that have been concealed, from others, and often from ourselves, can be unleashed via the dramatic role. The role enables previously unacknowledged or untolerated parts to be given voice, and at the same time to be contained within the safe arena of the dramatic act.

In the process of expressing unlived and unacknowledged parts of ourselves, we discover our shared humanity. Whether we are playing fictitious characters or playing ourselves, whether we are acting or witnessing the act of others, drama invokes our capacity to empathize and identify with others. Professional actors are intimately familiar with this capacity: in interviews with psychologist Brian Bates (1987), Marlon Brando states that each of us contains the seeds of all the characters we will ever play; Sybil Thorndike says that "when you're an actor. . . . you're a person with all the other persons inside you" (ibid, p. 80); Liv Ullmann declares that "if we fail to know others, we fail to know ourselves" (ibid, p. 114). The acting process promotes a consciousness that everything outside of us is in fact within our realm of understanding and possibility—a consciousness that intimates a deeper level of compassion, spirituality, and connectedness.

Given the complexity and challenge of living, we cannot afford to exist without a highly developed sense of empathy and perspective. We need to understand not only ourselves but the motivations, drives, and feelings of the other players in our lives—in order to improve our interactions, relationships, and social structures. I know of no better way to understand the experience of another than by putting myself "in his or her shoes." Becoming another person through dramatic enactment is much more powerful and effective than imagining in my mind that person's situation. *Drama, by its very nature, induces empathy and perspective.*

Perspective also has to do with time. Painful and trying periods are eased when one has a "larger perspective." Sometimes it is only through conceiving the future and remembering the past that we can bear the present. The future holds the possibility of change; we are momentarily relieved by the knowledge that later we will not be stuck in the same place. The past helps us comprehend the present, and enables us to draw from a myriad of experiences that have challenged and enriched us. If we view the present from the vantage of the future, our perception or appreciation of our current situation is often altered or heightened. In the dramatic mode, time is easily manipulated. We can be ourselves in past, present, or future tense. A person, for example, may step outside of her current predicament by enacting a scene that takes place five years from now. From this standpoint, she may be directed to reminisce about her experience of "five years ago."

While acting, we are both participant and observer; we are emotionally engaged in the reality that is being portrayed, and at the same time we are witness to what is taking place. The degree of identification and distancing, of subjectivity and objectivity, varies according to scene and individual, but both factors are always at play. Even as we are "caught up" in the action, we are detached enough to respond reflectively.

A balance is needed in our lives between underdistancing (overly identifying to the point of mergence with others or becoming overwhelmed with feeling we cannot control) and overdistancing (maintaining overly rigid boundaries or losing touch with our emotions). Robert Landy, in *Drama Therapy: Concepts and Practices* (1986), views the notion of distancing developed by social psychologist Thomas Scheff (1981) as useful for drama therapists. Scheff's notion is based on both psychoanalytical and theatrical models. Landy describes what Scheff calls "aesthetic distance" as being the achievement of effective drama therapy: "At aesthetic distance one retains a piece of the overdistanced, cognitive observer and a piece of the under-distanced, affective actor. When the two parts occur simultaneously, a psychic tension arises which is released through catharsis . . ." (p. 100).

To be and to watch ourselves at once, to live a new reality and the existing one at once, to relinquish and penetrate ourselves at once . . . such are some of the paradoxes that make this form of art and therapy so powerful. My clients in psychiatric treatment centers have frequently referred to the drama therapy group as "the place where we *get out of ourselves*." This expression implies an expansion of role and behavioral responses; it suggests getting past limitations. But "getting out of ourselves" also implies discovering about ourselves. "Paradoxically, the more one lets go of oneself, the more one becomes oneself," writes Michael Barnett (1973). "By trying to preserve oneself, one limits oneself, for I cannot preserve myself but only an image of myself—which is bound to be far less than what I am" (p. 31). If drama is viewed by some people as an escape, it is at least an escape that leads to greater self-awareness. Interestingly, the second most common description clients have for the drama therapy group is: "the place where we really *get into ourselves*."

The use of drama as therapy fosters liberation, expansion and perspective. Drama therapy invites us to uncover and integrate dormant aspects of ourselves, to stretch our conception of who we are, and to experience our intrinsic connection with others.

The process begins with the dramatic mode. But eventually the curtain lifts, and we find that what was revealed under the protective auspices of theatre no longer needs a stage.

Introduction

My first experience with drama therapy occurred at a state mental hospital in 1972. Drama therapy did not yet exist as a field in this country (and would not for another seven years), and it was only several years later that I even heard the term used officially—when I found that training in "dramatherapy" was offered in England, where I eventually studied. But it was at that state hospital, in the context of a university work-study position, that I discovered for myself the transformative power of drama. I was 19 years old.

Intrigued by the colorful, inviting posters I hung throughout hospital corridors to "sell" the drama workshop, chronic, depressed, lethargic, shock-treated patients meandered into the auditorium where the sessions were held. And within one hour, liberated from their role of patient via the dramatic mode, they exhibited facets of themselves that no one in the hospital had ever witnessed. Patients considered to be severely withdrawn interacted enthusiastically with others; those who "normally" manifested minimal emotional affect expressed themselves with gusto. Patients viewed as unmotivated and irresponsible came faithfully to every session.

It was at once astounding and not at all surprising. Social psychologists and theatre directors had had similar experiences when using theatre with special populations. In 1961, social psychologist Erving Goffman wrote: " In prisons and mental hospitals where some inmates may constantly sustain a heroic edifice of withdrawal, uncooperativeness, insolence and combativeness, the same inmates may be quite ready to engage in theatricals in which they enact excellent portraits of civil, sane, and compliant characters. But this very remarkable turnabout is understandable too. Since the staged circumstances of the portrayed characters are not the inmate's real ones, he has no need to exhibit distance from them" (p. 132). In 1968, renowned theatre director Peter Brook, leading a drama workshop at an asylum, wrote: "Two hours after any session begins all the relationships between the people present are slightly modified, because of the experience in which they have been plunged together. As a result, something is more animated, something flows more freely, some embryonic contacts are being made between previously sealed-off souls. When they leave the room, they are not quite the same as when they entered" (p. 134).

I knew that the sessions I was conducting at the state hospital were not simply theatre workshops, because a potent healing force, impossible to ignore or to classify only as "side benefits," ignited the stage. I knew that it was different from psychodrama, because there was no reenactment of individual patients' real-life issues. On some level, I knew, too, that this would be the work I would be doing for a long time to come. But there were countless questions to which I had no answers. I wondered about the striking behavioral changes: Would they become integrated with or remain discrepant to the person's off-stage self? Given such dramatic changes in a short time period, often within a single session, what stages of progression would be involved in long-term treatment? Which theatrical processes and techniques would have the most therapeutic potential? What kinds of interventions would be possible within the dramatic mode that would deepen the therapeutic experience?

The lack of models or mentors, which was the experience of those individuals practicing drama therapy prior to the founding of the National Association for Drama Therapy in 1979, has certain advantages. One is forced to find answers to one's own questions, capitalize on intuition, "reflect-in-action" (Donald Schön's [1983] term for the conscious and constant reflection on one's intuitive decisions and judgments), invent techniques and processes uniquely suited to the needs of particular clients, extract learning from every relevant experience, and draw from related disciplines.

This book explores some of the questions and answers that have grown out of my years of practice as a drama therapist. The motivation for writing the book stems from a desire to: 1) provide an integrative framework for the practice of drama therapy, bringing coherence to the field both in terms of concepts and techniques; 2) present the skills that are fundamental to the practice of drama therapy, regardless of one's orientation or specialization within the field; 3) introduce a comprehensive compilation of drama therapy techniques in conjunction with organizing principles and therapeutic implications so that techniques are not fragmented, but rather used with clinical artistry and integrity; 4) articulate the developmental process of long-term drama therapy as well as the process of a single session, and offer a view of the drama therapy session as a cohesive "piece of work," providing a therapeutic aesthetic; 5) describe how clinical interventions are made in the dramatic mode; 6) illustrate via case examples the incredible power and beauty of this modality.

Acting for Real begins, in Chapter 1, with an exploration of the primary, multidisciplinary sources that are at the roots of drama therapy, followed by a presentation of an integrative theoretical framework for drama therapy and an outline of central therapeutic goals. Conceptual sources have more meaning when one can understand their relationship and application to the practice of drama therapy. In Chapter 2, the primary conceptual sources—dramatic play, theatre, role theory, psychodrama, and dramatic ritual—are linked to five distinct phases in drama therapy, and the progression of treatment in long-term drama therapy is delineated. The case stories in Chapter 3 elucidate these stages, demonstrating the way in which the process of drama therapy affects people's lives. Following this overview of the process of drama therapy, Chapters 4 and 5 break down the process into its discernible parts: Chapter 4 analyzes the development of the drama therapy session and Chapter 5 analyzes the development of the drama therapy scene.

Once one has a grasp of the process of drama therapy, one can apply the techniques. Part Two of *Acting for Real* is comprised of a systematized description of drama therapy techniques. Most of the techniques are drawn from improvisational theatre, but they are adapted and revised to serve therapeutic purposes. Many are original; I devised them out of necessity as I worked with clients. The techniques are based in clinical work, integrated with therapeutic considerations, and categorized in accordance with therapeutic objectives as well as phases within the session. Clinical examples are interwoven throughout all sections of Part I and Part II, in an attempt to concretize and vivify drama therapy process and techniques.

Although drama therapy is typically process- rather than product-oriented, the culmination of a drama therapy series in a public performance is one component of drama therapy. Part Three of *Acting for Real* examines performance-oriented drama therapy by relating the story of a group of seven clients and the play they created about their lives.

Process, techniques, and performance—indeed, drama therapy itself—are not nearly as significant as the quality of the interaction between therapist and client. In the final analysis, the effectiveness of models and modalities, of approaches and tools, hinges on the personal characteristics of the practitioner who applies them. I agree with Carl Rogers (1951, 1961), founder of client-centered therapy and the leading figure in applying humanistic psychology to the counseling situation, that the most important aspects of treatment are not the therapist's knowledge of theory and techniques, but rather his or her capacity for genuineness, acceptance and caring, and deep understanding of each unique client.

Part I

PROCESS

1

SOURCES

CONCEPTUAL BASES IN DRAMA THERAPY

Drama therapy is the intentional and systematic use of drama/theatre processes to achieve psychological growth and change. The tools are derived from theatre, the goals are rooted in psychotherapy. Although drama therapy can be practiced within the theoretical framework of almost any existing school of psychotherapy, it also has its own unique heritage; its conceptual roots can be traced to various multidisciplinary sources, the most obvious of which is theatre. The following section includes a discussion of five conceptual sources that in my view have the most fundamental relationship to drama therapy, and that are most germane to my own practice. Work by prominent drama therapists that is clearly associated with these sources is integrated into the discussion. The second section of this chapter examines the psychotherapeutic dimension of drama therapy and presents an integrative theoretical framework for the practice of drama therapy. The chapter's final section delineates the primary therapeutic goals in drama therapy.

Aside from *theatre,* the most obvious and influential conceptual source is drama therapy's immediate predecessor, *psychodrama.* A third source, more primary than theatre in terms of human development, is *dramatic play;* a fourth source, more primary than both theatre and psychodrama in terms of the development of civilization, is *dramatic ritual.* The fifth source, *role play,* takes a central position: The experimentation with and embodiment of roles is at the core of drama therapy. These five conceptual sources will be linked, in Chapter 2, to five distinct phases in drama therapy treatment. The sources are presented in this chapter in the chronological order of the treatment phases to which they are linked, beginning with dramatic play and ending with dramatic ritual.

Dramatic Play

"To play it out is the most natural self-healing measure childhood affords," writes psychoanalyst Erik Erikson (1950, p. 222). Children use drama as therapy spontaneously, with no outside direction or preimposed structure. Dramatic play is the child's method of: symbolically expressing and resolving internal conflict; assimilating reality; achieving a sense of mastery and control; releasing pent-up emotions; learning to control potentially destructive impulses through fantasy; expressing unaccepted parts of the self; exploring problems and discovering solutions; practicing for real-life events; expressing hopes and wishes; experimenting with new roles and situations; and developing a sense of identity (Courtney, 1968). These functions, fundamental to the lives of children, are also relevant to people of all ages. The field of drama therapy is, in many respects, simply the outcome of an examination of what Erikson refers to as the "autotherapeutic nature" of the dramatic play of children.

Dramatic play is a primary component of general play, distinguished by its basis in impersonation and identification (Courtney, 1968) and projection (Landy, 1986). Dramatic play includes such processes as puppetry, storytelling, improvisation, and role taking. The media of children's play (e.g., dolls, puppets, toys) are for the most part inherently dramatic (Landy, 1986). Play therapy and drama therapy are closely connected, although in drama therapy the focus is specifically on *dramatic* play. The proliferation of the use of play in child therapy occurred at approximately the same time that pioneers of child drama (Slade, 1954; Way, 1967; Ward, 1957) stressed the significance of the process of drama in child development, and began incorporating drama in children's education.

Over many years, drama educator and specialist Richard Courtney (1964, 1967, 1968) has conducted exhaustive multidisciplinary research into the nature of drama. He found dramatic play to be a central process in thinking, learning, and healing—indeed, in all dimensions of living. Drawing on research in psychoanalysis, Courtney describes dramatic play as a stage in ego development that follows acting-out behavior and eventually leads to sublimation. In his seminal book, *Play, Drama, and Thought* (1968), he states that "dramatic play has a central position, relating the unconscious to the intellect. . . it is the link between instinctual gratification and mature thought" (pp. 92–93).

The distinction between acting out and acting is a critical one, and has been clearly articulated by psychodramatist and psychiatrist Adam Blatner in his book, *Acting In* (1988a): "Acting out is a psychological defense mechanism by which the individual discharges his internal impulses through symbolic or actual enactment. . . Since the rationale for this mechanism occurs largely outside of consciousness, the individual experiences no sense of mastery or growth or self-understanding through his behavior. If the drive toward action could be channeled, the person might be able to make better use of his feelings" (p. 1). In drama therapy, the experience of *acting* diminishes the need (of the client of any age) to *act out.*

Robert Landy (1986), a drama therapy educator, practitioner, and re-searcher, refers to dramatic play as a "dialectic between the actual, everyday reality and the imaginative one...(In play) the former context is explored through the latter" (p. 63). A core concept in drama therapy is this exploration of real life via the *fictional mode* of drama. Acting or playing out a situation, *as if* this situation were real, while at the same time knowing it is in fact *make-believe,* is the primary mode of the dramatic play of children as well as of the process of drama therapy. A dual level of consciousness, which humans are capable of at a remarkably early age, is at place; the player exists simul-taneously in the imaginary realm and the objective realm.

When I watch children absorbed in dramatic play, I marvel not only at their dual level of consciousness, at all that is communicated and revealed, and at the growth and healing that takes place, but also at the delight and pleasure the players indisputably experience. Likewise, the incorporation of dramatic play in therapy results in a process that is most often pleasurable, at the same time that it is personally beneficial. This is a radical departure from the association many clients have to psychotherapy as useful but agonizing! Creating a positive association to therapy by providing a process that is enjoyable augments motivation and commitment, as well as an open-ness to engage, later in treatment, in more painful self-examination.

In *The Art of Play,* Adam and Allee Blatner (1988) attribute the pleasure in dramatic play to the dual level of consciousness described above. "The mind seems to experience a kind of pleasure in being able to encompass (the) seemingly irreconcilable opposites (the real and the not real); it's a form of mental juggling" (p. 29). The Blatners add that the experience inherent in play of overcoming apparent paradox may be an expression of Freud's pleasure principle. Noting that adults have as much of a capacity and need as children do for the kind of pleasure that dramatic play provides, the Blatners prescribe play for people of all ages and offer an excellent guide for reclaiming the imagination and spontaneity of childhood.

The work of David Read Johnson (1981, 1982a, b, 1986, 1991), one of the most prolific researchers in the field of drama therapy, is clearly linked to dramatic play. The element of spontaneity, fundamental to dramatic play, is perhaps for Johnson the most critical component of drama therapy. Working from a developmental model and utilizing improvisational processes, Johnson creates a "free play" environment in which the clients' feelings and thoughts are reflected in the improvised roles. Analysis of degree of spontaneity, style of improvisational role play, and maintenance of boundaries exhibited by clients in their play are some of the elements he employs in diagnosis (which is an important part of his research and practice). He has developed a drama process called *transformations,* in which "roles and scenes are constantly transformed and reshaped according to the clients' ongoing stream of con-sciousness and internal imagery" (Johnson, 1991, p. 11), and which parallels much of the fluid and metamorphic nature of the dramatic play of young children.

The work of Eleanor Irwin (1975, 1981, 1983), another prominent drama therapist, is also very much influenced by dramatic play, although her model is psychoanalytic rather than developmental. Drawing from play therapy as exemplified by Anna Freud (1928), Melanie Klein (1932), and Margaret Lowenfeld (1935), Irwin emphasizes projective devices such as puppetry, storytelling, and sandplay in the diagnosis and treatment of clients. In many respects her approach is closer to the distancing model of Robert Landy than to the more direct improvisational approach of David Johnson. The dramatic play occurring in Johnson's sessions is typically *personal play,* whereas Irwin and Landy emphasize *projected play.* The terms personal and projected play were developed by Peter Slade (1954), a pioneer in the fields of child drama and educational theatre. Slade defines personal play as a physically active utilization of one's own self/body, in the taking on of roles. Projected play, on the other hand, involves projecting an imagined dramatic situation outwards onto objects (e.g., dolls, puppets). Irwin and Landy are also more often in the role of an observer of the client's play than Johnson, who is generally immersed in the play with the client. Landy's model of distancing in drama therapy is helpful in ascertaining the kind of dramatic play that is most ap-propriate in a given therapeutic situation. Projective play typically provides a greater degree of distance, which clients who lack discernible boundaries and emotional control or who are dealing with an issue that is highly threatening often require. Personal play, on the other hand, provides an environment of greater freedom and expressiveness.

The incorporation and influence of dramatic play, particularly personal play, is most clearly evident in my own work during the early stages of a drama therapy treatment series, which I identify in the next chapter as Phase One. At the beginning of a drama therapy process, I emphasize the establishment of a creative, playful environment, wherein the sense of freedom and pos-sibility that children experience when they play is reconstituted. Pressure to perform is avoided; spontaneity and interaction are encouraged.

Perhaps all therapists are drawn to approaches that correspond to that which was most healing in their own lives, or that relate to their own person-ality. From ages seven to 15 I had a best friend, Sarah, with whom I played regularly. While many children during these latency and early adolescent years stop engaging in dramatic play and begin instead to play competitive games with rules, our play continued to be dominated by drama and dance. (According to Piaget [1962], *symbolic play,* often in the form of dramatic play, shifts to *practice play,* which typically involves rule games, at about age seven, though in fact the *symbolic play* is accessible to the individual throughout the life span.) At times, Sarah and I wrote skits and choreographed dances, some of which were performed for our mothers or the neighbors. But most often we improvised scenes about our hopes and fears and conflicts, and for these we had no scripts and no audience. Whatever was troubling or compelling to us, based on our stage of development, our subculture, or our familial situations, became material for our creations. We playfully enacted, sometimes directly and sometimes symbolically, the various issues with which we were grappling. Although our lives from late adolescence on took very different paths, our eventual career choices were similar: Sarah became a dance therapist. Interactive dramatic play and creative dance were profoundly autotherapeutic aspects of childhood for each of us. In adulthood, Sarah and I drew upon our own early healing in our work with others.

Theatre

"Man is least himself when he talks in his own person; give him a mask and he will tell the truth," Oscar Wilde said (in Ellmann, 1969, p. 389), not knowing the significance this statement would have for the field of drama therapy. The theatrical role or character, like the mask, is both protective and liberating, enabling the expression of what lies buried beneath our real-life roles. "Given the dangers of expression," writes Goffman (1961), "a disguise may function not so much as a way of concealing something as a way of revealing as much of it as can be tolerated in an encounter" (p. 77). The element of disguise inherent in theatre is considered by drama therapists to be an invaluable source of psychotherapy. Having something to hide behind is a vehicle, rather than an obstacle, to self-exposure. Illusion in theatre does not lead to elusion of truth but to confrontation with truth.

"The play's the thing, Wherein I'll catch the conscience of the king." Quoting Hamlet, drama therapist Sue Jennings (1990) underscores the significance of both the play within the play in theatre and in drama therapy: "Essentially the drama therapy model creates a play within a play within a play—in other words, the drama within the drama therapy group within the theatre of people's lives as a whole. . ." (p. 25). This is the point in drama therapy "where consciences may be caught and truths revealed" (ibid, p. 22).

Theatre can be viewed, in many respects, as an extension of dramatic play. The distinction between role and self is more explicit in theatre than in dramatic play. In dramatic play, roles are spontaneously assumed and discarded, in a natural and fluid manner, and the development of a single role and scene is relatively inconsequential, whereas in theatre, role and scene development are emphasized. A further difference is that theatre implies the presence of an audience. Dramatic play, on the other hand, typically consists of collective creations, in which everyone is simultaneously involved in the action. In process-oriented drama therapy, the audience is composed simply of other group members or, in individual work, of the therapist alone. The watchful presence of one or several others results in an increased awareness, albeit often on an unconscious level, of aesthetic properties. Improvisational theatre, which incorporates principles of creative drama and extends playful interactive theatre games (Spolin, 1983) into performed dramatic enactments, can be seen as a segue from dramatic play to theatre.

Dramatic play, predominating in the early sessions of my work with clients, gives way to theatre, in what I describe in the next chapter as Phase Two of a drama therapy series. The more developed enactments at this stage accord fuller expression to the aspects of the self that are embodied in the roles and scenes. The permissiveness inherent in dramatic acting facilitates this expression. One is released from the burden of owning the parts of the self expressed via the role and of carrying the weight of consequence to one's actions. Pretending provides a unique experience of liberty and exoneration.

Experimental theatre in the past several decades has paid increasing attention to the process of acting, rather than focusing only on the product or performance. The ways in which various theatre directors and theorists have viewed acting and performance have had an important influence on the development of drama therapy. For the renowned Russian theatre director, Constantin Stanislavski (1924, 1936), acting was an emotional and psychological process. The actor was to find and expose the "inner truth" of the character by reaching for a part of himself that identified with the character. Identification was key, not only between actor and character but between audience and character. Stanislavski's concept of the *magic if,* in which the actor projected himself into the character's life circumstance, was designed to stretch the actor's imagination and identification. Through an improvisational process in the rehearsal stage, the actors recalled experiences in their own lives that evoked emotions similar to emotions required in the character.* By the same token, the audience, in identifying with the character, was led to a state of emotional evocation and often to the recollection of personal experiences associated with these emotions.

---

*The Method, an approach to acting in which the actor draws upon his emotional experience, was brought to America by Stanislavski's protégés, Richard Boleskusky and Michael Chekhov, and developed by their students, Lee Strasberg and Stella Adler.

The German director Bertolt Brecht, on the other hand, discouraged his actors and audiences from emotionally identifying with the characters. Brecht's aims were social rather than psychological. According to Brecht, emotional distance was required to help people think objectively instead of responding subjectively, and objective thinking was necessary to activate social and political change. In rehearsal, Brecht's actors were asked to refer to their characters in third person, a direct contrast to Stanislavski's personalized approach in work with actors. In performance, Brecht created an *alienation effect* by using distancing devices such as interrupting the action, projecting slides bearing a message in the midst of the action, terminating a scene before its climax, displaying masks and puppets. These devices, along with the actors' presentation of their characters in an objectified manner, were intended to foster the audience's capacity for critical reflection (Willet, 1964; Roose-Evans, 1970; Landy, 1986).

Both of these seemingly discrepant approaches have important application in drama therapy. Those of us who are detached from emotions associated with past experiences, who tend to intellectualize rather than feel, or who have difficulty identifying or empathizing with others, can probably benefit more from a Stanislavskian approach. On the other hand, those of us who are easily overwhelmed by emotion, or who have trouble viewing personal situations with the objectivity that is often needed to make clear decisions or changes, would benefit more from a Brechtian approach. The Stanislavskian approach emphasizes emotional expression and release, whereas the Brechtian approach emphasizes emotional containment and the development of the observing self, both of which are primary therapeutic goals in drama therapy.

An example of the use of the latter approach—emotional containment—is with acting-out adolescents. Once past the initial resistance to engaging in drama, adolescents will easily become highly emotionally involved in their scenes. Rather than allowing an emotionally charged and potentially volatile action to continue, I will shout *freeze!* in the middle of the action, at which point I will incorporate a distancing device, such as: 1) directing the client/actors to reverse roles (thereby lessening their identification with their character, and facilitating deeper understanding of the other character); 2) asking the client/actors, or the clients watching the scene, to think about what has taken place and to decide what should follow (thereby fostering reflectivity and the capacity to perceive choices and options); 3) asking the client/actors to speak about their characters, in the style of a television interview show (promoting objective analysis of the characters).

Robert Landy's model of distancing in drama therapy provides a helpful framework for the drama therapist, who must constantly ascertain the client's fluctuating needs on the distancing scale. Landy's model draws upon Brecht's notion of distancing in epic theatre and social psychologist Thomas Scheff's notion of aesthetic distance, which is based in both psychoanalysis and theatre. Scheff (1981) conceives aesthetic distance as the balance between overdistance (a state of repression in which the primary mode of experience is cognitive) and underdistance (a return from repressed emotion, in which the primary mode of experience is affective); it is at this median point that catharsis occurs, and toward which the drama therapist strives for in her work with clients. Although in general the more theatrically stylized devices lead to overdistancing the client, and the more realistic, naturalistic devices lead to underdistancing, there are no rigid formulas (Landy, 1986). Landy explains how the mask, for example, though usually overdistancing, can at times be underdistancing. Techniques have different effects on different occasions. Moreover, the distancing needs of clients fluctuate, which means the drama therapist must be wary of prescriptions. Although the work with acting-out adolescents described above is typical, there are times when the same group may need a less distanced approach, or when the same devices may have a different effect.

Another theatre director whose work has had a profound influence on drama therapy is Jerzy Grotowski (1968). Grotowski's approach is closer to Stanislavski than to Brecht, in that he focuses on the actor's emotional process; like Stanislavski, to whom he acknowledges his debt, he believes in the essential creative power of the actor. But for Grotowski, acting is more than an emotional and psychological process: it is a spiritual process. He compares acting to sculpting; in both, one chisels away all that is excess as a means of discovering and revealing the innermost form. The work of Grotowski's *holy actor* entails the elimination of blocks rather than the accumulation of skills. The actor's intensive training leads to the progressive discarding of everyday masks, until he reaches the essence, the core. In performance, the actor, serving as a kind of high priest/priestess, exposes and sacrifices this core, or truth, to the audience, in the hope of inviting the audience to embark on a similar journey of *self-penetration* (Grotowski, 1968) and purging.

Grotowski's Polish Theatre Laboratory was influenced by the work of the French director, Antonin Artaud (1958), whose actors invited the audience on a magical journey in which truths were revealed and emotional and spiritual purging occurred. Artaud used the language of dream, image, gesture, and poetry, breaking away from the theatre of his time, which was dominated by words and linear plot. He was deeply affected by the ceremonial and ritualistic nature of Balinese theatre, which is far closer to religious rite than to entertainment. Artaud's work influenced many other important directors (whose work in turn influenced drama therapy), including Julian Beck and Judith Malina, founders of The Living Theatre.

The significance to drama therapy of the work of Grotowski and Artaud, including the many theatre artists and companies they inspired, lies in the self-awareness it promotes and the spiritual needs it serves. This kind of theatre is not an escape from reality, but rather a means of unraveling the falsehoods that surround and entangle us. This kind of theatre is not a way out (of our problems, pain, dilemmas, longings, etc.), but a profound journey inward. Acting with integrity, or being audience to others who are acting with integrity, is a path toward deep knowing and healing. Although Grotowski has never to my knowledge explicitly mentioned the use of theatre as therapy, healing seems to be implicit in some of the paratheatrical experiments and ritualistic vigils conducted by his laboratory in the past decades. Approaches to drama therapy influenced by Grotowski, like those influenced by Stanislavski, are generally underdistancing. Approaches reminiscent of Artaud's surrealism, imagery, and non-naturalistic style contain elements of both underdistancing and overdistancing.

Drama therapy has not only been influenced by, but has itself influenced experimental theatre; in many cases it is difficult to discern which came first. Theatre and performance artists are increasingly cognizant of the healing dimensions—for themselves and for their audiences—of their work.* Autobiographical theatre, in which the roles one plays are either aspects of oneself or of others in one's life, is on the rise. There are many more plays that address pressing social and psychological issues (e.g., substance abuse and sexual abuse). There are many more performances by nonprofessional actors, many of whom are identified as "special populations," e.g., developmentally or physically disabled groups, emotionally disturbed people, and prisoners. All of these changes in the world of theatre implicate, and are implicated by, drama therapy.

The theatre I was exposed to as a child was a form of entertainment. This was before The Bread and Puppet Theatre went out into the streets of New York with gigantic puppets and free bread, before the Living Theatre confronted and shocked its audiences, before Anna Halprin engaged masses of people in public dance rituals. But there was one off-off-Broadway play I saw

---

*In *The Way of the Actor*, Brian Bates (1987) imparts the awareness of many contemporary actors of the psychological and therapeutic impact of their medium. Bates, a psychologist, says that "...acting, moving, speaking 'inside' a created persona is a liberating, startling, and sometimes deeply revealing experience both to oneself and to others" (p. 98). Liv Ullmann, in an interview with Bates, states, "There are days when, during a rehearsal or performance, unknown secrets within myself come forward, sparked by the shaping of a role, a dialogue with a fictitious character" (p. 100). Marlon Brando is more specific: "Acting has done as much as anything to make me realize my violence and get rid of it. And when I finished *The Wild Ones* I think it was gone forever" (p. 4).

when I was 12 that was totally anomalous to the musicals to which I had until then been taken. The performers were a group of recovering drug addicts (as they were then referred to). In a small, dark room—hardly a theatre—before an intimate audience of about 30 people, five African-American men revealed their real-life struggles. They told of their desire for numbness, for love, for renewal. Toward the end of the performance, one of the men suddenly stepped off the miniscule stage and walked to the front row. He looked right at me. My heart pounded as I sensed the invisible fourth wall, the wall that separates actor from audience, theatre from life, gradually crumble. He stood just a few inches from me and reached out his hand. At that moment in which our hands and eyes locked, the vast differences between us—in age, race, gender, and class—dissolved. He and I were simply two people who recognized and grappled with pain, two people who experienced intense longing and hope. I remember thinking that the show had not ended but had melted into reality.

My new perspective on theatre and its relationship to life, launched by this experience, stayed with me. Fifteen years later I was to form my own theatre company, composed of former psychiatric patients who performed plays for the public about their lives (described in Part III). And although I remain particularly enthralled by autobiographical performance, I find that whether or not public performance takes place, and whether or not dramatic enactments revolve around personal experiences, drama as therapy sets a stage in which truths are revealed, deeper levels of communication and understanding are reached, and the personal becomes the universal.

Role Play

Experimentation with roles is fundamental to the process of drama therapy. The early stages of a drama therapy series involve dramatic play and theatrical scenes. The roles one plays are largely fictional, whereas in latter stages the roles are drawn directly from one's real-life experience. Whether fictional or actual, the playing out of a multitude of roles serves to expand one's role repertoire, foster an examination of the many aspects of one's being, and increase one's sense of connectedness with others.

Jacob Moreno (1946, 1959), the founder of psychodrama, saw people not only as role takers, as social psychologist George Herbert Mead had proposed (1934), but as role players, a distinction underscored by Landy (1990): "Mead's conception is primarily a cognitive one: I become a self to the extent that I can internalize the roles of others and see myself as they have seen me. Moreno's conception is a more active, dramatic one: I become a person to the extent that I can play out the many roles of myself and also play out the roles of others through the process of role-reversal" (Landy, p. 224).

Inspired by Moreno's seminal contribution to role theory, psychodramatist Adam Blatner (1991) has expanded and systematized Moreno's work by developing a theory of role dynamics. The concept of role, according to Blatner (1988b), implies "a separation between a psychic identification with a complex of behavior and the potential of the self to choose alternatives" (p. 103). By naming our roles, we achieve some distance from them. The resulting objectification of the roles enables us to become more conscious and accepting of them, as well as to reevaluate and revise them. The objectification implies a detachment, reminiscent of spiritual traditions in which disentanglement from thoughts and feelings is practiced, often through meditation, with the aim of moving from a state of imprisonment to one of freedom.

Blatner (1988b) emphasizes the multidimensionality of human experience. We all play a multiplicity of roles. An enhanced capacity to both understand and be flexible with these roles validates and expands our sense of self and enriches our experience in living. Affined with Blatner's perspective, my own work with clients emphasizes role dynamics, particularly as clients enter Phase Three (described in Chapter 2).

Most social actors—that is, people playing roles in real life—are unconscious of the parts they play and of the influence their actions have on fellow players. Mangham (1978), speaking about social actors in an organizational context, proposes that social actors in organizations "utilize the dramaturgical framework and adopt a 'metatheatrical' perspective whereby they can recognize the inherent theatricality of much of social life and see themselves as parties to social drama—as creators of scripts, as directors, performers, audiences, and critics. In recognition and awareness lies the possibility of change: the possibility of creating new scripts, new directions, and new performances" (p. 28)—a formulation analogous to Blatner's role dynamics theory.

The use of theatre as the metaphor for examining social behavior was developed by social psychologists, most notably Goffman (1959), who argued that people, as actors, perform various roles, utilizing set routines to make particular impressions on particular audiences. Drama therapy takes the concept that theatre is a useful metaphor for observing and analyzing our behavior from terminology into action.* In Phase Three of a drama therapy process, participants replay and rehearse actual interactions and situations— not abstractly (in their minds, as we all do), but concretely, via dramatic enactment. The enactment of dramatic scenes leads to greater self-awareness

---

*Shakespeare was perhaps the first to use this theatrical metaphor with his famous (and very relevant to *Acting for Real*) quote: "All the world's a stage, And all the men and women in it merely players. They have their exits and their entrances, And each man in his time plays many parts. . ." (from *As You Like It*).

and insight into roles, responses to others, ways of trying to control the responses of others, patterns, and habitual scripts. In real life we are so busy playing our parts that it is difficult to be conscious of our actions. Drama, on the other hand, has built into it points of reflection—the scene ends, or is "frozen" by the director/therapist at any given moment. At these points, it is natural to talk about what took place, how one felt, what one observed. Theatre, according to role theorists, helps us to understand real life, as real life reflects theatre. Real life, according to theatre artists, helps us to understand and create good theatre, as theatre reflects real life. In drama therapy, both are true: Our dramas reflect our lives, and we come to understand our lives better via our dramas.

The work of Goffman (1959, 1961, 1967), Mangham (1978), and McCall and Simmons (1978), are relevant to a humanistic approach to drama therapy, in that they challenge the outlook of many role theorists that we conform to social situations in prescribed, determined, and basically immutable ways. In *Identities and Interactions,* McCall and Simmons (1978) compare life roles in life situations to improvisational theatre, as opposed to scripted plays (particularly the more rigidly specified scripts of classic drama). This is an important distinction, denoting their view that humans are a combination of determined and determinative; while there are some constraints, the humanistic notion that people have an active part in shaping themselves is taken into account. Likewise in drama therapy, participants make use of improvisational drama not only to understand themselves better, but to explore and practice new roles, behaviors, and responses.

An increased role repertoire implies an expanded sense of self, especially if one adheres to the view that our "self" is simply composed of the roles we play. This was essentially Moreno's view. Psychodramatist Peter Pitzele (1991) uses an apt metaphor to describe Moreno's notion: "He seems to be saying that we might as well regard ourselves as a collective of roles, as if we were a kind of theatre company, containing within ourselves many possible actors" (p. 15).

Landy (1990), who has focused much of his recent work on the relationship between role and self, has revised his original view of self as the container of a myriad of roles. He now argues that the concept of self is mythical, and that the roles themselves are the "containers of all the thoughts and feelings we have about ourselves and others in our social and imaginary worlds. . . . It is in the doing and seeing and accepting and integrating of all the roles, the 'me' parts, that the person emerges intact" (p. 230).

Drawing on the works of social psychologists who, along with Goffman, advanced the notion of life as theatre, Landy highlights the relevance to drama therapy of Sarbin and Allen's (1968) identification of three dimensions of role enactments: number of roles one plays, organismic involvement, and preemptiveness or time. Number of roles one plays relates to the goal in drama therapy of facilitating an expansion of the client's role repertoire. Organismic involvement, meaning the degree of intensity or distance in role playing, relates to the aim of helping the client achieve aesthetic distance, the balance between the emotional and cognitive. Preemptiveness or time, having to do with the amount of time spent on a single role in relation to other roles, relates to the goal of helping the client create a healthful balance among the various roles she plays.

Though role theory has largely been the domain of social psychologists, the concept of role is originally a dramatic one (Moreno, in Fox, 1987; Landy, 1990). Advocating the need for drama therapists to make fuller use of their roots in theatre, Landy (1990) has conducted extensive research on the use of role in theatre and on the archetypal roles that have appeared in various forms throughout the history of theatre, and has analyzed the application of this study to drama therapy.* For Landy, role and story are the two bare essentials to a drama therapy process. Role is "the container of those qualities of the individual that need to be enacted in drama therapy. Story is the verbal or gestural text, most often improvised, that expresses the role, naming the container. The client as creator invents stories. . . . as a means of revealing role. At the end of one's story, sometimes unfolded through months or years of therapy, one should be able to answer the question, Who am I? And the answer involves both an identification of individual roles I play and an integration among my many roles" (p. 223).

Landy's interest in story has been influenced by Sarbin (1986), who in recent years turned from the metaphor of life as theatre to that of life as story. Humans are not only role players, according to Landy's (1990) description of Sarbin's work, "but storytellers who make sense of their lives through taking on the dual roles of storyteller and protagonist in their own stories" (Landy, p. 227). Based on this metaphor, Sarbin and his colleagues have postulated a new field called Narrative Psychology. The relationship between story and healing has relevance to many disciplines, including psychology, sociology, literature, theatre, and philosophy. Sarbin's work is akin to that of many others who are drawn to storytelling, including philosopher and writer Sam Keen, who has of late proposed interrogating one's own life as a way of bringing into awareness unconscious scripts, and from there consciously writing one's life story at the same time that one lives it.

---

*Landy has written a new book on the subject of role: *Persona and Performance: The Meaning in Theatre, Therapy, and Everyday,* to be published by Guilford (1993).

Drama therapy essentially activates key ideas expressed by Keen and Valley-Fox (1989): "One fruitful way to think of neurosis is to consider it a tape loop, an oft-told story that we repeat in our dialogues with ourselves and with others. 'Well, I'm just not the kind of person who can . . .' 'I never could . . .' To remain vibrant throughout a lifetime we must always be inventing ourselves, weaving new themes into our life-narratives, remembering our past, re-visioning our future, reauthorizing the myth by which we live" (pp. xiv–xv).

These ideas are particularly compatible with a humanistic approach to drama therapy, in which the belief in the capacity of humans to make choices and changes is paramount. A heightened self-awareness (or perhaps I should say role-awareness) is a necessary precursor to authentic freedom and transformation. This role-awareness and story-awareness is not a simple endeavor, given the multiplicity of roles we play, the complexities of each role, the numerous themes and sub-themes in our life stories. A client may enter treatment with a seemingly clear sense of who she is, and often find out that this sense was not so much solidified as simplified and rigidified, that there is far more "than meets the eye"– even her own eye. Ram Dass (1989) has said that when two people meet it's like a cast of thousands! In drama therapy, dramatic enactment and role play are used to help us unravel and discover the many roles we play, and to achieve a synthesis of our inner cast of characters.* The client finds she is a kind of one-person band, capable of playing many more instruments than previously thought, while still being able to create one coherent piece of music. The presence of the (internal) conductor, analogous to the observing self, is crucial. In drama therapy, the person practices being simultaneously musician and conductor, character and writer, actor and director, and audience.

In my youth, I was aware that very different parts of me emerged in my interactions with different people, to the extent that some people's perceptions of me were at times quite dissimilar to that of others who knew me equally well. This was most striking during my adolescence. In the striving for a sense of identity, most adolescents join, if not fuse with, a distinct peer group. This group, often a clique, serves to reflect both to others and to oneself one's identity, as well as one's place and status in the larger community of peers. Rather than merging with a single group, I aligned with several groups. I was both attached and detached, and I had close friends who were themselves

---

*"The notion that we have a single 'personality,' coherent, integrated, and stable, is one of the most limiting myths of everyday life," writes Bates (1987). "While we each have a personal essence, an essential self, we also have within us a wide variety of subselves, aspects of ourselves that normally remain hidden, locked away, even repressed . . . But the way of the actor releases these elements" (pp. 80–81).

parts of very contrasting groups—including the most and least "popular." Indeed, some of my friends were unlikely to ever cross paths with other friends of mine. Each relationship, each role I played, each impression I made on others, felt authentic. I did not feel split (as those with the label of multiple personality disorder do); rather the parts of me felt like different shades of a single color, with each part maintaining an awareness of the existence of the others. Nonetheless, the sheer quantity and range of ways of being was sometimes overwhelming and confusing. Over time, in later years, I became better able to grasp the many different *mes*, to take them all into my guardianship, to choose to highlight and develop some and let others retreat, to discern which are more essential—and these are probably now witnessed in any audience from any walk of my life. In Blatner's terms (1991), I developed a good "inner manager" that ensures "multiple personality order." This process is an ongoing one, and includes the anticipation of new emergences and the unearthing of buried roles, a process which I also attempt to facilitate in my clients.

Psychodrama

The most widely known utilization of theatre for curative purposes since early civilization was psychodrama (Moreno, 1945; Cole, 1975; Johnson, 1982a). The founder of psychodrama, Jacob L. Moreno, M.D. (1889–1974), was a brilliant, prolific, and visionary man. He not only brought to psychotherapy the use of acting and action, but developed a formulation for group psychotherapy and a method for assessing group dynamics (called sociometry), stimulated an awareness of the significance of spontaneity and creativity, advanced the understanding of role theory, and changed the view of the therapeutic relationship (via his transformation of therapist-patient roles to that of director-protagonist). The scope of his work is extraordinarily vast and far-reaching, not only contributing to other disciplines (including education, sociology, philosophy, and the arts), but also addressing all aspects of living. He was profoundly concerned with our spiritual roots, our interdependence and co-responsibility, our need to find internal sources of creative replenishment. In his book *Who Shall Survive? Foundations of Sociometry, Group Psychotherapy and Sociodrama* (1953), he writes: "My position was threefold: first, the hypothesis of spontaneity-creativity as a propelling force in human progress. . . second, the hypothesis of having faith in our fellowman's intentions. . . of love and mutual sharing as a powerful, indispensable working principle of group life; and third, the hypothesis of a superdynamic community based upon these principles" (p.xv).

Originated by Moreno in the 1920s, psychodrama is a form of psychotherapy in which a person enacts personal issues rather than simply talking about them. The *protagonist* (the subject of the enactment) is guided by the *director* (the therapist), and other people in the group serve either as audience to the enactment or as *auxiliary egos* in the enactment (portraying other people in the protagonist's life or the protagonist's alter ego, referred to as the *double*). The protagonist depicts and explores his life dramas via the live enactment. This externalization of his internal world enables him to witness and to have others witness his dilemmas. "Because we cannot reach into the mind and see what the individual perceives and feels, psychodrama tries, with the cooperation of the patient to transfer the mind 'outside' of the individual and objectify it within a tangible, controllable universe. . . . Its aim is to make total behavior directly visible, observable, and measurable. The protagonist is being prepared for an encounter with himself. . . . The second phase begins; it is to resubjectify, reorganize, and reintegrate that which has been objectified" (Moreno, 1977, pp. xii–xxii).

The enactment of life dramas implies a kind of *reliving,* through which both protagonist and audience experience emotional catharsis. Psychodramatic scenes tend to be deeply emotional, dealing with painful memories, childhood traumas, unresolved conflict and critical life dilemmas (though lighter, playful enactments also take place). Moreno traces the catharsis for the audience/group to the Aristotelian concept of catharsis, in which the spectator is emotionally purged by witnessing tragedy. Catharsis for the protagonist is traced to the self-purging of the saint or savior of the Eastern religions, in order that he may later serve others (Moreno, 1946). Psychodrama thus draws on both the power of the stage and of religious ritual.

Given the obvious and profound similarities between drama therapy and psychodrama, it is natural to ask how the two differ, and indeed this is the first question typically asked of a drama therapist. Although drama therapy cannot (and need not) be fully separated from and conceptualized outside of psychodrama, significant distinctions do exist. Psychodrama focuses on one person in the group at a time, the central protagonist, who reenacts real-life scenes, or scenes that at least have a clear relationship to his actual life dilemmas. Though the group is involved as audience or as actors in the protagonist's drama, the therapy is nonetheless individually oriented.

Drama therapy, on the other hand, is more group-oriented; the focus is on the group process and group interaction, rather than on a single person. Furthermore, the scenes in drama therapy are not necessarily directly related to people's real-life experience. Rather, drama therapy utilizes far more improvisation of fictional scenes, capitalizing on the notion that to play and to pretend enables a sense of freedom and permission, and promotes expression and self-revelation, albeit obliquely. A wide variety of theatre processes are used in drama therapy, including not only role play, reenactment, and improvisation, but theatre games, storytelling, puppetry, mask work, panto-mime, and scripted scenes. Drama therapy grows out of the art form of drama and, unlike psychodrama, does not have a single founder. To become reg-istered, drama therapists are required to have a background in theatre (similarly, dance therapists in dance, art therapists in art, etc); significantly, this theatrical experience is *not* a prerequisite for certification in psychodrama.

These distinctions are more patently evident in the way in which psy-chodrama is commonly practiced today than in Moreno's initial intent and orientation. With his interest in group dynamics, theatricality (e.g., staging, stage lighting), and spontaneity, one might consider Moreno to be more of a drama therapist than psychodramatist! On the other hand, Moreno does clearly acknowledge the individual focus of psychodrama: "Even the so-called group approach in psychodrama is in the deeper sense individual-centered . . . and the aim of the director is to reach every individual in his own sphere, separated from the others" (Moreno 1946, in Fox 1987, p. 18). The *warm-up* in psychodrama is often more interactive and playful than the ensuing scene-work, but it is goal-driven, serving the purpose of selecting a protagonist and preparing the group for the psychodramatic enactment. Furthermore, it is my impression that the role of the classical psychodramatist is that of director in every sense, whereas the drama therapist is generally more of a fellow player. Naturally, individual practitioners have their own style, and some psycho-dramatists do directly involve themselves in the action. Nonetheless, drama therapists tend to place themselves along a wider "continuum of distance from the playspace" (Johnson, 1991), ranging from full participation in the drama (while simultaneously functioning as guide) to offstage witnessing of the drama. Elements of drama therapy have become increasingly incorporated by con-temporary psychodramatists (most notably Blatner, 1988b; Sternberg & Garcia, 1989; Fox, 1987; Leveton, 1991); that psychodrama has been a funda-mental part of the work of most drama therapists goes without saying. Psychodrama is central in my own work, particularly at certain stages in the process, which I describe in the following chapter as Phases Three and Four.

Moreno also originated sociodrama, an intermediary form in which the focus of the enactments is on issues pertaining to the group as a whole, rather than on an individual's personal situation. For example, a group of psycho-therapists might examine the theme of countertransference, or a group of male batterers might deal with physical abuse. Sociodrama is often used to help communities tackle social problems. A crisis in the community (such as antisemitic occurrences within a neighborhood) or ongoing issues (such as racism, sexism, or homophobia) can be powerfully explored via sociodramatic processes.

Participants in sociodrama assume social roles in hypothetical situations related to the issue they share, but do not play roles specific to their own personal lives. Moreno conceptualized roles as having both collective and private components. Sociodrama revolves around the collective components, those which people share in common; psychodrama revolves around the private components, those which are unique to the individual (Sternberg & Garcia, 1989). Sociodrama is more similar to drama therapy than to psychodrama in that it is group-oriented, but it is still different from drama therapy in that the sociodramatic scenes are overtly about real-life concerns, even though these concerns are collective rather than individual.

Like psychodrama, sociodrama is an invaluable source for my own work, one that I use most in adolescent groups. Adolescents are best engaged by realistic enactments about issues directly pertaining to their life stage (conflicts with parents, peer pressure, drugs, dating, etc.), and yet in their struggle for peer identification and peer acceptance, they are often threatened by more personal self-disclosure. Thus, the sociodramatic mode is particularly relevant and effective for them. With groups of children, imaginary scenes that are neither sociodramatic nor psychodramatic predominate. With many groups of adults, the retreat from one's real world into imaginary worlds is an essential component of the drama therapy treatment process. In groups of emotionally disturbed adults, the creation of a nonthreatening and highly interactive atmosphere is critical to a sense of well-being and a gradual establishment of trust and commitment. With these groups, sociodrama and psychodrama are not integrated until Phases Three and Four, respectively, of the treatment process.

At the core of psychodrama, sociodrama, and drama therapy, lie role play and role reversal. These essential processes, for which we are indebted to Moreno, are about putting ourselves in the shoes of others, increasing our understanding and empathy, and not only *seeing* but *experiencing* the world from a perspective outside of our own. More profoundly, these processes are about acknowledging our differences and locating our commonality, our connectedness as human beings. Here we find ourselves not only at the border between the psychological and the social but between the psychological and the spiritual. Moreno advocated both expression and transcendence of our individuality, a higher consciousness of our interrelationships, and—more profoundly yet—the psychodramatic embodiment of the divinity within ourselves. And this leads us to the realm of the sacred—and to the final source of drama therapy, that of ritual.

Dramatic Ritual

Although drama therapy is considered to be a new profession, with the National Association for Drama Therapy founded as recently as 1979, it is in fact an ancient mode; in early societies, drama and healing were inseparable. Dramatic rites and rituals were ways in which communities confronted fears, symbolized hopes, celebrated joys, prepared for real-life events, and achieved a sense of control and empowerment. Rites and rituals were also a unifying force, connecting individuals to the group—as well as to nature, God, and the spirit world, and instilling a sense of harmony within the community.

Anthropological practices, therefore, are an important source of drama therapy. The origins of theatre itself are in early shamanic and religious rites and rituals which exemplified the interrelationship between drama and healing. The wearing of masks and costumes, the impersonation of human figures, animals, and dieties, and the enactment of stories have existed throughout time (Schechner, 1973). Arts therapist Shaun McNiff (1988) believes that of all the arts, the "action-oriented art form of theatre is closest to the shamanic archetype." The links between theatre and shamanism, according to McNiff, "account for the way in which the theatre tradition has carried on the continuities of artistic depth psychology throughout the history of Western civilization" (p. 286). Cole's (1975) analysis of theatre and performance from the perspective of ritual and shamanistic practices has had a significant influence on the development of drama therapy.

In ritual dramas led by shamans (from prehistoric times to contemporary nonWestern cultures), the internal and often unconscious struggles of the individual or the community are symbolically represented, helping participants and observers to release emotion and achieve catharsis. The symbolic and metaphoric language transcends the constraints and limitations of verbal language and usual frames of reference; multiple meanings and multidimensional levels of feeling and experience can be conveyed. Bates (1987), referring to shamans as "primitive actors," describes the trance state in which the shaman/actor perceives and embodies the "illness," adding that the shaman "heals in a manner very like highly intensive drama therapy" (p. 22). Shamanic cultures define illness as a loss of soul, and the arts, "from rock and roll to the creative arts therapies," according to McNiff (1988, p. 291), "attempt to bring back the abducted soul."

Healing rituals have the capacity to express and embody the emotional, the mental and the spiritual, the personal and the universal, the secular and the sacred. The person, group, or community to be healed is viewed holistically; the many aspects affecting one's state are not compartmentalized. Similarly, there is no compartmentalization of the arts; drama, dance, art, music, and poetry are integrated forms of expression. Drama, however, is the art form that most clearly encompasses the others, and from which the others stem: "Drama is the oldest of the arts—drama as a danced movement impersonating a spirit, animal, or man. From it comes the dance (the movement when acting), music (the accompaniment to acting), and art (the illustration of acting). At least this is how artistic activities were regarded by the most primitive man" (Courtney, 1968, p. 159).

The suspension of disbelief is central to both ritual dramas and theatre, and paves the way for the departure from everyday reality and the embarkment on a journey of discovery. On this journey, the ordinary, or the secular, is left behind, and one enters the unknown or *limen,* the realm of chaos. The ensuing process of facing the chaos and darkness and of gradually creating order and finding light is a transformative one. Affected but unharmed, one returns from the journey, bringing back to the real world the discoveries that could have been unearthed only outside of it, in the domain of the magical and the sacred.

Dramatic ritual creates a structure within which the liminality can be contained and the transformative journey can take place. All people, whether they are from so-called primitive societies or from contemporary cultures, whether they are clients or therapists, travel through (or attempt to avoid) the chaos and darkness, the emptiness and woundedness, the murkiness and ambiguities, the anxieties and fears. Yet, herein—if one can tolerate the liminality, trusting, if not in oneself, in one's guide—lies the fertile ground for creative and spiritual nourishment, for psychological insight and strength, for illumination and purification, for replenishment and renewal. Campbell (1988), referring to myth (and ritual, according to Campbell, is the enactment of myth) says that it is only at the bottom of the abyss that salvation occurs, only from the darkness that the light emerges. The shamanistic journey is parallel to the process of in-depth psychotherapy and—more specifically, given its use of dramatic expression and embodiment—to the process of drama therapy.

Dramatic ritual is incorporated in my own work throughout the drama therapy series, but highlighted during the culminating stage, Phase Five. At this final stage, ritualistic processes facilitate the review, encapsulation, and celebration of what has taken place. The mental, emotional, and spiritual places within the individual and the group that the drama therapy series has touched can be expressed in their full intensity and complexity via these rituals. The expression entails a process of both internalization and externalization—integrating and assimilating (within oneself) the experience, and concretizing and sharing the experience (outwardly).

Rituals serve as a container for the powerful and often untranslatable feelings, images, and unconscious associations that emerge during the therapeutic process. They can be viewed as a vessel within which the life of the group—with its various shiftings and transitions, conflicts and crises, feats and joys—is embraced. Various dramatic rituals are interspersed throughout the treatment series, like refrains that one returns to, particularly at the endings of sessions. In this way, a kind of acknowledgement and purging of all that takes place becomes customary, reminiscent of the function of ritual in early cultures, in which dramatic processes provided a vehicle for expressing and expelling negative forces, as well as for acknowledging and celebrating positive forces.

The circle, which is used in most ancient rituals and in the goat dance, an early form of Greek theatre, is also the most common formation for dramatic ritual in drama therapy, as well as in psychotherapy groups in general (Jennings, 1987). The circle is a powerful religious, spiritual and psychological symbol, reflecting the psyche (Jung, 1964; Campbell, 1988). Further, it represents totality—in time and space, leaving and coming back, the adventure outward and the return home, birth and death and rebirth (Campbell, 1988). The circle connotes the cyclical.* In drama therapy, the dramatic rituals, beginning and ending in a circle, celebrate the cycles and stages within the group process. The circle formation contributes to the sense of containment and continuity provided by the ritual; it *holds* the group—with all its intricacies—in simplicity. More significantly, the circle embodies and intensifies the sense of unity and interconnection within the group.

The parallels between ancient dramatic rituals and those used in drama therapy, as well as between shamans and contemporary drama therapists, obviously have their limitations, given the vast differences in social context. Nonetheless, significant learning can be derived from the examination of the ways of other cultures. The integration of dramatic ritual is increasingly central in my work with groups, as well as in my personal life. In both cases, I strive to devise rituals that mark significant points in time, bring about the acceptance and healing of painful periods, contain chaos and confusion, and celebrate the positive.

As a modern day practitioner, my role is in most respects different from that of the shaman; I am not a priestess, and there is no fusion between my practice and religious experience. Unlike the shaman, I facilitate the clients' enactments of their inner worlds, rather than taking on their illnesses myself. Yet I do enter their worlds enough to be profoundly affected; their suffering and their courage informs and inspires me. And like the shaman, I am a kind of wounded healer, bringing to the work my own experience with suffering.

---

*In ancient and many contemporary nonWestern nontechnological cultures, the life cycles are marked by rituals; in fact the word ritual comes from rtu, Sanskrit for menses. Menses means, in Latin, month. The earliest rituals were connected to the women's monthly bleeding, which was considered a sacred and cosmic event, holding magical power (Gadon, 1989), and symbolizing nourishment (of the unborn) and replenishment.

Though compassion and empathy are possible without personal suffering, they are surely deepened by it. The shaman acquires knowledge from direct experience (Halifax, 1982). "An elder from San Juan Pueblo in southwestern United States describes the process thus: 'What I am trying to say is hard to tell and hard to understand . . . unless, unless . . . you have been yourself at the edge of the Deep Canyon and have come back unharmed" (ibid, p. 10). Emotional growth through suffering has been compared to the tree that has been pruned and then bursts with new growth (Strauss & Goldfischer, 1988). The bruises in life provide us with the opportunity for inner growth and expansion. Whether shaman or therapist, we bring to the journey with those we are to heal what we have gleaned from our own life experience, with all its trials and triumphs.

Like all full circles, we return to where we began, from ritual back to dramatic play. The origins of dramatic play lie in the dramatic ritual of early cultures, according to Courtney (1968), who links the spiritual, psychological, and sociological functions of ritual to the play of children. Linkages and interconnections can be found not only between the first and last source, but throughout the circle of sources: The richly symbolic and dream-like *theatre* of Artaud is after all reminiscent of the *ritual* journeys of shamans (Landy, 1986); Moreno's development of *psychodrama* largely grew out of his observation of the *dramatic play* of young children, the analysis of *role theorists* relies on theatrical constructs, and so on.

There are of course other influential sources, many of which are related to the five conceptual sources discussed in this section. These include drama-in-education and child drama; play therapy, gestalt therapy, and other creative arts therapies; and therapeutic recreation. A more elaborate discussion of the five sources and other related sources is beyond the scope of this book, given our focus on process and techniques.

Various schools of psychotherapy have also had an important influence on the development and practice of drama therapy. The following section presents a theoretical framework for drama therapy that integrates central concepts of the three major forces in psychology.

AN INTEGRATIVE FRAMEWORK FOR DRAMA THERAPY

Drama therapy is informed by each of the three major forces in psychology: psychoanalysis, behaviorism, and humanism. The incorporation of certain key principles and values of each of these three forces, in conjunction with a synthesis of the five roots of drama therapy described in the previous section (dramatic play, theatre, role play, psychodrama, and ritual), comprise what I refer to as an *integrative framework for drama therapy.*

The integrative framework provides a core foundation, or essential theoretical basis, for the practice of drama therapy. From this foundation, one can move to a more specialized approach, such as developmental drama therapy (Johnson, 1982b, 1986), psychoanalytic drama therapy (Irwin, 1983), or an emphasis on projective techniques (Landy, 1986). The integrative framework contains elements of all of these approaches.

The integrative framework is process-oriented (shaped by the ongoing dynamic issues emerging at any particular point in treatment), humanistic, depth-oriented, and action-oriented. It does not offer formulas; each client and each therapeutic relationship gives rise to new insights and perspectives on the psychotherapeutic process and—more broadly—on the human condition.

Psychotherapy is as much a healing art as a healing science. In artistry, one is attentive to subtlety, complexity, and incongruency. In the art of therapy, one must be observant of the uniqueness of each person; as Erikson (1958) said, "the patient is a universe of one." The multifarious aspects of each person form such a distinct and unparalleled being, demanding the therapist's utmost attentiveness and perceptivity at all times, that the superimposition of a model holds the risk of being a blinding rather than a guiding force. The experience for the client of being truly seen for what he is by another is a central component of effective psychotherapy. When this does not occur, the client may become resistant, which is, according to Maslow (1968), "a healthy response to being 'rubricized'—that is, casually classified, deprived of individuality and uniqueness" (p. 126).

Drama therapists use many perspectives, organized within the integrative framework, in order to access the many aspects of clients. The dynamics of specific individuals and groups, the issues of special populations and age groups, and the setting and length of treatment all influence the clinical methods. In my own practice, I often find that the struggles of certain individuals will be best described by the exponent of a particular theory of psychotherapy.* The relevant theory then guides my understanding and treatment of the individual. A theoretical structure is developed around each therapeutic situation, rather than fitting each situation into a fixed, predetermined structure (Schön, 1983).

The challenge for the experienced clinician is to remember that the process of helping people is a constant act of discovery.

---

*Although concepts drawn from psychoanalysis, behaviorism, and humanism predominate in the integrative framework, other theoretical models are also incorporated. These include, but are not limited to, Jungian analytic therapy, gestalt therapy, family systems, and of course psychodrama.

Humanistic Psychology

Of the three major forces in psychology, humanistic psychology contributes most significantly to the fundamental practice of drama therapy, providing an essential therapeutic stance and paralleling much of what is witnessed and valued in the process of drama therapy.

Humanistic psychology emerged in the late 1950s as an alternative to psychoanalysis and behaviorism, which were the two dominant schools at the time. Termed the "Third Force," humanistic psychology aimed to address the fullness of the human potential, the capacity of humans for creativity, art, spirituality, self-realization, and transformation. Humanistic psychology contains no absolutes or definitive answers. It encompasses rather than excludes central aspects of many other psychological theories. Maslow, one of the founders of humanistic psychology, claimed to also be a Freudian, behaviorist, and existentialist; at one point he stated that he saw himself developing a "psychology of transcendence" (1971).

Humanistic thinking grew out of European existentialism and phenomenology, especially as represented by Rollo May's (1961, 1975) work. Existentialist and humanistic approaches to psychology are similar in that both respect the client's subjective experience, trust the client's capabilities, and affirm individual freedom and choice. But while existentialists posit that "we are faced with the anxiety of choosing to create a never-secure identity in a world that lacks intrinsic meaning," the humanists feel that "we have within us a nature and potential that we can actualize and through which we can find meaning" (Corey, 1986, p. 101).

The notion of an actualizing tendency, that is, a movement toward growth and health, underlies humanistic psychology. Alfred Adler (1924, 1939), the founder of Individual Psychology, first introduced the concept of the creative self. In his holistic view of people and his belief in their striving to self-actualize and their ability to change, he is seen as a forerunner of humanistic psychology. "The life of a human soul," he stated, "is not a being but a becoming" (Adler, 1963, p. ix). Jacob Moreno, the founder of psychodrama, can also be viewed as a forerunner of humanistic psychology. As early as 1920, Moreno brought to the attention of psychiatry the importance of creativity, and the notion that the phenomenon of spontaneity is key to developing personal freedom and responsibility (Blatner, 1988b). Moreno believed that "what characterizes human nature is an unlimited capacity for spontaneous and creative action" (Fox, 1987, p.39).

Humanistic psychologists view each person as both actuality and potentiality; as in European existentialism, there is a gap between what is and what could be. Humanistic psychologists are concerned with how far humans can go in realizing their potentiality, in actualizing themselves. While acknowledging the influence of personal history, they believe that people have the faculty to take an active part in shaping themselves. Maslow (1968) writes that "we both discover and uncover ourselves and also decide on what we shall be" (p.13).

One of the primary relationships between humanistic psychology and drama therapy is that dramatic enactment can create a bridge between human limitations and human aspirations, between who we are and whom we hope to become. Dramatic enactment is an in-between state, an intermediary stage between fantasy and reality. The mode is fictional and yet the experience is very real. The fictional mode enables us to do what is still out of reach in real-life, e.g., to express feared emotions, change behavioral patterns, or exhibit new traits. Once we have lived the experience, albeit in a fictional mode, this new experience can become part of our real-life repertoire. The enactments in drama therapy are composed not only of our present selves and our past selves, but of our future selves. Drama therapy draws upon the human capability of influencing one's behaviors and modifying one's life script—a tenet of humanistic philosophy.

Maslow (1968, 1971), Rogers (1951, 1961), Buhler (1962), May (1961, 1975), Moustakas (1966, 1967), and other humanistic psychologists base their work on models of health rather than pathology, and they view human nature as intrinsically good and healthy. Illness, according to Maslow (1968), is the result of deficiencies, of a lack of gratification of basic needs. In group therapy, which is my focus, many of the needs that have not been satisfied in the person's early life can be addressed. Clients can experience safety, acceptance, respect, support, a sense of belonging, and intimacy. The fact that one has interactions with many others, rather than with the therapist only, intensifies the reparative experience.

In drama therapy groups, the initial focus is on interpersonal interaction in the context of a safe and nurturing environment. Once the client has received and assimilated nourishment, and given the same to others, she explores giving this nourishment to herself. Many of the dramatic enactments at this later stage in treatment reflect processes that are intrapsychic, in that the person enacts various parts of the self, plays one part addressing the other/s, takes on the role of a "higher self," or simply improvises a realistic scene in which she is alone. Psychological health rests both on being able to receive support from others and on being able to give support to ourselves. We must be able to tap inner resources, turn inward for reassurance and strength, and ultimately rely on ourselves.

Maslow describes two innate forces: fear of the unknown (leading to clinging to familiarity) and the desire to grow and change. The desire for growth emerges out of a sense of safety, just as healthy infants take risks when they sense the reassuring presence of their parents. We dare to move forward when there is a secure base from which to operate,* and when retreat to this base is always possible. Without the secure base, the desire to grow is obstructed. In my sessions, I first create this safe place, which many of my clients have unfortunately never experienced. The work is very gradual and paced, so that the fear is lessened and the desire for growth is heightened. Each step paves the way for the next step, affording clients a feeling of anticipation combined with readiness.

Humanistic psychologists hypothesize that if the right elements are present (in early childhood or in the therapeutic situation), the growth impulse will be manifested. The concepts of self-actualization (Maslow, 1968) or what Rogers calls "fully-functioning" people (1961) are, according to both Maslow and Rogers, close to being synonymous with creativity. Referring to the creative process as opposed to creative product, Maslow sees creativity as implying a capacity to be spontaneous, playful, expressive, absorbed in the present, and in touch with one's childlikeness. Rogers equates the motivation to create with the drive toward self-actualization, and May (1975) writes that the creative process represents "the highest degree of emotional health . . . the expression of normal people in the act of actualizing themselves" (p.40).

The qualities frequently evoked in the drama therapy process correspond to those that describe the creative, self-actualizing individual. The person's spontaneity, playfulness, expressiveness, resourcefulness, imagination, humor, empathy, and childlikeness are drawn forth. These qualities not only correspond to Maslow's description (above), but also to descriptions of the "inner child" (which grew out of studies in the fields of alcoholism, child abuse, and family therapy), the "real self" (Horney, 1939), and the "true self" (Winnicott, 1958; Miller, 1986). In accordance with humanistic psychology, the healthy parts of the person are always witnessed, highlighted, and developed in drama therapy. Severely disturbed clients frequently astound staff members—who have viewed them only from a pathological perspective—with the strengths they exhibit in this context. Within all clients, including those who have been badly traumatized, a pilot light of health remains, and it is for this light, however dim, that the therapist reaches.

---

*This notion is in keeping with that of object relation theorists, including Winnicott (1958, 1960) in his description of "good enough mothering" and adequate "holding environment," and Mahler (1975), in her analysis of separation and individuation.

Psychoanalysis

Recovery of the authentic, spirited, childlike part of ourselves also means recovery and "working through" of the hurt, wounded childlike part of ourselves. Along with deficient attention to basic needs, pathology is the result of narcissistic injuries (Kohut, 1971) and traumas of early childhood. Nowhere more fully than in psychoanalysis do we find an appreciation for the personal history and suffering of the individual, the complexity of inner life, and the role of the unconscious. In long-term drama therapy, I believe that the psycho-analytic emphasis on uncovering the past and connecting it to the present is necessary, and is not contradictory to concepts in humanistic psychology. Maslow (1968) himself speaks of needing to enter our depths, to access more of ourselves — including primary process, memories, dreams, the unconscious. He says that "by protecting ourselves against the hell within we also cut ourselves off from the heaven within" (p. 142).

The dramatic mode provides a vehicle for the symbolic expression of repressed feelings. Aspects of one's inner life that cannot yet be articulated, assimilated, or even tolerated on conscious, verbal levels can be safely approached via drama and other creative arts processes. Many dramatic techniques involve free association, most notably *Transformations* (Johnson, 1991). Other dramatic approaches, in particular psychodramatic enactment, involve the reliving of progressively primal scenes, leading to emotional as well as cognitive connections between one's past and present.

Central features of psychoanalysis and of psychodynamic psychotherapy, a derivative of classical psychoanalysis, can thus be integrated with a humanistic approach to drama therapy. Attention is given to the early mother-child interaction and issues of self-esteem (Kohut, 1971), to processes of separation and individuation in infancy and early childhood (Mahler, 1975), to social and environmental factors in development (Horney, 1939), and to the reality of child abuse and the need to safely relive primal trauma (Miller, 1986). The emotional exploration of the past and the cultivation of insight and ego strength are essential components of long-term drama therapy treatment. Interpretation by the drama therapist is selectively incorporated, within the context of a therapeutic relationship of trust and acceptance. Transference is recognized and heeded, though not accentuated as in psychoanalytic theory. In group work, the multi-leveled responses that group members manifest toward one another and the learning derived from these interrela-tionships are given equal consideration with the transferential relationship to the therapist (Yalom, 1985).

Empathy, central to Carl Rogers' humanistic, client-centered approach to therapy (1961), is a primary aspect of the integrative framework for drama therapy. In contrast to the neutrality and therapeutic distance characteristic of the client-therapist relationship in classical psychoanalysis, the drama therapist actively expresses her empathic responses to the client's pain and often participates in the enactment of the client's life dramas. The gap between psychoanalysis and humanism has in many ways been bridged by contemporary psychoanalysts such as Heinz Kohut, who insists that empathy, respect for the client's subjective experience, and "corrective emotional experience" are crucial to the therapeutic process (Alexander & French, 1946; Kahn, 1991). "The best definition of empathy," writes Kohut (1984), ". . . is that it is the capacity to think and feel oneself into the inner life of another person" (p. 78). This definition is reminiscent of the proposition by Rollo May, coming out of the humanistic, existentialist tradition, that the therapist not only listen but "experience" the patient's communication on many different levels (Ford & Urban, 1963).

In my own practice, once enough ego strength is fostered and enough support and trust within the group are developed, I try to help clients access, embrace, and parent the wounded parts of themselves. To support this process and to deepen and communicate my empathy, I will at times play an aspect of the client, or *double* for the client (Moreno, 1946), or even take on the role of the wounded child (within the client) myself. But regardless of whether or not enactment is used, nowhere more powerfully than in acting do we learn about truly entering the world of another while simultaneously maintaining our own boundaries. The drama therapist's training in acting equips her to manifest the kind of empathy that every client (and every wounded child within) deserves.

Beneath the wounded child, according to Miller (1986), lies an even more authentic inner child. The elicitation of the client's health in drama therapy supports the capacity to express primal pain and longing, and the contact with primal pain and longing leads to deeper levels of self-actualization.

Behaviorism

Drama therapy is not only concerned with the unearthing of primal pain and hidden strengths. Drama therapy is also concerned with concrete, behavioral manifestations of internal growth. Drama therapy is action-oriented, aiming toward not only insight and emotional maturation, but also practical change. Classical behaviorism, though seemingly contradictory to psychoanalytic thinking and to drama therapy in its rejection of underlying unconscious conflicts and its minimization of subjective experience, has nevertheless influenced the fundamental practice of drama therapy in its emphasis on visible change. The attention given in behavioral therapy to the breaking of maladaptive patterns and the acquisition of new coping skills is very akin to goals in drama therapy. Communication skills, interpersonal dynamics, and habitual responses are all actively examined in the drama therapy session. Change is not only envisioned but literally practiced. Behavior therapy, with its tradition of incorporating role play of simulated situations in treatment in an attempt to give the therapist a clear sample of behavioral dynamics and to offer the client a chance to discover and rehearse alternative courses of action, is an important component of the integrative framework for drama therapy.

Cognitive therapy, maintaining that how one thinks largely determines how one feels and behaves (Beck, 1976), is related to behavior therapy in its orientation toward the present and toward problem-solving. However, cognitive therapy, unlike behavior therapy (and like psychodynamic therapy), assumes that behavior is influenced by beliefs outside of one's conscious awareness (Corsini & Wedding, 1989). The combined cognitive-behavioral approach to therapy is relevant to the integrative framework for drama therapy in its examination of the client's interpretations of events and in its active attempts to modify perceptions that limit the client's capacity for well-being and self-actualization.

In sum, drama therapy is an active and creative form of psychotherapy that engages the person's strengths and potentialities, accesses and embraces the person's buried woundedness, and enables the practice and rehearsal of new life stances. The integrative framework for drama therapy is guided by these central concepts in humanistic psychotherapy, psychodynamic psychotherapy, and cognitive-behavior therapy. In my own practice, emotional catharsis and mastery, cognitive insight, and behavioral change are all essential and intertwining parts of the therapeutic process. The distinctive nature of the particular client or group determines the course of treatment, along with my belief in the profound import of early familial, social, and developmental experiences and in the unique capacity of human beings to change throughout the life cycle.

GOALS IN TREATMENT

Therapeutic objectives are formulated in conjunction with an ongoing examination of the particular issues, needs, and strengths and weaknesses of individual clients or groups. Nonetheless, there are certain general goals that transcend particular cases. Representing my own clinical experience and perspective, the following is a brief overview of primary goals in drama therapy treatment.

The first goal revolves around the *expression and containment of emotion.*

Drama offers an outlet for the expression of intense and diverse emotions. Feared emotions can often be expressed with a sense of safety in the dramatic mode. This is partly because there is no real-life consequence to the expression, but also because drama affords a distance or separation from what is being enacted. The actor simultaneously experiences strong emotion and being in control of her expression. Drama therapy emphasizes the interplay between emotional release and emotional containment. Containment does not imply suppression, but rather mastery over one's emotion, enabling one to release strong feeling through appropriate and acceptable channels. Some people need more help with accessing and expressing feeling or achieving a greater connectedness with their emotions; others are easily carried away by emotion and need more help with containment or self-mastery. For many, the two are intertwined: Resistance to emotional expression is due to a fear of losing control. Such individuals need to experience emotional expression and emotional containment concurrently, in small doses, until they begin to recognize and trust the level at which they can tolerate the influx and discharge of feeling.

A related goal is that of developing *the observing self*—the part of us that can witness and reflect on the rest. Deikman (1982) distinguishes the observing self from the observing ego as being a more transcendent part of ourselves. I would call this part the director within us. The director has a broad overview and is able to think rationally even in the face of emotional turmoil. The director is detached enough to respond reflectively and to perceive choices and options. S/he has an enlarged perspective—encompassing past, present, and future, fellow players, the self in relationship to all that exists outside and beyond the self, "the larger picture." This kind of perspective often implies hopefulness, if not a kind of spiritual consciousness and faith, an important though frequently overlooked aspect of psychotherapy. By hopefulness and faith I am not referring to that which is unrealistic or unattainable, but to all that in fact *could be,* whether in the realm of outside experience or in internal change.

A third goal is the expansion of *role repertoire.* Our real-life roles, responses, and dynamics in interaction with others are limited; we become imprisoned by our own patterns and the expectations held by others that we behave in certain ways. In drama, however, the possibilities are limitless. We have permission to experiment with identity, discover and express dormant aspects of ourselves, practice new ways of relating. Expansion of role repertoire involves not only playing a greater number of roles, but playing each role with greater flexibility, commitment, and integrity. An expanded role repertoire equips us to deal with a broader range of life situations, to cope with new tasks, and to respond to old tasks in new and creative ways. Rigidity gives way to fluidity, and the spheres in which we felt stuck, actors in our own predetermined scripts, are imbued with new possibility. We become more *available to* life experience, experience that may otherwise have seemed out of reach. Even more significantly, we become increasingly available to all that lies within us.

A shift in self-image results from the expansion of role repertoire (when this occurs in an active and integrative fashion). The *modification and expansion of self-image* make up another goal in drama therapy. There is a dynamic, interactive relationship between role and self-image: Our self-image determines our repertoire of roles, and our repertoire of roles determines our self-image. Many clients have had parental figures in their childhood who reacted to them as though they were bad and worthless. Tragically, these clients developed a self-image that matched the image others projected onto them. This self-image determined their repertoire of roles, but the exposure to far more roles, along with the witnessing and reflecting back of others—heightened in group therapy—who see the person in a broader and increasingly positive light, gradually results in a modification in their perceptions of themselves. The expansion and enhancement of self-image bring an increased sense of self-worth. This includes coming to know, understand, accept, and respect the many diverse aspects of our being.

A final goal is the facilitation of *social interaction* and the development of *interpersonal skills.* The fact that drama is primarily a collective and collaborative art form makes it ideally suited to these aims, especially in group work. This goal is highlighted in drama therapy with clients who are withdrawn or socially isolated, a common symptom in psychiatric settings. Confidence and competence in modes of relating, both verbal and nonverbal, are increased. The close relationships and the trust developed in the group become a microcosm for what is possible in the world, reducing the deep sense of alienation with which so many people enter treatment. Even when socialization is not a problematic issue, drama therapy provides a means of exploring the intricacies of human intercourse. The use of drama in and as therapy leads to a process that emphasizes relationship, an aspect of life that warrants—for all of us—the deepest possible level of examination and understanding.

The principal therapeutic goals—emotional expression and containment, the development of the observing self, the expansion of role repertoire and self-image, and the enhancement of interpersonal relationship skills—are evidenced thoughout each stage of a drama therapy treatment series. The following chapter examines the progressive stages in long-term drama therapy, linking each phase to one of the five primary conceptual sources discussed at the beginning of this chapter: dramatic play, theatre, role play, psychodrama, and ritual.

2

STAGES
Five Sequential Phases in Drama Therapy

In long-term drama therapy, I have noted progression—both in the clients, and in the course of treatment itself—represented by the content and nature of the dramatic work. This chapter describes five phases of a drama therapy course of treatment. The description of phases grows out of extensive observation of groups, rather than being a pre-imposed structure or design. In general, I have found the movement from one phase to the next to be a sign of the therapeutic growth of the group or, in individual drama therapy, of the positive development of the process.

The five phases delineated in this chapter are linked to the five conceptual sources described in the previous chapter. While elements of all five conceptual sources are evident in each phase, each source is most correspondent to a particular phase. Phase One is most influenced by dramatic play, Phase Two by theatre, Phase Three by role play, Phase Four by psychodrama, and Phase Five by dramatic ritual. The processes incorporated in the five phases progress from interactive dramatic play, to developed theatrical scenework, to role play dealing with personal situations, to culminating psychodramatic enactments exploring deep-seated issues, to ritual related to closure. The phases have thus been subtitled: I. Dramatic Play; II. Scenework; III. Role Play; IV. Culminating Enactment; V. Dramatic Ritual.

PHASE ONE: DRAMATIC PLAY

The first phase lays the groundwork, or foundation, that can support the work that is to follow. A nonthreatening, playful environment is established. Processes include creative dramatics, improvisation, playful, interactive exercises, and structured theatre games. Many of the techniques are physically active, and most are socially interactive. Individual and group skills are developed; these skills, in turn, promote self-confidence and self-esteem, along with an awareness of and appreciation for the qualities of co-participants. Phase One is based on a health model. The strengths and healthy parts of the client are elicited; in keeping with the humanistic paradigm, qualities such as expressiveness, playfulness, creativity, spontaneity, humor, and aliveness are nurtured. These qualities develop the clients' ego-strength, enabling them to tolerate the more regressive work, involving often painful self-examination, later in the treatment series.

During Phase One, trust begins to develop—trust in one's own capacities, trust between group members, and trust in the therapist. Acceptance of self and others, a growing connectedness between group members, and group cohesion are central features of a successful group process. Although these features evolve naturally over a period of time, following an often slow and rocky course, drama offers particular means of accelerating and strengthening this course. Interaction between members, which can be so awkward and minimal in beginning phases of verbal groups, can be facilitated via drama therapy. Drama is a collective, collaborative art form. This aspect of drama is central to the work in Phase One. The unifying capacity of drama is drawn upon; collective creativity is encouraged. Group interaction and collaboration help develop a sense of group identity and mutual supportiveness. In individual drama therapy, the interactive dramatic processes in Phase One facilitate the development of the relationship with, and trust in, the therapist.

The other aspect of drama central to the work in Phase One is spontaneity. Spontaneity is the key ingredient in improvisational drama. The word spontaneity comes from the Latin root "sua sponte," which means of one's own free will or accord, coming from within. The spontaneous person is in contact with, and able to act upon, her innermost desires, rather than conforming to the expectations of others. Without spontaneity, one cannot act in the present moment; one is tied to the past, held back by the future. New situations elicit habitual responses and patterns remain unbroken. "Through spontaneity," writes Spolin (1983), "we are re-formed into ourselves. It creates an explosion that for the moment frees us from handed-down frames of reference, memory choked with old facts. . ." (p. 4). Says Maslow (1967): "Full spontaneity is a guarantee of honest expression of the nature and the style of the freely functioning organism, of its uniqueness" (p. 54).

Dramatic play, the most influential conceptual source of Phase One, generates spontaneity and facilitates relationship and interaction. The majority of dramatic processes used in Phase One are linked to dramatic play. Participants play out personally or socially significant themes symbolically, creatively, and collaboratively. Familiar themes and issues are also left behind, as participants enter the world of the imagination.

Phase One can be the most or the least structured part of the treatment series. It is the least structured when working in a mode of free-associative and nondirective play. By observing and participating in the client's dramatic play, the therapist gains a deeper understanding of underlying issues and themes. Informed therapeutic interventions can thus be made later in the treatment series. Phase One is the most structured part of the series when the therapist takes the role of active facilitator, easing the clients into the drama therapy mode and treatment process, rather than emphasizing diagnosis and interpretation. Structured dramatic play and theatre games (both adapted for drama therapy) tend to diminish potential reluctance, fear, and self-consciousness, especially with adult clients who have lost touch with the dramatic play of childhood. In either case, unstructured or structured, the role of the therapist and the techniques s/he incorporates at this point significantly influence the process of treatment, whereas later in the treatment series the interventions s/he makes are far more important than the choice of techniques.

The degree of structure depends not only on the needs of particular clients, but on the approach of the therapist. My own approach leans toward the structured at this early stage, especially in group work with emotionally disturbed adults. A higher degree of structure alleviates anxiety and diminishes resistance (a priority for me, whereas other therapists may instead choose to focus upon and interpret the resistance), facilitates interaction, and paradoxically releases spontaneity and creativity. The structure gradually decreases throughout the course of the treatment series—until the structured rituals of the final phase. Accordingly, a major portion of the techniques I have devised are geared toward Phase One.

It is important that initial activities are simple, engaging, failure-proof, *and age-appropriate*. The drama therapist needs to be especially attentive to age-appropriateness, not only because of the heightened caution (if not suspicion) manifested by clients at this early stage, but because of the thin line between dramatic play and "childish" play. (A further distinction can be made between bringing out *childlikeness,* or the child part of the client, and *childishness.*) The use of unsuitable techniques at this point may increase the clients' inhibitions and resistances, which often results in wavering commitments and drop-outs. Acknowledgment of and sensitivity to the clients' initial anxieties are critical. In addition to the fears associated with beginning any therapy process and of joining a group, there are particular fears associated with *drama* therapy. These include the fear of appearing childish, of having to perform (and failing), and of being asked to be other than oneself (or other than how one actually feels). The therapist should avoid any techniques that could confirm these fears. The trust of the clients needs to be earned during Phase One; the establishment of a positive therapeutic relationship is paramount. Later in the series, the clients' commitment and connectedness to treatment is sustained also by peer relationships and the overall sense of group identity.

With sensitive leadership during Phase One, clients experience a sense of permission, freedom, and joy, reminiscent of the experience of dramatic play in childhood. This sense of permission expands into a sense of liberation in Phase Two, with the more developed dramatic acting and scenework.

PHASE TWO: SCENEWORK

Phase Two progresses from the spontaneous improvised play and structured dramatic games in Phase One to sustained dramatic scenes, composed of developed roles and characters. The primary dramatic process used in this phase is scenework, which is generally improvised (although some drama therapists use existing scripts). While the link to dramatic play remains present, the conceptual source at the heart of Phase Two is theatre. The format and techniques of Phase Two are very similar to theatre workshops, though adapted for therapeutic purposes. It is startling to witness the degree to which ordinary people who have never before participated in theatre can, in fact, *act* despite their initial claims to the contrary. Given a safe, supportive environment and sensitive pacing and guidance, all people can express and reveal themselves via the theatrical process.

In contrast to psychodrama, in which protagonists play the roles of themselves in a variety of situations, the scenework of Phase Two involves playing roles other than those reflecting one's own life. This allows for greater role distance and less immediate self-disclosure, a useful step in the development of trust and spontaneity.

The aspect of drama central to Phase Two is the notion that acting gives permission to "be different." Diverse scenes and roles afford clients the opportunity to experience and exhibit new sides of themselves. The "stepping outside of oneself" and into a role is freeing; it provides relief and release from the constraints, both internally and externally induced, that are experienced in everyday life. Within the dramatic context, latent aspects of the self can emerge and suppressed emotions can be expressed. Wished for qualities or characteristics can be tried on and embodied. The "shadow" part of the person can be tolerated and given voice via the sanctioned theatrical role.

The critical point of awareness for the therapist at this stage is to ensure the freedom that promotes self-expression and role-expansion. More specifically, the therapist should not insist on verbal "processing" or "ownership." Forcing the person to own everything that emerges spontaneously or within the context of the role will be inhibiting, and the beginning of Phase Two should be one of liberation, not inhibition. It is important not to destroy the very context that is enabling the "transformation" to take place.

By the middle of Phase Two, clients begin naturally to comment on or discuss their enactments. Often there are manifestations of surprise at the emotion they displayed in the scene or the type of character they played. Typical remarks are: "I can't believe how much anger I expressed in that role," "I've never acted like that in my life" or "That's so different than the way I usually behave." Toward the latter part of Phase Two, clients relate yet more personally to the role they played. Comments here may be: "That's a pattern of mine, so it felt familiar to play that role," or "That part helped me to express the sadness I really feel." This is an exciting point in the series, because it is the point at which clients really make the connection between drama and therapy. For them, it is often an "aha" experience; for the first time, they simultaneously apprehend this activity as both drama and therapy. At the state mental hospital in which I had my first experience with drama therapy, I witnessed the remarkable transformation in affect and behavior of patients while they were acting, but my groups never reached this latter stage of Phase Two. The permission and liberation afforded by the theatre processes of Phase Two unquestionably occurred, but the discussions in which the linkages between acting and real life are made did not.

The end of Phase Two is marked not only by the responses of the "actors" but by that of the "audience." Clients watching the scenes begin expressing associations they had to the scene and feelings or memories that were evoked. An improvisation about a couple arguing might remind someone of his divorce; a scene about loss might elicit sadness and even tears, in much the same way that watching a movie or play affords cathartic release. Scenes also help people recall positive moments in their lives and give occasion for these to be shared with the group. Verbal processing is not forced, but spontaneous; clients manifest the desire to review and discuss the scenes.

Because of the personal disclosures and potentially intense emotional reactions arising at this point, it is important that Phase Two occur only after some degree of trust in the group and therapist has already been established. The skillful therapist is not merely patient, allowing for the emergence of each phase, but appreciates what each stage has to offer, much as a parent might enjoy the particular nature of each developmental stage of her child.

In the first two stages of drama therapy, the dramatic medium provides the safeguard, or disguise, which enables self-revelation. Participants in this context often seem to both expose more of themselves *and* feel safer than in normal everyday encounters. Gradually, though, as trust continues to develop between group members and toward the therapist, the need for a safeguard dissolves, and what is exposed can be *consciously* tolerated and integrated. The verbal processing at the end of Phase Two steers the scenework in a more personal direction. In the latter stages of drama therapy, the dramatic medium is used to explore personal material more directly.

PHASE THREE: ROLE PLAY

Phase Three is marked by the shifting of the dramatizations from the imaginary to the actual; clients are now ready to make use of the dramatic medium to explore situations in their own lives. Current predicaments, conflicts, and relationships are presented and examined. The thin line separating drama and real-life is particularly apparent at this point. The scenes, based on real life, seem *"so real,"* and yet the fact that they are fictional enactments rather than real-life occurrences is of critical significance in terms of therapeutic possibilities. The stage becomes a laboratory setting in which real life can be explored and experimented with in safety. Within the world of make-believe, one can confront difficult situations, try out new options, prepare for real-life events—all without consequences. Central to Phase Three is the notion of drama as rehearsal for life.

The primary dramatic process in Phase Three is role play. Clients may replay confusing or disturbing interactions with friends, practice job interviews, express feelings to significant people in their lives, confront people with whom they are angry. Common themes shared by a particular group are often explored. For example, a group of substance abusers may role play skits revolving around coping with the temptation of alcohol or drugs. The dramatic examination of interpersonal issues within the group is also largely the domain of Phase Three, a phase which incorporates many aspects of psychodrama and sociodrama.

Role play and role theory comprise the most influential conceptual sources of Phase Three. Through dramatization and ensuing discussion, clients gain a clearer view of the roles they play in life and the patterns that emerge in their interactions. Moments from real life are magnified and elucidated under the illuminating lights of the theatrical stage. Clients simultaneously act and watch themselves in action, a feat difficult to accomplish on a regular basis in real life. The bit of distance from reality afforded by drama stimulates the functioning of the self-observing ego. This distance can be capitalized upon by pausing in the midst of a scene or just after the scene ends, at which point the players examine each person's role and behavior, how each interpreted and was affected by the other's role and behavior, how effective each person was in her role, etc. Mangham (1978) speaks of the predictability of most (inter)actions, even given the rehearsal of the mind, for we tend to have a limited repertoire. For example, "he who defines things pessimistically is unlikely to rehearse a course of action which departs radically from such definitions, and therefore he selects actions which tend to confirm these definitions" (p. 28). In drama therapy, not only is the person likely to be more conscious of such choices made within the theatrical mode, but the presence of an objective observer, the drama therapist, helps ensure that patterns do not go unnoticed. The drama therapist gradually makes interventions, under the auspices of theatrical directions, that facilitate awareness and change, rather than unending repetition.

It is important for the drama therapist to clarify, when necessary, the distinction between scenes that serve as actual practice for real life and ones that promote healthy catharsis within the session but are not intended as preparation or prescriptions for real life. This clarification is usually called for when clients confuse the latter category with the former. For example, a rageful confrontation with an abusive parent may be helpful for a particular client to experience within the fictional mode, but may be either nonconstructive or deleterious in real life. If the therapist suspects that the enactment is potentially prompting the client (or members of the group watching the scene) to actualize the situation (that is, to go out after the session ends and "do it for real"), or if the client is reluctant to perform an enactment because she views it as encouragement to do something that she would not want to do in real life, then clarification is essential.

Clients play not only themselves, but other people in their lives. For example, adolescents may be interviewed *as* their parents, followed by enactments of relevant parent-teen conflicts. In playing the role of others, the client gains perspective, and the responses and motivations of others are better understood. Additionally, as was discussed in the previous chapter in relation to the role theory of Mead (1934), role playing others in one's life relating to oneself (that is, seeing oneself through the eyes of others in one's life) contributes to the development of self-concept and identity. Taking on the role of another person in one's life relating to oneself (for example, if I play the role of my brother while someone else plays me) enables one to encompass and assimilate the multitude of roles and facets of self that are manifested in relation to others.

The work in Phase Three is often on a behavioral level; role play in assertiveness training, for example, is considered Phase Three material. But with skillful intervention on the part of the drama therapist, insight into roles and behavioral patterns, as well as experimentation with alternatives, is also achieved. The therapist at this point needs to pay careful attention to the direction of the scenes, ensuring that the client is taken further—toward understanding or discovery of options—rather than simply repeating real-life performances. Verbal processing is generally very integrated with dramatic work at this point. Dramatization and discussion help clients not only vent feelings and practice new behaviors, but understand and change underlying dynamics. Most importantly, at this stage clients experience themselves not only as actors, but as directors, playwrights, audiences, and critics of their own life dramas.

It is toward the end of Phase Three that clients often begin to clearly experience a sense of hope for change in their lives. The hope comes as a result of experiencing (as opposed to only imagining) themselves responding (via the dramatic mode) to personal situations differently from the nonconstructive patterns of response they fall prey to in actuality. The implication is that if they could act that way in scenes that are *almost real,* perhaps they could act that way *for real.* The importance of the development of acting skills in Phases One and Two must be reemphasized here. Without a certain level of dramatic proficiency, the scenes are not "real enough" for this dynamic to take place. It is at this point, too, that clients frequently report that they responded to a difficult real-life situation in a new or uncharacteristic way. Many clients have told me that this was accomplished by pretending they were acting a scene. Put in other terms, these clients made use of the capacities they had manifested in drama to cope more effectively and healthfully with the trials of real life.

PHASE FOUR: CULMINATING ENACTMENT

The examination of roles, relationships, and conflicts in current life situations gradually leads clients to a deeper level of introspection. The increased level of consciousness regarding role and life patterns achieved in Phase Three facilitates entry into the unconscious. The journey into what lies beneath the surface of one's daily life, along with the questioning of who one is, how one sees oneself, why one acts the way s/he does, what circumstances influenced one's emotional development, are natural outgrowths of what has taken place in the preceding phases. Phase Four is marked by the shift from concrete, present-day issues to more core issues in one's life. The past comes closer to the surface, and unconscious material becomes more accessible. Memories, dreams, associations, and images—some involving family constellations, childhood traumas, significant events—shed light onto unresolved issues, recurrent themes, ongoing struggles. Scenes in Phase Four often revolve around experiences that have affected or disturbed the person's present. Some scenes entail revelations about oneself that were until now kept hidden from the group, the therapist, or even from oneself.

The primary conceptual source of Phase Four is psychodrama and the primary dramatic processes are psychodramatic. There is an increased focus on the individual within the group, as the inner lives of *protagonists* are

dramatically explored and their stories relived. Many of Moreno's psychodramatic techniques, such as *doubling,* are vital early in Phase Four. By the
middle of Phase Four, clients are enacting what I call *culminating scenes.* The
culminating scenes are elaborations, deeper explorations of themes that have
emerged or patterns that have been exposed during the preceding phases.

Though the culminating scenes of Phase Four resemble psychodramatic
scenes, they have two unique features. First, the scenes are performed only
at a point at which clients have already developed proficiency in drama, as
well as a high level of trust in the group. Second, the content of the scenes
is emergent, growing out of the process thus far. These features enable a
degree of depth, subtlety, and complexity which is often not possible when
one begins a treatment series with psychodrama. The scenes are enacted
with a particular sense of authenticity and possess intense power on a theatrical as well as a therapeutic level. In performance-oriented drama therapy
groups, the final performances, particularly of autobiographical plays, are
usually composed of culminating scenes.

In my own work with clients, there is an evolution to this phase, largely
because I believe it is critical that the degree of self-exposure and emotional
intensity be matched by the level of group cohesion and support. (In psychodrama, the scenes often reach a level of power and profundity that far
surpasses the level of connectedness between the group members; indeed
intense scenes are not uncommon in one-time-only or "drop-in" sessions. One
of the risks here is a post-enactment feeling of alienation.) Also the gradual,
paced process in drama therapy, in which significant issues (which cannot
be predicted or prescribed in advance by the client or the therapist) emerge,
facilitates a journey of surprise and discovery. The notion that to pretend or
be disguised enables revelation and exposure, a notion capitalized upon
in the early stages, is important to reemphasize here. In drama therapy one
begins by *acting* rather than by *re-enacting.* The acting steers one away from
initiating therapeutic work on predictable and familiar issues that often are
unconsciously presented as a shield against dealing with more authentically
significant issues. The gradual, paced process also enables the therapist to
both gauge and develop the client's tolerance for emotionality and self-
exposure before embarking on the intense culminating scenes of Phase Four.

The culminating scenes are a climactic point in the group process.
Revelation, disclosure, and sharing are heightened; insight is deepened. As
buried emotions emerge and are given an outlet for expression, a powerful
experience of catharsis occurs. The therapeutic intensity is matched by the
theatrical power of the scenes; both are matched by the level of group support
and cohesion. Inner resources, creative reserves, and untapped strengths are
drawn upon in developing these scenes. There are often various stages and

levels of exploration, and one client's culminating scene may have several parts and take more than one session to unfold. The enactments result in a unique sense of both artistic achievement and mastery over often very painful content.

The aspects of drama central to Phase Four are multiple: 1) Reliving events (rather than talking about them only) accesses the sensations that one experienced at the time the event took place. The enactment revives suppressed emotions. These emotions were often squelched because the individual was unable at the time to cope with them, and/or because emotional expression at the time would have resulted in punishment or other negative consequences. But the suppression has had damaging effects and uncovering the source is part of the healing process. The defense mechanism of intellectualization (or other forms of distancing), so common when talking about an emotional experience, is circumvented. As psychodramatic scenes integrate sensation, emotion and cognition, the client cannot remain on a cognitive plane only when dealing with emotional issues. The fact that the language of drama is very rich, often conveying far more nuances and intricacies than can be communicated with words alone, facilitates this integrative process. 2) The immediacy and potency of this kind of dramatization heighten the empathy of the other group members and the therapist. Empathy is central to therapy, not only in terms of the therapist's understanding of the clients, but because the clients' experience of the empathy of others enables them to empathize with themselves. 3) In dramatizing, the internal is externalized. In this process of sharing and showing one's internal world, a burden is lifted, an inner weight removed. What was private is now witnessed. This often leads to an experience of intense acceptance and forgiveness, as clients expose what had previously been hidden, even from themselves. A sense of exoneration and of communion ensues—in individual therapy by and with the therapist, in group work within the group, and in performance-oriented drama therapy with the outside world. This sense is reminiscent of the ritual purging ceremonies of primitive cultures, in which evil spirits were expelled in the presence of the entire tribe (Collomb, 1977, in Emunah & Johnson, 1983). The ritualistic aspects of drama pervading the end of Phase Four create a segue to the final stage of the drama therapy treatment series.

PHASE FIVE: DRAMATIC RITUAL

After the climactic, culminating scenes of Phase Four (the duration of which varies widely), the series begins to come to a close. This closure is in itself an important developmental process, facilitating the integration and assimilation of the therapeutic progress made in the preceding phases. The work of Phase Five assists clients in carrying the changes made within the context of drama therapy into the outside world. The connection between one's achievements in the group and changes within oneself is strengthened, meaning that the client comes to realize that these changes will not cease to exist when the treatment process is terminated. At the same time, the multiple and complex feelings regarding termination are explored. Phase Five is about transition and closure.

Phase Five is conceptually linked to ritual, and primary dramatic processes are dramatic rituals. In early societies, dramatic rituals were ways in which communities marked points of transition, shared wishes and successes, and celebrated events. The celebratory aspect of drama is central to Phase Five. Rituals and other dramatic processes are incorporated to help clients review the series, evaluate progress, give each other feedback, experience the rewards of accomplishment, and express both the sadness and joy of completion. The processes also serve to reflect and intensify the sense of unity and kinship within the group. The unique *entity* formed by the group and the particular interrelationships within the group are acknowledged and honored.

Dramatic rituals can often communicate that which cannot be expressed through language alone. The intense feelings evoked by the therapy process and its conclusion, along with the deep level of intimacy that has been experienced within the group, can sometimes be best conveyed via dramatic ritual. Collectively developed and repeatable group creations, composed of powerful images, metaphor and story, rhythmic sounds, and poetry and movement, enable the expression of a seldomly mentioned dimension to the therapy process—the spiritual dimension. I am referring to the sense of awe one may encounter during a process that entails uncovering layers, discovering what was previously unknown, accessing the unconscious, transforming pain into art. In the course of treatment, there have been transformations— on small and large scales—witnessed in others, experienced in oneself, and shared with the group. These transformations can be perceived not only from psychological and aesthetic standpoints, but from the spiritual domain.

Much of the description of Phase Five applies, too, to the final phase of each session within the series. Closure of the treatment series and of each individual session is not a matter of implying that there has been solution or even necessarily resolution. Rather, closure provides an arena for reviewing what has transpired, recognizing the steps that have been taken, and making the transition from the drama therapy session to one's outside reality. The drama therapist devises and utilizes creative techniques to facilitate this review of the process. Significant points in time, powerful scenes, trying periods, critical conflicts or challenges, important insights are all recalled and further digested. This retrospection deepens the level of introspection, of awareness of all aspects of the process. The entire journey is, in a sense, encapsulated, helping the client to *grasp* and *own* the experience, with all its impact. The rituals in Phase Five provide a kind of *framing* of the treatment session and series.

By the end of Phase Five, clients feel very validated for the process they have been through. The dramatic rituals help achieve this, for—like all rituals—they mark life events, rather than letting events fade into oblivion. They enable us to take hold of our experience, rather than letting experience slip through our fingers unregistered, unacknowledged, unassimilated. In this way, there is a sense not only of loss for what is over, but of appreciation for what has been gained. When experiences and the termination of these experiences are validated, there is in the end not so much a sense of emptiness, but one of fullness in living.

The intensive and carefully designed process of closure in Phase Five not only helps clients reflect on and integrate the past, but creates a sense of opening to the future—pointing to the steps that lie ahead, the possibilities, and the hope as one continues the journey.

CONCLUSION

The five phases are best viewed not as rigid entities, but as an analysis of the gradual unfolding of a therapeutic process. The phases are fluid and often overlapping. Phase One, for example, remains present on some level throughout the series; it is important not to drop the playful component, even as the clients enter more emotional terrain. Elements of several phases are often present within a single session. The phases are not intended to be prescriptions for drama therapy, but rather helpful guidelines, which can assist the drama therapist in pacing, identifying needs, assessing progress, and determining appropriate techniques and interventions.

There is no set formula for the way in which a group progresses through these five phases. In some cases, the first two phases may be very brief; in others they may comprise the bulk of the series. Some populations may be best served by an emphasis on a particular phase. For example, groups of children or developmentally disabled may benefit most from Phase One work. Phase Three work, on the other hand, may be most appropriate for support groups (dealing with specific issues) composed of high functioning adults. A particular phase may also be most in keeping with the therapeutic orientation of a facility or the length of treatment provided, and thus most suitable.

Moreover, different drama therapists, because of their own orientation and skills, may feel most affinity with a particular phase, and their work may incorporate little of the other phases. Those with a stronger creative drama background or belief in the importance of play and spontaneity, for example, may lean toward Phase One work, and an entire series with such a therapist may remain in this phase. Drama therapists with a stronger background in psychodrama and a preference for in-depth psychotherapeutic work may focus on Phase Four. Those who are more comfortable with "here-and-now," concrete approaches to psychotherapy will probably make most use of Phase Three. Theatre-oriented drama therapists may find Phase Two work the most natural and interesting. Thus, the phases can be viewed not only as stages of group development, but as models of practice. In my own practice, however, I have made equal use of all phases, with different phases being emphasized with particular groups. My groups with emotionally disturbed and acting-out adolescents tend to center on Phases Two and Three; with high-functioning adult clients the emphasis leans toward Phase Four. But it is not only population that determines emphasis, but the unique configuration of clients within a given group. In the majority of cases, I find in retrospect that all five phases have been present to a surprisingly equal degree.

British drama therapist Sue Jennings (1983) describes three models of practice in drama therapy: the Creative/Expressive, the Learning, and the Therapeutic. The first is considered a "health model," stressing the "healing nature of active participation in the creative process through drama" (p. 4), as well as the communal aspect of sharing creativity with others. This model would be most correspondent to what I have described as Phase One, with some connection to Phase Two and Phase Five. Jennings' Learning model emphasizes the acquisition of skills via dramatization, specifically role flexibility and repertoire. To the extent that it centers on "the drama of everyday life," it corresponds to Phase Three. The Therapeutic model focuses on latent and unconscious issues, and is described as "a form of psychotherapy where enactment is used as well as talking in a closed group setting" (p. 5). This corresponds to Phase Four, though in my estimation all phases are therapeutic as well as creative.

Although the model of five phases is based on work over a period of time (generally speaking, at least 20 sessions) with a fixed group membership, the model can also be applied to short-term treatment and/or to groups with rolling admissions. In short-term treatment, there is often a faster-pace progression from Phase One to Phase Three. The group rarely will enter Phase Four, and Phase Five is given less weight than in longer-term, fixed-membership groups. The relative absence of the last two phases does not lessen the importance of short-term drama therapy; even several sessions can often serve as a critical catalyst for progress in other areas of treatment or for making changes in one's life. With rolling group membership, there is an increased fluctuation in the phases (as the group dynamics and needs shift from session to session) rather than the more steady progression typical of fixed-membership groups. With changing membership, Phases Four and Five are rarely apropos. My own preference is for fixed group membership to allow for progression and to foster the interrelationships and group cohesion that I believe play a most significant role in the journey toward health and well-being.

Phases and models, concepts and techniques mean little until one can see what they signify in the lives of actual people. While this chapter has focused on the progression of the drama therapy series itself, the following chapter illustrates the progress of individual clients within a drama therapy series of fixed group membership. Four case stories are told, stories of people undergoing a process of struggle and of change.

3

STORIES

Individual Growth in Process-Oriented Group Drama Therapy: Four Case Examples

The four examples in this chapter are taken from group drama therapy with adult clients in a psychiatric day treatment setting. The four clients, all in their twenties and thirties, each attended two to four drama therapy series, totalling six months to one year of treatment, with groups meeting twice a week. Each drama therapy series consisted of 90-minute sessions over 12 weeks (approximately 25 sessions per series). The case stories highlight the culminating scenes in Phase Four. Names and certain facts have been changed to assure confidentiality, although descriptions of the sessions and of particular scenes are as close to what actually took place as possible; in most instances, dialogues have been recorded verbatim.

The day treatment center in which the treatment took place serves a diverse population, in terms of age, race, class, and level of functioning. The majority of clients have been hospitalized at some point (some for only a brief period and others for extended periods or on multiple occasions) as a result of emotional disturbance including schizophrenia, manic-depression, and borderline personality disorders. Most clients take psychiatric medication on a continuous basis. Many live in board-and-care homes and are subsidized by social security; others live independently and hold responsible jobs. Enrollment in the center is voluntary, though most clients are referred by outside therapists. Once members are enrolled, attendance is mandatory. Clients participate in a multidisciplinary treatment approach (including group, individual, and family therapies; dance and drama therapies; biofeedback; arts and crafts; and informal outings and social events) for seven hours daily, three to five days a week. Length of stay in the day treatment center ranges from three months to two years. The center encourages the assumption of responsibility, the cultivation of social skills and interaction, the identification and expression of feelings, and the development of self-esteem.

Though the four individuals described in this chapter have a psychiatric history and diagnosis, to view them only as patients is at best limiting and at worst dehumanizing. Each one is a complex and multifaceted person, a player of many life roles, a "universe of one" (Erikson, 1958), a fellow human being challenged—as we all are—by the circumstances that profoundly affected their development. My background in acting taught me to find parts of myself in every character. Likewise, being a therapist involves reaching inside myself, in search of what it is in me, in my experience, that will enable me to understand and connect with the client more deeply. The boundaries between self and client in therapy as between self and character in acting remain clear. But they are boundaries, not barriers.

In Shawn, Ivan, Lisa, and Christine, I witnessed layer upon layer of pain and layer upon layer of beauty. At each unfolding of our work together, my respect, care, and love for them grew. These are stories of struggle, of courage, and of victory.

SHAWN

I worked with Shawn twice a week for a year, in four three-month series. Shawn was among the more socially interactive, verbally sophisticated, and creative members of the day treatment center. At 32, she was an exceptionally bright, sensitive, and attractive Australian woman. Long, wavy red hair framed her strikingly beautiful and expressive face. Shawn was divorced; she had been married for four years during her mid-twenties to an artist who was 15 years her senior. She had a seven-year-old son who lived with his father during the week and with her on the weekends.

Shawn lived in her own apartment, had an advanced degree in Art History, and had achieved some success as the assistant curator of a small museum. She also had undergone two brief psychiatric hospitalizations for suicide attempts. At times she was anorectic, and even more frequently gave in to impulses of self-mutilation in the form of cutting herself. Her psychiatric diagnosis was Borderline Personality Disorder. Shawn came from a wealthy, professional family. Both of Shawn's parents had been alcoholic and incapable of providing her with sustained care. Her mother, now deceased, had been neglectful and emotionally unavailable, and her father, a radiologist, had been emotionally abusive as well as seductive with her. (There had not been explicit sexual molestation.) She had an older sister who was a talented musician and also a drug abuser, and two younger brothers—one an alcoholic and the other a successful attorney. One set of grandparents was still alive and seemingly supportive, but lived in Australia, where Shawn had spent the first 10 years of her life.

In our early work, Shawn was depressed, but the sessions brought out her natural though rather buried playfulness and spontaneity. For the duration of the session, at least, the depression lifted. Her skits during Phase One (Dramatic Play) were wonderfully imaginative and creative, and she was surprised by the validation she got from others for her skills. She was drawn especially to dramatic play which allowed her to express anger safely and playfully, such as *Gibberish* (using sounds or made-up language instead of actual words), and this expression of anger further reduced her depression.

But as the group moved into the more developed improvisational scenes of Phase Two (Scenework), associations and feelings related to Shawn's childhood were easily triggered, and she quickly became overwhelmed. For example, after another client played an alcoholic stepmother in a fairy-tale scene, Shawn grew silent, and later I found out that that night she cut her arm with a razor. Her cutting seemed to be a way of inducing physical pain to distract her from emotional pain, and also to make the emotional pain more tangible and palpable. At this point in treatment (after approximately eight sessions over a month period), I began encouraging her to identify feelings as they came up in the session. This was difficult for her because she tended to have a delayed reaction; she put feelings aside and later felt devastated. In childhood, Shawn had never been allowed to express feelings, nor had she witnessed her family express feelings directly. Rather, her parents had used drinking as a way of avoiding and denying feelings. I tried to "check in" with Shawn frequently during the session and to give her extra support at the end of the session. Any feelings she acknowledged were validated. This process also served to develop her trust in me and in treatment.

But as her trust in me increased, so did her fear of abandonment. Her transference toward me was manifested by the degree of her upset and the feelings of abandonment she expressed when there was a change in schedule. For example, when I announced that I needed to end one session 15 minutes early in order to catch a plane or when, a month in advance, I announced that we would not meet the Friday after Thanksgiving, Shawn accused me of not caring about her or the group. Rather than interpreting the transference, I chose to reassure her, in an attempt to provide some consistent support and care.

Much of the work as the group moved into Phase Three (Role Play) revolved around helping Shawn to predict the situations that would precipitate overwhelming emotion and thus the cutting. She either had little sense of when this might happen or didn't care enough about herself to try to protect herself. For example, she had been planning a trip at Christmas to see her father, whom she had not visited in several years. I had her direct other members in the group in an enactment of what the visit might be like. As she watched the playing out of her father's drinking and seductiveness, two things gradually became clear to her. First, dealing with the feelings evoked by the enactment was difficult enough and she was far from ready to cope with this visit in reality. Second, she realized that her anorexia and self-punishing behavior were linked to guilt over her father's stated preference for her over her mother, and specifically his sexual comments about her body.

At this stage, I followed any scene evoking past feelings with a scene about how she could deal with these feelings. After the scene about the visit with her father, we enacted a scene about how she would feel alone that very evening and what she could do to cope, without resorting to the cutting. This served to help her anticipate her reactions, as well as practice new ways of responding to her pain.

Insight into the cutting deepened in an exercise entailing the creation of a sculpture depicting parts of oneself *(Self-Sculpture)*. The dominant role in Shawn's sculpture was the punishing part of herself. I had her enter the sculpture and assume this part. While playing the role, she surprised herself and the group by spontaneously exclaiming, "I'm your mother!" At the following session, she made a dramatic phone call *(Telephone)* to her deceased mother, whom she contacted in hell. Using some humor as a distancing device, she confronted her mother's negative and punitive attitude toward her. She also addressed her mother's self-destructiveness and the feeling she had that her mother wanted her (Shawn) to emotionally die with her. Shawn reported at the next session that as the impulse to cut herself had arisen a stronger impulse had taken over, which she had succumbed to: to buy herself a doll. It was to be her first doll. As a child, she said, she had never wanted dolls; she hadn't known what to do with them.

By the end of our fourth month, the self-mutilating and self-destructive behavior had ceased. The work from this point on centered largely on the theme of nurturing herself. Her rejection of her inner sad and wounded child was linked to the self-mutilation; she had wanted to get rid of this child. As she started to understand and accept this part of herself, and to experience the empathy that others had for this part of her, she began, via scenework, to find ways of taking care of herself. A great deal of sadness was expressed for the way she had been abandoned and the way she had abandoned herself. Now she struggled to reach this child inside her. There was a scene in which she desperately tried to place a long-distance phone call to her inner child, insisting on getting through despite the difficulty or cost. There was a scene in which she used her creativity and imagination to devise a planet *(Ideal Planet)* in which people cared for themselves, or as she put it, there were no self-child abusers. There were many scenes in which she played the role of a child needing care. And she was increasingly able to play a nurturing parent, albeit in scenes of other members of the group.

There were still days of hopelessness, or times in which emotions overwhelmed her. Any pain of the present triggered tremendous pain from the past. On one occasion, she had just found out that a neighbor had been diagnosed with AIDS. At this time, as at other times of increased emotional stress, she was asked to identify and direct others to play out all the feelings she had. She watched and conducted, which helped her to develop an observing self and to acknowledge and contain all of her emotions. This process also helped her to make the distinction between present stress and feelings left over from her past. I gradually encouraged Shawn to make modifications in the scene—for example, to direct the anger outwardly, instead of inwardly toward herself, or to introduce a nurturing part that could tend to the sad child part of herself. One day, I had Shawn enter the scene and assume the role of this sad child part of herself. I, along with two members of the group, sat next to her. "Doubling" for her, we repeated and added to the feelings she was expressing. Our presence enabled her to relive some of the desolateness she experienced in her childhood, but this time with supportive, understanding people at her side.

As the contact with her neglected inner child developed, Shawn was also drawn to examine her relationship with her son. Through role play, she reviewed challenging interactions with him and practiced communicating more openly and expressing her love more fully. Her skills at mothering her son clearly surpassed her skills at mothering herself, but Shawn was as motivated to enhance the former as she was to discover the latter.

The more playful work also continued and she manifested an increasing zest for improvisation. She seemed to be using this aspect of the group process to experience a childhood she never really had had. Shawn proved to be remarkably expressive. The roles and characters she improvised became increasingly strong and assertive. I directed her in scenes to apply the qualities displayed in character roles, such as assertiveness, toward situations in her own life that were difficult for her. Dramas were enacted in which she had to turn down requests for help by her peers at times in which she really needed all her energy to take care of herself, or in which she had to politely refuse men's invitations that did not interest her.

By the end of our seventh month Shawn was able to perceive her own strengths. She was also able to trust me and her peers without an excessive fear of abandonment. Despite anxieties, especially about separations and endings, she experienced more hope and optimism for the future. She began enacting in scenes (and thereby visualizing and emotionally preparing for) some of the future work and life situations for which she yearned.

In emotionally laden scenes, Shawn no longer needed to stay in the role of director. The observing part of herself was internalized enough so that she could now be the actor. She could handle emotionality without the need for distancing, though she still needed some help taking hold of her pain. For so long she had had a punitive attitude toward her inner child. Now she needed to embrace this child, with all the gentleness and compassion that she was so able to manifest toward other people in the group.

One of Shawn's *culminating scenes* in Phase Four was about saying goodbye to her mother, and not saying goodbye to herself. In the scene, she played herself expressing a multitude of intense feelings toward her mother, including rage and love and disappointment, all of which she could now tolerate. Her capacity to be in touch with and express emotion was matched by her capacity to contain emotion.

"I don't understand why you never lived," Shawn says, gazing toward the empty chair. "You've been dying for as long as I knew you. With the smoking and the drinking and the running and everything. And now when you're dying you don't want to die. It's a little late, don't you think? I don't want to be here watching you die. I've spent my life watching you die."

The tone of sadness is transforming to anger. "Why couldn't you ever live, damn it? And why couldn't you ever see me? Why did you leave me in a car because you couldn't remember I was there? And leave me in a store, and do all the other shit you did."

Now the sadness again, embedded in rage and hurt. "Was I that bad?"

There is a long pause, and I can see that an inner turn is being made. My directions are minimal because by this point in treatment Shawn is remarkably self-directed; the self-actualizing impulse within her, which Maslow describes as an innate force (that is often inhibited by fear), is clearly manifested—Shawn wants to get well. "But the fact that you're going to die doesn't mean I have to die. The fact that you spent your life dying doesn't mean I have to make the same choice." I ask her to repeat this last line. She does, and then thoughtfully adds: "I've sort of done that in the last two years, but I don't have to keep doing it. I'm learning to have my feelings now. Something you never did. That's what everyone in the family was afraid of—all the drinking, all the suicide—running from feelings. But now I'm having mine, and it's not easy. But it doesn't have to kill me to have my feelings."

I now ask Joanne, a very sensitive member of the group with whom Shawn is close, to assume the role of Shawn's neglected inner child. This is the part that Shawn has tried in the past to destroy. Gently, I direct

Shawn to take hold of this part of herself. She does so physically, holding Joanne in her arms. Soon she does so with her tone and her words. "You're very special and you're very loveable. Sometimes I have trouble seeing that, but it's getting easier. When I have trouble it isn't because of anything you've done. It's just that I learned things a whole lot differently, and it's hard doing them the new way. But you're an important and special part of me. And you deserve to be held. And you deserve to be loved. And you deserve to have all the feelings you have."

Without interrupting the scene, I softly suggest to Shawn that she assure her child that she will never say goodbye to her again. There is a very long silent pause as Shawn struggles with this direction. This is by far the most difficult challenge yet: to promise never to abandon herself again. But slowly she reaches inside, until she finds the words. "I know we had to say goodbye to a lot of people in our life, and there will be a lot more. But there is one goodbye I don't ever have to say. And that's to you."

In the closing rituals of Phase Five of her final series of drama therapy, Shawn was able to say goodbye to me and to the group without the sense of abandonment she had experienced in previous endings of our group series. At this ending, what she expressed was gain rather than loss, because this time she was taking herself with her.

IVAN

Ivan was a 31-year-old Caucasion gay man who completed two series of drama therapy. When he was 19, Ivan had attempted suicide by jumping out of a window. The result was paralysis from the waist down, a permanent disability that left him confined to a wheelchair. Although not psychotic, he had undergone six psychiatric hospitalizations since his attempt. He was also a recovering alcoholic. But for the five years preceding our work together, Ivan had functioned without need for hospitalization and had been sober. His decision to attend day treatment at this time was precipitated by a separation from his lover.

In the day treatment center, Ivan was among the more social members; he was friendly, supportive, and spoke openly about his problems. This came easily to him, he said, because of his years of "practice as a patient." Ivan was bright and witty, with a "tough" persona. He was intellectually insightful but emotionally disconnected from the personal issues about which he spoke so articulately. On some days, his usual sociability was superseded by a display of anxiety, depression, or diffuse anger.

In early scenes, Ivan consistently played the role of a rebellious teenager in improvisations. He claimed he loved acting, though it seemed what he really loved was playing this role. With each scene, more anger surfaced via the character of the teenager, until, in the sixth session, he exhibited surprise at the degree of anger that had "come out." At the following session, he acknowledged that he gravitated toward this role because it allowed him to express his own anger.

During the next few weeks, as the group progressed toward the latter part of Phase Two (Scenework), Ivan continued to play a teenager, but the scenes grew more complex. There was an improvisation in which a teenager asked permission to join an extracurricular modern dance club, but his father refused, explaining that he needed instead to devote more time to his studies. "Besides," the father added when I asked Ivan to switch to this role, "it isn't right for boys to be interested in dance, they should be playing sports." There was a scene in which a teenager's request to see a therapist was declined by his parents, who claimed, "Our family is perfectly normal; we don't need any shrinks." The themes continued to revolve around the teenager's frustration at his family's concern for image and the lack of acceptance of his feelings and needs. His emerging sexual feelings toward men combined with the familial and cultural homophobia with which he was surrounded were further sources of frustration, confusion, and pain. "This scene is really close to home," Ivan finally said one day. "It's bringing back memories of my childhood, and how angry and frustrated I got."

Ivan's depression seemed to lift as he expressed anger in scenes and discussed his identification with the enactments. But the intensity of the scenes was still mounting. In one improvisation, he played an alcoholic teenager who desperately attempted to get attention, though his parents did not even notice that he was drunk at the dinner table. By now I had the clear sense that Ivan needed to relive the deep pain and cries for help that preceded his tragic act. Through the dramatic medium, he was struggling to understand and come to grips with the event that changed the course of his life.

In one session, during the transition between Phases Three (Role Play) and Four (Culminating Enactment) of Ivan's first series in drama therapy, I asked the clients to create a sculpture (using others in the group) that reflected a significant aspect of themselves or their lives. Ivan "molded" another client in the position of a person slashing his wrists. The scenes of the past weeks, recalling ever more vividly and intensely the emotions Ivan had experienced over a decade ago, now brought him to the point of his suicide attempt. His sculpture was testing ground for himself and for the group: Can the suicide itself be confronted?

In the following session, clients were asked to sculpt their three most central or frequently experienced emotions *(Self-Sculptures)*. Ivan's sculpture contained only two emotions: anger and sadness.

I directed the sculpture to "come alive," with each actor emoting his or her given part. After a few minutes, I asked Ivan to take over one of the parts. Not surprisingly, he chose the part he had come into closer contact with in our sessions: Anger. As Anger, he began to push Sadness away. He would not tolerate any communion between the two parts. When I suggested a role-switch, he froze.

The deep sadness and loneliness that preceded his suicide attempt had been long buried, and was far more frightening than anger. And there was grief, which had never been expressed, for the body he lost.

I asked Ivan if a third part existed.

"No, but I wish there was one."

"What would it be?"

"Acceptance."

We added Acceptance. Ivan watched, visibly touched. When he later physically embodied this part, there was a surge of vulnerability, all the vulnerability his anger guarded against. In the role of Acceptance, tears surfaced. As he played this role more fully, the tears gave way to full-fledged crying. The dam had been broken.

At the following session, I opened a *Magic Shop.* Clients entered the shop and bargained for human qualities or emotions. Sure enough, Ivan asked for Acceptance.

"What sort of Acceptance do you want?" I questioned as the shopkeeper.

"The forgiveness kind of Acceptance. Forgiveness of myself."

It was toward this forgiveness that the scenes of the series had been leading. It could be avoided no longer. And this is what his *culminating scene,* which he was nearly ready for, was to be about.

I ask Ivan at the following session to create a scene in which he uses his new purchase from the magic shop. We both have the same scene in mind. He says, "I want to be with my self at 19, to talk with him, with forgiveness."

At moments like this, I am once again deeply moved by the desire and capacity of human beings to heal themselves.

Ivan chooses Jesse, a very empathic member of the group, to be Ivan at 19. I suggest that Jesse respond without words, so as not to steer or distract from the scene. I want the scene to belong to Ivan.

The result is a deeply exquisite moment of theatre and of therapy, indeed, of life. One can see Jesse being slowly transformed, in Ivan's eyes, to a younger and deeply troubled Ivan. At the same time, one can feel, throughout this transformation, Jesse's actual presence remaining intact, offering support and love to the adult Ivan.

In addressing his 19-year-old self, Ivan passes through many stages and layers of feelings. First, there is anger, soaring into rage: it is because of this 19-year-old boy that Ivan must spend the rest of his life paralyzed. There is unbearable frustration and regret. But there is also understanding—for the pain that drove the boy to jump, pain relived by the adult Ivan in the past six weeks. The suffering is now shared and with that comes compassion. Although the adult can still not condone the act of the child, and wishes it had not happened, there is love for this child he once was. It is not easy, but ultimately there is forgiveness. Ivan addresses himself with forgiveness only when he can do so without pretending. This moment is for real.

Jesse in his silence exudes more empathy and kindness than could possibly be expressed in language.

As Ivan reaches out to himself, he also reaches inward, for more forgiveness, and he finds this, this hidden well of forgiveness, in his adult self. His tears are joined by ours, and by the time he finishes, there isn't a dry eye in the house.

I say *a moment of theatre* because the scene could have been performed on any stage. It contained the authenticity, depth, and power that is the essence of good theatre.

I say *a moment of therapy* because here is a man who, because the pain was too great, had become disconnected from his emotions. Here is a man who had been at war with himself—the self that tried to kill and the self that survived. In forgiving himself, he is flooded with feeling, but without the risk of drowning. The forgiveness is an embrace of life.

Another *culminating scene* occurred toward the end of Phase Four of Ivan's second series of drama therapy. His 10-month participation at the day treatment center was coming to a close; he was to be discharged as soon as this drama therapy series ended.

Ivan said he wanted to do a scene dealing with the ending of his relationship with his lover.

I knew that they had been separated for two years, and that Ivan spoke frequently in verbal therapy groups and individual sessions about their relationship and separation.

What he wasn't talking about was his feelings about leaving the day treatment center. He was anxious about the upcoming transition, but it seemed easier for him to bring up the more familiar topic of a previous separation, rather than to face his current situation. Given his high level of trust in me and in treatment, I felt it was possible (and important) at this time to be directive: "The theme you're initiating is one of separation and transition, and certainly each separation brings up feelings about other separations we've been through. But why not begin with the one you're about to face—leaving the center—and see where that leads?"

As he nods in agreement, I notice that his expression has shifted; he looks more vulnerable. I ask what he fears about this separation. He describes being alone in his apartment.

"Sometimes at night I have periods of loneliness, a loneliness that really aches. It's almost an existential feeling. I get very sad and empty. I'm afraid that without the day treatment, which has given me so much structure and contact with people, these periods may be harder to bear. It's not just loneliness. It's being alone with my feelings."

I suggest that he *show* us what this state is like, alone in his apartment, beginning with an exploration of how this state is triggered.

He arranges several chairs, a table with a plant, the phone prop on the floor near a cushion, creating some semblance of his apartment. Then he places himself in the scene. I am impressed by the way he takes his time; it reminds me of the way an actor trained in Stanislavski's "Method" might concentrate with his whole being until the character, fraught with senses, emotions, motivations, becomes real. Only here the character Ivan is trying to build is himself, himself in a particular state of mind.

Ivan wanders, looking a bit lost. Then he struggles out of his wheelchair, sits down on the cushion, and dials the phone. From his monologue, it is clear that he has called a friend who is busy studying for an exam and doesn't have time to talk. Ivan hangs up, dejected.

After a long interlude, Ivan breaks out of the scene. "What would make me feel even worse now is a call from my father." I have the phone ring. Ivan picks it up, once again concentrating on the scene.

"Hi, Dad. Yeah. No, nothing's new. *(long pause)* I don't want to be busy, Dad. No, that doesn't interest me. *(pause)* Dad, you're always telling me I should be busy, I should get involved in this and that. That might work for you, but I need to leave time for me to *feel what I'm feeling,* not to escape it."

As he sets the receiver down, it is clear that he is now fully engrossed in the scene; in his imagination, *this is actually taking place,* at this moment. For the audience, it almost seems like eavesdropping; we are witnessing Ivan's private life and inner state. Except that we have been invited to do so. In this way we can *feel with* Ivan. As audience to this drama, our senses, too, are involved, enabling us to understand much more fully than when we hear Ivan *talk about* this state. It is a quiet, subtle scene, devoid of plot or action, so very different from his early feisty scenes. And yet, because the scene is played with truthfulness, it is rich and captivating. Ivan begins to cry. Softly, I ask what he might do with these feelings. Without breaking his concentration, Ivan, now back in his wheelchair, opens a drawer, takes out a candle, and slowly lights it. He goes over to the stereo, puts on a Bob Dylan record. The music he has selected intensifies his mood. He cries some more. The room is silent.

A bit later, again in a low voice that does not disrupt the ambiance he has created, I ask him what might follow. "I might go out. I'd like to go to the beach, look at the waves."

"The ocean is out that way," I point to the far corner of the room. Ivan wheels over slowly. Then, for what seems like a long time, he looks into the ocean.

This stillness and languor, unusual in dramatic scenes, contributes to the sense that life is being mirrored on our stage. The external simplicity is purifying. For the audience, the poignancy of the scene lies in being with someone who is alone. For the actor, it is in sharing his aloneness with others.

Stanislavski would have been proud: Here is a someone with no script or plot, few props, no persons to "play off of," fully recreating a moment in time. The presence of the ocean, so keenly felt by the player, is transmitted to the audience. One senses the solace it offers. Soon Ivan's state seems to be more one of meditation and reflection than of pain.

Now he wheels over to what becomes a café. He orders a cappuccino, which soon we can nearly smell, and begins writing in a journal. Clearly, he is converting feelings into words, using the void he has been courageous enough to face as material for creation. Again, there is almost no action on stage—just a man writing. After a few minutes, he puts his pen down. He is ready to communicate more directly with us. He finds the perfect way to make the transition out of the scene: He reads to us the poem he has just written.

It is a poem about pain and strength. About emptiness and fullness. About acceptance of the totality of what we have been through and whom we have become.

The group is touched, but in some faces I can see the settling in of depression. Ivan's pain and loneliness have mirrored their own. The scene has subjected many clients in the group to feelings they usually suppress; Ivan's confrontation with these feelings impels them to do the same. The session is nearly over. I motion for us to sit in a circle, and initiate a discussion about how each of us experiences and copes with the state of emptiness and aloneness. Group members begin to speak about what they do, or would like to be able to do, at these times. Some describe methods of escape, some of discharge and release, others of expression and creation. To enter more deeply into this state and experience its full intensity, rather than attempting to rid oneself of it, is a new idea to some. But I can see depression melting into hopefulness as the group's association to this inner confrontation shifts from desolation and relapse to consolation and renewal.

Ivan's culminating scenes were about facing himself with tenderness and strength. The culminating scene from the first series focused on his past; the culminating scene from the second series on the present. It was my hope that he would be able to draw on these scenes in future times when real life tested him, as sometimes it takes recalling experiences on-stage to handle the challenges of real life.

LISA

Lisa was fair-skinned with blond shoulder-length hair framing her young and almost childlike features. She was from the South, and still retained a Southern drawl. Her style was simple and natural; she wore corduroy pants, tee shirts, no make-up. She looked right at you when she spoke; there was an intentness in her gaze. Her eyes were an unforgettable aqua color. At times, Lisa projected impishness, at other times there was a waif-like quality about her. I was surprised to learn she was 27; she looked about 17. Her voice and mannerisms were even younger than her physical appearance.

Her chart revealed that she first began seeing a psychotherapist in elementary school, had come close to completing a college degree in philosophy, had undergone several brief psychiatric hospitalizations during the past 7 years, and was currently diagnosed with Atypical Paranoid Disorder and Borderline Personality Disorder. She refused all psychiatric medication and maintained a strict macrobiotic diet. Lisa was brought up by a combination of foster home placements, aunt and uncle, and, in her early childhood, a schizophrenic mother. Lisa's parents had married when her mother became pregnant at 17. Her father, a military man, left her mother when Lisa was a year old. There was one piece of Lisa's history that was startling: When Lisa was five years old, her mother had suffocated Lisa's twin brother in his bed.

The staff in the day treatment center often viewed Lisa as moody, withdrawn, regressed, and manipulative. They were frustrated with her seeming unwillingness to "work on" significant issues in her life and with her flat unemotional affect. Lisa's firm opinions about so many things—diet, fluorescent lighting, superficial conversation—contributed to the staff's perceptions of her as rigid and controlling. Lisa interacted little with staff or fellow clients. She preferred reading or meditating in the corner of a dark room.

To me, she had magical charm. Her eyes sparkled, her speech was often poetic—in a way that made precise sense if one listened attentively enough, and she was delightfully creative. I saw the brooding and ultrasensitive side of her too, but in the drama therapy group the lighthearted and imaginative part of her prevailed. In pantomime, she invented fanciful objects; in improvisation, she created colorful characters. She developed scenes with ease and humor. The staff were amazed at how actively she participated in this group.

There were also sessions, during her first series of drama therapy, in which she withdrew, sometimes to the point of catatonia. On these occasions, she refused to participate, speak, or move. But even at these times, she remained in the room throughout the entire session. In fact, Lisa never missed a single session.

At times she stopped me in the hallway before the group began and with a mischievous grin asked, "Can we be rambunctious today?" In leading *Mirror* exercises, she sometimes started with slow simple movements and then suddenly let out an earth-shattering scream, startling the group. Or she beat the floor, and then stopped as abruptly as she had started. There was a sense of shock in the way she conducted these expressions of fear and anger, devoid of sustainment, development, emotional affect. A kind of trauma, with no "follow-up." Indeed, this is what her *culminating scene* was to be about.

First there were months filled with creative skits. The characters and scenarios she devised during Phases One and Two (Dramatic Play and Scenework) were vivid and humorous, though strikingly devoid of emotion. I remember her characterization of a peculiar suburban housewife who complained about her neighbor's peacock trespassing her backyard. Or the untidy roommate who considered her sloppiness to be a sign of her capacity to "let go." Or the prison guard who couldn't stay awake. I remember how surprised and pleased Lisa was when I complimented her on her creativity. She said she had never thought of herself as creative.

She became increasingly consistent and the nonparticipative bouts ceased. As her trust in me, in the group, and in herself developed, and as the group entered Phase Three (Role Play), she began initiating scenes related to her personal experiences. When I brought in telephones, she "got up the nerve" (as she put it) to play a scene in which she placed a long-distance call to her father to wish him happy birthday. She claimed she needed the practice; it was already past his birthday and she hadn't been able to "psyche herself up" to call him. After the call, she spoke of the awkwardness of their barely existent relationship. Her father had rarely been mentioned in this or other areas of treatment. Her spontaneous association to the telephone was that of distance and the desire for contact, both primary elements in her remote relationship with her father.

Toward the middle of Phase Four (Culminating Enactment) of her second series of drama therapy, just before her 35th session, Lisa approaches me to say she wants to work on her brother's death. I sit down with her privately and ask her what made her think of dealing with this event at this time. I do not take for granted that the reenactment of traumatic events is necessarily beneficial. I do not take for granted that catharsis will occur and, even if it does, that it is in all cases healing. When, how, and *whether* to work on a scene needs careful consideration. Lisa explains that a staff member recently confronted her on cutting off her feelings. While giving this some thought, Lisa began to suspect that this process of aborting feelings had originated at the time she witnessed her brother's death. Perhaps if she went back to this moment, she would start to feel again.

I ask her to tell me the story. I want to know what her memories are and I want to know the extent of emotional severance.

"Well, I was five years old," she begins in her flat, childish voice. "My brother showed me a Christmas card he had made for my mother. He made me promise not to tell her; it was to be a surprise. Then my mother came in and said she was going to read my brother a bedtime story. He went into his bedroom. I called my mother to put on the record player for me. When she came to the living room, I sneaked out the Christmas card and showed it to her. Then she went back to the bedroom. I went to my bedroom, which was next to my brother's room. I heard my brother coughing and choking and then saying 'Stop, I can't breathe.' I went to his bedroom door and saw her pushing a pillow down on his face. She shut the door on me. I went back and sat on my bed. My mother came out sobbing and called the fire department. I thought, 'What's she crying for? *She did it.*"

Although she has related the story in a monotone, I detect a trace of feeling. "Can I do the scene today?" she asks.

The session is about to start and my mind is racing. It is Friday; I am nearly certain it would be better to wait until the following session, on Wednesday. I am reluctant to work on such loaded material (for Lisa *and* for the other group members) just prior to the weekend. The midweek sessions allow for immediate follow-up and support should that be needed. Also, waiting until Wednesday would enable me to check on her continued interest in working on the scene, providing some assurance that she will be able to handle the ensuing emotions and that her present eagerness is not based solely on impulse. It would give me time to consult with others on the treatment staff and reflect on ways of approaching the scene. The obvious drawback in waiting is that Lisa's "ripeness" for the work may be lost. As the other clients enter, I consider their needs too. I had planned on trying to engage some of the quieter members today. In Lisa's case, "ripeness" is not a critical factor, and I decide it is best to wait. I explain this to her at the end of the session.

I can tell even before she says anything on Wednesday that she is as ready as she was on Friday. I am further reassured by the stability of her mood and the cohesive, supportive feeling in the group. Lisa has never shared this event with any of them. Before she describes what is to take place, I intimate to the group that the forthcoming scene may be painful and distressing.

As she selects the players, I recognize the perceptiveness of her choices.* For her mother, she selects the most disturbed member of the group, a young, attractive woman who is diagnosed as paranoid schizophrenic. Marie is sometimes warm and friendly, sometimes cold and hostile—very unpredictable. She is also the mother of two young children who have been placed in a foster home. As her brother, Lisa casts a mildly brain-damaged young man whose behavior is very much like that of an innocent, loving child. Lisa will play herself, 22 years ago.

By the detailed way she sets up the stage, representing the living room and bedrooms, I can tell that she will remain "overdistanced" (that is, on the side of emotional detachment). Indeed, as the scene is enacted, she is as much in the role of director as actor. The distance is a necessary safeguard for her at this point. She has the event played out as she had described it to me, adding only some motivation for the murder: Her mother is mad at her brother about something, so she grabs him and pushes the pillow over his face.

There is a surreal quality to this drama. It is directed and enacted as if the events taking place were not at all extraordinary. The squelched emotion comes out in the form of obsession for detail and order. The clarity and specificity of Lisa's direction make the scene almost simple to carry out. Yet somewhere beneath the unbearably smooth exterior of the scene, I can hear the startling screams that erupted from Lisa in

---

*Often the choice of *auxiliaries* manifests a subtle intuitive process between group members that Moreno (1969) called "tele."

free-form sound and movement exercises. Feelings from a long time ago—aborted. Or nearly.

The audience is still. I know I must get them involved, for to sit and watch this atrocity only elicits feelings of helplessness. I direct them to enter as the fire department crew. Lisa adds that the firemen must take her mother away: "That's what happened."

With the hysterical mother and lifeless brother hauled off, Lisa is left alone on stage. I stand at her side. She explains that at this point her foster mother came and got her. As I begin suggesting that someone take this part and talk with her, she immediately insists that this never took place: No one spoke to her about what happened or bothered to ask how *she was feeling*. This is a difficult transition point: letting go of what actually took place means letting go of her control over the scene. Her control and obsessiveness finally abate, and she allows me to be the director.

I tell her she is still five years old and there is an understanding adult at her side, to whom she can express any feelings or thoughts she may have. I place Jane, a strong and caring woman, in this role. A moment after the scene begins, Lisa halts, repeating that this never happened, but then—with my continued acknowledgment—she goes along with the drama. Her voice is even more childlike than usual. Some words come, but there is little emotion. Jane is visibly uncomfortable. But suddenly, stuck in the bits of dialogue, I catch Lisa murmuring, *"I want my brother back."* Attached to these words is a faint tremor. I know it will hurt, but I gently ask her to repeat this line. She does, and this time her voice cracks. The third time she says it there is moisture in her eyes.

This line now becomes the backbone of the fragmented dialogue. At one point she leaves the word *back* out and half the emotion leaves with it. I ask her to maintain the line in its entirety. Now she is on the verge of crying, and along with her tears, buried for so long, are the tears of the group. Jane looks at me helplessly. "I don't know what to say." "You don't have to say anything," I respond. "All I can think to do is hold her," she says. "Yes, do that."

Lisa has been the child long enough. Approaching the stage area, I ask her now to play the adult. As I do this, I am also aware that playing the child will be too difficult at this time for anyone in the group. Though generally I remain on the outside, directing and overseeing, there are times in which it is best (for the protagonist or for the group) that I assume a role. This is one of those times.

As I enter my role as a five-year-old child who has just witnessed her mother killing her brother, I am aware that the therapeutic choice for the enactment is to have the part be played with emotion—the emotion Lisa herself has just begun to express. There is a wound here that desperately needs acknowledgment. I am now both actress and therapist. I say the line that I know will evoke the feeling: *I want my brother back.* Now I find the thoughts that will amplify the feeling. Alongside Lisa's pain, I am thinking of my love for my own brother, I am thinking of a death suffered in my own childhood. I say the line again, this time like a five-year-old. I sense the tears welling up in my eyes and choose to let them surface.

It is a strange phenomenon. Therapists are trained to maintain clear boundaries between themselves and their clients and to monitor the degree of emotion they express with (and for) their clients. Yet here, via my dramatic role, I have the sanction to embody Lisa's pain and to let the pain I feel for her, and for all suffering children, be manifest. Through me, Lisa recognizes emotional pain—her pain.

My script is composed of what she said, or almost said, when she played this role. There is fear and confusion. Stored in the word *back* is not only deep sadness but the intimation of anger. As I draw on these emotions, Lisa as adult tries to reach out to me, but it is hard for her. She is brave; I know she is fighting a desire to retreat. Soon I will grant her this, but first, there is one more feeling that I think is important to broach.

"Should I have done something to stop her?" I ask meekly.

Lisa's intent look seems to convey: Yes, I have this question. Instead she says, "What could you have done?"

"I don't know, what should I have done?"

Lisa drops her role for a moment and says to me softly, "I always wondered if I could have stopped her." Before I can respond, she is back in role, asking, "Were you scared?" I nod. "Real scared."

"Scared she'd do something to you?"

"Scared she'd hurt me too."

I leave my chair and curl up on the floor. Lisa is silent. I look up at her and ask if I did anything wrong. She shakes her head gently. I look up at her again, still confused and torn. "No?"

"No, there was nothing you could have done." And now there are real tears as she whispers, "Believe me, it wasn't your fault. You were only five years old."

And then she holds me.

That deep inner well of emotion that confounds, frightens, pierces, and challenges us is also a source of primal sustenance. In drawing from it, we are enlivened, rejoined with the life force within us. But for Lisa, emotions were suffocated the day her brother was suffocated. Now she had access to this well once again. It was a well she drew from continuously, with both caution and curiosity, during her remaining three months in drama therapy.

CHRISTINE

I have to go back to my videotapes to remember what Christine looked like when I first met her. The image that installed itself in my memory is of Christine three years later, when she looked entirely different. At 37, she had the appearance of a chronic mental patient. She was stooped, unkempt, withdrawn. She frequently wore plastic masks to guard against germs, as her environmental allergies were severe. Naturally, the masks further isolated her socially. After I got to know her, I understood how she had come to be so wary of people and so desperately in need of protection. Can we expect a child traumatized as deeply as she had been to grow up trusting the world?

At 40, Christine looked 10 years younger. Her cropped hair had grown out Afro-style, her dress was casual and attractive, and her face glowed with the intelligence and warmth it had always possessed beneath its many masks. She was wonderfully radiant and engaging as she described to me her adventures on a recent two-month trip through South America.

The staff at the day treatment center had not referred Christine to drama therapy. Her attendance was too inconsistent and her avoidance of people too extreme. Judging from her overall lack of motivation and commitment to treatment, they felt she would not benefit from drama therapy. In fact they thought that her lack of progress since she began the program (five months earlier) might warrant dismissal. But Christine had spoken with me briefly in the hallway once, expressing some curiosity about "what goes on in the drama therapy group." "Would you be interested in being in the next series?" I asked her. Her response was, "I don't think I'd be any good, but I might try it." I don't know if it was a flash I caught in her eye, giving the subtlest hint of the worlds that lay braced beneath her exterior, or some inexplicable sense I had of prospective relationship between us. Could it be that what is described as chemistry in coupling is an aspect of all relationships, including therapeutic alliances? I told the staff that I wanted to give Christine a chance. It was one decision no one ever regretted.

Christine, who was biracial, had a long history of psychiatric hospitalizations since age 18. The nine hospitalizations were precipitated by severe depression, suicide attempts, and catatonic episodes. Christine had been adopted when she was six years old by a Swedish couple. Until adoption she had lived with her emotionally unstable and sporadically neglectful Caucasion mother and a loving though not fully available grandmother. Her biological

African-American father had left before Christine was born. Christine's adoptive mother was addicted to valium and had attended a residential drug rehabilitation program for close to a year when Christine was 10. Her adoptive father was a successful and caring but "workaholic" businessman. Christine lived with her adoptive parents until she was 35 (and they were in their 70s), at which time she obtained her own apartment. Despite this achievement, she had difficulty emotionally separating from the symbiotic family and developing peer relationships. Her allergies were considered to be psychosomatic and, along with numerous other physical ailments, they limited her participation in day treatment activities and in life.

During the first few drama therapy sessions, Christine withdrew. The physically active and socially interactive games of Phase One seemed to overwhelm her. There were sessions incorporating exercises such as *Ball Throws,* in which we tossed imaginary and then real balls; *Gibberish* exercises, in which the whole group spoke in made-up languages; *Emotional Greetings,* in which members shook hands according to various emotions I called out. Christine stood on the sidelines, though I noted that she watched the others intently. In trust exercises, she refused to shut her eyes and in *Nurturing Falls* (in which one leans backwards and is caught by the group), her rigid body wouldn't budge. When encouraged to try, her only comment was, "I've fallen too many times."

But when we began improvisational scenework at the fifth session, marking the transition to Phase Two, I caught a glimpse of her stored creativity. In her first scene, which took place in a restaurant, she played a waitress and a go-between. A young female customer, who was too nervous to order anything, confided in the waitress that she was very attracted to the gentleman eating crepes at a neighboring table. Though Christine's role was brief, she was witty and imaginative as she moved back and forth between the two customers, encouraging their interest in each other. For example, when the woman eagerly asked the waitress, "What does he do for a living?" Christine retorted, "Oh, he owns a couple of uranium mines." That which emerges spontaneously in improvisation often relates to one's own world. When asked why the gentleman wasn't wearing any shoes, Christine quipped, "He's allergic to them. His pores like to breathe."

Her next improvisational scene stemmed from the exercise, *Line Repetition* (in which two people dialogue using two lines only), with the given lines being "I want it" and "You can't have it." Christine played a storekeeper who refused to sell a punch bowl that was on reserve. But her customer, played by Charlie (a 21-year-old man with a sociopathic history) was adamant, insisting on purchasing this particular bowl. Here Christine sustained her role much longer than in her previous scene. When finally I asked Christine and

Charlie to come to a resolution, Charlie's immediate response was, "You better give me the fucking punch bowl before I break it over your head." Christine's response was to shout, "Police, police!" I wasn't surprised. Charlie's way of handling the conflict was typical of the acting-out adolescents I work with, using a threat of violence or destruction to assert power. Christine's was that of many passive and dependent adults—to cry for outside help.

Video was an integral part of this series. Aside from taping and viewing segments of most sessions, the clients were asked three times during the series to sit before the television monitor and address their own live image (described in Chapter 7 as *Confronting Yourself on Video*). They were left alone in the room for this intimate encounter. Christine's stance was one of attack and self-deprecation.

Looking at herself on the screen, she spoke disdainfully: "Dumb idiot. You look real stupid. Look at you, you're fat, you're ugly. You're a bitch. *(long pause).* Say something. Look at me when I talk to you. Don't you obey? What's the matter with you? You're really stupid. You make me nervous. I don't like you at all. As a matter of fact I hate you. I wish you were dead."

Despite her self-hatred, those creative sparks that seem capable of hibernation in humans for decades, if necessary, emerged. In exercises such as *Transforming the Object* (in which one creates objects in pantomime, or uses actual objects in novel ways), she was inventive and funny and her use of props was imaginative. In one session, participants were given several props with which to create an improvisation. Christine turned a pink sheet into a pink Volkswagen, and herself into a drunken old lady who had just crashed. Alone on stage, half covered by the sheet, she shrieked, "Heeellpp," interspersing her unforgettable cries with hiccups. The rescue team, consisting of two men, arrived. As they began hosing down the car (with long balloons!) and taking out the crowbar (in pantomime), Christine's cries for help turned into pleas to be left alone. She used the actual mistrust she lived with daily in her role as the delirious and paranoid drunk. "Don't come near me, leave me alone, heeellpp, don't touch me. You bad men, you!" Aside from expressing an inner conflict—both wanting and distrusting help—the scene brought the audience to fits of laughter.

It was in the 10th session that Christine confronted herself again on video. Her tone was more gentle, and her affect sad. "I like you a little better than I did before. But I'm still not satisfied and I don't think I'll ever be satisfied. You should have been a success and you're a failure. You're even failing at this. You make me want to cry for a hundred thousand years. And that's a long time."

Once the veil of anger and self-hatred lifts, there are layers upon layers of sadness. I've seen this process over and over in my clients. Grief seems to be a territory that has no limits. "A hundred thousand years . . ."

At the 12th session, as the group seemed to be entering Phase Three, I brought telephones as props. Christine spontaneously improvised a conversation with her adoptive mother. Her portrayal was wonderfully expressive and strikingly believable; it was as if someone were indeed on the other end of the line. After numerous "uh-huh"s, Christine exclaimed, "Yeah, I'm listening. No, don't get mad, I'm listening!" Distressed, she pulled the phone away from her ear for some momentary relief.

I directed her to role play her mother, and another client to play Christine listening. As soon as Christine switched chairs, she slipped into the role:

"My back hurts, and my legs, they ache so bad. Are you listening to me? You don't know how much pain I go through. Nobody cares a damn about me. Your father and you—you're both alive—but you're not taking care of me like I took care of my mother. You're probably not even listening. Well I have all those pills in my drawer, and one of these days I'll take them all and I'll be dead."

When Nancy as Christine tried to intercede, Christine as her mother reversed tactics:

"I worry about you. What's going to happen to you after I die? Who's going to take care of you?"

I asked them to switch roles.

"I can do all right by myself, Mother. Look, I've been living on my own for the past two years."

Nancy as Mother challenged this. "I worry about you living on your own. That's why I have you call me every day. You should move back in with me, so I would know you're all right."

Christine practiced asserting her independence from the symbiotic relationship, both in terms of taking care of her mother and being taken care of. "Look, aren't we better friends since I moved out? I'm doing OK by myself. I'd like to take care of you and Daddy but I can't do it myself. Maybe you should have adopted more than one kid."

And then, in her self-deprecating fashion: "Or maybe you should have adopted someone else. I can't help it if I'm mentally ill. You think I'm stupid, don't you?"

"Well, if you were smart you wouldn't have ended up in day treatment." Nancy has picked up the critical tone and stance of Christine's mother.

"You were in a rehabilitation yourself. Besides I've done a lot of improving since I've been here. I've started to work hard on my problems. And Mom, I can do all right by myself."

I heard Christine trying to convince both her mother and herself of her new state, which was in fact in a formative stage. I told her, "This is your only or main line, Christine. Keep saying it." She looked at me for a second, the sides of her mouth curling slightly in a near smile; she was pleased to have permission for this feeling.

"I can do all right by myself. I get lonely sometimes and I call you up, but I get by now on my own." There was more strength in her voice now, and a hint of anger. "I'm not you and you're not me. And Mother, listen, I can do all right by myself. Do you understand? I CAN TAKE CARE OF MYSELF." I cut the scene on this powerful note, but not before Christine had interjected an emphatic, "I CAN!"

Christine now asked that the mother be played in a more provocative manner. Sensing that she wanted uncensored incitation to facilitate her own emotional expression, but with protection at hand, I assumed this role. Christine responded by exploding with repressed anger.

"You don't know what you're doing," I challenged. "You can't take care of yourself."

"I do too!" she shouted.

"Watch the way you talk to me. Do you realize that I'm sick and in pain. My back, it . . ."

"Sick shit!"

"What? Christine, am I hearing right?"

"Oh shut up, I can't take anymore."

"Do you know I'm getting old? You know what I could do? I'll go and take my bottle of pills . . ."

"Go ahead and take it. I don't give a damn. I wish you were dead anyway." She slammed the receiver.

The intense emotional energy, reverberating in the room, needed further discharge. To talk now about the feelings would create distance; instead I wanted to provide an outlet for the unspeakable. Those irrational, inarticulate, sometimes preverbal feelings are usually set aside, tucked away, stored in the body. But in Christine they had reached the surface, demanding release. The release must come from the body, and from the voice.

I asked everyone in the group to find a partner and I stayed with Christine. Face-to-face, as in *Mirror* exercises this group had done before (in which one person moves identically to her partner, as though she is a mirror-image), I joined her, so that our movements and vocalizations were synchronized. There was screaming in unison, pounding and stamping. I wanted to be with her, literally, as she vented feelings that could seem overwhelming and dangerous. My partnership in this primal territory facilitates expression partly by creating a container, a safety valve. I am a follower, but a magnifier; what she initiates is instantly doubled. I extended and expanded any movements or sounds she hesitantly began, encouraging her to see where it led. Now we were on all fours, growling and snarling like raging dogs. Later, our worn-out movements, droopy with signs of relief, gained a second wind. Hanging arms began to swing, stretches distended into reaching gestures. Each shift I detected in her body was captured and mirrored in my own, with slight exaggeration, concretizing the new physical state. Her chest, usually so concave, was now open and, as if a burden had been lifted, her breathing was slower, fuller. Our movements became lighthearted, with a trace of gaiety.

There were more *Mirror* exercises in subsequent sessions. Christine seemed to enjoy leading and emoting, both of which she had been unwilling to do earlier in the series. I gave her many opportunities to lead the group, knowing it enabled her to experience a degree of control and importance.

During one session, a *Mirror* exercise called *Circle-Mirror-Transformation* (in which individuals initiate, transform, and mirror repeatable sounds and movements), had snowballed into such highly emotive physicalizations that I had kept it going for about half an hour. Christine came toward me with a singsong, "Let's quit, I say," repeated with playful assertion and conviction. I joined her and then ended the game. I noted her ability to come forward with her needs, to take charge. Christine would soon be ready to direct.

She was no longer wearing allergy-protection masks and her attendance at the center was now consistent. In fact, she hadn't missed a single drama therapy session since the third week of the series. There were other striking changes. In trust exercises such as *Nurturing Falls,* she let herself fall nearly to the floor before being caught. Given that her body was more relaxed, her movements more fluid, and her trust in others greatly increased, this was not too surprising. But the change was so impressive that the group sometimes broke into a spontaneous applause.

In one session, Charlie (the client who had played the belligerent customer in the store scene) was confronted on his inconsistent attendance. In an effort to deal with his resistance to me and to the group in a nonthreatening and playful way, I reversed roles with him. He became the group leader and I role played him. During the scene, the group members gave me (as Charlie) feedback on my behavior, something they had been unable or unwilling to give Charlie directly. Christine was among the most vocal participants. In the discussion following the scene, she addressed Charlie in a firm but gentle tone: "You're a part of us, part of the group. Like an arm is part of the body. When it's missing, what can you do, you miss that arm, it affects the rest of you. When you're not here, we miss you. We want you here."

In the following session, the group members, intrigued by the role play in the previous session, asked for the opportunity to role play each other. Christine made an interesting choice. She decided to become Carmen, a seductive woman whose sexuality was quite apparent. As the scene began,

Christine walked sultrily over to Daniel, a young, tall, attractive, and high-functioning client in the group. "You're really good-looking, you know that," she said, looking straight into his eyes. Later she sat down next to Alex, an attractive and sociable man in his late forties. She stroked his Afro, admiringly. Catching on, he said, "I like you too. I got this apartment, you want to come over some time?" A little embarrassed, but still in role, she said, "Sure, that'd be real nice." After the scene, Christine commented: "I picked the person the most different from me. I tried to be as sexy as I could. Because you're pretty sexy, Carmen. It was fun and scary at the same time. I never would have done that as myself."

Her phrase, "I never would have done that as myself," is striking because in fact she did *do it,* and because what we choose to play, consciously or unconsciously, is an aspect of ourselves. The disguise—be it in the form of character, mask, or role—enables self-revelation. At 37, Christine's sexuality was just surfacing. She had never had a lover. Her appearance and, indeed, self-image was asexual. But what she displayed in the scene was soon to become, in a more subtle and integrated fashion, a part of her. Often in drama I detect the first traces of emergent issues, feelings, and behaviors. In this and other scenes, Christine was testing new ground, within the safe world of make-believe. She was beginning to try on new roles, experiment with new sensations, practice new behaviors. Ten months from now Christine would embark on her first relationship with a man. A year from now she would take her first step outside of California, on a trip with her boyfriend through South America.

One afternoon, Christine privately asked me if she could direct a scene in the group. Sure enough, the scene she described was the scene that had the most profound effect on her life. I thought it over, considering her readiness, potential ramifications, ways of handling this traumatic material. Probably I would keep her in the role of director, rather than having her become the protagonist, though only the evolution of the drama-in-progress could indicate its ultimate course.

It is the 18th session of the series. The group has become quite close, and is on the threshold of Phase Four (Culminating Enactment); the dramas have been increasingly related to deep concerns and conflicts of individual members. Christine tells the group about the scene she would like to direct: "There is a child, seven years old, sitting with her grandmother. Her mother is in the bedroom. The girl doesn't suspect anything. But then her grandmother tells her that a couple is coming over soon to take her away for a while. The girl keeps asking why till her grandmother says it's because her mother can't take care of her anymore.

The girl doesn't want to go but the couple come and take her. She has no idea that this is the last time in her life she will see her mother."

The group is silent. Then Charlie asks, "What is this from?"

"It really happened."

Charlie: "To who?"

Christine: "To me."

I ask Christine to choose her players. She casts Charlie as the six-year-old child, whom she decides to call Chris. She has Alex play the grandmother and Gil, the participating staff member, the mother. All the originally female roles have been assigned to men. Clearly this affords her an added degree of emotional distance from a trauma that was perpetrated by women.

"Mother" is told to remain in the bedroom, putting on nail polish, throughout the entire scene. She is not to react to the events taking place in the adjacent living room except to occasionally stop and listen. "Granny" has the major task: breaking the news to little Chris. David and Nancy, cast as the couple, are to wait outside until Christine instructs them to knock on the door. Christine stands just outside of the playing area—half in, half out—ready to give cues. Her body is taut and alert.

The scene begins. Chris sits on the floor, clutching a teddy bear.

Alex, as Granny enters. "Some people are going to come and take care of you for a while."

"Why," asks Chris, surprised.

Granny repeats the same thing.

Chris protests. "But why, I don't want to go away. I want to stay here with you and Mommy."

Finally, Granny, who is continuously cued by Christine, says, "It's not that we don't love you. It's just that I'm getting too old and your mommy can't take care of you anymore."

"But why?" Chris repeats, growing alarmed.

"Well," Granny replies, "your mommy's no longer able to manage taking care of you."

Christine cuts the scene. "More whiney," she directs Charlie. "More upset, like I DON'T WANT TO GO. OK, action."

Chris protests more intensely, and suddenly the scene is like a flame that has just caught fire. Christine has the couple knock on the door. The tension mounts. Granny goes slowly to answer the door, and motions to the couple to enter. They act friendly but Chris is sulky and unresponsive to their overtures.

They try enticing him. "We've got a nice big house and a big brown dog."

Chris looks away. "But I don't know you. You're taking me away from my mommy and my granny and I don't want to go with you."

"We can go out and get you a big sundae, how's that?"

"No, don't take me away," Chris is now pleading.

Christine cuts the scene. She wants Charlie to be even more emphatic. Charlie, ordinarily so detached and "cool," tries for yet more emotion.

He achieves this easily when Christine directs Granny to leave the room, the couple to become more insistent, and finally to take hold of him physically. He panics and screams.

Christine gives him his line. "Scream, 'I want my mommy.' " Somehow she is still managing to direct, even as she is entirely wrapped up in the action.

Chris is crying out with his his whole body now, "LET ME GO . . . I WANT MY MOMMY . . ." over and over.

Christine, watching him intently, is crying too. Both inside and outside of the scene, feeling for and as the child, she echoes, "I want my mommy, louder, Chris, I want her."

The mother continues to put on nail polish, layer upon layer, in the bedroom.

Chris' piercing cries reverberate, as they drag him out of the room through the door. "I WANT MY MOMMY, I WANT MY MOMMY, I WANT MY MOMMY, MOMMY, MOMMY . . ." The cries, now rising from his gut, have become a deep wail.

It is not yet time to talk; words would not match the pain felt in the body. Being the director has provided Christine a degree of distance and control over a trauma which as a six-year-old child she had no control over. But even as she directs, she is also a player; even as Christine watches the drama from the vista of adulthood, she has reentered her childhood. Herein lies the potency of enactment: to talk about a memory keeps it at a distance; to reenact it brings it to life, reawakening the feelings and sensations one experienced at the time. The suffering of the child cannot be undone. But now there is someone who can bring comfort and understanding to the hurting child: the adult she has become. Christine will need to draw on all the adult strengths and skills she has acquired in tending the aching child.

I ask Charlie to remain in the scene, in a role that has filled him with intense emotion and enabled him to express, for the first time perhaps since his own childhood, vulnerability. He sits on the floor, clinging to the teddy bear. I ask Christine to enter as an adult capable of helping the child. Her entrance into this role marks her shift back into adulthood, but without the necessity of distancing herself from the pain she feels for/as the child. Calling herself Annie, she kneels at Chris' side. And in a tone of deep recognition, she quietly says, "I know how you feel." Chris protests, "No, you don't!" More to herself than to convince him, she murmers, "I do."

Chris appeals to her. "Why do I have to go? Do they have to take me away?" "Yes," Annie replies both firmly and gently. "I'm afraid it's something that has to happen." Chris whimpers, "But why, did I do something wrong?" Annie looks at him intently. "No, you did not do anything wrong. It's just that your mommy is no longer able to take care of you. She loves you. But she doesn't have a husband, and she has a lot of problems. It's not your fault, but there's nothing you can do to change it. It's not fair, and I know it hurts, I know it hurts a lot." Chris looks up at her, as if to see if this knowledge may be genuine. She meets his searching gaze. "God, I know it hurts."

I can now end the enactment; the bridge to expressing feelings in words has been made. While they are still in the physical postures of their roles, I ask Charlie how he feels, and he describes the sadness and hurt and anger. I ask Christine what it is like to play the adult trying to help the child. "It's hard. How can you explain to a child that he's going to lose his mother forever? That his mother maybe doesn't want him." As if struck by what she just said, she whispers, "That's too horrifying even to think about."

Once we are out of the stage area, I ask Christine in what ways this trauma affects her today, how this past event influences present-day reactions. "I carry it out almost every day of my life. If I don't get my way, if things don't go just right, I get very upset and depressed. I say, 'Screw the whole world, I don't need you. I don't need you, world. I don't need anybody. I don't need you, Mommy. I can get along ok by myself. If I can't, I'm going to shoot myself."

"So you don't just say I can do all right by myself, you add, 'If I can't, I'm going to shoot myself.' "

"Yeah," she admits with a sheepish grin. "See, it's pretty lonely. And it's interfered with my trying to get close to people. Because she was the only one I was ever really close to, ever. And I feel like, damn it, I'm not going to get close to anyone else because they'll do the same thing that she did. It's hard. I know this in my head, but it's harder to live it. I mean to get it in the gut that everyone's not my mother."

"What's a situation that could happen today, or has happened, that would make you say 'Screw everyone, I can do all right by myself, if I can't I'm going to shoot myself'?"

As Christine reflects, Charlie suddenly reminds her of a recent situation that had triggered in her feelings of abandonment. Her psychiatrist had gone on vacation.

"Oh yeah, my doctor was gone and I wasn't sure who was substituting for him. I found out that the doctor I thought was his alternate wasn't and so I didn't know if I had just been left."

In an attempt to strengthen the connection between the past and present, we enact the situation Christine just described. She chooses someone to play the assumed alternate psychiatrist. After a brief role play using telephones, Christine easily slides into the response she had to this occurrence just several weeks ago. She sits on the floor, head in her lap, immobile. I ask Charlie and, a few minutes later, another group member to enter the scene asking Christine how she is doing. Christine doesn't answer or stir. When the state she is now portraying was slightly more extreme, she was diagnosed with catatonia.

I cut the scene and ask Christine if she might experiment with, and thereby practice, an entirely different way of responding. "I could maybe tell friends who ask how I'm doing what I feel, even if it's anger," she offers. After a brief replay of the phone call, she does just this. Her affect is animated as she expresses her distress and irritation. She also realizes that in her anxious state she overlooked several possible reasons for the confusion with the alternate.

"It felt much much better, but it was hard—especially at first, because it was like breaking a long-term cycle that seems to almost run on its own."

After years of psychotherapy, Christine had achieved a measure of insight, but this remained largely on an intellectual level ("I know this in my head, but it's harder to live it"). Drama can help bridge this common gap between intellectual awareness and practical change. As the progression of the culminating scene in this session demonstrates, in-depth therapeutic work is multidimensional; emotional catharsis, insight, and behavioral change are equally valued.

In a final improvisation five sessions later, with the group well into Phase Five (Dramatic Ritual), Christine and Charlie were directed to improvise running into each other five years from now at a bus stop (Reunion). Christine's acting was remarkably believable, from her expression of faint recognition to the moment she exclaimed, "Charlie!!!" They talked about what had taken place over the past years: Christine was married; Charlie had become an electronics engineer! As he began to invite her and her husband over for a drink, he recalled her allergies, but Christine immediately responded, "Oh, I'm all over those allergies now." Then, as they reminisced about the old days in day treatment, Charlie suddenly started howling, "Heeelpp," interspersed with hiccups. The group/audience laughed along with Christine as she exclaimed, "You know, I knew I was never going to live that scene down. And after five years, you remember!"

During our celebration marking the end of this series, Christine shared with other members her feeling of sadness about the ending of the group. With emotional affect that clearly matched her words, she spoke about how much she would miss working with the other group members. "I never trusted anyone like I trust the people here in this group," she added.

In her third and final dialogue with her image on the video monitor, Christine said, "I found out that you are a nice fun-to-be-with person. That you have a sense of humor. I found out in drama that you are actually likeable. In fact, I discovered a whole new side of you I didn't know existed. I found that you can do things you'd never even thought you'd ever be able to do, ever."

Christine's unfolding self-image made me think of an experience I used to love: working in a darkroom, soaking and tending blank photographic paper in developing fluid until an image emerged. The best part was witnessing the gradual solidification of the image until it could be removed from its fluid and called a photograph.

I worked with Christine for two more series, totalling approximately 60 sessions over eight months. During the second series, feelings regarding her adoptive father, who had rarely been mentioned during the first series, surfaced. Enactments also revolved around Christine's fear that her mother's dependence on her would increase after her father's imminent death. Via dramatic scenes, she continued to assert and communicate her need for autonomy. She also began to identify feelings about her biracial identity, feelings that had been stifled and confused by her upbringing in a Caucasion home. She began to deal with feelings of abandonment by her biological father. Anger and grief related to the pain and injustices in her life were expressed, largely nonverbally. Her capacity to access an internal nurturing parent developed, and there were many enactments in which she tended to the wounded child she had been and still carried within her. Most importantly, Christine gained trust again—in a new group of people. During the third series, Christine reveled in her play with characterization. It was apparent that she was experimenting with her rapidly expanding self-image. Increasingly spontaneous and playful, she excelled in improvisation. And a new role was added to her dramatic repertoire: She could play a girlfriend or lover or wife. In fact, her sexuality, which had emerged ever so subtly via the role of Carmen in the first series, was manifested in many scenes.

The first of the three series (the one described in detail) was the most catalytic, in that it helped Christine to get past her impasse in therapy and paved the way for her to benefit from various forms of treatment. This included the individual sessions with a psychiatrist she had been seeing for about seven years as well as the overall milieu approach of the day treatment program. In both situations, she had been at a prolonged standstill, resulting in a poor prognosis.

Following the completion of the third series of drama therapy, Christine enrolled in a junior college. She continued to attend day treatment, but switched to a part-time basis. In college, she took courses in stenography, African-American culture, and drama! And, for the first time in her life, she embarked on a relationship with a man. After five months of part-time status, she left the day treatment center, but I saw her about every six months for the next seven years; she visited the day treatment center and gave an update on her life. In one of the early visits, her face was glowing as she described her adventures during an eight-week trip to South America with her boyfriend. Her appearance kept changing drastically; at each visit she looked younger, more vibrant and healthy. Her severe allergies were gone, and she no longer took psychiatric medication. She continued to live independently, and eventually supported herself without the assistance of disability funding. She completed secretarial training and obtained full-time employment. And she coped with the death of both of her parents.

But when her two-year relationship with her boyfriend ended, there was a setback. What throws us back to childhood abandonment more than separation from a mate? Christine voluntarily hospitalized herself for four days. When she was discharged, her life resumed without the need to re-embark on the long cycle of the mental health system (a cycle that seems to be the pattern for so many people who have undergone repeated hospitalization). Even with the loss of both parents and her partner within a short time, Christine was not about to let all the progress she had made disintegrate.*

My clients are some of the most inspiring people I know. In them I witness the confrontation with pain more intensely than elsewhere in life; I witness the courage to descend into dark unknown territory; I witness the craving to find the lost self. I will never forget Christine. She taught me to what extent, with enough spirit, we can all change.

---

*The other clients in this chapter, too, have maintained the progress they made. In the recent contact I had with all four clients (representing a follow-up of between four and 15 years since the time we worked together), I was moved to hear how well each one was doing — in terms of social relationships, rewarding work or projects, healthful coping with emotional strain, and independent living.

4

SESSIONS
The Development of a Single Session

While the previous two chapters have attempted to provide an overview of drama therapy treatment, describing and illustrating the process over a course of time, the following two chapters aim to bring into focus, from a practical and clinical perspective, the components of the treatment process: the session and—more circumscribed yet—the dramatic scene.

This chapter begins with an analysis of the progression of the session, from the leader's internal preparation prior to the onset of the session to the closure of the session. A brief look at resistance to drama therapy and ways of responding to this resistance follows. Common choices facing the drama therapist in the course of a session are then examined.

In an attempt to give the reader as close to a live experience as possible, the final section of the chapter provides a detailed description (essentially a transcription) of two complete sessions. One of the clients whose story was told in Chapter 3, Shawn, took part in these sessions, affording a close-up view of her early work in treatment.

PROCESS AND PROGRESSION

The work of the drama therapist begins prior to the onset of the session, with her own internal preparation. This preparation is not unlike that of the actor before a performance. Both actor and therapist need to achieve a mental and physical readiness, which includes a dissolution of egoism so that one can be truly receptive to another (the character or the client). At times when the therapist is preoccupied with personal matters, this preparation is all the more critical. Each individual should find her own way of inducing a state of openness, energy, and presence.

"Begin where the group (or patient) is" is a common statement in creative arts therapy. The drama therapist must be able to pick up the mood and subtle cues of the group (or individual), so that she can be genuinely sensitive to their needs, rather than imposing her own agenda. At the same time, she must take an active role in "setting the stage," that is, in establishing an environment in which the clients feel permission to be and to act in new ways. Once the door to the drama therapy room is closed, a special space can be created.

The balance between following the clients' lead and taking initiative, or having what might be called a more strategic approach, is a delicate one. Sometimes the balance may tip more to one side: for example, in early stages of work with withdrawn and passive psychiatric patients, the drama therapist may intentionally design and lead exercises that are likely to reduce the initial depressed affect, as well as use her own energy to stimulate activity and interaction. But even at these times she is careful not to overwhelm the group with her own enthusiasm. As she facilitates movement from one state of being to another, she simultaneously demonstrates to the clients that she perceives and understands the state in which they have entered the session.

Before the session begins, the leader should make some kind of contact with each individual in the group. This establishes (or reestablishes, in an ongoing group) a connection with each client. During this contact, even if it is just for a brief moment, the therapist gains a sense of the client's state and, equally important, the client picks up the attitude of the therapist, which is hopefully one of acceptance, care, and genuineness (Rogers, 1961). In groups of disturbed populations, and in early phases with any population, the significance of this contact is intensified, because the clients are less able to convey this attitude to one another. With resistant populations, such as disturbed adolescents, the significance of the pre-session contact cannot be overestimated. On innumerable occasions, belligerent teens who have entered the room prepared to fight with any authority figure have completely backed down at the moment of our contact. In that moment, they perceive my care and respect, regardless of their behavior, and they also perceive that I will not be defeated by their responses. The diffusion of resistance, anxiety, fear and alienation prior to the onset of the session, via the therapist-client contact, is one of the most critical, and subtle, tasks facing the therapist.

Following or concurrent with the contact with individual clients, there is usually some rearranging of the room with the assistance of the group. In most cases, this entails moving furniture and chairs to the side in order to create as much open space as possible. In other cases, as with nonambulatory groups, it may mean moving the chairs into a circle in the center of the room. With resistant clients, it is often best to leave the room unchanged, although one or two chairs may be discreetly placed at one end of the room, to initiate a potential performance area. The rearranging of the room is symbolic as well as practical. The stage is being set for new possibility. A distinction between the outside (world) and inside (the drama therapy session) is also made by the next practical steps: taking off shoes and closing the door. The closing of the door marks the official beginning of the session.

The first activity usually involves the entire group and takes place in a circle. This is not a rigid principle; the best beginning for some groups could be for everyone to walk around the room, or lie down each in his own corner, or even to immediately initiate a performed scene by one or two members. Resistant groups in particular defy any norm, as will be described in the following section. But in general the very beginning of the session is a time for the group to (re)unite, and the circle is a traditional symbol for unity. The leader is very active during this first exercise, as her presence serves to energize the group and to help the members (re)connect to the process and to one another. The most common objectives at this early stage are to facilitate emotional expression, physical activation, trust, observation and concentration, and group interaction. In many cases, these objectives overlap. The therapist determines the objectives based on information gathered prior to the session or as the session begins, as well as at the previous session. The techniques described in Part II for beginnings of sessions are categorized according to these objectives.

The second activity usually takes place with the group in pairs. The partner work facilitates the development of relationship between group members and enables the leader to step aside and become more of an overseer than a central participant. The transition from work with the entire group to work in pairs is a smooth one, often involving the same process or technique but in a different format. For example, with an emphasis on trust, the session may begin with the entire group in a circle, catching one person (see *Nurturing Falls,* p. 171), and be followed with the group in pairs, with one person catching the other.

The beginning two or three processes/techniques serve as a prelude to the mid-session, which is generally the "main course" or most developed part of the session. The most typical process in the mid-session is scene enactment. The most typical format is to have the group divided into small subgroups of about three people. Each group prepares a scene which is then enacted for the whole group. The scenes can instead be conducted in pairs, or with the entire group acting at once, or with one individual as the sole performer or central protagonist. Applause is used after most scenes not only to boost self-confidence and provide a sense of achievement but to clearly mark the end of the scene, thereby underscoring the distinction between fantasy and reality. Most dramatic scenes, from the end of Phase Two through Phase Four of the treatment series, are followed by or integrated with verbal discussion. The most common objectives for the mid-session are expression and communication, character and role development, group collaboration, and/or self-revelation. As with objectives for beginnings of sessions, these goals often overlap. The techniques described in Part II for mid-sessions are categorized according to these objectives.

What takes place during the mid-session is influenced by the process in the earlier parts of the session. For example, a session emphasizing emotional expression may begin with the entire group using sound and voice and eventually repeating in unison an emotional line such as, "I want it!" The group may then divide into pairs, with one person saying, "I want it" and the other insisting, "You can't have it" *(Line Repetition).* Each pair then discusses situations or relationships that came to mind as they engaged in the *Line Repetition* technique and, based on this discussion, plan a scene to enact before the group. The important point here is that there is a sense of flow and progression to the session. Each exercise paves the way for the next. There is a natural transition between processes, spiralling the session toward increasing depth and complexity. A drama therapy session should never be composed of isolated techniques. It is the interconnection and progression of techniques that result in a *process* that contains therapeutic and aesthetic possibilities. The experience for the clients during a carefully crafted session (whether preplanned or developing spontaneously) is of time going by very quickly and, by the end of the session, of fullness and completion. Resistance during the session is rare, whereas in a "choppy" session comprised of un-related techniques resistance may recur at the onset of each new technique or phase within the session.

Smooth transitions are generally achieved in one of three manners. The first is through the development of a single technique. The example given above is such a transition: The repetition of two emotional lines is first con-ducted by the entire group, then by pairs, and finally scenes are created from these lines. An entire session could be based on a single technique, which is modified, developed, or extended in diverse and increasingly complex ways. The second manner is through theme or content. For example, trust exercises are followed by scenes that deal with the issue of trust, or beginning tech-niques that facilitate the expression of anger lead to scenework in which anger is expressed. The third manner of achieving transition is through spatial form. For example, a technique in which the group stands in two rows facing one another is followed by another technique in this two-row form. This manner of transition generally works best in conjunction with one of the other two manners—development of technique or continuity of theme—although some-times form alone can create enough of a *flow.* A technique that takes place in a circle, for example, can at times be effectively followed by an unrelated technique that also takes place in a circle.

In planning the session, the drama therapist may be most influenced by a conception of the mid-session. She then "works backwards" in designing beginning techniques that effectively lead to the main part of the session. Or she may have only a sense of a beginning that would be most suited to the group's needs and this beginning then influences the rest of the session. This "sense" often arises in response to her initial interaction with the clients. Sessions with smooth transitions are not necessarily preplanned; with experience, the drama therapist is able to achieve a *flow* even when working entirely spontaneously. Most sessions, however, are partly planned (or at least reflected upon beforehand) and partly evolving in-the-moment.

At the end of the session, the group is reunited, often by forming a circle, as in the beginning of the session. In an energetic session, the closure allows for a period of calm; in an emotionally charged session, the closure provides further release as well as containment; in a session that led to new insight, the closure facilitates review and integration; in a session that involved fantasy play, the closure provides "grounding" and eases the transition from the drama therapy group to the *real world* that lies outside the door. The end of the session reinforces significant aspects of the session or acknowledges and reflects feelings that are present in the group, often via dramatic ritual. Most closing rituals or techniques are designed to facilitate giving and receiving between group members, sharing their perceptions, collective creativity, and review and celebration. The techniques for closures of sessions are categorized according to these objectives.

Parallels exist between the progression of a single session and that of a series of sessions. Like that of a session, the progression of a series is marked by a gradual increase in depth and complexity. At the same time, the degree of structure provided by the drama therapist gradually decreases over the course of the series, as clients are able to take greater initiative and develop processes more fully on their own. The therapist is also more actively involved in activities early in the series, whereas later on, as the clients' interaction and connection with one another increases, she becomes more of an overseer and director. Many of the objectives of beginnings of sessions correspond to those of beginning of series, mid-session objectives correspond to mid-series objectives, and objectives of closure of sessions correspond to those of the closure of series. Most of the techniques described in Part II under *Beginning of the Session* are particularly relevant to Phases One and Two of the series, *Mid-Session* techniques are particularly relevant to Phases Three and Four, and *Closure of Session* techniques to Phase Five.

There is an aesthetic quality to the structure of the session as a whole. It has a beginning, middle, and end, yet each part flows naturally into the next in a seamless fashion. There is a gradual and subtle progression throughout. Many sessions have a climactic point or denouement. The end of the session

both highlights and encompasses the rest of the session. The very final moment is often a poignant or poetic one. Usually the tone at this point is quiet,
although the session might also end with a forceful and dramatic "zap!" If
any announcements need to be made, they should occur prior to this final
moment. The significance of the very end of the session for the clients is
analogous to the significance of the final moment of a play for its audience.
The final moment reflects, and contributes to, the aestheticism in the process.
This aestheticism is emotionally and psychologically stirring, reaching a place
inside the person that often cannot be expressed in words. The aestheticism
also engenders a stillness, a kind of inner pause, before the movement toward
whatever comes next ensues. The client is left with a blend of completion and
anticipation—completion with what has taken place in this session, and
anticipation for the next session, as well as for the internal churnings and
changes that may transpire in the interim.

RESISTANCE

Resistance, a classic response to embarking on (and encountering difficult
or painful stages within) a therapy process, has been described by Laplanche
and Pontalis (1973) as the client's organized attempt at opposing the processes of becoming aware and of the emergence of unconscious forces. (Less
psychoanalytic interpretations of resistance include: a reluctance to be in
treatment; wariness about the method; lack of support by the therapist and/or
group; lack of a sufficient warm-up.) Though resistance is a fairly universal
phenomenon, occurring among most clients at some point of (any kind of)
psychological treatment, there are particular populations, most notably adolescents, for whom resistance—especially at the onset of treatment—is pre-
ponderant. Moreover, different forms of treatment may elicit particular
anxieties and resistances.

The three primary resistance-inducing anxieties pertaining to drama
therapy, based on associations many people have to *drama,* are: 1) having
to perform; 2) appearing childish; 3) having to become someone other than
oneself. Performance raises fears about failure, inadequacy, and ridicule. For
adolescents dealing with the self-consciousness and insecurity engendered
by the profound and rapid physical and psychological changes occurring at
this life stage, the idea of "standing out" or "being put on the spot" is especially
uncomfortable. The thought of engaging in a childish activity brings out fears
of looking foolish or silly, or of wasting one's time.* Given the adolescents'

---

*Many of these considerations also apply to adults and senior citizens.

attempt to define their position and identity by defying adult authority and at the same time asserting their adulthood as they fervently push childhood behind, resistance to activities that appear childish is heightened. The association of acting with discarding one's own character and emotions in order to portray someone else (and someone else's emotions) elicits feelings of loss and nonacceptance (of one's real self). When identity is tenuous, as in adolescence, the notion of becoming someone else can be frightening and threatening.

Although all of the above associations do represent actual aspects of drama, they are not fundamental to drama or to drama therapy, but rather are small components of the very broad spectrum of possibilities within this medium. The recommended means of dealing with these associations is to dismantle them from the onset of the session. In being sensitive to the clients' initial anxieties, the therapist avoids those processes and techniques that involve performance, characterization, or a childish appearance.

One other association to drama that can evoke anxieties, if not completely deter a prospective client, is having to be extroverted, or be a "ham." Indeed, most people assume that actors are extroverts, a fallacy pointed out by Bates (1987), who clarifies that in fact "the actor needs to be at one and the same time extremely introverted and extremely extroverted. Actors are required to be absorbed in self-understanding and simultaneously, yet paradoxically, oriented towards the outer world, social stimulation, audiences . . ." (p. 54).*
Prospective clients who perceive themselves as being too introverted for drama therapy should be assured that they need not be/have in any given way. The drama therapy process is adapted to the person, rather than the reverse.

In response to the clients' fears related to having to be extroverted, play someone other than themselves, or alter the state of mind in which they enter the session, the drama therapist not only allows, but encourages and gives outlet for the expression of *self*. One *acts* as one feels or, put in other terms, one's actual feelings and behaviors become the dramatic material. For example, if the clients enter the session acting hostile or aggressive, the drama therapist may ask for a dramatic display of hostility and aggression. Withdrawn or shy clients may become engaged in a dramatic activity that requires acting withdrawn or shy. (Examples of techniques to facilitate this process are *Emotional Greetings and Group Mood*.) The dramatization of

---

*Bates believes that the actor's psychological stretching to encompass the wide continuum from introversion to extroversion (involving different challenges for different actors, depending on whether one's natural tendency leans toward introversion or extroversion) is one of the growth-inducing or healing forces inherent in acting (1987).

actual emotion or behavior, particularly when exaggerated, tends to promote a sense of acceptance and acknowledgment, cathartic release, an atmosphere of playfulness and humor, and a capacity to observe oneself in action.

Dramatic activity is well suited to this open and permissive approach; drama provides an arena in which all kinds of behaviors, attitudes, and emotions can be expressed within a controlled, structured setting. Because drama affords natural boundaries within which enacted behaviors and attitudes can be self-observed and contained, a great deal of permission can be safely granted. This permission creates an environment in which clients will eventually feel free to experiment with alternate behaviors (Emunah, 1983).

Thus, the client's resistance is incorporated into the dramatic activity; resistant clients *play out* their resistance. This strategic approach is analogous to Erickson's pioneering work in hypnosis and psychotherapy (Haley, 1973), and to Jay Haley's (1973, 1980) and Salvador Minuchin's (1974) work with families. The client's resistance is, paradoxically, cooperative, since what s/he is being asked to do is to be resistant (via the dramatic mode). The activation of the resistance, as opposed to suppression of the resistance, releases energy which can be channeled constructively and creatively (Emunah, 1985).

In one of my early experiences in working with adolescents, I remember being greeted by a new group of hospitalized acting-out teenagers with hostile cries, "Get the fuck out of here, lady, we're not doing no dumb drama group." Fighting an impulse to flee and struggling to maintain my inner equilibrium, I encouraged the group to keep telling me this, to keep repeating their words. I asked them to get louder, to be more emphatic, no matter what I said. Then I began retorting, "C'mon and try it." Soon a provocative but communicative dialogue was established, with the group beginning to respond to the variation in my intonation and volume. At one climatic point, I suddenly shouted, "I'm not doing no dumb drama group." Spontaneously, they shouted, "C'mon and try it" (Emunah, 1983).

The above example illustrates the paradoxical approach, in which the client's resistance and rebelliousness are encouraged, and in place of a power struggle between therapist and client, a playful relationship is initiated. Also illustrated is the technique, *Line Repetition* (p. 129), in conjunction with the psychodramatic tool, *Role Reversal* (p. 125), but more importantly evidenced by the example is the way in which techniques and tools emerge out of particular therapeutic situations, rather than being superimposed. The techniques and the process of drama therapy can be viewed as convergent, in many cases indistinguishable from one another. An impromptu response on the part of the therapist will often also lead to the discovery or development of a new technique, as will be demonstrated in Part II.

In work with adolescents it is helpful to make the distinction between resistance and rebelliousness. Adolescent rebelliousness is a "developmentally appropriate reaction to both the seeming childishness of latency and the entrenched authority of adults; it is a necessary aspect of the adolescent's dramatically changing self-identity. The way in which adolescents initially resist the treatment process is by acting rebellious. It is an attempt to conceal feelings of frustration, pain, and fear of being hurt, misunderstood, rejected, or betrayed. Disturbed adolescents in institutional treatment groups struggle to maintain a mutual conformity via their shared rebelliousness, which of itself is a resistance to the treatment program" (Emunah, 1985, p. 72).

The therapeutic approach that I have used in work with disturbed adolescents is to "join with and support their rebelliousness, thereby engaging their interest and nurturing the sense of group identity, while minimizing or even bypassing the underlying anxiety and resistance to treatment." (ibid, p. 72). A power struggle is averted by the playful manner in which the client's rebelliousness and aggression are permitted, mobilized, and creatively channeled. In essence, the client is enabled to act out his feelings and attitudes within the context of the dramatic activity, thereby converting *acting out* to *acting*. Acting, unlike acting out, implies self-observation and self-mastery as well as the possibility of discovery and change. "The client experiences success at drama rather than at defeating the structure" (ibid, p. 78).

In addition to the containment provided by the structure of the dramatic activity, particular theatrical devices are incorporated to ensure control at all times. Examples are the use of "cut" and "freeze." When the drama therapist shouts, "Cut!" the dramatic scene (or game) instantly ends. When "Freeze!" is called out (in the midst of scenes or warm-up techniques, especially those of a physical nature), the clients instantly "freeze" in the physical position they find themselves in, forming a momentary statue or tableau. At all times, the drama therapist makes certain that the boundaries between the fictional and actual are maintained. The action is always stopped or redirected if the drama therapist senses that the clients may be on the verge of losing control. At all times, the therapist assumes responsibility that no one in the group gets hurt, physically or emotionally.

Once initial resistance to the structure has been relinquished and the clients are actively engaged in the dramatic activity, rebelliousness may nonetheless persist—via the content of the dramatic creations. The behavior portrayed in early scenes and games often duplicates destructive life behavior. The therapist's capacity to witness and accept this behavior (e.g., using or selling drugs, committing crimes, etc.), in the context of acting, is being tested and challenged. If the therapist can tolerate this material rather than censor it, all the while ensuring that boundaries and control (as stated above) are maintained, the relationship between client and therapist will be strengthened.

A sense of collaboration develops; the clients are the actors, whose material is respected; the therapist is the director, and her directions are respected. It is under the auspices of theatrical direction that therapeutic interventions with such clients can be made, as will be discussed in the following chapter.

In addition to the dramatic mobilization and channeling of rebelliousness, empowering roles can be offered to clients. The sense of helplessness many resistant clients experience, leading them to attempt to render the therapist helpless (at the same time that they are terrified of succeeding), can be responded to by giving them dramatic roles in which they possess control or authority. Examples of such roles are a judge (see *Court Trial,* see p. 206), a parent, teacher or therapist, or the director of a scene.

Another strategy for dealing with initial resistance is to begin the session in a surprising and intriguing manner. Verbal instructions that might be taken as cues for resistance are bypassed. One such example is to have a ringing telephone (the ringing sound is played on audiotape—see *Telephone,* p. 186); answering the phone tends to be irresistible. Another example is to have cups with juice laid out on a table, which clients will spontaneously gravitate toward and drink; at the bottom of the plastic cups are directions regarding how to act (see *Party with Secret Roles,* p. 163).

The attitude of the leader is the most crucial element in working with initial resistance. In addition to the care and respect, along with the firmness, described earlier in this chapter (under *Process and Progression*), it is important that the therapist's own boundaries be clearly maintained and that she not be personally threatened by the clients' manifestations of resistance. The selective use of humor is also invaluable, in terms of diffusing a charged moment, demonstrating a toleration of the clients' stance, and often—by catching the clients off-guard—leading to a shift in their stance.

Resistance arising in the midst of a session or scene, as a reaction to the encounter with painful or stressful material, can also be responded to in the dramatic mode, and the exaggeration of behavior described earlier can be incorporated. Blatner (1988a) proposes having the client exaggerate his defensiveness, as a way of making his defense mechanism/s explicit, conscious, and thereby more likely to be mastered or modified, if the client so chooses. In Johnson's work (1991) with *Transformations* (see p. 205), any fears or anxieties arising during the course of play are utilized, magnified, or transformed. The client can even flee the scene by transforming it, all the while remaining in the "playspace."

The playful acknowledgment and active engagement of resistance in drama therapy, in conjunction with sensitivity to clients' particular fears and anxieties, afford many options for both client and therapist, thereby facilitating the commencement and progression of the session.

CHOICE POINTS

The heart of the session lies in the subtle choices the drama therapist makes during its course. Dealing with choice points is one of the most challenging and engaging aspects of the therapist's work. Multiple factors and needs exist throughout the session, especially in group drama therapy, and the therapist's undivided attentiveness and perceptiveness are required at all times.

The most common choice point in group work involves group versus individual needs. At times what is best for the group as a whole may not be best for an individual member, or vice versa. The therapist is constantly juggling and balancing these needs. In general, there is a movement in the session (and also within the series) from the group to the individual, and then back to the group. The session begins with a focus on the group; group needs are addressed via group activities. Gradually, attention shifts to individuals within the group; one or several individuals are often the focal point of the mid-session. Attention then shifts back to the whole group, often in the form of verbal processing, in which group members discuss how they related to the individuals' scenes. The beginning group work lays the foundation for the more individual work by providing the supportive environment and emotional container within which individuals can take risks. The individual work spirals the group work toward greater depth and intensity, as each person's risk-taking and self-exploration encourage and inspire the others. The return from the individual focus back to the group further supports and contains the individual work, and restores the foundation of the process. In this sense, the group work can be viewed as a refrain, repeated between each new stanza of individual work.

The movement from the individual back to the group may occur through dramatic work rather than through verbal processing, and may occur over several sessions rather than within a single session. An example of this can be found in the story of Christine (Chapter 3): After the session in which I role played one of the clients in the group (Charlie) in an effort to give him feedback on his behavior, all of the clients (in a group scene) role played each other. Another example from this particular series (but not described in Chapter 3) took place the session after Christine's *culminating scene* about being given up for adoption. Affected by the scene, the entire group discussed and improvised scenes related to abandonment. After the emotionally cathartic work of these two sessions, the group appeared unburdened and the tone lightened. In the session following these two sessions, the group members, Christine included, joked and laughed as they playfully enacted skits about psychiatrists going on vacation, and their (the patients') subsequent feelings of abandonment and rejection. Sharing feelings and situations familiar to all of them further increased their sense of closeness and kinship as a group (Emunah, 1983).

Some of the choice points between group versus individual needs relate to degree of readiness. An individual within the group may be emotionally ready to enact a significant scene at a time when the group as a whole or certain individuals within the group are not yet emotionally ready to witness it. For example, one 25-year-old client, Deborah, wanted to explore and practice an emotionally laden scene that she was considering undertaking in real life: confronting her father on recently surfaced memories of being sexually abused by him during her early childhood. Deborah's capacity to both express and contain powerful emotions was greater than that of other members of the group. I had to forego enabling her to enact this important scene because I knew the other clients would not be able to tolerate the emotional intensity or the evocation of their own memories and feelings, and would not be able to offer Deborah the support she would need.

However, I devised a compromise that would permit Deborah to express some of her feelings, but at a greater distance. I directed her in a *fictional* rather than in a *psychodramatic* enactment, by having her confront a friend who has betrayed her. Deborah imbued this simple scene with passion. The enactment gave her some of what she needed and, equally important, it developed the group's toleration of emotionality and courage to approach emotional terrain. In the discussion following the scene, Deborah and the other group members shared emotional responses and personal associations to the enactment. While there is no formula for making such choices, the identification of phases in treatment (discussed in Chapter 2) can serve as a guide. Viewing the above example from the perspective of phases, it is apparent that the group was in Phase Two (Scenework), explaining why Deborah's potential Phase Three (Role Play) or Four (Culminating Enactment) scene was not appropriate.*

There are times in which work with the individual does take precedence over group needs. Usually this choice occurs in the form of development or extension of an individual's enactment, rather than as the choice of embarking on an enactment. The individual scenework continues even when the group is losing its attentiveness, given the significance and healing potentiality of

---

*The drama therapist should never feel pressured to generate psychodramatic scenes. When in doubt regarding a patient's or group's readiness for a psychodramatic scene, the therapist should consult with either: 1) other therapists who work with the client; 2) a co-therapist or supervisor; 3) the client herself. In a multidisciplinary treatment program, other mental health workers should be notified when a client has undergone emotional scenework, so that follow-up care (or attentiveness to the client's belated responses) can be provided.

the process for that individual. The therapist is constantly weighing benefits and risks, establishing priorities and, most of all, using his intuition. Once a choice is made, he incorporates processes and techniques that can mitigate the drawbacks inherent in that choice. For example, to help the group retain its attentiveness during a prolonged individual scene (or series of scenes), he may introduce the intervention, *Taking Over the Role* (p. 128), in which group members watching the scene can "tap out," and thereby replace, actors in the scene. Group members (or even the entire group at once) may be asked to *double* for the protagonist, or to help direct or redirect the scene, or to feed significant lines to the protagonist. The active involvement of the "audience" members helps them to sustain their interest and engagement, as well as to experience some mastery over the emotions that are being evoked.

The choice between individual and group needs also arises when an individual suggests an activity that is not in keeping with the therapist's plan or notion of what will benefit the group, a fairly common occurrence in groups of children and adolescents. The choice is difficult because the encouragement of initiative among group members is very important, and offering this initiative may have been especially significant for the particular client. Here, too, compromises can often be made. For example, the therapist may be able to begin with the client's suggestion, and then devise a segue into his plan, or creatively adapt the client's suggestion, or incorporate it at some other point in the session.

Other choice points in the session involve pacing and timing. Exercises that engage the group can be developed or prolonged, or the therapist can use the energy generated from one activity or phase of the session to make the transition to the next activity. Exercises that are unsuccessful can be dropped, or the therapist can stay with his plan and try to find ways of promoting involvement despite the initial reaction. Many of the decisions about pacing and timing are based on the attention span of the particular group. Some groups (and populations) have poor attention spans and are more likely to remained engaged in a fast-paced session. With these groups, a high level of energy evoked during a particular exercise will quickly fizzle out if the exercise is prolonged, and it is far better, especially during early phases of the series, to progress to the next exercise before this occurs, so that the clients feel successful and their energy is capitalized upon. Other groups are able to sustain involvement easily and derive more benefit from a slow pace in which there is time to absorb and develop each experience. Decisions about session pacing relate to decisions about degree of structure. In both cases, the identification of phases can be helpful. Sessions in earlier phases of a series generally require more structure and are faster-paced, whereas later in the series the sessions are less structured and slower-paced.

Another common choice facing the drama therapist is whether to incorporate dramatic enactment or to promote verbal discussion. Often a combination is most effective. For example, when a group of acting-out adolescents stormed into the session, screaming about a fight that had just taken place, I first asked them to explain (verbally) what had happened, but within minutes moved into the dramatic mode. Typically, a verbal discussion will serve as a prelude to dramatic enactment, giving the necessary information and clarification of the significant issues. The enactment facilitates emotional expression and containment, and enables both client and therapist to apprehend the subtleties and complexities surrounding the issue. The progression from verbal discussion to dramatic enactment is not only relevant to real-life situations. One session spontaneously began with a discussion about a fantasy planet. Through responding to the many questions I asked the members about the planet, it was established that the name of the planet was Glockenspiegal, that Glockenspiegal was devoid of rape or crime or violence, that people here had no desire to hurt themselves or others, and that a regular custom on Glockenspiegal was to undergo a special emotional *cleansing process.* When I heard this, I simply asked whether an earth person could be given a tour of Glockenspiegal and taken through the cleansing process. Thus began the shift from discussion to enactment.

The choice between verbal discussion and dramatic enactment also arises following scenework, at which time the client's emotional and cognitive responses can be further integrated either through discussion or continued enactment. When further emotional release or resolution is needed, enactment is usually preferable, whereas when insight and cognitive understanding is primary, discussion is usually preferable. These choice points will be elaborated upon in the following chapter, in the context of directing and developing dramatic scenes.

As in other forms of psychotherapy, the therapist is often faced with deciding how much interpretation to offer the client. In a scene that illuminates a pattern of response, but in which this illumination bypasses the client/actor's awareness, the therapist has the choice of giving the client feedback, or simply using the new information to understand the client better. I agree with Yalom (1985) that interpretation should be delivered selectively, and only within a context of a therapeutic relationship of trust and acceptance. The client's awareness can also be facilitated via the dramatic mode rather than through verbal feedback, thereby fostering the assimilation of new insights on an emotional as well as cognitive level. For example, occasionally a highly significant line or word will spontaneously slip out during a scene. Rather than ask the client later if he heard what he said, I will intervene during the scene by directing the client to repeat that line or word (*Repetition*

p. 129), thereby bringing it to his full attention.

In reviewing the session after it has taken place, often in form of written *process notes,* the therapist can assess the choices he made as well as uncover choice point moments within the session that he may have missed. This analysis helps guide the choices he makes at the following session with the same group, as well as enhancing his overall capacity to spontaneously make effective choices within the drama therapy session.

DESCRIPTION OF TWO ACTUAL SESSIONS

The following is a description of the first session of a series of 32 sessions (twice weekly over four months) at an adult psychiatric day treatment center. The second session described is of the same group of eight clients, at their 15th session.

This series was the first of the four series that Shawn, whose story was told in Chapter 3, attended. The eight clients are Dan, Ginny, Ramon, Rhonda, Leroy, Carolyn, Anna and Shawn. Their age range is 24 to 48. The descriptions of the sessions also elucidate some of the techniques included in Part II, giving a contextual picture of their usage. The first session illustrates a number of the techniques designed for the beginning of the session and series, delineated in Chapter 6. Session 15 revolves around one technique, Self-Sculptures, *delineated in Chapter 7.*

Session One

There are eight people in the room, sitting quietly, apart from one another, each in his or her own world. The sense of isolation is palpable. From far away, as if using an imaginary telephoto lens, I try to read some of the faces. Is it apprehension or suspicion I detect? As I scan the faces and bodies of these new clients, I reach for the part of myself that has felt, or feels now, some of what I perceive in the clients. At the same time, I am aware of my current state of energy and readiness. I move, as unobtrusively as possible, toward a few of the individuals, to initiate some contact. For some, the greeting seems to bring relief; I have not been too threatening. For others, the greeting makes no dent in their high level of anxiety; for these clients, facing a new person, a new group, and a new venture is overwhelming.

I want to change the atmosphere from one of passivity to activity, from deadness to aliveness. My own level of energy is critical in this process but its manifestation is delicate: I need to *begin where the group is at,* to be *with* them and not *at* them, to demonstrate that I recognize and understand their current internal state. I view the process that is about to take place as gently lifting the clients, and carrying them, ever so slowly, to a somewhat different place/state, one they may have long left behind. I am conscious of the responsibility I am assuming and that some may criticize *lifting* or *carrying* as promoting dependence or strategizing change rather than letting be what *is.* My belief is that some weight must be carried by the therapist during the beginning stages of work, especially with severely depressed clients who have lost their own initiative. Just enough to give them a glimpse of another place, which is really another *part of themselves.* Just enough to give them a choice—to embark on a journey they may otherwise have not known was possible.

We are about to begin the session. There is growing tension and I know that any delay with verbal instructions or discussion will only increase the tension. The activity itself will alleviate anxiety, and the sooner we start the better. I ask that shoes be removed and that a large circle be formed.

In pantomime—and here is where the magic begins—I pick up a ball. After clearly establishing its weight and size, I throw it to someone in the circle, as I call out that person's name. The instructions have come through demonstration, rather than words. Shawn spontaneously *catches* the imaginary ball, then tosses it to Ramon, calling out his name. When it comes back to me, I transform it to a different weight, size, and shape. Within minutes, there are smiles and then laughter, as the clients watch their peers pretend—*so realistically*—to throw a ball that weighs a ton, or shrink a beachball to a marble and gradually to a tiny speck that nearly disappears. After several more minutes, there are more creative modifications, this time in the throwing of the ball; it is being punched, hurled, rolled, and blown. The practical function being served by the exercise, *Ball Throws,* is that the clients in this first session are learning each others' names, and observation and concentration are being developed; the symbolic function is in the representation of transformation.

I have deliberately begun with a clear structure because I believe that a structured framework facilitates the reemergence of creativity and imagination among people whose creativity has been stifled. Had I begun with a very free-flowing exercise, such as asking each person to make a movement and sound expressing how s/he feels, imagination would have, in my view, instead been arrested. There would have been too much freedom, abstraction, and performance in such an opening—precisely what these clients fear. Later in the series the session may well begin with an expression, or dramatized exaggeration, of what the group feels. At this point however, the clients' feelings, predominantly anxiety, are obvious. The priority is alleviating that anxiety, providing a sense of safety, and establishing an atmosphere of play.

I discreetly slip out some real balls that I have brought. They are large, light, colorful, and balloon-like. Before the group even realizes the exercise has been modified, I toss a ball to one person in the circle, saying his name, and then throw another ball to a different person. Soon there are four balls in the air, which before long I increase to six. No possibility for "spacing out" here; one's name is being called at very frequent intervals, always a split-second before a ball—or two or three—arrive in one's arms.

The clients appear very alert and energized. It is time to leave the circle and to move. I suggest we all walk around the room, in any direction. People begin to shuffle hesitantly. I say, "Walk as if you're the only one in the room, you want to be alone. Avoid other people." This is easy, familiar. Soon I add: "Take up more space. You want the *entire room* for yourself" (*Dodging*). As I speak, I move, grabbing space myself, instigating physical interaction with individual clients. Now the group is moving more purposefully and with a touch of mischievousness. "You're really greedy. You want to own the whole room. Grab the space! Don't let anyone get in your way; collect all the space for yourself. Dodge people." The power in my voice increases in relation to the energy in the room. Everyone is now running, stretching their arms and legs, dodging, laughing. There are a few near-collisions.

"Now begin to slow down, and as you walk, notice the other people in the room. Start shaking their hands, saying their names. Shake hands with everyone you see" *(Emotional Greetings)*. Nine people are shaking hands with each other. "Faster. Move from one hand to the next." My directions are always given in conjunction with action; the activity never stops while I speak. I am constantly *doing* the activity myself, rather than directing from a distance. "Use both hands, shake with one person on one side, and another person on the other. Always have two people, and then move on. Faster." The activity is becoming reminiscent of a film played at fast-speed. At a peak moment, I shout "Freeze!!" A tightly woven mass of people has formed in the center of the room.

"Stand back-to-back with someone whose hand you are holding. In a second, you're going to turn around and greet each other, according to the feeling or attitude I call out. OK, *Shyly*." All turn around, face their partner, shake hands and introduce themselves—in a very timid fashion. "Back-to-back. This time greet each other *Nervously*." The anxiety and timidity that many have felt *for real* is being given an outlet, in a playful and nonthreatening context. The underlying message is one of permission and acceptance: it is OK to feel, to be, this way. "Back-to-back. *SUSPICIOUSLY*." Eyes narrow, heads tilt, hands drop. "Back-to-back. *AGGRESSIVELY!*" The level of noise and temperature in the room rises. Pent-up anxiety is being further dispelled. *"ENTHUSIASTICALLY!"* People who have met less than a half hour ago are hugging each other as if they were old buddies at a reunion.

I now ask for a volunteer to leave the room, explaining that when she returns, the entire group will be *acting* a certain way *(Group Mood)*. After observing for a few minutes, she will try to identify the emotion, mood, or attitude of the group. As Rhonda leaves the room, I bring the group into a huddle and ask for suggestions. Smiling, one person says, "depressed." Immediately I support this suggestion and ask the group to try to make clear in their acting the distinction between depression and similar words, as sadness. The choice of emotions are often reflections of actual current states. Everyone goes off to a corner; as I let Rhonda back in, I note that the group appears remarkably as it had just before the session began. Before long, Rhonda says, "This looks very familiar. . . . depressed." Spontaneously, the group applauds.

Ramon volunteers to go out. While he is out of the room, there are several suggestions at once. I select the most energizing of the suggestions, to balance the depression we have just done: "angry." This will also be a good follow-up to the depression, allowing for the expression of feelings that frequently lie just beneath the surface of depression. One man in the group, Dan, says, "This will be hard, I'm not used to expressing my anger." Several people nod in agreement. "You can show it any way that you like, even if that's by hiding it," I respond. I let Ramon in. Some clients still look depressed, but something in their bodies or faces divulges the anger—a clenched fist, a look in the eyes. Others, including Dan, are physically stomping and verbally raging at each other. Ramon guesses correctly and the group applauds. Dan wants to be the next *guesser,* but before he leaves, he exclaims, "Boy, that felt good!"

The next selected word is more subtle (a typical progression—from simplicity to complexity): "ambivalence." We speak briefly about how ambivalence is expressed in our lives. Dan returns and watches with curiosity and delight, though he is unable to guess. I ask him to direct two or three specific people to interact in the manner of the word, while the rest of the group watches. Shawn and Anna are funny and entertaining as they discuss their *ambivalent* feelings (without using the word of course) about the first drama therapy session! Dan identifies the word.

There are other words—ashamed, manic, arrogant, distracted, flirtatious—and other mini-improvisations performed to give the *guesser* clues, until the last person has had an opportunity to leave the room. During this last round, Ginny, a very timid, withdrawn middle-aged woman suggests "uninhibited." It doesn't much matter whether the suggestions are in fact emotions; the important thing is to accept, as much as possible, the clients' ideas. During the enactment, Ginny's stiff posture loosens and she becomes very gregarious. I pray at these instances that the door won't inadvertently be opened by someone outside of our group, for this would break the spell of dramatic transformation. In less than 45 minutes, a space has been created in which people are *unlocked* from their usual patterns of behavior. Any sudden confrontation with "reality" at this point could evoke shame or fear. By the end of today's session, I will gradually bridge the gap between the magic of this moment and the reality they will face, in the world and within themselves, as they leave the room. But until then, the dramatic space is protected.

As a way of further developing the activity and the interactions between clients, I divide the group into three subgroups and whisper to each group an emotion to enact *(Emotional Mime)* and a setting in which this will take place. To one group, I say, "You're all *anxious,* at an exam"; to another, "You're all *excited,* at a rock concert"; and to the third, "*engrossed,* watching a tennis match." My suggestions are adjusted to the group's level of sophistication. At this early stage, it is crucial that the clients experience success at the activity. (An example of a more simple suggestion would be "frightened at a scary movie"; a more sophisticated suggestion would be "preocccupied in a park." With some groups, I would give no suggestions, but rather have them immediately come up with their own ideas.) Each group nonverbally enacts, in their places, the miniscene, after which the other groups try to identify the emotion and setting. The use of guessing diverts the focus from the performance and thereby diminishes potential self-consciousness. The format of remaining seated, improvising with others, and using mime rather than needing to think of words to say also serves the purpose of reducing self-consciousness. Performance can be especially frightening for people whose self-esteem is low, and it is critical that it be initiated gradually and gently, ensuring success at each step.

After the first round of enactments, I whisper another setting to each group, but this time they themselves come up with the emotion. The other modification is that the enactments will now involve movement rather than being sedentary. The new places include a bus stop, a roller coaster, and a dog pound. The clients are increasingly engaged and creative in these enactments. I am moved as I witness isolated and depressed individuals collaborating with obvious delight. In the last enactment, two of the members become the puppies who are anxious for homes and love. Real feelings and needs can be expressed even via the most playful and humorous dramatizations. By now the enactments, though still simple, have a greater sense of *realness;* the clients are *imagining,* rather than *pretending.* For the final round, I ask the clients to conceive an idea of their own. They come up with *resistance* in a group therapy session, *anxiety* in the waiting room of a maternity ward, and *pleasure* in a hot tub!

Rather than having the last group (which is still in a huddle after its hot tub scene) disperse, I ask the rest of the group to join them in a small circle on the floor. I compliment the group on their enactments and ask what they enjoyed in the playing or watching of these last scenes. After a brief exchange in which positive aspects of each others' scenes are identified, I ask the group members which of the feelings portrayed in the last scenes also apply to feelings they have about beginning our drama therapy group. The clients' reflection at this point marks the transition from the fun just experienced to the reality to which they will soon return. Some are able to acknowledge feelings of resistance to beginning a new group process, anxiety as well as excitement about this process, and pleasure in the warm contact with others in the group.

I ask more specifically about fears they have, or had, about the process, as well as expectations and hopes. "I was afraid it was going to be childish and make me feel silly," Rhonda says, "but it didn't. I actually had fun, and that's pretty rare these days." Ramon speaks next. "I was really anxious before we began, that we would have to act and perform, which I'm no good at. I'm glad we didn't do anything like that." Others add that they were relieved they didn't need to get too "heavy" or expose too much. Here is an opening for me to say more about the group. I explain that we will take time to get to know one another, to build trust, and that all along the way we will experience our creativity and capacity for enjoyment, and that gradually we will also use drama to cope with actual feelings and problems in our lives.

The group now responds to the latter part of my initial question—their hopes. "I want to feel more comfortable being around people," says Ginny. A few others nod their head in agreement. "I think this may help me to be more spontaneous when I'm with people," Carolyn remarks. Anna speaks quietly, with her gaze on the floor. "I hope the group can help me get in touch with my feelings, instead of feeling numb." Leroy adds, "For me, it's a problem of how to express my feelings without losing it. Like when we decided to do anger in that game, I was afraid I'd get out of hand, but it was all right. But in real life it seems I can't express anger without breaking something or going crazy."

I remark that here we will be able to express many emotions, safely and playfully. I add that it is most important for everyone to attend every session, twice a week for the next 12 weeks, so that we really get to know each other, that this will make the whole process comfortable for everyone. I stress that the commitment, regardless of how one feels on a particular day, is critical. Everyone seems to understand, though in some faces I sense anxiety again. Perhaps they are wondering: "Will I be able to keep this commitment? Will I get too frightened to come? Will I let others down? Will others let me down?" All I can do at this point is to let the clients know, through verbal and nonverbal language, that they can come *as is,* that they need not be prepared or *in the mood*; they will be accepted regardless of the state in which they enter the session. I must convey that at the same time that I perceive their potentialities, I also recognize the emotional challenges this process poses for them.

I want to end on a playful note, bringing back the spirit of the session, and to create a closure that is in some way reminiscent of the opening of the session. The session began with an exercise that involved giving and receiving, and transforming. I create an imaginary object, steaming hot, and pass it quickly to the person on my right, Rhonda, exclaiming, "It's very hot, pass it on!" *(Passing the Substance)* She immediately tosses it to her neighbor, Shawn, who does the same. It comes back to me within seconds. I transform the object to something ice cold, indicating to the group that after they receive it, they can either pass it on as is or transform it. Before long the ice becomes sticky, then gooey and slimy. The depressed faces I had encountered before the session began are now vibrant. From the disgusting substance gradually emerges something delicious which everyone wants to taste, to something precious which everyone wants to keep, to something live — a butterfly, I think, which we finally set free. This moment marks the end of the session.

Session 15

Five minutes before the session begins, Shawn tells me that a neighbor has just been diagnosed with AIDS. She wants to "do something about it" in our group, though she has no idea how. Her eyes are wet and her tone shaky, as she says, "I just feel so overwhelmed with pain." Tentatively, she adds, "There are so many feelings, I can't keep track of them. I don't know what kind of scene I would do." I ask, "Is it that it's hard to know where all the feelings are coming from, because there are also so many emotions stemming from the past, that a present crisis brings up all the past pain?" "Yeah," she replies, "I'd like to be able to separate things. It's enough to deal with the present."

There is no time to design a session or scene; the group members are already in the room with their shoes off, waiting to begin. It is clear that Shawn needs help today, and our brief interchange has given me clues about the issues with which she is struggling. Work with Shawn is delicate; her insight and intelligence mask her fragility. I think back to early sessions in which childhood memories were indirectly evoked. Shawn had remained engaged and participative during the sessions, but on two occasions she had gone home and slashed her wrists.

I bring the group into a small circle. One person volunteers to be in the center, then falls and is gently caught and contained by the group. After some time, others volunteer, until everyone has had a turn. *Nurturing Falls* establishes the gentle tone and nurturing atmosphere that will be needed for this session's work.

Still in a circle, we sit down on the floor. I ask Shawn to tell the group what she is going through; I want to get a better sense not only of her state but of the group's. Before embarking on any emotional scenework, it is important to assess the group's tolerance for emotionality. Shawn begins speaking of her neighbor and then of the the myriad of feelings with which she is bombarded. Other clients respond, mostly referring to their own anger at the injustices of life. For all of us, new pain triggers unhealed past pain. Shawn's predicament evokes the sense of helplessness my clients experienced as children, when they were unable to control the *bad* that was happening to them. Not only were they powerless then to change their circumstance, they had no outlet for the feelings with which they were inundated. There is some fear in the room now. One woman, Rhonda, asks, "How can we protect ourselves from bad things happening?" I say that many events in life are beyond our control. But what we can have some control over is the way in which we handle or respond to those events.

An image of a tight knot of emotions that needs unraveling flashes through my mind. The identification and separation of each emotion, a kind of sorting out of one's internal state, may be the first step in achieving a sense of mastery over this state. Both Shawn and the group appear ready to embark on emotional scenework. But I also sense that as the issue is one of mastery versus powerlessness, of coping versus being overwhelmed, our work will be geared more toward emotional containment and cognitive insight than toward emotional catharsis. Shawn needs to step outside of her internal state in order to view it, and the role of director can help her to do this. As for the rest of the clients, keeping them as actively involved as possible in the drama will help them not only to sustain emotional engagement, but to feel empowered rather than victimized. Remaining a passive audience can at times engender feelings of powerlessness and immobilization.

I ask Shawn to depict all the feelings she is experiencing with regards to the news of her neighbor's illness by selecting a group member to embody each feeling. This process entails not only self-reflection but a gradual concretization of each potentially amorphous and undefinable piece of the internal knot. Not surprisingly, given her perceptivity, Shawn makes her selections very carefully:

Shawn: *Anna, you be my six-year old self. You're sad, endlessly sad. You feel abandoned and rejected and unloved. There's no one to take your feelings to—so you stay by yourself, isolated and withdrawn.*

(Anna has become Shawn's closest friend in the group. Like Shawn, Anna is sensitive and bright and playful, and there is a deep sadness in her eyes. Like Shawn, Anna was emotionally abandoned as a child.)

Rhonda, you be my feeling of being bruised. Every negative feeling brings back other pain. You take everything, everyone's pain, onto yourself.

(Rhonda had just described this feeling herself in our earlier discussion. And in recent sessions, Rhonda has enacted scenes dealing with unclear boundaries between herself and others.)

Let's see (tentative tone, which becomes tremulous). Leroy, would you play the part of me that wants to hurt myself? The part that wants to smash the walls and slash myself with a razor?

Leroy nods. He has only recently been willing to enter emotional territory. I am not certain whether Shawn is aware that what precipitated Leroy's admission into the day treatment program was driving his car, deliberately, into a post. I quietly ask Leroy if he is comfortable assuming this part, and he nods again.

Dan, you're my anger—at the injustice of it all—at all the negative stuff in the world.

(Dan had spoken in recent sessions about beginning to get in touch with his own anger. Earlier in this series Dan made an angry phone call to "Circumstances of Life.")

Carolyn, you're my nurturing part—comforting myself. Taking care of myself.

(Carolyn is a simple, gentle, and sweet woman who in a recent session came to our Magic Shop asking for self-love.)

The selected actors stand in a row in the stage area.

Shawn: (at a loss, a little frightened) Now what do I do?

Myself: Why don't you place the feelings in different parts of the room. Decide where you want each person and in what position. Who's in the fore-front, in the background, moving or still.

Seeming a bit relieved at having some direction, Shawn places the Sad-Child in the back of the room, huddled on a sofa. Anger is set in center stage and instructed to pace. Bruised is told to stand just right of center and Self-Destruction to lean with palms against the wall. Self-Nurturance is instructed to walk around and engage with the other feelings. I sense some relief for Shawn in externalizing these emotions, as if in casting her peers in these roles she has been granted some temporary respite from bearing them all herself.

Myself (to actors): It's going to be demanding to play these emotions. But try to play your role in as real a way as possible, allowing for the part of you that really has felt this, or understands what Shawn is going through. Shawn will decide which feeling is in focus, and that person can express him or herself with words or sounds or movements. Even when your part is not in focus, stay with the feeling.

Shawn now orchestrates her creation. She zeroes in on Rhonda playing Bruised first, then on Anna/Sad-Child, then on Dan/Anger. Carolyn/Self-Nurturance is given only a brief moment. I am impressed with each person's level of concentration and authenticity in expression. Shawn's body grows tense just before she calls out to Leroy/Self-Destruction; it is frightening and perhaps also embarrassing for her to witness and share this part of herself. Leroy surprises everyone with his intensity. He pounds the wall and yells, then stops abruptly. As if fraught with fury, he reaches for the imaginary razor.

Shawn now calls on everyone simultaneously. Each expresses his or her part in isolated unison.

Myself: *Would you like to make any adjustments to help your crew come closer to showing the way you feel inside?*

Shawn: *They're doing great. But maybe . . .* (She goes over to Anna and places her in a more curled-up position, puts Leroy's hands in a fist and moves him closer to the forefront.)

Oh, and maybe this time Dan could show a little more anger.

Dan growls, clearly appreciating the permission this direction gives him. There is some laughter, offering momentary comic relief from the emotional intensity of the scene.

Shawn sets the readjusted cast in motion. She watches the action until, like someone who has just recognized a face in a composite s/he had drawn, she whispers to me, *"That's exactly the way it feels inside."*

Having disentangled, depicted, and observed her emotional state, Shawn may now be able to transcend it. As the director to her own internal drama, she is no longer enslaved by it, but empowered to make changes.

Myself: *What would you like to see happen, or change here?*

Shawn (somewhere between humor, sarcasm, and seriousness): *I'd like to get rid of some of them—at least I wish Leroy wasn't in the picture.*

Myself: *Probably you can't get rid of any of them entirely; they're all a part of you. But why don't you step into the scene and rearrange things as you'd like, or create new interactions between the parts. You can do this as the director or you can take over one of the parts for a while.*

I intentionally give Shawn a number of options, as I sense that the self-directive part of her has been accessed. Her own instincts, in which I have trust and faith, are very important to the evolution of the scene.

Shawn: *I think I'd like to take over the comforter role as I do this.*

Myself: *Good idea.*

Shawn takes Carolyn's place. She goes over to Anna/Sad-Child, who is actually tearful, and puts her arm around her. Spontaneously, she leads Anna over to Leroy/Self-Destruction. Leroy looks away.

Shawn (to Leroy): *Face her. It's not her fault. Let her be.*

Leroy: *I can't look at her.*

Shawn: *By hurting yourself, you're hurting this child. You must want to hurt her.*

Leroy looks down.

Shawn (pressing): *She's innocent. Don't try to get rid of her. See her, accept her.*

Leroy (glancing at Anna): *I don't really want to hurt her. It's just easier to slash myself so that I can feel physical pain instead of feeling her emotional pain.*

Shawn (nodding knowingly): *I know. But with my help we can be there for her, instead of trying to destroy her.*

Still with her arms around Anna, Shawn now walks over to Rhonda/ Bruised. The three women face each other. Then Shawn stops and looks at me.

Shawn: *I don't know what to do or say here.*

Myself (entering the playing area): *Maybe this part of you* (indicating Rhonda) *needs also to recognize the Child, to realize the pain of the Child leads her to feeling so bruised.*

Shawn: *Yeah. The overwhelming feeling she has comes from the sadness and helplessness of the child.*

Myself: *Maybe she could help ease that feeling by helping the child. Try having her connect with and comfort the child.*

Shawn facilitates this interaction. Rhonda and Anna begin walking gently arm-in-arm.

Shawn (looking at Dan and smiling faintly): *I don't know what to do about him.*

Dan snarls.

Myself: *Well, let's watch him for awhile.*

We stand back together. Dan paces, ranting and raving. In the meantime, Leroy is facing the wall, fists clenched.

Shawn: *It seems that this part* (indicating Dan) *expresses anger outwardly and this part* (Leroy) *turns the anger onto myself.*

Myself (nodding, then adding): *Why don't you take over Dan's part and see what it's like.*

Hesitantly, Shawn dismisses Dan and begins to pace in his place. In a loud angry tone she starts complaining about the paucity of funding for AIDS research, the cruelty of the disease, the injustice. But soon the boundary between her role and Rhonda's weakens. I spot the first traces of wallowing in Bruised and also regressing to Sad-Child.

Myself: *You're doing great. But you're on the verge of also taking over Rhonda's part and maybe Anna's too. Try to keep your part distinct—just pure anger.*

Shawn: *Oh yeah, OK.* She continues to speak about AIDS, but her tone is now more fervent and the anger seems more concentrated. The content of her monologue begins to shift to a personal domain, but her affect remains that of Anger, not Bruised. This is the first time I have seen Shawn—in or out of the dramatic mode—clearly express anger. In the coming months of my work with her, this expression would occur with increasing frequency and intensity.

Wanting to support and sustain Shawn's direct expression of anger and, even more importantly, to involve the two group members who have until now been in the audience, I ask Ramon and Ginny to join Shawn, as if merging into one all the more powerful part.

For several minutes, the three of them ignite the stage with a vigorous outpouring of anger. Finally Shawn stops, exclaiming, *"That felt good!"*

Myself: *This seems to be a very dynamic and healthy part of you.*

Shawn: *It felt scary at first, but it was a great release. I couldn't do that as a kid. I'm really getting the difference between this part and Leroy's. When this angry part can express itself, I think Leroy's part is more in the background, less fueled.*

Myself: *Let's step outside again and see what you've created—with the changes.* (Ramon and Ginny step back too.) *What feelings are central to this current situation with your neighbor having AIDS?*

Shawn: *The anger is in focus, closer up front, in the center.* (Dan reenters the scene.) *I want Leroy to still be against the wall, but now watching the other parts instead of facing away. He was looking away because he's afraid to feel anything. Now he's going to face the feelings and especially see Anna, recognize her. But he should sit with his hand underneath him, to be sure he doesn't hurt himself. Rhonda is with Anna, with her arm around her, way in the back of the room. And Carolyn is comforting and nurturing both of them. Then I want her to approach Leroy. I'm usually so afraid of coming near this part of me.*

The actors carry this out.

Shawn (seeming somewhat surprised, very alert, pleased): *Wait, can I add a part?* (I nod.) *Ramon, will you play the part of me that appreciates life?*

Given that Shawn has been suicidal, I am very moved by this spontaneous addition. Wanting to underscore what she has just said, I ask: *Do you mean a part that can see that the things in life you appreciate still exist, even when the going gets rough?*

Shawn: *Yes.*

Myself: *Can you name a few things in particular that this part appreciates and enjoys?*

Shawn (reflecting): *Nature, music, art.*

Ramon enters the playing area. Shawn sets them all in motion for a brief time, and once again observes her creation.

Shawn: *Three months ago I wouldn't have had that part. I probably wouldn't have put in Carolyn's part either. I guess I am changing.*

The scene ends. We applaud Shawn and all the actors, and return to our familiar circle.

Shawn (with humor): *Now I'll have names to call my feelings when they come up. When I start feeling like a six-year-old, I'll think of Anna. I'll say to myself: Now I'm Anna, or Rhonda—when I'm in touch with the bruised feeling, or Leroy—if I feel a surge of self-destructiveness. They'll diagnose me as having a multiple personality disorder!* (laughter in the group). *But really, it'll be more like having all of you with me, and telling me it's ok. Thanks everyone.*

Group members praise Shawn for her courage and insight. I too compliment her and the group, and then ask the group to talk about their relationships to the roles they played.* Anna tells of the pain she experienced while in the role, of sensing the sadness of her own inner child, of how good it felt to be comforted by Carolyn, and of the emergence of a new and somewhat surprising feeling—of *deserving* nurturance. Rhonda says that she strongly identified with her role and that the exaggeration of it made this part of her seem clearer, and thus perhaps more manageable. Dan exclaims that he loved his role and wants to be cast in such roles more often! Ginny concurs. Ramon says that he felt privileged to be cast in his role, which reminded him of his own buried joy in living. Carolyn and Leroy, less at ease with verbalization, are quiet, though when prompted do offer some words: Carolyn, that she liked her role because she felt she was able to give something to Shawn and also because she wants to be more in touch with this part of herself. Leroy, that the moment that was initially the most frightening—being told to face the other emotions—was in fact the most liberating; until that moment he had felt very alienated.

The scene foreshadowed much of the work Shawn was to do in the following nine months of her participation in drama therapy, via several different group series. Her story was told in Chapter 3.

Wanting to end the session on a more active and expressive note, I ask the group to stand in two rows against the wall, facing me. I tell them to pick a role in Shawn's drama, but not the one they had just played. I lift an imaginary baton and begin conducting the orchestra. When called upon, each person emotes sounds or words that express his or her role, carefully watching for my cues regarding volume and speed, starting and stopping. Sometimes there is one "instrument" at a time, other times several—or all

---

*In psychodrama this is called the sharing phase—a supportive process that circumvents tendencies to analyze and encourages people to speak emotionally and personally.

the Angers (since several people have selected this part!) concurrently. I end the piece with everyone emoting in unison, followed by a single note coming from the part that appreciates life. The group spontaneously applauds. I suggest we do one more piece, this time with each selecting any emotion at all, not necessarily from Shawn's scene. Our *Emotional Orchestra* is now more forceful, teeming anger and love, pain and hope. Each instrument is at once distinct and able to blend with the others, and in the end all the voices rise together with fury and passion, as if bellowing that this is the human condition, and we are all in it together.

5

SCENES
Development, Direction, and Resolution of Improvisational Enactments

TYPES OF IMPROVISATION

Dramatic scenes form the cornerstone of the drama therapy session. These scenes are generally improvisational, rather than scripted.* In comparison with the enactment of scripted scenes, the improvisational mode is better suited to: 1) reflecting the client's inner state, conflicts, or associations as well as providing diagnostic information; 2) enabling the expression of actual feelings; 3) developing spontaneity; 4) affording the freedom to experiment with diverse roles and responses; 5) promoting insight into patterns and dynamics; 6) building skills in relating to and collaborating with others. The improvisational mode is closer to real life, in which there are no set scripts or prepared lines. Our experience with improvisation in real life prepares us to improvise in drama. Scripted work, on the other hand, requires special skills, including reading, memorizing, and bringing the written word to life. The resemblance of the improvisational mode to real life also creates a more natural progression into psychodramatic scenes in which actual life situations are reenacted.

The improvisational mode is very flexible, yet various degrees of structure are possible within it. The following types of improvisation represent three levels of structure:

---

*Scripted scenes, nonetheless, have a place in drama therapy, especially when the clients themselves manifest an interest in them. The drama therapist brings to the session scenes which correspond to individual or group issues, which help particular clients express suppressed emotions, or which simply bring out the clients' strengths. When scripts are used, they are incorporated during Phase Two, the phase in which self-expression and expansion of role repertoire are facilitated via the enactment of fictional scenes. The use of scripted scenes is elaborated upon in Part II, p. 203.

1. The Planned Improvisation

In the *Planned Improvisation,* the clients/actors decide in advance what is to take place. This is the most structured type of improvisational scene. The planning is usually brief (the actors simply agree on the basic scenario), though it can also be extended and detailed. The resolution or ending of the scene may or may not be decided upon in advance. Much is left to surprise, including the actual lines within the scene, which of course are not set. However, the clients enter the scene with some sense of identity and direction.

The drama therapist's instructions for the planning of this type of improvisation are guided by the previous exercise or warm-up activity, or by the theme of the session. For example, following the *Line Repetition* exercise, in which conflictual lines such as "I want it" and "You can't have it" are repeated back and forth, the drama therapist may ask each pair to devise a scene that involves a conflict pertaining to these lines. Or in a session focusing on roles, each subgroup may be asked to plan a family scene composed of given roles. At times the drama therapist's directions serve simply as a catalyst for the clients' planning of the scene. For example, she may give each small group a setting and a relationship, which become the basis for a scene devised by its members, or she may hand out several objects that are to be utilized within a scene, thereby stimulating the group's imagination in the creation of the scene.

2. The Extemporaneous Improvisation

There is no planning stage preceding the *Extemporaneous Improvisation,* but the clients decide on (or are told) the parts they are to play. For example, two teenagers decide to enact a mother and a teenage daughter at home on a Saturday night. Rather than discuss before the scene begins what will take place, they immediately embark on the improvisation. Thus, the action within the scene is entirely spontaneous. Another example is a group of children who shout, "Let's all be animals escaping from the zoo" and then proceed to enact this. The difference between the *Planned Improvisation* and the *Extemporaneous Improvisation* is simply that in the former the clients discuss and reflect on the scene prior to the enactment.

A range in terms of structure and complexity exists within the *Extemporaneous Improvisation,* depending largely on how much information the actors have about their scene. For example, the actors may know only that they are mother and daughter, or they may know also that they are home on a Saturday night, or they may know also that the daughter, unbeknownst to the mother, is pregnant. Public performances of improvisational theatre, typically based on audience-suggestion (the actors ask the audience to tell them who and where they are, and then immediately begin a skit), would generally be categorized as *Extemporaneous Improvisation.*

3. *The Impromptu Improvisation*

The *Impromptu Improvisation* contains no planning stage and the actors have no prior knowledge as to role or setting. They are left entirely to their own resources, imagination, and ability to let something emerge in-the-moment. Each person adapts to the other's input. For example, two clients are asked to begin a scene. Spontaneously, one begins to pace. The other paces with him. They pass an imaginary cigarette back and forth. One mumbles, "I wish like hell we could get out of here." The other responds, "Forget it, we're stuck for life." Gradually, it becomes clear to the actors (and audience) that they are prisoners in a cell, serving a life sentence. But this relationship and situation evolved during the playing of the scene, rather than being decided upon at the outset. Improvisations that use movement and sound only are often in this category. The players relate to one another nonverbally, gradually developing an interaction and relationship.

Of the three types of improvisation, the *Impromptu Improvisation* is the least structured, and the most demanding in terms of spontaneity. In that it is the most unpredictable, it involves for many clients the greatest degree of risk-taking. It is also the closest to free association, and therefore can be the most reflective of the client's inner (and often unconscious) struggles.

Catalysts such as music or props can be used to help clients embark on the *Impromptu Improvisation,* or the therapist may give a general suggestion such as "start the scene by walking." The entire group can engage in an *Impromptu Improvisation;* this often eases the way for more individual scenes. One example of a group *Impromptu Improvisation,* stimulated by the therapist's direction, is to ask one person to begin performing some kind of activity in pantomime. Another group member enters the scene, at which point both people can speak. One by one, the rest of the group enters, gradually establishing, developing, embellishing, and finally concluding the scene (identified in Part II as *Join the Scene*).

The therapist chooses which type of improvisation to use based on the strengths and needs of the group, along with her overall objectives, orientation and personal strengths. I find that adults who have not *played* in a long time usually feel more comfortable, at least initially, with the *Planned Improvisation.* Adolescents often have little patience for planning, yet are eager to present ideas for scenes. Once the idea or impulse is voiced, they are ready to embark. Thus, with this age group I most often utilize *Extemporaneous Improvisation.* Children have the most ease with *Impromptu Improvisation.* Young children play in this unstructured manner naturally, often moving quickly from one scenario to another in a spontaneous and free-flowing fashion. The use of *Impromptu Improvisation* in a fluid fashion, with one scene transforming into another in an uninterrupted flow, is essentially the mode of *Transformations,* developed by David Johnson (1991, see p. 205).

With children, the scenes may begin as *Impromptu Improvisations* and over the course of a treatment series progress to *Planned Improvisations,* whereas with adults the sequence may be reversed. I find that, generally, the creativity of adult clients emerges within a structured framework. At early stages of treatment, *Impromptu Improvisations* can be inhibiting and anxiety-producing for adults. Given that my objectives revolve more around process and treatment than around diagnosis, I prefer beginning with more structure.* On the other hand, I may use very brief *Impromptu Improvisations* early on, as an outgrowth of the dramatic play in the first phase of a treatment series. There is no set formula; rather, the group itself dictates which type of improvisation is the most appropriate.

Enactments that are directly linked to real life are most often either *Planned Improvisations* or *Extemporaneous Improvisations.* If the scene is a reenactment of an actual event, it would be considered a *Planned Improvisation,* because the player/s know in advance what is to take place. Of course, the feelings or particular lines that emerge during the scene are unprepared for, and are often surprising and revealing. A scene that is geared toward practicing or preparing for a particular real-life situation is also generally a *Planned Improvisation,* although if the enactment is unspecific, and the client has little idea as to what will transpire (e.g., a client saying, "I'd like to try expressing anger to a friend"), it may be an *Extemporaneous Improvisation.* A scene in which the protagonist projects into the future (e.g., playing oneself five years from now) is generally an *Extemporaneous Improvisation;* the setting and role are clear, but the rest is unknown.

One type of improvisational scene may switch to another type, as a result of the therapist's directions and interventions. For example, following a *Planned Improvisation* reenacting an unexpected encounter with an ex-spouse, I asked the client to perform an *Extemporaneous Improvisation,* in which he returns to his apartment and voices all the feelings that have been evoked. After some discussion, he (along with three other group members

---

*This is not contradictory to Johnson's developmental approach; Johnson, too, believes that greater structure is needed initially, until "members can tolerate greater reliance on their own abilities to structure the experience" (1982b, p. 184).

who identified with the scene) was asked to do an *Impromptu Improvisation* using sound and movement only. What emerged at this point was an abstract creation, using repetition and echo, of the feelings of loss, pain, and aloneness than can recur over many years.

In the following section, the therapeutic direction and development of improvisational scenes will be examined.

THERAPEUTIC DIRECTION OF IMPROVISATIONAL SCENES

One of the primary means of intervention in drama therapy is through the direction of improvisational scenes. The drama therapist intertwines theatrical and therapeutic skills in determining the most beneficial ways of developing the enactments. An exciting aspect to the directing of scenes is that the theatrical and therapeutic needs usually coincide. That is, direction from an aesthetic perspective will often elicit deeper psychological content, or lead the scene toward deeper expression or resolution. And directing from a therapeutic perspective will often result in a more impactful theatrical creation.

Although the possible objectives in directing scenes are innumerable, the following section describes four common objectives and gives examples of each, in the hope of giving a sense of the ways in which improvisational scenes can be developed therapeutically. The objectives can be applied to any of three types of improvisational scenes described in the previous section. The first objective, *uncovering the meaning of the role,* is most used in scenes that take place in Phase Two (Scenework). The second objective, *finding alternatives or new behaviors,* is most common in Phase Three (Role Play); the third, *heightening or containing emotion,* in Phases Three and Four (Culminating Enactment); and the fourth, *introducing an internal nurturing parent,* in Phase Four.

First Objective: Uncovering the Meaning of the Role

One objective in the development of a scene is to uncover its symbolic meaning or expression. This intent is most likely to take place in Phase Two (Scenework), in which the scenes are fictional, though it may also occur within the dramatic play of Phase One (Dramatic Play). Such scenes often begin with the client playing a particular role in an impromptu, or extemporaneous, or planned improvisation. Rather than asking the client about the meaning of the role or trying to determine this meaning in advance, the therapist facilitates the playing-out of the scene. During the course of the scene, the meaning (or multiple meanings) gradually surfaces. This new understanding then guides the therapist's direction of the scene. The unfolding of the scene, along with the uncovering of its meaning and the therapeutic direction dictated by this meaning, is a gradual and interactive process. It is through the telling of the story or the enactment of the scene that nuances, tone, and levels of meaning are conveyed. This results in a far richer process of creation and understanding than would result if an interpretation regarding the client's choice of role had been prematurely made or solicited. (Uncovering the meaning of the role in a scene is analogous to uncovering the meaning of the role in a dream; it is through the *playing-out* of both that the interpretation or multiple interpretations gradually achieve transparency, without sacrificing complexity and texture.) The following three examples illustrate the way the meaning of a role becomes clear as the scene is enacted:

Stanley, an extremely withdrawn, passive, and socially isolated 60-year-old man who has spent most of his adult life in psychiatric hospitals, rarely takes any initiative in drama therapy. But one day he surprises me by saying he would like to play the *role of a mailman*. Immediately, I place a bag on his shoulder, and ask the rest of the group to become the people on the street who are waiting for their mail delivery. Stanley goes over to each house, looking pleased as he drops off the mail. But there is little dramatic action or interaction in the scene, and I can see that without direction it will soon end. I whisper to the remaining group members particular roles to play when the mailman shows up. One is desperate for a letter from her boyfriend, another has a barking pit bull dog, a third invites him in for coffee. This direction leads to greater interaction between Stanley and others, and allows time for Stanley to *live out* his role. It also gives me time to observe the scene and realize its meaning: Stanley wants, and perhaps is now ready for, contact with others. He wants to feel needed, to have something to offer, *something to deliver.* On an even more concrete level, the role of the mailman gives him permission to visit people in their homes, something this man has rarely done in his life.

Lenny, a six-year-old emotionally disturbed boy, places my student intern in the *role of a wife*. Prior to this, he has always had her play authority roles of mother, teacher, or police officer, or occasionally a baby role toward which he was alternately cruel and affectionate. The student had an understanding of these roles, but is confused by the sudden shift to the wife-husband scenes. I encourage her to go along with the scene in her sessions, following the child's lead. In their improvisations, Lenny obsessively insists that she stay in bed, while he feigns making coffee, going to and returning from work, running errands. She is not allowed to budge. Every so often he returns to bed and snuggles beside her. Throughout a number of sessions, the same scene is repeated over and over. In supervision, I have the student enact her client playing the husband. In role, she becomes aware of his high level of anxiety and his desperate need to control—to keep her (his wife) *in place*. The meaning of the scene becomes apparent. The student had recently explained to her clients that she was an intern and would be working with them only for a limited period of time. To this boy, a wife symbolized someone he could keep forever. As a husband, he could be the one to come and go, explore his growing world and identity, and always have someone to come back to—an experience he unfortunately had not had with his actual parents. At night, in the loneliness of his bed, he could rely on her comfort. I suggest to the student that she make an interpretation after the enactment. At the following session, after the familiar enactment, she says (as herself), "This scene makes me think that maybe you're worried about me leaving and want me to stay with you forever, but I can't. I care about you deeply, though our work together is only for the next few months."* This was the last time Lenny cast her in the role of wife (Emunah, 1989).

Gina, a depressed 24-year-old client, lives with her mother with whom she has a symbiotic relationship. One day, Gina suggests playing the *role of a Highway Patrol officer*. I have no idea what, if any, significance her scene will have, but I help her to set up a drama in which she stops speeding cars and gives the drivers tickets. Gina becomes very engaged and animated while giving the tickets. Her tone and behavior are not ones I have seen her display before: bossy, authoritarian, guilt-provoking. After the scene, she exclaims, "That felt good!" I ask her whether her tone reminded her of anyone or anything. Her response: "Yeah, my mother." I have her enact another scene, continuing the tone of the patrol officer, but this time playing her mother. She does this easily, and after a while is ready to role-reverse. When she is playing herself, I see the more familiar Gina reemerge: quiet, depressed, apologetic. As soon as the scene ends she mutters sadly, "At home I always feel like I'm being given tickets." This session paves the way for an exploration of the dynamics of her relationship with her mother, which until now she

---

*In retrospect, a better suggestion to the student would have been for her to find a way to express this sentiment during the scene, in role.

has not been ready to do. After many mother-daughter scenes in subsequent sessions, Gina's desire to move out and live on her own becomes apparent, along with her fears about being more independent, and her guilt about leaving her mother. These feelings are acknowledged, and scenes projecting into the future—in which she has her own apartment, and at the same time maintains a relationship with her mother—are dramatized.

Second Objective: Finding Alternatives or New Behaviors

In many scenes, the therapeutic objective and direction are to help the client discover alternatives (in terms of perspective, emotional response, or behavior), or to *practice* new behaviors. Most often such scenes occur during Phase Three (Role Play), beginning with a reenactment of a real-life (or *realistic*) situation. Following the reenactment, the drama therapist asks the client to *replay* the scene, this time experimenting with a different way of responding, rather than the one that actually took place.

Such an intervention is also possible in scenes occurring in Phase Two (Scenework) or Phase Four (Culminating Enactment). For example, a scene in Phase Two, albeit fictional, can nonetheless reveal the way in which a client would respond to such a situation in real life. The therapist can then direct the client to play the same scene in a different manner (or, when greater distance is required, ask that the *character* try a new behavior). This intervention does not necessarily involve replaying the same scene; the intervention can be interjected in the middle of the scenario, or lead to a follow-up scene. For example, a belligerent character in a Phase Two scene, who has just got into a fight with his buddy, returns the next day to apologize, or Cinderella musters up the courage to confront her stepsisters rather than remaining subservient. An emotionally laden scene in Phase Four may be followed by enactment and discussion which help the client to derive deeper insight and a heightened understanding of behavioral dynamics. But given that even with the greatest awareness and insight changing behavior is far from automatic, many such scenes are followed by practice with the new behaviors. Christine's *culminating scene,* described in Chapter 3, provides an example of such a sequence of interventions.

It should be noted that by *replay* I am not referring to following a reenactment of a painful situation with a scene depicting the client's fantasy of how this situation could or should have been—an intervention which is sometimes used in psychodrama. Although such a replay may feel good to the client in the moment, I believe that soon afterwards there can be negative repercussions, because of the extreme gap between the reenactment which was *real* (that is, based on real life) and the replay which was *not real.* The client's actual past cannot be erased or changed or magically transformed. A person who endured an abusive father, for example, cannot change the abusive parent into a caring one. But what can change are the *client's* response, coping mechanisms, affect, insight, perspective, behavior. In the therapeutic direction of such scenes, it is more beneficial to help the client explore the pain, rather than to recreate a scene in which there is no pain.*

If, however, the scene is about a client's own blunder or regret (as opposed to being subject to pain incurred by others), a replay in which he enacts how he would have liked to respond, or how he would respond to such a situation in the future may follow. The difference is that here the focus is on change within the client, rather than on changing another person in his life. Such scenes are quite useful in dealing with long-standing patterns of behavior. The initial scene illustrates and illuminates the client's pattern, and enables the client to achieve a heightened or meta-level of awareness about this pattern. The therapeutic directions of such a scene have two underlying objectives: first, helping the client achieve insight into the pattern/dynamic and, second, practicing a new behavioral response.

While the direction of many scenes enables clients to enact behaviors that they are consciously striving to incorporate in their real lives, in many cases the scenes are more about discovering alternative behaviors (or courses of action) that may not have occurred to them before, as the following two examples illustrate:

> Angela, a 21-year-old Hispanic client with a very low self-image and a history of self-abuse, primarily in the form of cutting herself, enters one session looking very drawn. In an exercise involving being pulled on both sides by two opposing parts of oneself (described in Part II as a prelude to *Identifying the Conflict*), Angela has the two people at her sides represent her conflicting attitudes of self-negation and self-acceptance. After a while, I stop the physical enactment and ask Angela to clarify what the self-negating part of herself says. She responds that this part of her always insists that she take her medicine. Then she confesses that the previous evening she cut her wrist with a razor to punish herself for getting a traffic ticket. She refers to this cutting as her medicine.

> Using Angela's own language, I decide to set up a medicine store, except that it is to be an *alternative* medicine store. I invite the entire

---

*On carefully selected occasions, portraying an ideal scene does have value in terms of helping the client get in touch with what is desired.

group to join Angela in a visit to this special store. Playing the shop-keeper, I ask my new customer what her usual prescription is. "Blood and a knife," she responds. "And how is that curative?" I inquire. "It sticks in the mind, it scars permanently, and it reminds you never to make the mistake again." "And what are the drawbacks of this medicine?" "It's dangerous and it can make you feel worse and it can send you to the looney bin."

"What would be a whole different kind of medicine that would work in a different way," I ask her. She is silent. After a long pause, I add: "You can ask your friends for ideas."

The group reflects on the kinds of new prescriptions they would like to give themselves, and that they would recommend for Angela. It isn't an easy topic, because most of the clients in this group have far more self-destructive tendencies than self-nurturing ones. To facilitate this process of reflection, I ask Derik, who is skilled at drawing, to draw for us a large-scale medicine cabinet. This is done on butcher paper and hung on the wall. When it is completed, everyone in the group writes on the whimsical drawings of jars and bottles and tubes the labels for their new medicines. Before long, we have boundary tablets, its-ok-to-make-mistakes liquid, safe sadness, and room for imperfectione (deliberately spelled wrong!). Angela takes an active part in filling in this cabinet, and also notes on a pad of paper the ingredients she particularly wants to remember, so that she can take these back home with her.

Derik, the artist in the previous example, is a very creative but restless and easily agitated 35-year-old African-American man with a history of alcoholism and depression. He had given up his artwork six years earlier. Although the group is in Phase Three (Role Play), Derik rarely brings up any personal issues. But one day, not long after Angela's medicine store scene, Derik asks to enact a scene about his ex-girlfriend. He claims that despite the fact that they have been separated for two years and that she now has a new boyfriend, she continues to beseech and pester him for money and cigarettes, to which he always acquiesces. He wants to practice being more assertive and "able to say no."

Derik chooses a young woman in the group, Diane, to play his ex-girlfriend, Linda. As the scene is to take place at Derik's apartment, I direct Diane to begin outside the room, knocking on the door. The enactment that follows *shows* us, dramatically, what Derik has just described verbally. It also becomes clear by the enactment and the brief discussion that follows that Linda stops by Derik's apartment frequently. We then replay the scene, with Derik attempting to explain to Linda that he has little money of his own and cannot keep giving her cash. As I watch Derik play this role, I have the sense that his difficulty is not so much in refusing to give Linda money but in letting go of her company. Even with the annoyance caused by her presence, it is nonetheless a presence. Giving her money and cigarettes assures him that she will come back.

I ask Derik to continue the scene, only now it is later in time, after Linda has left. He looks confused at first, and I too am uncertain as to what will take place in this solo scene. But just as uncovering the meaning of the role takes time, so too uncovering the meaning of the scene or discovering its emotional essence occurs gradually, through the playing out of the scene.

Now Derik is alone in his apartment. We have rearranged the space a bit more, to give greater semblance to his living room. I ask him to try to really imagine he is alone here, but to voice his thoughts out loud, so that we can also be with him, as witnesses to his long evenings. He turns on the imaginary television, clicks from channel to channel, visibly upset that there is nothing of interest on. He shuts off the T.V., fidgets, turns it on again, then off. He looks at me for help.

"Where's your cat," I ask, knowing he has one. He smiles and looks around, then spots her on top of the bookshelf. "Will she come if you call her?" "Oh, sure," he responds quickly. "Then call her and talk to her, tell her everything that's going through your mind."

She comes, and he tenderly places her on his lap. Now it is easier for him to speak out loud. "It's so quiet here, isn't it Furry? So lonely. Even the T.V. has nothing good on tonight. And you probably want to go off and meditate by yourself again, right?"

It is a big step for Derik to voice his inner feelings, to acknowledge and share his loneliness; this is a far greater challenge and authentic therapeutic issue than the original issue of working on assertiveness. His loss for words now is not so much due to self-consciousness as to not knowing what he feels. Derik is used to being distracted, often by Linda, and not paying attention to what lies within. I am tempted to join him in the scene or to invite others in, but I sense it is important, however difficult, for him to remain alone, with himself.

He tells Furry a little more: "I wish the phone would ring. There's nothing to do, no one to see, it's just you and me. And there's the bottle, but I don't want to do that." He caresses Furry but after a short while shows in mime that she has slithered out of his arms, and is now lying on the coffee table. He looks up at me again. "Even my cat's rejected me."

"What can you do?" I ask.

"I can't force her to sit on my lap, I can't make the phone ring, I can't make a good T.V. program appear, and I don't want to drink."

"Right. Why don't you just sit where you are, watch Furry from a distance, and see what happens."

He does just that. And after a long pause—a pause that holds both dramatic tension and therapeutic potentiality—he reaches in mime for a sketchbook and begins to draw. Furry is the object he is concentrating on, but it is clear that the sketch will be one of this moment, in its many facets, of what lies within him at this time. This is the healing point: Derik is finding that something does lie within, that out of the vacuum there can be creation. On a behavioral level, he is *finding an alternative* to filling that void with television or alcohol or catering to his ex-girlfriend's unremitting needs for pocket money.

Third Objective: Heightening or Containing Emotion

The therapist's direction of the scene can heighten its emotionality or can create emotional distance. The monitoring of emotionality occurs throughout the series, but it is most commonly a central objective in the more personal scenes of Phases Three and Four.* The decision to help the client become more emotionally invested or more emotionally contained depends on: 1) the therapeutic issues and overall treatment orientation for that client; 2) the particular content of the given scene; and 3) the phase of treatment during which the scene takes place. Robert Landy's (1986) concept of distancing in drama therapy is helpful in assessing the optimal degree of distance. A client who easily becomes overwhelmed by emotion will need help with containment, whereas a client who has difficulty accessing and expressing feeling will need help getting in contact with emotions. The drama therapist carefully gauges the degree of distancing that is required and, via her directions, steers the scene accordingly.

Sometimes both heightening and containing emotion are needed within the same scene. In this case, the therapist first guides the client toward emotional affect and catharsis. When the client has reached his tolerance point of emotional expression, the therapist helps him achieve some distance, so that he can master and cope with the emotion that has been evoked. At times the process is reversed: more distancing devices (as Landy's projective techniques) are used first, as a kind of warm-up or preparation for personal and cathartic enactment. Or, within the same scene, the therapist interweaves

---

*Only trained, experienced practitioners should engage in these more psychodramatic phases of therapy.

both directions: Initial containment sets the foundation for a heightening of emotion, which is followed by containment; the containment is then followed by a move toward a deeper level of expression, etc. The following example demonstrates the heightening of emotionality, followed by helping the client achieve mastery and containment:

Angela, the client mentioned above, has long suppressed emotions as a means of self-protection during a neglectful childhood. She stuffs herself with food as a way of avoiding feelings. But soon I discover far more problematic symptoms. After another group member's emotional scene, Angela sometimes cuts off all feeling, claiming she feels nothing and never has feelings. As previously indicated, Angela is also prone to self-mutilation. I know that when she finally does express some of her emotional pain, there will be tremendous relief and catharsis, but there will also be the risk that she will "split off" from the experience (withdrawing or denying it in some extreme fashion), or that she will try to distract herself from the emotional pain by inducing physical pain.

Despite several setbacks, Angela progresses well through Phases One, Two, and Three of the series. She is able to express feelings playfully, enjoys acting in fictional scenes, and is able to handle small doses of emotional expression related to current conflicts in her relationship with her emotionally disturbed mother, with whom she lives. But I know that the beneath her anger toward her mother are even deeper levels of rage and pain related to abandonment by her father, who had died in an automobile accident several years earlier. The scenes that other group members perform during this fourth phase of our series, dealing with unresolved feelings toward deceased parents, evoke Angela's own issues. She cannot hide much longer.

Finally, she is ready to enact her scene. She chooses Harold, a kind man whom she has grown to like and trust, to play her father. As we set up the scene, I ask Angela where her father would be when she is trying to contact him. She responds, "in the bathroom." Creating a semblance of a closed door out of chairs, I have Harold be in a bathroom, and instruct him to say little in the scene. This direction is designed both to reflect reality and to heighten Angela's sense of frustration about the lack of contact, as well as to focus the scene on Angela's expression of feeling rather than on a dialogue between father and daughter.

With Angela just outside the bathroom door, the scene begins. "Dad, you've been in there for hours. When are you coming out? How come all you want to do is live in the bathroom? Why won't you spend time with us?" And after a long pause: "Don't you care about me? You only have one kid. How come you never spend time with me?"

Little emotional affect underlies these words, until the last question, at which point I detect a kind of descension into a deeper level of engagement. Despite the emotional distance, Angela now seems very intent. I decide to *heighten the emotion.* Following her format of asking her father questions, and knowing how much Angela was abandoned in her childhood, I ask her to say, "Why did you leave me?"

Without any interruption in her concentration, Angela repeats the line, "Why did you leave me?" This line is followed by one question after another, each one slightly more specific and spoken in a slightly more emotional tone than the previous one: "Why'd you leave me at Linden Hospital? Why'd you leave me at Astin Children's Program? Why'd you leave me at the group home? Why'd you leave me in foster care? Why'd you leave me alone with Mom? Why'd you leave me when you were alive?"

As she names residential program after program, event after event, her level of engagement and emotionality continue to increase. "Why'd you always believe what everyone said about me? You never even asked what I felt, what I wanted, what I needed."

Now there are tears. "You always ignored me. What do you think that did to me? I just wanted your love. If you loved me, you wouldn't have made me beg for your attention and your love."

This is the first time I have seen Angela cry, and I sense that it is new for her, too. I let her continue a bit longer, especially as she is now making statements, rather than asking questions, but soon I intervene. I want to be sure to curb this process *before* she becomes frightened and overwhelmed. It is time to help her *contain* all the emotions with which she has gotten in touch.

As I enter the stage and gently touch her shoulder, she says to me with surprise and a hint of alarm, "I'm getting emotional." My response is reassuring. "I know. That's fine. That makes sense. That's human." Then she sputters, "God I feel weird, I feel hate and I feel love, and I hate myself for loving, and for hating, and I'm scared. . . ."

I interrupt. "You know what? Let's take one at a time. Let's get all the feelings out there. The first thing you said was hate. Pick someone who will play hate." Angela points to a member of the audience, who enters the stage area. "Now pick someone to play the love that you feel." She does so. "What else do you feel?" "I feel tied in knots, like I'm gonna be someone else, because I don't want to feel this." "The part of you that would rather shut out feeling," I say calmly, in an attempt to clarify and underscore this dynamic. "Yes." "OK, pick someone to play shutting out feeling." "What else?" I ask. "Scared," she says.

In identifying and directing others to play out all of her feelings, Angela achieves the distance necessary for her to contain emotion rather than becoming overwhelmed. She externalizes, as opposed to splitting off, her emotional self. Even her tendency to deny feeling is acknowledged, by being given a part in this drama. But because she will now be the director, she will not be controlled by it.

Angela directs and is audience to her own internal drama of emotional responses. She watches a dialogue between the conflicting feelings of love and hate. She observes the feeling of being scared (which she has relabelled, "scared child") respond to the dialogue, and the looming presence of the part that shuts out feeling, who is ready to take over should "scared" become too overwhelmed. During this part of the process, Angela is deeply engaged, but the roles of director and audience allow her to be less emotional than in the previous scene. In these more objective roles, she achieves not only distance but clarity and understanding.

I now ask Angela to enter the scene, and to address each of her emotions with acceptance.

There is a striking level of intentness, immediacy, and authenticity as Angela sits beside each part of herself, and reaches for words that come from her heart. She has attained "aesthetic distance," which Landy (1986) describes as the midway point of the distancing paradigm, the point at which there is a balance of thought and feeling.

First she speaks to the hate and anger: "It wasn't right for all that to happen. It's OK to be angry. You have every right to hate him, because none of this should have been that way. I understand why you feel so angry."

To the love she says: "You have a big capacity to love, even people that hurt you or desert you. Your capacity to love is good. And I'm glad I have you."

To the scared child: "I'm going to try to take care you of you. And maybe give you some of the love that you never had."

To the part that shuts out feeling: "Your help saved me a lot of times. I needed you because without you I would have gotten overwhelmed." I intervene. "What about now, do you still have the same need for that part ?" Still looking at the person playing that role, she says, "You did a good job, but I think you're going to have to retire soon!"

In directing Angela's scene, my first aim was to heighten emotionality. Once Angela did get in touch with and express strong feeling, the scene was steered toward containment. In the final part of the scene, the emphasis was first on helping her reintegrate the various emotions/parts of herself (that had been externalized during the distancing part of the scene), and then on guiding her toward self-acceptance. This last intervention will be clarified in the next section, as it relates to the introduction of an internal nurturing parent.

Fourth Objective: Introducing an Internal Nurturing Parent

In many of the scenes during Phase Four (Culminating Enactment), the woundedness experienced in childhood is brought back to life. Alice Miller (1983, 1986), a psychoanalyst who has criticized Freudian drive theory for not giving credence to the reality of childhood trauma, advocates reliving early trauma. She is not referring to using dramatic enactment, though enactment facilitates her aims, which are to help the client uncover the truth, and acknowledge and accept the past. Miller describes the wounded child as a part of oneself that has been split off and yet is the source of acting out, repetition compulsion, and unhappiness. In Phase Four scenes, the emotions and sensations lodged in the past are accessed and once again experienced in the body, but this time within the safe confines of the dramatic mode and among supportive others. The secret pain that has imprisoned the child, leading to guilt and alienation, is now witnessed by and shared with others. During such scenes, the drama therapist allies herself with the wounded child, which helps the client to eventually do the same. At the same time, the therapist encourages the development of an internal nurturing parent.

It is only after the strengths and healthy sides of the client have emerged in the drama therapy process that the client will be able to bring into the scene an internal nurturing parent. This is especially true for people with low self-esteem and little sense of self-worth, which is unfortunately the case among most psychiatric patients. Their sense of badness may otherwise be overwhelming, and the therapist's premature attempt to introduce an internal nurturing parent may fail or be superficial. This intervention must also be made only after the client has experienced, and begun to internalize, the empathy of the therapist and the other group members toward the wounded inner child. Bradshaw (1988) speaks of having his clients, while they are in touch with their inner child (via a trance-like state, which is not dissimilar to dramatic enactment), hear nurturing words spoken by others in the group.

In drama therapy, once the client has heard and internalized the love and acceptance of others toward the child within, he is ready to give this love and acceptance to himself. At these times, it is almost as if the client is embodying two roles simultaneously: the needy hurt child and the nurturing parent. The introjection of an internal nurturing parent, with the assistance and direction of the therapist, is an important intervention, especially within scenes enacted by clients who have difficulty coping with their pain or tending to themselves in a nurturing rather than a self-destructive fashion, as the following example illustrates:

In the same group as Angela (and as Shawn, from Chapters 3 and 4) is a 40-year-old man named Harold. Affected by the capacity of many in the group to confront their painful pasts and increasingly trusting of the group, Harold finds himself ready to do the same. As a child, Harold had been severely abused, emotionally and physically. Harold's mother had committed suicide when he was only eight, leaving him with her sadistic second husband. Harold carried into adulthood the sense of worthlessness and guilt instilled in so many abused children.

Shawn assumes the role of Harold's deceased mother, though I ask her to say little in the scene. Her presence, however silent, helps Harold (who does not yet possess the same level of dramatic ease and concentration as Shawn) to embark on the scene.

"How could you have left me without saying goodbye? I'm pissed as hell." There are long pauses between the lines. "Why'd you have to pick a relationship with a sick man? I loved you. But I'm tired of fighting him off of you."

The temporary switch to present tense indicates Harold's increased level of emotional involvement in the scene, and his underdistanced state. "I always try to put myself in the middle so you won't get hurt, and I get hit. I don't mind any of it if you just would stay with me, instead of checking out, you cheap bitch!"

Sensing that Harold has reached his tolerance point of emotional expression, I enter the playing area to help create some distance. At the same time, my intervention will assist him in reaching out to the hurt child he was, with the adult strengths he now possesses. With my hand on his shoulder, I ask, "Harold, how old are you at this time?" "Eight." "Pick someone to play you at eight."

Harold chooses Joanne. She is instructed to sit in a separate space from the one in which the scene with his mother has just occurred. I ask adult Harold to approach eight-year-old Harold.

Kneeling down and placing his hand on Joanne's hand, Harold speaks slowly and gently. "I know this whole thing has put you through a lot. It's not right. You don't deserve this. You deserve a whole lot better. None of this is your fault." To underscore this last line, I ask Harold to explain to the child why it is not his fault. Taking my instruction to Harold as a cue, Joanne says, "She wouldn't have left me if I hadn't done something wrong." Harold is visibly moved. "No, you didn't do anything wrong. It wasn't because of you. I know she loved you. But she was sick. She had a disease. Called alcoholism. And it didn't have anything to do with you."

Given his capacity to achieve some emotional distance and to become a *nurturing parent to himself,* Harold is equipped to take the scene further. He reenters the initial playing area, in which there is now an empty chair. By the wet, angry flash in his eyes, it is clear to whom he will now speak.

"You bastard! You ignorant shithead! Don't you know what you just did. At least she knew something about love. But you never loved me. You have no concept of what love is." Before me, I see both adult and child. The torment of the child is apparent, and his rage, released by the adult he has become, is rising. It is clear that these lines are new—the real child had never dared confront his stepfather. "Every time I do something small or little, you beat me with your belt. You beat me when I cry. And the time you beat me with a dog chain. I hate your guts. You're the reason she's dead. You make me sick. I'm sick of you. I don't want you in my life." And now he is screaming. "I WANT YOU OUT OF MY LIFE. PERIOD."

I go over to Harold, longing to hold the little boy, but knowing that that time is long past, and it is the large burly man before me now who must find his way back to the boy.

"Did you ever say back then what you were able to say now," I ask, wanting to support all the feelings he has been able to express and to acknowledge his capacity to express them. "No, never." "How was the eight-year-old you?" "Trying to be good, so it wouldn't happen. I couldn't cry, or be angry, or anything." "So all the feelings you're able to express now, you weren't able to express then." "Yes." "Go over to the little boy."

Harold returns to the area in which Joanne still crouches. He speaks with more conviction than before. "He had no right. No right to make you work, or to beat you when you cry. It's not your fault. He's a sick man. But there's nothing you can do about it. You don't have to try to be good. You can't control this. You aren't bad. You're hurt, because you've been treated so badly. I accept you the way you are."

"Can you tell him a little about what it's like to grow up, and what he has to look forward to?"

"I don't want you growing up thinking that everyone's like this. Because not everyone is. There are people you can trust and love. I know it's hard to imagine now, but there are people you will love, and people who will love you. And you can trust me, and I love you."

After a few minutes, he speaks to me and to the group. "For generations this has been going on in our family. This horrible mistreatment of children. This lack of respect for human life. But I'm going to be the link, no matter how hard, that stops that chain, that has a good family relationship, that loves his children. And I'm going to start with myself."

TOOLS AND TECHNIQUES IN SCENE DIRECTION

Many of the techniques utilized in the direction of improvisational scenes are drawn from psychodrama. There are many excellent sources on these psychodramatic techniques, including books by Blatner (1988a, b), Kipper (1986), Goldman and Morrison (1984), Sternberg and Garcia (1989), Yablonski (1975), and Leveton (1991). Described below are six frequently used techniques, the first two of which are staples in psychodrama. An entire session can be based on a single scene which is developed in diverse ways, with the aid of Role Reversal, Doubling, Playing with Time, Adding or Eliminating Characters, Taking Over the Role, or Repetition.

Role Reversal

In Role Reversal, the participants in the scene switch roles. It is important that they be asked to physically change places with one another and to assume the other's position, posture, and attitude as closely as possible. Role Reversal is not limited to psychodramatic scenes or to scenes that occur during Phase Three or Four. Cinderella, for example, can switch places with her mean stepsister, or a mama and baby can reverse roles—as children do all the time in their play.

Role Reversal facilitates the development and enrichment of a scene. More specifically, it can be used to help: 1) understand the other's perspective or point of view. This building of empathy is especially appropriate when a scene is about communication and relationship. On the other hand, when the perspective of the other is irrelevant to the scene, Role Reversal is not indicated (because the therapeutic aim is giving the protagonist free reign to express his feelings, unimpeded, as in the case of Harold speaking to his stepfather); 2) demonstrate how a role should be played. It is often important at the onset of a psychodramatic scene for the protagonist to play the role of another person in his life in order to demonstrate to the person who will assume the role (the *auxiliary*) how it should be played. Sometimes Role Reversal occurs during the scene, to assist the auxiliary in playing the role more closely to the protagonist's experience; 3) increase role repertoire. The switching of roles often enables a client to behave or express himself in an uncharacteristic way; 4) give feedback on how one is perceived by others. When a client watches himself being played by another client, he can see how he behaves or how his behavior is perceived by another; 5) provide distance. When emotional distancing is needed, switching to the other role (usually entailing switching from playing oneself to playing a character or auxiliary) is helpful because in so doing the client shifts to a more objective state. Frequent switching back and forth between roles prevents an emotional attachment to any given role and prevents the deepening of emotional affect (and should only be used when this in fact is the intention); 6) work through an impasse. When there is a standstill in the scene, Role Reversal can circumvent a premature ending of the scene, or alleviate an uncomfortable moment (although at times it is better to have the clients "stay with" this uncomfortableness); 7) enable one to answer his own questions. When a therapeutically significant question is brought up, Role Reversal is an opportune way of having the person himself respond, to himself. Often *in role* one can find answers that were previously blocked or inaccessible.

Doubling

In Doubling, the protagonist is joined by another person in the group (or by the therapist), who expresses out loud what the protagonist may be feeling or thinking but not saying—that is, voicing the protagonist's inner feelings or thoughts. In a scene in which the protagonist is freely expressing himself, the Double simply repeats or elaborates upon the protagonist's words. Doubling is best used to: 1) provide support and encouragement; 2) help the protagonist become aware of and eventually voice suppressed feelings or thoughts; 3) heighten, deepen or sustain the protagonist's emotional engagement or affect; 4) enable others in the group who identify with the protagonist to become an active part of the scene.

As in Role Reversal, Doubling is not limited to psychodramatic enactment. Characters in fictional Phase Two (Scenework) scenes can be joined by a Double. The double generally stands behind or to the side of the protagonist or character, and in more emotional scenes often makes some physical contact. Because the Double represents inner thoughts, other people in the scene do not respond to the Double's words, only to what the protagonist or character voices.

At times, rather than there being only one Double, several group members, or even the entire group, can join as Doubles. The use of multiple Doubles serves to: 1) magnify the sense of support for the protagonist; 2) actively involve the group during a scene that is otherwise individually focused; 3) enable expression and catharsis by audience members who strongly identify with the protagonist. (A variation is for the group members to double from their seats, or to shout lines for the protagonist to repeat, if he wishes. This variation enables the protagonist to remain alone on stage and at the same time have support and direction from the group.) It is also possible for both parties in an interactive scene to have Doubles, though if the therapeutic emphasis in the scene is on the protagonist's expression of suppressed emotions, it is best to have only that side represented.

When a protagonist is stifling feelings that the therapist senses are on the verge of expression, it is often best to switch the protagonist to the role of Double, and have someone in the audience take over the role of the protagonist. As the Double to himself (or to the character he was just playing), the client is given the permission and distance he needs to express his inner feelings. (If he remains stuck the therapist and/or other group members can join him in the doubling.) After this emotional expression is achieved, the client may be asked to resume his original role, and now express his feelings directly to the other person/s in the scene. The role of Double is eliminated from the scene; once the inner feelings are openly expressed, the Double is no longer needed. If it is not in the client's best interest to communicate these feelings to the other person/s in the scene in real life, it is often better to have his expression remain under the auspices of the Double (which is more removed from reality, more in the imaginary realm), rather than revert back to playing himself in the scene.

The following tools are not drawn from psychodrama literature, but are frequently used in my own work.

Playing with Time

Similar to Moreno's technique of Future Projection, Playing with Time enables a scene to be shifted into the past or the future. In Future Projection, the scene is set in the future so that the client can explore a forthcoming event. In Playing with Time, a given scene is developed by moving it forward or backward in time, depending on the particular therapeutic objectives. The move backward tends to promote insight and understanding, whereas the move forward tends to foster the exploration of consequences and options. For example, after a scene in which an adolescent proudly enacts getting into a car drunk and driving full speed, the drama therapist rewinds the scene by one hour. The resulting scene may be one in which a fight the teen had with his father is depicted, leading the client to make a connection between his behavior and his emotions. Or, the drama therapist fast-forwards the scene by one hour. The resulting scene may be one in which the teen is taken into an ambulance after he has crashed into another car, leading the client to

consider consequences to his actions. The future scene aborts the glori-
fication of drunk-driving that occurred in the original scene, and helps the
client learn to think ahead.

A more drastic move backward or forward in time can intensify these
objectives: For example, a 35-year-old woman engaged in a scene about
rejection by her husband is asked to revert to her 10-year-old self, experiencing rejection by her father. Or a 13-year-old delinquent boy engaged in a scene
about a robbery is asked to portray himself at 23, looking back on his adolescent years. The projection into the future also expands role repertoire, and
helps the client achieve perspective on the present. This intervention is
particularly useful with clients who are feeling depressed and hopeless. Within
the context and role of a scene in the future, the client gains a degree of
distance from his current state of mind, allowing for the possibility not only
of hopefulness but of the discovery and articulation of positive aspects to his
current struggle and pain.

Adding or Eliminating Characters

A scene can be developed by adding more characters to the original
interaction, or by asking some of the original characters to leave the scene, so
that the focus is on a particular relationship. In general, the addition of characters adds scope and new perspective, whereas the elimination of characters
deepens the scene; the former tends to increase emotional distance and the
latter to decrease emotional distance. For example, in a Phase Two scene involving two parents at home with their angry 15-year-old daughter and compliant 10-year-old son, the drama therapist senses a particular emotional charge
between the mother and daughter. He asks the father and son to find a reason
to exit the scene, leaving the mother and daughter alone with one another. The
originally light scene suddenly becomes emotionally compelling. Or the therapist may choose to add breadth to the original scene, by having the grandmother come for a visit. The grandmother's relationship with her daughter, son-
in-law, and grandchildren adds complexity to the scene. Both directions can
occur within the same scene, particularly in conjunction with Playing with Time.
The original family scene, for example, is rewound a few hours, at which time
the mother and daughter are engaged in a confrontation. It is then fast-
forwarded a few hours, at which time the grandmother arrives at the door.

Taking Over the Role

Those watching the scene are invited to "tap out" one of the actors and
take over his role, at which point the original actor returns to the audience.

Generally, the person who has taken over the role is expected to embody the original character as closely as possible, and to continue precisely from where the original actor left off. A modification is to suggest that once entering the scene the new actor can play the role in a completely different manner. In some scenes, any of the characters may be tapped out; in others, the tapping out may be reserved for a particular character.

Taking Over the Role serves to: 1) actively engage the group members watching the scene. It is especially useful when the therapist wants to heighten the group process, or senses that many people in the group personally identify with the enactment; 2) allow the original actors to watch the scene they created. This can provide useful feedback, and expand options and perspectives. It can also rescue an actor who is feeling self-conscious or at a loss; 3) enhance role flexibility. Participants weave in and out of roles. They may reenter the scene several times, each time tapping out a different character; 4) create emotional distance. Any technique that involves switching back and forth between roles or having a number of people play the same role tends to prevent the players from becoming very emotionally identified with one given role.*

It is often best to end the scene (or sequence of scenes) with the original actors back in their respective roles. This provides cohesion and closure, and allows the originators to be acknowledged for their initiation of the scene, as well as express some of what they derived from watching the evolution of the scene.

Repetition

When a particularly significant word or line has been spontaneously uttered, the drama therapist may ask the client to repeat what he just said. She may even suggest that the client continue the scene using only that phrase, and no other words. Repetition serves to: 1) underscore something of significance, so that the client hears and assimilates what he has said, rather than letting the utterance slip by unnoticed; 2) heighten emotion. Often a particular set of words contains an emotional charge for the protagonist. Repetition helps the client get more in touch with the emotion and steers the scene toward a deeper level of emotional engagement.

It is important that the therapist give the direction to repeat what has just been said in a discreet and gentle manner, so as not to interrupt the client's

---

*For this reason, Taking Over the Role is most often used in Phases Two and Three, and rarely in Phase Four. In Phase Four scenes, Doubling is more likely to be incorporated, as a way of addressing other group members' "act hunger" (Moreno's term).

concentration and the flow of the scene. The objective in Repetition is to decrease emotional distance, and any clear interruption of the scene would have the opposite effect.

Repetition is also used in bringing a scene to a conclusion, as will be discussed in the following section.

Additional Tools

Other tools and techniques that are frequently used are: 1) having the protagonist *direct* the scene rather than be an actor within the scene. This is recommended when a significant degree of distance is needed and the therapist wants to ensure that the client does not become overwhelmed. The client may also be led to weave in and out of directing and acting in the scene. (The drama therapist functions as a coach/co-director); 2) having the audience direct the scene or aspects of the scene. This helps the audience feel more involved in the scene and more in control of what they are witnessing; 3) having the audience become a chorus within the scene. This too helps the audience become actively engaged. It can also serve to dramatically heighten or emphasize aspects of the scene, or to diminish performance self-consciousness that the protagonist may be experiencing, or to enable the protagonist to hear the support of the group.

The drama therapist utilizes her intuition, insight, and creativity in directing and developing improvisational enactments. She is constantly assessing the clients' needs and capacities, making choices, drawing from her repertoire, and inventing on the spot new means of advancing enactments toward their therapeutic potentiality.

SCENE RESOLUTION

Scene resolution refers to the final portion of the scene as well as to the very last line or moment. A sense of completion, dramatic power, or realization is necessary from both aesthetic and therapeutic perspectives; indeed, these two perspectives are often inseparable. An aesthetic ending is likely to be a therapeutic one, and vice versa. The closure to the enactment affects the overall impact of the scene, the way the actor/s feel about the scene, the way the audience views and responds to the scene, the degree to which the scene is digested or assimilated into the actor's experience, and the degree to which the actor/s are able to make the transition from the dramatic mode to reality.

Since clients engaged in a scene are often unable to think about or find a way of ending the enactment, the drama therapist's attentiveness is paramount at this point. The drama therapist may: 1) steer the actors toward a resolution by giving directions during the enactment; 2) "pause" the scene as he asks the actors to think about, or improvisationally arrive at, a resolution; 3) have the actors decide in advance (before the scene is played out) on a resolution; 4) end the scene himself on a powerful or poignant moment that occurs spontaneously during the enactment. It is important to note that resolution of a scene does not imply a necessarily positive outcome. The steering of a client toward a happy ending will only be artificial and alienating. A resolution simply means closure to the enactment.

In scenes that involve conflict, the first two interventions listed above, steering the scene via directions by the therapist or pausing the scene, are the most typical interventions. Many clients tend either to walk away from conflictual scenes or to create a pat resolution. Both of these should be discouraged, if not circumvented. The experience of dealing with conflict within a scene affords important practice in dealing with conflict in life. If the actors are not content with the resulting resolution, it can always be magically erased and replayed in a different way. The audience, too, can direct, or redirect, the actors toward a resolution. A contrasting option for scenes that involve conflict is for the conflict to be punctuated or encapsulated rather than resolved. For example, at the point of deadlock, the therapist pauses the scene long enough to ask each of the actors to come up with a final statement reflecting his position. He then gives them the sequence in which the final statements will be made, choosing carefully which character/person is last. Although there is no clear outcome, the conflict is not avoided.

The process for clients of formulating in advance an ending of a scene and particularly of choosing final lines or moments helps crystallize the issues of the scene. The work of creating an ending forces the clients to consider what the scene is really about, what they want to communicate, and with what feeling they want to leave the audience—and themselves. Both insight and mastery are facilitated.

Theatrically and therapeutically impactful resolutions of scenes often manifest transitions, hopefulness, or succinct encapsulation of the scene's essential meaning or message. Transition injects the scene with a dynamism, revealing not only what exists now but what is in process of *becoming*. Both transition and hopefulness at the end of a scene give form to the actor's striving. Hopefulness is not the same as a positive or happy ending; rather it is a way of reaching for and expressing the part of oneself that will not succumb, that will not be a victim, that has determination or faith. Succinct encapsulation punctuates what has transpired in the scene, driving the point home in a powerful or poetic fashion.

Irony is one way of achieving the succinct encapsulation of a scene. An example is the closing lines of a scene from the autobiographical play *Inside*

Out by the group *Beyond Analysis,* discussed in Part III (page 280). In the scene, as friends of the family ask Stacey questions about how she is doing, her mother consistently responds for her. Not only is Stacey prevented from speaking for herself, but many of the mother's responses are untrue. When the guests ask Stacey what she is doing now, her mother immediately answers, "Oh, she's working as an occupational therapist. She really enjoys it." Stacey has given up on trying to speak for herself, but after the guests leave she confronts her mother. The final lines, devised by Stacey herself, encapsulate the scene with irony: "Why did you do that? Why did you tell those lies?" Poised and assured, her mother responds: "Well, Stacey, you've been a *patient* in occupational therapy for the past six months, I figured it was the only thing you could *talk about!*"

The last intervention, that of having the therapist end the scene on a line/moment that occurs spontaneously within the scene, occurs by calling out at the choice moment, "Cut!" In Phase Two scenes, the therapist's choice point at which to cut the scene is often at a line/moment that is punctuative or humorous. In Phase Three scenes, the line/moment is often one that is synoptic or empowering. In Phase Four, the line/moment is often one that is emotionally potent or poignant, or that highlights a particularly significant aspect of the enactment. (As repeatedly stated, these are not formulas.) An alternative to "cut" is "freeze," at which point the actors freeze in their positions, forming a kind of statue or tableau, which becomes the ending to the scene. The use of freeze is recommended in scenes that are more physically than verbally oriented, or when the actors' positions at a certain point in the scene are especially telling of their emotional stances or interrelationships.

When a client utters a line or statement that holds particular significance or emotionality, the drama therapist may ask for this line to be repeated (see *Repetition,* p. 129) or she may ask the client to return to the significant lines at the very end of the scene. Another option is to ask the client to play the entire scene using only these words, and then cut the scene at a point at which the lines are spoken with particular conviction.

The ending of the scene captures and frames whatever was taking place at that final moment, similar to the process of catching a revealing expression in a photograph or freezing an image on video. The precise ending point need not be on a line or word. An expression or gesture, or a nonverbal interchange, such as a hug between two people, is often more meaningful than words. Sometimes, a few moments of silence just prior to the final ending point creates a more impactful ending; the "pause" allows for a "seeping in" or registering of the scene's emotionality or message.

In scenes of Phases Three and Four that involve a central protagonist, the therapist needs to ensure that the protagonist has the last line, rather than one of the auxiliaries. In scenes (of any phase) that do not have a central protagonist, it is often still important to decide which actor/role should have the last line. Sometimes, one actor (or the character he is playing) has been stifled within the scene and can be allowed not only the last line but the last *monologue.* The other actors are told to simply listen (or be frozen, if the intent is to give the impression that they do not hear the speaking actor), while the selected actor has free reign to speak his heart.

There are exceptions to the guideline of giving the last line to the protagonist, rather than to an auxiliary (or a Double). Such an example can be found in a *Telephone* scene by a 40-year-old professional woman, Hannah, who had lost her father when she was 24. In the scene, Hannah telephoned her father in heaven. Her monologue consisted largely of questions concerning how he was doing. My sense was that she wanted a response from him — not really to how *he* was doing in heaven, but rather to what *she* was making of her life. I asked her to tell him how she was, who she was, what was important in her life now. Her affect became more emotional and her engagement in the scene deepened. It soon became clear that joys and positive experiences had rarely been shared in her family. There was much at this time in her life that made her happy, and she wanted the opportunity to express this joy to her father.

I asked her to reverse roles, and respond as her father to what had been said. In the role of her father, Hannah responded with surprise, but also with pleasure and acceptance. Her emotionality increased when (as her father) she said, "I'm glad to hear how well you are doing now. I'm proud of you. Go ahead and be happy. I accept your happiness. I want your happiness." Though the father she had lost 16 years earlier may not have responded in this way, it was clear that Hannah was compelled to give to herself what she needed to hear now.

As is typical in scene resolution, I had her come back to being herself. But I did not have her speak the last lines. The therapeutic essence of this scene was about hearing and absorbing words she longed to hear. Another member took over the role of the father and repeated the significant lines Hannah had just spoken. The final part of this scene consisted simply of Hannah listening — to the lines she had given to her father and, on another level, to herself. I ended the scene with a soft "ok" when I saw her facial expression manifest a deep gratification in hearing the words, "I'm glad for your happiness."

Whether or not there is an outside audience, the ending of scenes in group drama therapy is immediately followed by applause. Although there are pros and cons to the use of applause in drama therapy, I have generally found it to be valuable. The applause clearly marks the ending, fostering a sense of closure, completion, and achievement. It builds confidence in performance and establishes a mode of appreciation and acknowledgment within the group. Applause also provides a clear break from the fantasy enactment, after which discussion can be encouraged. It serves as a demarcation between the fictional and the actual, assisting the actors, and audience, in making the transition from the enactment which was *not real* to the *reality* that follows. This demarcation is critical in work with emotionally disturbed clients, whose boundaries between fantasy and reality, self and character, are often impaired.

In the scenes of Phase Two, the first objective—that of building confidence and demonstrating appreciation—is especially significant. In the scenes of Phase Three, which are very close to real life, the second objective—providing a clear demarcation—is particularly important. While the applause following Phase Two scenes is an expression of praise for the actors' skills and creativity, in Phase Three it is also for the actors' manifestation of new behavior, thus supporting and reinforcing whatever is being practiced in the scene. In Phase Four, too, the applause is for both the scene and for the actor/protagonist himself; the two are indistinguishable. It is a way of commending the protagonist for his courage and of conveying the empathy felt by the audience.

However, there are psychodramatic scenes in Phase Four, often ones that entail the reenactment of trauma, after which applause is not appropriate. These scenes are sometimes best followed by a few moments of silence. As always, the drama therapist follows his instinct; there are no rigid rules or formulas. Other potential drawbacks to appplause are: 1) creating competition in the group when one applause is greater than the next; 2) heightening performance anxiety; 3) unintentionally supporting "ham," manic, or narcissistic clients.

The ending of the scene, like the ending of the session, is a kind of sacred moment. An act has been completed, creating the space for what comes next—be it reflection (on conscious or unconscious levels), discussion, or further enactment. As one imaginary curtain is drawn, another one appears, waiting to be opened.

Part II

TECHNIQUES

Introduction

The techniques described in Part II are intended as resources for the therapist, not as recipes. All of the techniques are based in clinical work and most of the descriptions are integrated with therapeutic considerations, applications, and illustrations. In selecting techniques to incorporate into the drama therapy session, the therapist must carefully examine the needs of the particular group, as well as her own affinities and strengths. Any technique that is used should be appropriate for that group of clients, and should feel comfortable to that therapist. Since each client is unique, as is each therapist, modification of the techniques is encouraged. In fact, it is my hope that the techniques will stimulate the therapist's creativity, leading to new variations as well as to the invention of new techniques based upon discoveries made within particular therapeutic contexts. Moreover, as a drama therapy session is never composed of isolated techniques but rather of a progressive process comprising smooth transitions as described in Chapter 4, the therapist's creativity will naturally be challenged in devising sequences of techniques and in finding interconnections between techniques.

The techniques are categorized according to phases of the session and treatment series, and subcategorized according to therapeutic objectives. These categorizations are not rigid, and most techniques overlap more than one category and subcategory. But the majority of techniques described in Chapter 6 are most frequently utilized either at the beginning of the session and/or during Phase One (Dramatic Play) of a drama therapy treatment series. The majority of techniques described in Chapter 7 are utilized in the middle of the session and/or during Phases Two (Scenework), Three (Role Play), and Four (Culminating Enactment) of a drama therapy treatment series. The techniques in Chapter 8 are most often used at the end of the session, and/or during Phase Five (Ritual) of the treatment series.

The assessment of therapeutic needs and the application of techniques to meet these needs are complex processes. Most drama therapy processes and techniques serve multiple functions concurrently. Nonetheless, the majority of techniques emphasize particular objectives. It is my hope that the categorizations and subcategorizations will assist the practitioner in reflecting on the objectives that are most central, taking into account the particular point in the treatment series and the session, as well as the particular point in the journey for the group or individual client. (As repeatedly expressed throughout this book, the categorizations should not be viewed as rigid formulas.) For the drama therapist who prefers working spontaneously, without preplanning sessions, an increased familiarity with techniques, in conjunction with stages and objectives, will facilitate the capacity to incorporate appropriate techniques and interventions on the spot.

Within each subcategory, the techniques are listed according to my assessment of their overall applicability; the first techniques in each section are the ones that I find myself and my students using with the greatest frequency. A secondary consideration in sequencing the techniques is their interrelationship; I have attempted consecution in the listing of related techniques.

The techniques described in Part II can be applied and adapted to many diverse contexts. Though the techniques are geared toward group drama therapy, most can be applied to individual and family drama therapy. Additionally, practitioners in psychology who do not intend to conduct entire drama therapy sessions but who are interested in active approaches to therapy and who wish to incorporate some experiential processes will find many of the techniques useful. Practitioners working with clients who manifest difficulty with verbal communication, social interaction, or emotional expression/containment—be they children or adolescents, emotionally disturbed or socially disadvantaged, substance abusers, or prisoners—will find the techniques particularly relevant. Many of the techniques can also be used with people who have developmental or physical disabilities, who are suffering from post-traumatic stress disorder or eating disorders, or who are survivors of abuse.

As drama therapy is ideally suited to group work, group therapists can easily incorporate drama therapy techniques into a verbal group process. Many of the techniques can serve as catalysts to a verbal process not only in clinical situations, but in organizational development, teaching, and recreation. Some of the techniques can also be utilized at community events, social gatherings, and in the home; all people can benefit from dramatic play. Creative arts therapists and psychodramatists can naturally interweave many drama therapy techniques into their sessions. Last, theatre teachers who are not concerned solely with professional training or skill development but are interested in the personal growth that can be derived from acting will find many of the techniques germane.

I have devised the majority of the techniques in Part II myself as I struggled to find ways of meeting the needs of particular groups and therapeutic situations. The degree of originality varies; the development of many of the

techniques was naturally influenced by the sources of drama therapy delineated in Chapter 1. Some of the techniques are developed by specific other
people; in these cases the source is indicated. Most of the borrowed techniques are those of Viola Spolin (1982, 1983, 1985, 1986), pioneer of theatre
games. Many of the techniques by Spolin have a long-standing history in
drama workshops internationally. Some are also based on, or related to, techniques described by other drama specialists, including Way (1967), Hodgson
and Richards (1967), King (1975), Johnstone (1989), and Barker (1977). The
basis for inclusion of selected techniques of Spolin and others is the
applicability to a therapeutic context and to a particular therapeutic objective.
All borrowed techniques have been explored, and in many cases modified and
adapted, in my clinical work. Still other techniques in Part II have no single
originator to my knowledge, and may remind the reader of similar techniques
from a variety of disciplines, including theatre, gestalt therapy, psychodrama,
and dance/movement therapy.*

LIST OF TECHNIQUES

1. Beginning of the Session and Series

Emotional Expression

Line Repetition
    Group line repetition
Group Mood
Emotional Greetings
Mirror Exercises
    Partner mirror
        voice mirror
        voice and body mirror
        face mirror
        sounding the movement
        mirror with emotional suggestion
        activity mirror
        follow the movement

---

*Structured games have been used, too, in various group therapy settings (Russell, 1975:
Langley, 1983; Zweben & Hammann, 1970; Weathers, Bedell, et al, 1981), in family therapy,
and in the encounter groups and sensitivity training that were popular in the 1970s. Structure
facilitates containment and safety, which in turn facilitate expression and self-disclosure.
The techniques in Part II bring the particular healing properties of theatre to the psychotherapeutic arena.

Group mirror
    group sounding the movement
    who started the motion
    circle-mirror-transformation
Join the Emotion
Emotional Mime
Guess How I Feel
Masks and Mime
Emotional Statues
    Partner sculpting
    Sculpting a scene
Emotional Spaces
Emotional Orchestra
Voice Games
Silent Scream

Group Interaction

Categorical Groupings
Fast-Speed Handshake
Introducing Yourself as Another
Party with Secret Roles
    Roles that meet the occasion
    Surprise phone calls
Bubble War and Balloon Float

Physical Activation

Dodging
Back Pushes
Don't Get Up
Body Connections
Balls Between Backs
Back Dialogues
Four-Corner Dash
Break out of/into the Circle
New Musical Chairs
Rope Games

Trust

Nurturing Falls
    Circle falls
    Falling between two rows

Partner falls
Partner leans
People Lifts
Blind Walks Revisited
Partner Blind Walks
Head identification
Follow my sound
Follow my scent
Follow my directions
Identify your leader
Group Blind Walks
Creating a circle
Identify others
Find the same hands
Touch and Smell
Rag Doll

Observation and Concentration

Ball Throws
Circle ball throw
Get the ball
Guess Where We Are
Eating in Mime
Who Started the Motion
Three Changes
Guess Who's Guilty
Guess the Topic
People Puppets
Space Substance

2. Mid-Session and Mid-Series

Expression and Communication

Telephone
Hand Gestures
Gibberish
Calling Out Emotions
Dubbing and Silent Scene
Breaking the News
Video Lip-Syncing

Character and Role Development

Family Roles
Family Therapy
Therapist-Client
Restaurant Scenes
Newspaper
TV Interviews
Hidden Conflict
Scripted Scenes

Group Collaboration

Join the Scene
Transformations
Court Trial
Ideal Therapeutic Community
    Ideal planet
Let's Make a Play
Congratulations

Self-Revelation

Sculpting and Self-Sculptures
Self-Masks
Establish the Relationship
Person in Your Life
Yourself at Different Ages
Becoming Your Own Therapist
Magic Shop
Identifying the Conflict
Self-Revelatory Performance
Confronting Yourself on Video

3. Closure of Session and Series

Giving and Receiving

Hand-Squeeze
Transforming the Object
    Transforming the real object
    Transforming the newspaper
    Passing the substance

Pass the Facial Expression
Gifts in Mine

Collective Creativity

Magic Box
Theatre Ritual
Story-Building and Storytelling
    One-word-at-a-time
    Narrating and enacting a story
    Playback
    Mutual storytelling
    Personal storytelling
Fortunately/Unfortunately
Part of a Whole and Machine
Group Statue
Group Poem

Intergroup Perceptions

Poetic Associations
True and False Statements
Answer as Someone Else
Sculpt the Group
Secrets

Review and Celebration

Guess that Scene
Reunion
Parachute
Toasts
Diplomas
Group Photo
Re-Fortuned Cookies

6

BEGINNING OF THE SESSION AND SERIES

The objectives for the beginning of the session and series include: *emotional expression, group interaction, physical activation, trust,* and *observation and concentration.* The facilitation of *emotional expression* in drama therapy is primary, in contrast to the early phases of theatre workshops and classes, in which the development of observation and concentration, sensory awareness, and movement skills is typically underscored. *Group interaction,* central to group work, is particularly important in Phase One (Dramatic Play), during which the sense of group identity develops and peer relationships are formed. *Physical activation* eases emotional expression (and also, at times, group interaction), and serves to energize and enliven the group, as well as to establish a playful environment. The building of *trust* is an important goal throughout the series; the techniques aimed at building trust are used in early parts of sessions in all phases of treatment. *Observation and concentration,* necessary skills for the improvisational scenes that take place in later stages, heighten the focus and presence of the participants.

Most beginning techniques within a session interweave two or more objectives. For example, a session may start with a technique categorized under *physical activation,* and be followed by two techniques categorized under *emotional expression.* The session may then progress toward one of the objectives indicated under *Mid-Session,* such as *character and role development.*

The first section of this chapter, *Emotional Expression,* is the most extensive, as many techniques have been devised to meet this critical objective during early parts of the session and series.

EMOTIONAL EXPRESSION

Line Repetition

"I want it."
"You can't have it."
"Please, I really want it."
"You can't have it!"
(pleading) "I want it . . ."
(gently) "I'm so sorry, but you cannot have it."
(now desperate and screaming) "I WANT IT . . . I WANT IT"
(interrupting, shouting back) "YOU CAN'T HAVE IT!"

A dialogue restricted to two given lines produces, very simply, a powerful moment of theatre. The exercise immediately places the clients' focus on expression, communication, and emotion, rather than on worrying about what lines to say next. Clients are paired off, given the specific lines, and instructed to vary intonation, volume, and affect, but not to stray from the given words. The inherent structure in the exercise promotes a sense of freedom of expression, and the repetition of the lines tends to naturally elicit strong emotion. The exercise is an ideal warm-up for improvisation and is invariably followed by dramatic scenes that are rich with feeling and conflict.

Any lines or words may be used, from a basic "YES"—"NO" to a more complex "HELP ME"—"I CAN'T." "I WANT IT"—"YOU CAN'T HAVE IT" is one of my favorite sets of lines because it is simple and direct, and everyone seems to relate to it. This particular set of lines tends to evoke feelings of frustration, need, desire, and power, which are often associated to parent-child or couple relationships. The specific content and level of intensity of the scenes that arise from these lines hold a wide range of possibility. Some clients, during the exercise or in the scenes that follow, create a concrete, relatively impersonal, and often humorous conflict, e.g., asking a stranger for a cigarette. For others, deep feelings emerge. In one session, a 40-year-old professional woman let out a chilling, primal wail as she repeated, "I want it." Her voice became childlike, and her wails turned into cries. She had gotten in touch with the extent to which her emotional needs in early childhood had been unmet. The eldest of several siblings, she had been delegated by her unavailable parents to bear the responsibility of caring for the family.

Combinations of lines can be devised to address specific individual or group issues. A set of lines that I initiated to facilitate exploration of separation, loss, dependency, and need for autonomy is: "I WANT TO GO" and "I NEED YOU TO STAY." Extraordinarily powerful scenes have developed from these lines—scenes about children leaving home for the first time, symbiotic relationships, divorce. The addition of particular props, such as a suitcase (given to the person saying "I want to go") heightens the tension. Lines aimed at self-assertion are: "I CAN DO IT"—"NO YOU CAN'T."

The lines need not be conflictual. In fact, both partners can be given the same line. For example, as a warm-up to performance, I had a group in pairs repeat, "I'M SCARED." A few minutes later this was switched to "I'M EXCITED" and finally to "I'M READY." The lines were first said back and forth and then in unison.

Line Repetition is my most used drama therapy technique. It liberates clients from anxiety about acting, elicits dramatic skills, provides an outlet for intense emotion, and emphasizes relationship and interaction. When an entire group, divided in pairs, is engaged in this exercise, the room is electrified. On numerous occasions I have seen clients with a perpetual flat affect suddenly emote during *Line Repetition,* or severely withdrawn clients become animated, or clients disconnected from emotions begin to *feel.* Just as often, I have witnessed clients with a tendency to become overwhelmed by emotion express strong feeling while maintaining full control.

Line Repetition is best preceded by a physical warm-up that relates to the nature of the conflict to follow. For example, as a lead-in to the the lines, "I want it"—"You can't have it," each pair of individuals stand back-to-back and push against each other (see *Back Pushes,* p. 166) as if their backs are engaged in an argument. Or the group (as a whole or in pairs) conducts a tug-of-war. For "I want to go"—"I need you to stay," partners are instructed to hold opposite hands, as one person tries to pull away. The physical exercise stimulates the emotional state, evoking the desire to vocalize the feeling. Similarly, *Line Repetition* evokes the desire to use other lines, that is, to not remain restricted by two lines only. Thus, there is a natural transition from the physical exercise to *Line Repetition* to improvisational scenework.

During *Line Repetition,* directions entailing physical action may be added to develop and dramatically intensify the interaction. Such an instruction might be: "If you're saying, 'You can't have it,' try to run away from your partner. You're sick of him asking for it! But, if you want it, don't let your partner get out of your sight!" The other natural development of the exercise is for partners to reverse roles.

After the exercise, each pair can be asked to perform their interaction in front of the group. This is sometimes a gentle way of introducing clients to performance. It also allows them the full space of the room, within which they can move and shout freely. The vignettes, which usually end up having a unique quality, are entertaining to watch, and they tend to bring out the actors' humor, playfulness, expressiveness, and intensity.

Discussion following *Line Repetition* generally revolves around emotional responses and associations to the lines. I often begin by asking participants which side of the conflict felt more comfortable or familiar, and whether any particular relationships came to mind. Improvisational scenes can then be developed based on this verbal exchange. A more spontaneous approach to the development of scenes is to ask the actors *while* they are engaged in *Line Repetition* to begin to use other words when they are so moved, and to continue the interaction until the conflict and relationship become clear. With more advanced improvisors, this *Impromptu Improvisation* is both exciting and revealing.

VARIATION

Group line repetition
The entire group walks around the room, repeating one or two given lines, which are addressed to other group members as they encounter one another. As in *Line Repetition,* the instruction is to vary intonation or intensify expression as the line is repeated. The therapist may initiate lines that reflect actual feelings at the beginning of the session, e.g., "I'm anxious" or "I can't do it." After some repetition of the given line, half the group might be asked to respond with a corresponding line, e.g., "Yes, you can," followed by the reversal of roles.

Group Mood

One person volunteers to leave the room. The group gets into a huddle and decides on a particular mood (or emotion, attitude, behavior) to enact. The volunteer returns and observes the group's verbal and nonverbal language until s/he can identify the mood the group is portraying.

Group Mood enables participants to express actual feelings or anxieties within the safe and structured confines of the activity. The suggestions clients make for enactments are typically reflections of real feelings, or feelings with which individuals would like to be more in touch. Adolescent groups often eagerly propose, "Let's all act resistant," or "Let's be hostile." The resistance or hostility they may have displayed toward the therapist or the activity is thereby contained within the game. Depressed adults often choose passive states, as *lazy, bored,* or *depressed,* followed by *anger* (which is not surprising, as anger tends to underlie much depression). Since clients are *only acting,* they feel more in control of those emotions or behaviors that might normally, in real life, frighten or overwhelm them. And the exaggeration of the emotions, which is common early on in the activity, provokes a sense of humor and perspective and establishes a mood of fun and playfulness. Institutionalized clients, who have been plagued by years of diagnostic labeling, will spontaneously suggest acting *paranoid schizophrenic, manic depressive,* or simply *crazy.* The suggestion and enactment are attempts at understanding and mastering these terms, and perhaps at inoculating themselves to the stigmatization. It is interesting to note the way psychiatric clients enact *crazy,* but more intriguing is how quickly, once the word is guessed and the game is over, they stop acting crazy (Emunah, 1983).

The inhibition with regard to drama that participants understandably feel at the beginning of a session or series is greatly reduced by: 1) the format of guessing, which diminishes self-consciousness, because it gives a sense of purpose or objective; 2) the fact that the whole group is engaged at once, and therefore there is no audience; 3) the allowance to play out actual feelings, rather than being asked to be or behave as someone other than the self. Once a certain level of comfort is achieved, the therapist can suggest that the "guesser" direct two or three people within the group to enact the word. This focus on a smaller segment of the group facilitates further development of the enactment and becomes an excellent warm-up to improvisational scenework.

While the initial enactments of moods or feelings are often simplistic and superficial, they gradually become more authentic. I encourage participants to find the part of themselves that does feel that emotion, or to recall the way they normally behave when they are in that particular state. I ask the person attempting to guess to observe for a while before guessing, in order to allow the group time to enact the selected mood.

Group Mood enables participants to watch themselves in action; by experiencing various states and simultaneously observing themselves and others in these states, they achieve a meta-level of awareness. Another typical progression during *Group Mood* is from enacting actual feelings to enacting unfamiliar feelings. This corresponds to the notion that once clients are given permission to express their current state of mind, they are receptive to experimentation with alternative behaviors and affects.

Group Mood is an effective technique with any age group or population. A group of healthy latency-aged girls I worked with reveled in this game session after session. A group of developmentally disabled adults enjoyed enacting basic emotions such as *happy* and *sad,* while graduate students challenged themselves with more subtle words, such as *skeptical* and *vulnerable.* By facilitating emotional expression in a playful, interactive context, *Group Mood* offers participants at the onset of a session or series an immediate taste of the drama therapy process.

For groups that are threatened by any kind of emotional enactment, *Group Mood* can be modified to include general adverbs, rather than feelings:

The "guesser" requests that the entire group perform certain actions, which s/he calls out (as walk, talk, shake hands, pretend to eat, etc.) according to the adverb the group has selected (for example, *slowly, rapidly, softly, loudly, intensely*). This variation is particularly effective with children as a prelude to the use of more emotional words.

Emotional Greetings

Group members stand back-to-back. The leader calls out an emotion or attitude, at which point everyone turns around (facing her partner), and greets the partner in the manner of that emotion. Emotions that members are actually experiencing may be selected. I will usually use *Emotional Greetings* during a very first session, and call out words such as: shyly, anxiously, suspiciously, professionally, aggressively, enthusiastically. (The initial words/greetings reflect actual feelings; the latter ones are aimed at heightening the level of energy and interaction.) The tone in which each emotion is called out reflects that emotion.

Emotional Greetings is an excellent way of giving clients in early sessions a sample of the experience of expressing and dramatizing feelings in an interactive and playful context. The technique is active and fast-paced, moving fairly quickly from one emotion to the next (with partners reestablishing the back-to-back position between each greeting), taking into account the difficulty and potential awkwardness participants may have in sustaining and developing a dramatic interaction at this early stage. To prolong the nonverbal component of the interaction slightly, participants may be asked to stand at some distance from one another (rather than back-to-back), and then turn around and walk toward each other once the emotion is called out.

A natural follow-up to *Emotional Greetings* is *Group Mood*.

Mirror Exercises

The following descriptions attempt to convey the extensive and diverse application of *Mirror Exercises* to drama therapy. *Mirror Exercises* can be categorized under *Emotional Expression* or under *Observation and Concentration,* depending on which aspect of the exercise is emphasized. As I generally aim to facilitate emotional expression within *Mirror Exercises*, especially in *Group Mirror* and in the variations listed under *Partner Mirror,* I have placed *Mirror Exercises* under *Emotional Expression*.

PARTNER MIRROR

I know of no greater way to empathize with another person than to *become* him or her through a *Mirror Exercise*—through active imagination, dramatic role playing, or physically.

The traditional *Mirror Exercise,* which is a staple in dance/movement therapy and in theatre workshops, entails two people facing each other, with one designated as *leader* and the other as the *mirror image.* The mirror image attempts to follow the *leader's* movements as precisely as possible.

The *leader* is reminded to begin with slow, steady movements; the aim is not to challenge or trick the partner, but to achieve synchronization. After a while, if both parties are concentrating intently, the *mirror image* can almost predict, or intuit, the movements of the *leader.* I instruct participants to maintain direct eye contact throughout the exercise, rather than look at the part of the other's body that is moving. This helps participants to stay in touch with the whole person in front of them and heightens their sense of interconnectedness. A second stage occurs when the partners are asked to switch roles. (This instruction should be given softly, to avoid disrupting the flow.) A third stage of the exercise is to eliminate both roles; at this point one detects and immediately mirrors all subtle shifts in the partner, so that any leading and following is imperceptible on the outside, as well as at times to the partners themselves. This stage should only be added when simultaneity has been achieved during the first two stages.

Mirror Exercises require acute concentration and sensitivity; all nuances of expression are captured. There is a powerful sense of intimate sharing and communion, as the usual boundaries between people dissolve. Another powerful element in mirroring is that of magnification. When actions are multiplied by two (in *Partner Mirror*) or by many (in *Group Mirror*), the experience for the initiator is one of strong validation.

The nonverbal contact and communication in *Partner Mirror* are often quite intense, and the slow synchronistic movement of bodies is often beautiful to behold. It is touching to witness the degree of connectedness that is achieved between clients who are normally withdrawn and isolated, or the level of concentration and focus among clients who are usually hyperactive or restless.

Partner Mirror is not recommended for clients whose boundaries between self and other are very weak, but it can be very useful with clients whose boundaries between self and other are rigid. Many dance/movement therapists and drama therapists, including Janet Adler (1969) and Audrey Wethered (1973), have incorporated mirroring in their work with autistic children. Autistic children are extremely self-absorbed, and they let in little of the outside world. Rather than attempting to have the child join the therapist's world, the therapist enters the child's world, mirroring the child's naturally repetitive and ritualistic movements. At first, the child may not even notice, but gradually the child experiences, often on a subconscious level, a kind of validation and acceptance. After long periods of patient mirroring, which also serve to deepen the therapist's empathy with the child, the therapist initiates a subtle modification or extension of the child's movement or sound. A breakthrough occurs when the child incorporates this change in her own movements, for this may be her first manifestation of relatedness and reciprocity.

I will never forget a strange and powerful dream I had when I first began doing drama therapy. In the dream, I was leading a session in a huge studio space. The clients were exploring and moving playfully through the space, when suddenly I noticed in the far corner of the room a frightening sight. One client, Catherine, was "having a breakdown." The other clients were pre-occupied with their own explorations, but it was obvious that soon they, too, would see Catherine and panic. Catherine was now silently shaking, and her teeth were chattering uncontrollably. I knew I had to do something quickly. From across the room, I began shaking my body like hers, chattering my teeth, and twisting my face as she was doing with her face. The other members now stood still, staring in shock. But I was certain I had to continue. Moving slowly toward Catherine, I mirrored her every movement, gesture, and sound. She watched me and I watched her back. When she began crawling regressively, I crawled too, toward her, until we were face to face. Our joint chattering and screeching was intense, but I purposefully increased its volume, speed, and intensity. She too got louder, faster, and more intense. After a short while, I decreased the volume and pace until very gradually we came simultaneously to a stop. Catherine was calm.

I include the dream because it conveys my belief that what we do in drama therapy are not really techniques but *processes. Partner Mirror* is a process of entering the world of another, achieving connectedness, and physically expressing and transcending emotional states.

PARTNER MIRROR VARIATIONS

Voice mirror

Instead of body movements, voice and sound are "mirrored." With pairs seated on the floor, one person initiates sounds (or words), which the other simultaneously duplicates. The sounds may be soft or loud, high or low, extended or choppy. *Voice Mirror* not only is an excellent warm-up for the voice, but tends to energize the whole person, physically and emotionally. When synchronization is achieved and sustained, the amplification of voices can be exhilarating.

Voice and body mirror

Both voice and body are incorporated. This is the form of *Mirror Exercises* that I make the most use of, though I usually precede it with the use of body only and then voice only to facilitate a gentle progression. With *Voice and Body Mirror,* the sounds both reflect and intensify the movement. In my directions, I encourage the development, magnification, or extension of movements and sounds, rather than looking for diverse movements/sounds. This direction supports my other direction, which is to engage on an emotional level, allowing the sound and movement to express strong feeling states.

Face mirror

Rather than mirroring full body movements, the two participants mirror facial expressions only. They are seated on the floor (or in chairs), facing one another. Clients tend to begin by making funny faces, but after some time they create more subtle expressions, depicting feelings and attitudes. This variation requires more focus and is usually more intimate than the full body mirror.

Sounding the movement

In pairs, one moves while the other makes accompanying sounds, as though one person were the voice (or sound effects) for the other. Words can also be incorporated. *Sounding the Movement* is most effective when the focus is on emotional expression. For example, the "mover" may be physically expressing anger while the "sounder" expresses the anger in grunts or screams or words; each matches the intensity and responds to the nuances of the other. *Sounding the Movement* is a sophisticated variation, and is recommended only for participants who have practiced *Voice and Body Mirror.*

Mirror with emotional suggestion

During *Partner Mirror,* the therapist calls out suggestions for emotions to incorporate. Without breaking concentration, the participants' movements, sounds, or expressions begin to reflect and then to develop these particular emotions. This variation is helpful for clients who need encouragement to work on an emotional level.

Activity mirror

With participants who cannot yet engage in abstract movement or incorporate emotional expression into their movement, a more concrete version of mirroring can be used. Here the *leader* pantomimes a specific simple activity, such as putting on make-up or washing clothes, which the *mirror image* imitates. This variation emphasizes concentration and focus, rather than emotional expression.

Follow the movement

Instead of mirroring synchronistically, one person repeats (or in *Voice*

Mirror, echoes) the action/s of the *leader*. This variation is far less emotionally and interpersonally intense, and can thus be useful with individuals who are frightened by the sense of mergence that occurs in the standard *Partner Mirror*.

Spolin (1983) describes a number of other variations. As most of these are quite complex and require sophisticated skills, I have found them to be less applicable in a therapeutic context. Examples are a three-way mirror (as in a clothing store) and a distorting mirror (as in a fun house).

GROUP MIRROR

The entire group mirrors one person's movements. The emphasis is on working together to achieve synchronization. I usually begin initiating the movements, with the group following me, and after a while hand the leadership over to a group member.

As *leader*, I can express through movement, sound, or word actual feelings the group might be experiencing. I may repeatedly wring my hands in *anxiety*, jump around the room with *excitement*, vacillate between moving toward the group and then backing away in an expression of ambivalence about getting close, or stomp and shout in *anger*. Through the exercise, actual feelings are acknowledged, released, and shared—in an indirect, physical, and playful manner. A container is thus provided for expressions that may have otherwise been deemed unacceptable or unapproachable. My movements and sounds are influenced by what I perceive are group needs. I may run and dance through space if I sense that the group craves the sensation of freedom and expansion, or I may bring the group into a quiet huddle to promote contact and intimacy.

Typically *Group Mirror* is utilized at the beginning of the session, but it is also effective at the end of sessions in which physical release of emotions evoked in verbal scenework is needed. The emotions demanding further expression may be obvious, or may emerge gradually and spontaneously through the mirroring, in a transformational process. As *leader*, my flow of images is at times an attempt on the part of my unconscious to grasp and express the group's unconscious. Trusting my intuition, in conjunction with the nonverbal response of the group during the mirroring, I allow for the evolution of our expressions.

When the group has reached a state of connectedness, leadership can be diminished. Without stopping the activity, I ask the group to *pick up on any* group member's initiation or amplification of movement or sound, so that eventually we are all one flowing mass. There may be a fluctuation between chaos and order, disharmony and simultaneity. At some point I may again discreetly take on leadership, as a way of moving the group toward the next activity or, if it is the end of the session, toward a point of final closure.

GROUP MIRROR VARIATIONS

Group sounding the movement

One person expresses nonverbally—through movement, gesture, or facial expression—various emotions. The group makes sounds or voices words that correspond to the person's motions.

Who started the motion

In this Spolin technique, one person, placed in the center of the circle, tries to identify the (predetermined) leader, whom everyone is following. The participants try to remain perfectly synchronized and to maintain eye contact with all the other members, rather than watching the leader only. As the emphasis is on concentration and observation, *Who Started the Motion* is described in greater detail under the last section of this chapter.

Circle-mirror-transformation

The group stands in a large circle. One person enters the center of the circle, initiating a repeatable sound and movement. Gradually, she lets the sound/movement be transformed. When the new sound/movement is stabilized, she takes it to one of the group members, who immediately mirrors it. During the mirroring, they switch places, and the new member continues the sound/movement into the circle. Gradually, he transforms it, and once the new sound/movement is stabilized, he takes it to another group member, and so forth. Only the person in the center and the partner she chooses do the sound/movement; the rest of the group watches.

Circle-Mirror-Transformation works in a similar way to building a fire: It takes a while to develop, and sometimes it never ignites. But usually, with patience and good direction during the exercise, it eventually catches, at which point it can be sustained for a very long period of time. Often clients are initially inhibited or lethargic, but after some time they become fully engaged, expressing and sharing diverse emotions. The energy and intensity increase with each transformation, and the exercise seems to take on a life of its own. In fact, it is not uncommon for *Circle-Mirror-Transformation* to last an entire session. The therapist's directions early in the exercise should encourage: 1) allowing the sound/movement to transform, rather than forcing a change; 2) emotional expressiveness in the sound/movements; 3) immediate mirroring once a person in the outer circle is contacted; 4) amplification of the sound/movement during the mirror between the two individuals.

Join the Emotion

One person enters the playing or stage area and begins nonverbally conveying a particular emotion. When other group members have a sense of the emotion, they join in, until the whole group has become involved. The emotion may be expressed through manner of walking, gesture, movement, sound, facial expression, etc.

This technique can easily follow *Group Mirror,* and can be be a good prelude to *Join the Scene* (in Chapter 7).

Emotional Mime

One person chooses (or is given) a particular emotion to convey. He enters the playing or stage area and conveys the emotion nonverbally, through movement, gesture, or facial expression. The other group members attempt to guess the emotion that is being expressed.

Emotional Mime can also be played with participants seated in a circle. Each person takes a turn conveying an emotion in mime.

Guess How I Feel

Guess How I Feel is the same as *Emotional Mime,* except that participants convey actual feelings. *Guess How I Feel* enables participants to get in touch with, express, and exaggerate their current state of mind, as well as to closely observe one another. It is best utilized when the therapist wishes to create a more personal tone to the beginning (or ending) of a session, or when she feels that the group will be more comfortable with actual feelings than with imaginary feelings.

Masks and Mime

Masks and Mime is essentially the same as *Emotional Mime* or *Guess How I Feel* except that participants are given masks to wear. The wearing of the mask focuses the attention for the actor and audience on the body. As the client can no longer rely on facial expression to convey a feeling, he becomes more expressive with his body.

The element of disguise—the covering of the face—reduces self-consciousness and inhibition. Clients often develop their movement/mime into a mini-performance, which can be quite beautiful to behold; the expression of both strong and subtle emotion by a masked figure is naturally theatrical. It is exciting to witness the way in which the neutral mask is given life by the wearer of the mask. Each small gesture or motion imbues the mask with feeling and character.

Masks are theatrically and psychologically powerful, but should be used with caution with clients who are disoriented or have weak ego boundaries.

These clients may experience a loss of self when wearing the mask, or, as audience, a loss of the person who has just put on the mask. The wearing of a mask by the therapist can be particularly disturbing to such clients, who rely on the therapist's reassuring presence for their sense of safety in the group.

Emotional Statues

Everyone walks around the room until the leader shouts "freeze," at which time participants come to a halt and remain frozen, like statues. Once participants are accustomed to this process of moving and freezing, the leader calls out an emotion just before freezing the group. Participants spontaneously form a posture that expresses that emotion, and remain perfectly still until the leader asks them to unfreeze and walk around again.

To develop *Emotional Statues,* one or several particularly expressive people remain in the frozen position, while the leader "releases" (by tapping shoulders) the others. The group then meanders through the "statue gallery," observing the various statues. The stillness of the frozen people combined with the expressiveness in their bodies and faces produces exciting theatrical images. Sometimes there are several individual statues; other times a cluster of people forms a single statue.

VARIATIONS

Partner sculpting

In pairs, one person *molds* the other into a representation of an emotional state. The person being molded relaxes her body so that it is "like clay," making it easier for the other to manipulate.* When all of the sculptors are done, they walk through the room, looking at each others' works of art, and giving their impression about the conveyed emotions.

Sculpting a scene

One person molds three members of the group in a way that suggests an emotional scenario. Once the sculpture is completed, there are several possibilities: 1) The audience tries to identify what is taking place; 2) The sculpture comes alive, meaning that the frozen individuals begin to spontaneously move and speak; 3) The sculptor gives the frozen individuals their lines, and then has them come alive. In the latter two options, the actors are

---

*The image of a doll, rather than a sculpture, can be used, as suggested by Dayton (1990) in a technique she refers to as "Emotional Doll Game."

refrozen after a short period of time; the scene ends with them once again in a frozen tableau.

The sculptor may mold the three subjects into three emotional states, rather than creating a dramatic scenario. When this tableau comes alive, the actors express their emotional roles via sound, movement, or words. The sculptor may become the director, who conducts or instructs the actors in various ways. This variation is an excellent warm-up to *Self-Sculptures* (Chapter 7, p. 212).

Emotional Spaces

Particular emotional states are attributed to different corners or spaces in the room. The selected emotional states may represent actual (or latent) feelings present among participants. For example, one corner/area may be *anger,* another *sadness,* another *excitement,* etc. Participants move from corner to corner, or simply remain in the corner of their choice, with the understanding that when in a particular space, they are to encounter and express the emotional state of that space.

By bestowing physical spaces with feeling states (and the reverse), this technique literally provides containment. Clients can express emotions with greater ease given these boundaries, and given the knowledge that they can move on, when they choose, to a different part of the room.

Drama therapist David Johnson describes using this technique with a young man who was diagnosed catatonic schizophrenic. "Daniel" was initially mute and unable to communicate, but in the 15th week of his drama therapy treatment, he walked through the room, expressing feelings of *happiness, sadness,* and—most strikingly and importantly—*anger.* Johnson states that "clearly, the structuring of emotions in a *spatial* and *bodily* framework helped Daniel first to focus on one thought at a time, and then to verbalize his inner states" (1982a, p. 89).

Like most drama therapy techniques, *Emotional Spaces* can be applied in many different contexts, from in-depth individual drama therapy to large group events. At a party for the drama therapy program that I direct, I turned each *room* of a large Victorian apartment into an emotional state. The selected emotional states reflected the various feelings that students undergo during their course of study. For close to an hour, 30 students roamed through the apartment, interacting with their peers in given rooms. Some wandered from room to room, while others lingered for long blocks of time in a particular room that grabbed their emotional attention on that evening.

Emotional Orchestra

The group is clustered in two rows, facing the leader, who assumes the role of an orchestral conductor. Each person decides on an emotion to convey via a particular sound. The conductor then begins the orchestra by pointing to one or several people. At the conductor's artistic discretion, volume and tempo can be played with, solos and duets can be initiated, and at times the entire group can emote at once.

Emotional Orchestra can be composed of words rather than sounds. Each person is given (or chooses) an emphatic, emotional word or set of words, such as *I want it, You can't have it, Please, No, Help, I need you, Goodbye,* etc. The orchestra is most theatrically effective when several of the lines are interrelated or conflictual; the conductor can then instigate emotional inter-actions and dramatic exchanges between members. Clients may also assume the role of conductor, and in this role exercise their creativity. The choice of the final sound or word/s, for example, is very significant; like the ending of scenes, *Emotional Orchestra* should be terminated on a powerful note.

Voice Games

Most of my clients have been conditioned to suppress their feelings. An important aspect of treatment is giving clients "a voice." Relief from the burden of silence is often experienced as clients for the first time not only vocalize and verbalize their feelings, but learn to shout and scream, and to play with all nuances of voice expression.

One form of *Voice Games* is for the group to form two lines, facing one another. A specific sound or word is given by the therapist. The participants in each line together say the sound/word, followed by a repetition of the same sound/word by the participants in the other line. The idea is to gradually increase the volume, so that each subgroup repeats the sound/word slightly louder than the previous subgroup. This can be followed by work in pairs, again with the aim of increasing volume at each utterance.

Another form of *Voice Games* is to have both people vocalize at the same time, without listening to one another. The objective is simply to use one's voice, freely, at whatever volume, pitch, tempo, and quality one chooses. (This is an excellent prelude to *Gibberish*.)

Adolescents certainly bask in the opportunity to be as loud as they wish, and find some safety in the knowledge that their shouting is contained within a structured game. For clients who are more reserved or withdrawn, the liberation of the voice serves as an excellent warm-up to emotional scenework.

Silent Scream

In this technique described by Spolin (1983), participants are asked to scream without making a sound. They are coached to respond physically and muscularly as they would for a vocal scream. Once they are truly making use of their bodies and expressions, they are instructed to scream out loud.

While Spolin uses this technique primarily to help actors physicalize emotion and, more specifically, to rehearse for mob scenes, I have utilized it to facilitate the expression of rage and pain, first in the safety of silence, and then—at times—out loud. The latter is potentially more frightening as well as cathartic. The emotional intensity is *contained* by the fact that the scream is conducted in unison and for a limited time only. This exercise should be used with caution, given the sense of disturbance and incompletion it can engender.

GROUP INTERACTION

Categorical Groupings

"Find the other people in the room," I shout as the group walks around the room, "who were born in the same part of the country or world as you. As quickly as possible!"

Everyone mingles about, calling out his birthplace, asking others where they were born, until clear clusters are formed. I ask each cluster to tell us where it is from, not only as a way of sharing these facts with the group, but also as a means of making certain that everyone has found his group.

"Walk around again. Now find the other people in this group—as quickly as possible—who happen to have the same. . . . astrological sign as you." Again, everyone scrambles, shouting his sign, seeking counterparts.

Examples of other categories are: same number of siblings as you have, same sibling order as you, same city you currently live in, same living situation, same line of work, same color eyes (a good way to facilitate eye contact), same first letter of your first name (a good way for people to learn each other's names). Categories that require reflection are also possible, as "same primary reason for taking this workshop (or being in this group)" or "same way you feel right now," though these questions tend to slow down the physical momentum of the game. Some categories are well suited to certain groups but could make other groups uncomfortable. An example is "same age," which is appropriate in groups of children or adolescents but might make adult groups uncomfortable.

Categorical Groupings promotes a high level of group interaction, even among withdrawn clients. The exercise is nonthreatening and playful; most significantly, it establishes a beginning sense of group identity. Groups are fascinated to discover their own statistics—whether it is the preponderance (or dearth) of certain astrological signs, eldest children, or people born in foreign countries. The information is also interesting for the group leader to note, and cultural contexts often become apparent. When conducting groups in the midWest, for example, I've often been struck by the clusters of those with eight and nine siblings, in contrast to groups of high school age Californians in which there is generally a large cluster of "only children."

Categorical Groupings works best with a large group, of nine to 14 people. I have also used Categorical Groupings at staff workshops of 30 to 60 people. With this many people, there is initial chaos, but an energizing and exciting kind of chaos, followed by order, as the groups are formed. At the 1986 conference of the National Association for Drama Therapy, I incorporated an abbreviated version of Categorical Groupings in an experiential morning "Meeting" designed to help all conference participants meet one another! There were several hundred people. As participants had come from all over the United States, I began with, "Find the other people in the room who live in the same part of the country or world that you live in." As it was obviously impossible for everyone to find one another without more structure, I had the 10,000 square foot room be visualized as a map. Our geography was rough, but people very smoothly gravitated toward their general region (with the international participants being especially creative), and then grew more specific. The next category was "Find the people whose first name begins with the same first letter as yours." Again, the room was visualized as a map, an alphabetical map, with As on one side, Zs on the other, and Ms in the center. Later in the conference, it was interesting to observe small groups sitting together at an event or eating lunch, and then realize that their names were Diane, Debra, David, and Dina!

Categorical Groupings is effectively preceded by Dodging and followed by Fast-Speed Handshake and Emotional Greetings.

Fast-Speed Handshake

As the group members walk around the room, they are asked to shake hands with one another. Gradually they are directed to increase the speed of the handshaking, moving from person to person and using both hands for shaking, so that they constantly have one person on one hand and another person on the other hand. The facilitation of Fast-Speed Handshake occurs not through a lot of instructions, but through the drama therapist's interaction with the group; the group follows her lead. The speed continues to increase until the group ends up in a small cluster, at which point the leader shouts, "Freeze!"

I designed *Fast-Speed Handshake* to literally and physically promote a high level of group interaction. It is most effectively used with a large group, following a physically activating exercise as *Dodging.* To continue the momentum, while steering the session toward emotionality and dramatization, *Emotional Greetings* is recommended.

Different degrees of speed can be played with in *Fast-Speed Handshake,* including interacting in slow-motion.

Introducing Yourself as Another

I devised this technique for use in the very beginning of a first session with a group of people that has not previously met. It is well suited to a class on drama therapy or to work with any healthy group. Emotionally disturbed clients will find it disorienting and confusing.

The group divides into pairs. Participants are asked to introduce themselves to their partner, an instruction in keeping with participants' expectations. The unusual part is that they are not to tell the truth. Or rather, they are to tell not actual facts about themselves—but fabricated ones. What they "make up," however, can have some relationship to the truth. For example, the story they convey may be a path they *almost* took in real life, a path they would have liked to have taken, a path that represents an "unlived" part of themselves. *Introducing Yourself as Another* is more compelling when the stories are not outlandish, wild fantasies, but real possibilities—of what could have been. It should not only sound believable to the person listening, but feel believable to the person speaking; that is, as in any dramatic enactment, the person should truly imagine herself in that role/situation. I suggest that the person's real name be used, though everything else that she feels she can get away with changing (including age!) be altered. Though a small amount of time can be allotted prior to beginning the introductions, once people start speaking it is best that they do not think too much or censor, but allow the self-introduction to unfold spontaneously.

The first part of *Introducing Yourself as Another* entails both people speaking about themselves. In the second part, each one gives feedback to the other regarding her impressions or reactions to what was told, any truths she gleaned about her partner from the lies, and any observations or guesses she has about her partner's actual background. Finally, in the third part, each person responds to the partner's feedback, and tells her actual background (in relation to the particular areas of her life she spoke about in her introduction).

Workshops and group experiences commonly begin with people introducing themselves. Though informative, these self-introductions rarely surprise the speaker herself; she has told this story about herself many times before. Furthermore, the presented information is usually more than the listener/s can absorb or be truly interested in at this early point, especially in large groups in which there are many introductions. In *Introducing Yourself as Another,* the speaker is liberated from her familiar story. What emerges is striking and illuminating—to the speaker herself. To the listener, too, the speaker's projections and fantasies are revealing; those listening invariably claim they learned much more about their partners than if they had simply heard actual facts. In this sense, *Introducing Yourself as Another* serves as a demonstration of drama therapy itself, a microcosmic exposure to what will follow. In this one exercise, participants experience improvising, creating a fictional reality, drawing from themselves rather than acting a character foreign to themselves, and revealing aspects of themselves via the imaginal, dramatic mode.

Introducing Yourself as Another is best followed by sharing actual facts about people in the group. *Categorical Groupings* facilitates this aim, and is an ideal successor.

Party with Secret Roles

Plastic cups filled with grape juice are set on a table. The leader invites the group to a party, and each person takes a drink. On the bottom of their cups, visible only when they have consumed the drink, are instructions indicating how they are to behave at the party. (The leader has taped instructions on the bottom of the cups.) Everyone is to play his given role, at the same time trying to "meet" as many people as possible.

Some of the instructions might be: try to get attention; try to instigate arguments; try to impress people; try to seduce; try to make everyone feel comfortable; try to avoid everyone; try to make professional contacts; try to engage people in deep, philosophical discussion; try to introduce everyone; try to elicit sympathy; try to facilitate some kind of group interaction. When the scene is ended, participants make their guesses about the roles of fellow party members.

.The results are hilarious! The game promotes a highly dynamic and interactive group process and develops concentration and observation as participants must simultaneously play a role *and* pay close attention to others. The element of intrigue at the beginning—cups with secret messages— diminishes potential resistance and incites playful involvement.

Discussion and enactment of roles played in real life or roles participants wish to play more frequently, particularly in social settings, often ensue.

I initially devised *Party with Secret Roles* for a presentation entitled "Facilitating Interaction in a Passive or Resistant Group," held at a psychiatric conference. I have since used it with groups of staff, students, and clients. It works best with a group of 10–16 people. *Party with Secret Roles* is effective as an opening to a session, but not in a first or very early session of the series; it is best used toward the end of Phase One (Dramatic Play).

I have created many variations on both the theme of roles at parties and the use of secret messages. The following two offshoots are more appropriate for recreational than for therapeutic contexts:

VARIATIONS

Roles that meet the occasion

Roles that have significance to a particular occasion or group of people are devised. For example, at a get-together for my graduate students, the following roles were randomly distributed: you're a student at the drama therapy program at this school; you're a student at the drama therapy program at N.Y.U.; you're applying for a faculty position in the drama therapy program; you're the director of the drama therapy program; you're a psychoanalyst; you're an accomplished actress; you're a sex therapist; you're a documentary filmmaker, etc. Once each person had received a role, I set the group loose at the party within the party. The interactions were fascinating. The room was brimming with an electric party-like energy; there was joking, serious discussion, questioning, animated debate, gossiping, flirting.

Surprise phone calls

I once had a group of staff, colleagues of mine from a psychiatric day treatment center, over to my home for an "experiential get-together." I wanted to really surprise and delight them. I also wanted to create a natural transition between dinner and the workshop which was to follow. Here is how I accomplished these goals:

Toward the end of dinner, the phone in my kitchen rang. I went to answer it. The caller asked to speak to Anne, one of my guests. When I told Anne she had a call, she was very surprised, but went to answer it. A few minutes later, the phone rang again; it was for another guest. By the time the fourth or fifth person received a call, everyone started to realize something was up, especially as each person returned from his call acting just a little bit different. Soon everyone had received the mystery call, and the room was brimming with diverse interactions.

Naturally, I had a friend make these calls, in which he delivered a pre-planned message to each person at the party regarding how s/he should behave toward one or more specific other people. The plan was quite intricate, but designed to resemble, especially at the beginning, typical social interaction. The close resemblance to real life heightened the intrigue by creating a very subtle and gradual shift from real life to drama. For example, Anne was told to try to engage Arthur in a serious, intellectual discussion; John was instructed to try to distract Arthur; Arthur was told to act preoccupied with some personal matter; Nick was to encourage people to eat some more; Cynthia was to engage the whole group in a productive discussion about the day treatment center; Paul was to act resistant to any suggestions others had; Barbara was to be ultra-supportive to everyone; Andrea was to butt into any private conversations, etc. The last person to receive a call, Carol, was instructed to stop the game. At that point, everyone tried to guess the message each person had received.

For years, the staff talked and laughed about this experience. More importantly, a heightened consciousness was manifested in the workplace regarding the role/s each person played within the actual group dynamic.

Bubble war and balloon float

Everyone in the group is given a bottle of soap bubbles. A playful war, with bubbles as ammunition, is initiated. As participants blow bubbles at others and try to avert the ones directed at them, the room starts looking rather magical, permeating the aggressive play with a kind of lightness and beauty.

The aesthetic atmosphere created in the room by bubbles can also be created with balloons. In a warm-up designed to facilitate both group interaction and physical activation, the group attempts to keep many balloons in the air at once. Here the group members work as a a team, rather than in opposition; everyone helps ensure that the balloons don't fall or burst.

PHYSICAL ACTIVATION

Dodging

"Walk around the room," the leader begins. "Now walk faster. Even faster. And now, as you run, try to take up as much space as possible. Be greedy about it. You want the whole room for yourself! Keep moving. Avoid other people. Dodge people as you move."

In this simple exercise, energy is rapidly mobilized. Even depressed and passive clients, who may have seemed capable of very little participation when they entered the room, will generally become engaged. The dodging is a significant component to the exercise. Participants are asked to *avoid others* (often exactly what they feel like doing), but in fact the close contact and near-collisions (which demand dodging) facilitate interaction. The instruction to take up as much space as possible is also significant; participants usually delight in the permission to "be greedy!" The leader's own energetic and playful participation in *Dodging* is critical to the effectiveness of this warm-up.

Back Pushes

Two people stand back-to-back with their knees slightly bent. One tries to get the other moving forward; the other attempts to remain in place, perfectly grounded. They may use their feet, but it is important that they be instructed to keep their backs together at all times. (If one gives way, the other will fall.) After some time, they straighten their backs, stand still simultaneously, and then switch roles. In a third stage of the experience, both people push—and try to remain planted in their spot—at the same time.

The way in which clients use their weight and strength is often quite telling. Clients who are highly dependent, passive, or helpless typically will be unable to remain in a grounded position, and will easily be pushed forward by their partner, even if their partner is smaller or lighter than they are. These clients are unable to plant their feet solidly on the ground and unable to make use of any strength in their backs. I will often stand in front of such a client, as she is being pushed by her partner, and, bracing myself, place my hands against hers to prevent her from sliding forward. In this way, she can at least experience what it is like to remain grounded in one spot, and the pressure of my palms against hers helps her begin to find a way to push back.

Back Pushes energizes the group quickly and tends to be a lot of fun. It can also be an excellent warm-up to emotional work; I have frequently used it as a prelude to *Line Repetition*.

Don't Get Up

As I begin the adolescent session, a rebellious 14-year-old boy stubbornly shouts, "I'm not getting out of my chair." This response is typical of oppositional clients. Spontaneously, I approach Tom and, in a playful tone, say, "Try as hard as you can to stay in the chair." Gently, I take hold of his hands and attempt to pull him to a standing position as he struggles to remain seated. His aggressive and hostile stance transforms into a playful one and, through the physical contact, a relationship is established between the two of us. Another client, seemingly delighted at witnessing this match, grabs my place, claiming that he can lift Tom. Soon all the clients are pairing off with each other, alternating roles that represent resistance, surrender, and power (Emunah, 1985).

What began one day as an impulsive gesture on my part has since become an intentional game, used as a strategic approach (in which the client's resistance is encouraged rather than suppressed, an approach discussed in Chapter 4) to engage resistant clients. In *Don't Get Up,* clients can be paired with each other from the onset. Security and relief is experienced in being asked to stay seated, and an irresistible challenge is experienced by the clients who have to get their partners to stand. After a while, the roles are reversed, or several people are asked to try to lift a particular group member who has successfully resisted the efforts of his original partner.

Body Connections

In pairs, participants move through the room, connected by a body part, like Siamese twins. Backs, heads, elbows, hips—any part decided upon by the leader or the group members themselves—can be joined. The exercise is playful and engaging and requires concentration and cooperation; one has to synchronize one's gait and movements with that of one's partner, paying close attention to changes in rhythm, speed, and direction. Once participants are successful, they may be given new challenges, e.g., increasing speed of movement or conversing with each other as they move!

Balls Between Backs

In pairs, participants move through the room, connected by a very large ball between their backs. The objective is to keep the ball from falling. Similar to *Body Connections,* the ball can be placed between other body parts, and new challenges can be added. With clients for whom the physical contact in *Body Connections* would be too intimate or uncomfortable, *Balls Between Backs* is a good alternative.

Balls Between Backs is a good follow-up to *Ball-Throws* (p. 177).

Back Dialogues

Participants stand back-to-back with their partner. They are to have a nonverbal "conversation" or interaction using their backs only. The leader provides some structure by calling out the ways in which they should relate, for example: *playfully, aggressively, seductively, argumentatively.*

Back Dialogues is best used with a sophisticated group, as conversing with backs (or other body parts) is too abstract for many clients. *Back Dialogues* can be beneficial for clients who tend to overly rely on verbal modes of communication and need help in becoming more expressive nonverbally and physically. *Back Dialogues* playfully promotes relationship and communication. It works most effectively when it is kept brief.

Back Dialogues can be easily followed by *Back Pushes*.

Four-Corner Dash

Four-Corner Dash works best in a large room. After being told that all four corners of the room are *safety spots,* participants are instructed to go to a corner of their choice. The leader, or designated person, remains in the center of the room. The aim is for participants to switch corners, as often as possible, without being tapped by the leader.

While *Four-Corner Dash* is simply a variation on a children's tag game, it is applicable as a drama therapy warm-up because the notion of safety spots is emotionally provocative, as is the experience of taking risks—when moving from one corner to the next. But most of all, *Four-Corner Dash* is an excellent physical warm-up. The fact that there is an objective (not getting caught) helps diminish self-consciousness and challenges participants to move at their fastest. Playfulness and prankishness are elicited, as participants try to foil the leader by running silently when her back is turned, or by running across the room at the same time that many others are escaping. When the leader catches someone, that person comes to center and becomes the next catcher.

Break out of/into the Circle

This technique, described by Schutz in his seminal book *Joy: Expanding Human Awareness* (1967) and by many others since then, was used in the Encounter Groups that developed in the 1960s. One member of the group stands in the center of a circle. With their hands held tightly together, the other group members attempt to keep that person inside the circle as s/he tries to break out. Physical maneuvers are commonly used by the person trying to break out, but nonphysical tactics, e.g., verbal pleading, can also be encouraged. The less static the game, the better. As long as the group continues to encircle its prisoner, it can move around the room, extend or shrink its circle, alter its shape, playfully taunt and tease the person in the center.

The most powerful therapeutic use of this technique occurs when the group leader is in the center. I have placed myself in the center when I perceived unexpressed, feared aggression toward me, often occurring after I had to cancel a session due to an out-of-town trip. The group's anger and its desire to keep me confined, so that I will not be able to leave them again, is played out physically and symbolically. My acceptance of their feelings is demonstrated by the playful way in which I engage in and prolong our inter-action. As the group rallies against me, peer cohesion is fostered. In some cases, the activity is followed by verbal processing; in others, the physical catharsis suffices.

A group member, rather than the therapist, can be designated as the person trying to break out. It is interesting to observe the way in which individuals respond to the task of getting out. Some cannot conceive of any way out and give up easily. These are often people who feel power-less to effect change in their lives. Rather than allowing these clients to surrender, I challenge them to find new resources within themselves, until they do find a way out. Other clients are remarkably deft, ingenious, or persevering. The final victory—exiting the circle—appears to symbolize for some the possibility of overcoming a particular struggle in life. Still others seem to *want to remain* inside the circle. To these clients, the circle apparently feels less like a confinement and more like a safe haven or womb.

Break out of the Circle can be used as warm-up to dramatic enactments or can lead to the verbal articulation of emotions as one tries to break out. One client, whose attempts to break out of the circle were sporadic and ambivalent, talked about the wall she had built around herself, behind which she felt both protected and trapped. The group transformed itself into this wall. Speaking to the wall, Betty's terror of the outside world became increasingly apparent, though after some time her longing to find out what lay beyond her limited experience also clearly surfaced. Finally, with our gentle encourage-ment, she ventured—for just a moment—outside, a move she was on the verge of making in real life.

Rather than breaking out of a circle, the reverse process—breaking into a closed circle—can also be used. *Break into the Circle* tends to evoke feelings of exclusion and thus is most potent when an underlying theme in a group is that of inclusion/exclusion. The technique can also be modified by having more than one person attempt to break in or out (or a combination) at the same time.

Break out of/into the Circle is not appropriate with clients who have little physical control; one could easily get hurt during this exercise and caution should be taken, especially in its use with children and adolescents.

New Musical Chairs

New Musical Chairs can begin in the traditional way: With lively music playing in the background, the group walks around a row of chairs, which are facing in alternate directions. When the music stops, all participants try to seat themselves as quickly as possible. As the number of chairs is always one less than the number of participants, one person is too late and is thereby eliminated. The game continues, each round eliminating one person, until only two people remain, vying for a single chair.

Musical Chairs is useful as a physical warm-up because it so easily engages and focuses the group; the challenge of getting a chair in time seems to make everyone hyper-alert! The music too is stimulating, especially when irresistible dance music is utilized. In *New Musical Chairs,* the game is modified in various ways. Rather than walk around the chairs, the group is asked to skip, hop, or walk backwards, or to sing or talk as they walk. Each round can contain a new variation, contributing to the playfulness of the game and making it a more interesting and creative activity than the one everyone recalls from chiidhood.

Rope Games

One example of a *Rope Game* is a simple *tug-of-war,* which not only physically engages the group, but becomes a useful warm-up for emotional work that revolves around conflict (see *Identifying the Conflict* p. 222).

With the aim of developing concentration and skills in pantomime, the actual tug-of-war can be followed by a mimed tug-of-war. The group is asked to make use of the real sensations they have just experienced. If they do this authentically, the same level of energy will be utilized as in the real game. Another way of developing the tug-of-war is to follow the group tug-of-war by tug-of-wars between partners, using smaller ropes.

Small ropes can be used in diverse ways. Two people, in pairs, can grasp the center of the rope, and both lean backwards, using the rope and the weight of the other for support. The rope can be used simply for jump-rope; simultaneous jumping in pairs necessitates being in rhythmic sync with one's partner. Or participants, again in pairs, can be asked to use their imagination to devise creative ways of incorporating the rope in a sequence of creative movements.

TRUST

Nurturing Falls

CIRCLE FALLS

In this very familiar trust exercise,* one person stands in the center of a circle formed by the group and lets his body fall in any direction. The group catches (or more precisely, contains) the person falling. The circle can be "shrunk" or "stretched," depending on the trust level of the particular individual falling.

It is useful to have the group assume a physical posture that augments readiness to catch "fallers" of various sizes and weights. The best position is feet solidly planted on the ground with one foot behind the other, knees slightly bent, and hands prepared for catching. The "faller" needs to have his feet glued to one spot, as his body loosely sways.

Circle Falls is gentle and nurturing, at the same time that it develops trust. The circle format provides a sense of safety, boundaries, and unity.

A variation is for the falling person to utter a sound, which the group echoes, or to uttter words (usually ones of self-affirmation), which the group repeats. This variation works best with a group that has already reached a high level of intimacy.

FALLING BETWEEN TWO ROWS

Rather than forming a circle, the group stands in two rows, forming a narrow pathway between the rows. Each person takes a turn walking through this pathway and falling backwards. Participants on both sides are ready at all times to catch the person falling.

Falling Between Two Rows is a more playful version of *Nurturing Falls* than *Circle Falls*. Although the two-line format demands greater risk-taking than the circle, it is also less confining. Clients who are afraid to fall can always do more walking than falling; others can fall suddenly to surprise the group or abort a fall to "fool" the group. The lightheartedness evoked in *Falling Between Two Rows* makes it generally more suitable at earlier stages of the group process, before intimacy has developed. *Circle Fall* is far more intimate and should be used to reflect growing group trust and closeness. At later stages of group work, *Circle Fall* is also very effective at the end of the session or after an emotional scene, as a way of expressing group support and

---

*Many trust exercises were developed in the 1960s and 1970s as part of the Encounter Group movement. *Circle Falls* is essentially the same technique as *Roll and Rock,* described by Schutz (1967).

providing containment. *Falling Between Two Rows*, on the other hand, is recommended only at the beginning of the session. It is particularly effective with clients who enter the session preoccupied or withdrawn; the immediacy of the exercise demands active presence and responsiveness.

Some emotionally disturbed clients are initially very reluctant to fall, claiming they "can't trust anyone." With the patient support of the group, they gradually begin to trust and, over time, often make striking progress in their capacity to fall. Other clients initially fall too easily and too hard. Using all of their weight to resist the group's arms, they land on the ground, thus "proving" that indeed nobody can be trusted. Like the timid "fallers," these clients are frequently victims of abuse or neglect. Rather than withdraw, they tend to act out, test limits, and incite repetition by provoking others to respond negatively to them. If their resistance to treatment diminishes, these clients, too, often make striking progress, and the changes they make are physically manifested in *Nurturing Falls*.

PARTNER FALLS

Falling can be done in pairs: One person falls, and the other catches. The "catchers" should be reminded to retain the grounded position (described above, in *Circle Falls*). This position enables them to catch a partner who weighs more than they do. It is best to begin with a very minimal fall and have each subsequent fall be more daring, until both "faller" and "catcher" reach their limit.

This technique can also be done in a threesome: The person stands between two people and falls backwards and forwards.

PARTNER LEANS

While this exercise does not involve falling backwards, it is a related technique, and works well in conjunction with (or immediately following) *Partner Falls*. Facing one another, participants place their hands against their partners' hands. By putting pressure on the others' hands and leaning their weight forward, they support each other enough to be able to take tiny steps backwards, until they approach a horizontal position. The leader must remind everyone to "never let go." When they reach their limit, they gradually rise together, until they are back in a standing position.

People Lifts

The group members surround one person who lies on the floor. With their hands gently placed beneath him, they slowly lift him. A variation that involves less touching and is therefore less intimidating is to lift the person in a blanket. The person can then be rocked or carried around the room.

For people who have already developed a degree of trust, *People Lifts* can be intensely nurturing. *People Lifts* is especially useful at the beginning of a session that is likely to involve painful work, or at the end of such a session, or directly following an emotional scene. In this latter case, the protagonist of the scene is placed in the center and lifted. A group member who remained in the background during the session can also be chosen as the one to be lifted, as a way of affirming his presence in the group.

Blind Walks Revisited

PARTNER BLIND WALKS

The traditional *Blind Walk* is for one person to lead another (who is blindfolded or has his eyes closed) around the room.

With groups needing more structure and focus, adding the instruction of finding objects in the room for the blinded partner to touch and identify is helpful.

With groups needing more freedom, holding the exercise outdoors, in an open space, is recommended. Sensory experience is heightened outdoors, especially in nature, and trust is challenged to a greater degree when there are no clear-cut physical boundaries.

The following are variations on *Blind Walks,* created to lessen the familiarity of the exercise, add new challenges, and facilitate areas of growth in addition to trust. Because the variations are more complex than the basic exercise, it is usually best to first introduce the traditional *Blind Walk.*

PARTNER BLIND WALK VARIATIONS

Head identification

To stimulate group interaction, the leaders (sighted partners) are asked to place their partners' hands on the heads of other people in the room, rather than on objects in the room. The blinded partners try to identify the people whose heads they are touching. (The specification of one body part to touch, as the head, is important to avoid uncomfortable or inappropriate touching.)

Follow my sound

Rather than leading through touch (i.e. holding the blind partner's hand or arm), the leadership is through sound. Each pair decides on a particular sound. The sighted partner then makes that sound and, without any physical contact or guidance, the blind partner follows the sound. At first, the sighted person stays in close physical proximity, but after some time she may move further away or alter direction to challenge her partner.

Follow My Sound demands a great deal of concentration and enhances auditory sensitivity. With a large group, the whole space becomes filled with sound, intensifying the need for concentration on a particular sound and also creating a lively and playful environment.

To further increase the challenge and complexity of the game, I often become an *imposter* (or share this role with a group member—possibly a client who does not wish to have his eyes closed or who simply does not have a partner in an odd-numbered group). The particular sounds are imitated, thus testing the blind partner's ability to distinguish between the "authentic" sound of his partner and the imposter's version!

Bates (1987), working with actors, has augmented the challenge of *Follow My Sound* by having barriers placed in the room (after the blindfolds are on). The leaders are not restricted to one sound, but can use any vocalization (besides actual words), e.g., *Gibberish* language.

Follow My Sound is best used with large groups of 10 or more people (it can be very successful with groups as large as 30), and only for brief periods; it should be stopped just before the chaos drives everyone "crazy!" *Follow My Sound* should not be used with clients who are disoriented or psychotic.

Follow my scent

Rather than following a sound, a scent is used. Items with strong scents, e.g., coffee, baby powder, perfume, a cut onion, are brought to the session, and one is given to each pair. The strong-smelling item is held by the sighted partner for the blind partner to follow.

Follow My Scent results in a very humorous sight: The blind partners often end up crawling on all fours and sniffing as actively and eagerly as dogs. With children and adolescents, *Follow My Scent* can be conducted with one pair at a time, rather than the entire group at once, to create a simple but comical performance!

Follow my directions

The blind partner is led not by touch, sound, or smell, but by verbal directions. There is no physical contact. The sighted person may, for example, instruct his blind partner: "Take two steps forward. Now turn to your left. Now walk forward until I tell you to stop."

My favorite use of *Follow My Directions* is with latency-age children or adolescents. The exercise turns into a mini-performance, with two blindfolded people onstage and their two sighted leaders offstage. The leaders, in effect, turn into choreographers or directors. Young adolescents delight in the sense of power and control the role enables them to assume and their partners equally relish the opportunity to relinquish all responsibility and decision-making. Both stances reflect underlying and often indirectly expressed themes in early adolescence.

I will often encourage the *directors* to maneuver their *actors* into some kind of interaction. For example, the directors may lead their partners to shake hands or to sit down next each other. The resulting effect is often even more entertaining to watch than *Follow My Sound.* More significantly, important skills are developed: clear verbal communication (on the part of the directors), collaboration (between the two directors), and careful listening (on the part of the blinded actors).

Identify your leader

This variation is similar to the standard *Blind Walk,* with the added intrigue and challenge of not knowing who one's (sighted) partner is. Half of the group sits with eyes closed. Each member of the other half of the group selects a blind partner to lead around the room. It is important that the sighted person does not give himself away with his voice during the exercise. At the end of the walk, each blind person tries to guess, based on intuition and a sense of the nonverbal presence of the sighted partner, who his partner is. *Identify Your Leader* should be used only with groups that manifest trust and security.

GROUP BLIND WALKS

In the following variations *all* participants have their eyes closed.

Creating a circle

Everyone in the group walks around with eyes closed. The group leader and possibly one or two designated group members (often people who are not comfortable closing their eyes) ensure that there are no collisions or accidents. After some time, the group leader asks participants to begin to connect with others, until a circle is formed with everyone holding hands. She lets the group know when all group members are included and the circle is complete. At this point, the group (still with eyes shut) is asked to sit down in unison.

Identify others

Similar to *Head Identification* and to *Identify Your Leader, Identify Others* entails walking around with eyes closed, nonverbally interacting with another person or several people, and then attempting to identify them.

Find the same hands

Find the Same Hands, my favorite variation of *Blind Walks,* promotes group interaction as much as it develops trust and sensory awareness. After some mingling with eyes closed, participants are instructed to gradually find a partner (without speaking or peeking), and to hold this partner's hands. Once all participants have found a partner, the group leader encourages everyone to become very familiar with the partner's hands. ("Feel the texture and temperature of your partner's hands. Are there any rings? Are the hands larger or smaller than yours?" etc.) Participants are then instructed to let go of their partners' hands and to walk on their own again. After wandering alone for awhile, the group leader instructs participants to find the hands of their partner again (with eyes closed of course). This part of the exercise is wonderful to behold; participants reach, grab, and reject hands, until the joyous moment when they find the right hands!

The more passive people in the group often take longer to find their partner's hands (especially if their partner is also passive) and may need the group leader's assistance. *Find the Same Hands* works best with large groups; I have found it most enjoyable with groups of about 12 people.

Touch and Smell

As a way of both awakening the senses and developing trust, participants are asked to identify objects or substances by their shape or smell. It is best to begin with touch, which is less difficult and less potentially intimidating, and then progress to smell. The two main formats for this exercise are: 1) One at a time participants enter the stage area, close their eyes, and are given by the group leader an object to feel with their hands and to identify. 2) The group is divided into pairs, and one person hands his blinded partner given objects to feel and identify. The first format develops the relationship between the leader and participant, and establishes a simple performance mode (in which an audience watches the action). The second format develops the relationship *between* participants, and maintains a process mode, in which the entire group is actively engaged at once.

In selecting objects for touch, it is best to find contrasting textures (e.g., feather duster, pine cone, strawberry) and interesting shapes (e.g., hourglass, rawhide dog bone). In selecting substances to smell, it is best to find distinct and evocative scents (e.g., coffee, baby powder, cinnamon, lemon, cut onion, rubbing alcohol, mint).

Touch and Smell is very effective with passive clients, as it allows them to *remain passive;* they are simply handed an object, and eventually curiosity takes over. The sedentary and nonthreatening nature of the exercise makes it particularly suitable to work with the elderly. The textures and scents often revive dormant sensations and evoke memories.

Touch and Smell can lead directly to discussion or scenework or, more commonly, can be used as a prelude to pantomime. The *real* experience in *Touch and Smell* leads participants to bring a kind of reality to the forthcoming pantomime or dramatic scenes, so that they imagine rather than pretend, and thereby imbue the act with the rich presence of all five senses. An example of such a progression is to follow *Touch and Smell* with *Eating in Mime.*

Rag Doll

In pairs, one person lies on the floor and relaxes her body. Her partner sits at her side and gently lifts, then places back down, parts of her body— beginning with hands, then arms, feet or legs. The person on the floor should not help; rather, she should attempt to be completely limp, like a rag doll. Images of heaviness or dead weight can be used; the person lying with eyes closed is to relinquish all control and responsibility. With each of her partner's lifts or maneuverings, she relaxes more fully. After some time, when enough trust is developed, her head can be gently lifted. *Rag Doll* is generally a quiet, nurturing exercise, but it can also take on a more playful tone. This occurs when the rag doll's full body positions are altered, e.g., getting her to sit up (with the partner supporting her behind her back) or to roll over.

Some clients have difficulty letting go enough to allow their partner to maneuver them without their help. With these clients, who often manifest a need to be in control and a lack of trust in other exercises (as *Trust Falls*) and in their lives, *Rag Doll* would be better used at a later stage in treatment.

Rag Doll is best used with groups that have already established trust and that would not be threatened by the physical intimacy in the exercise. It should be used only with groups that are fully capable of caring, gentle, and appropriate touch. With these groups, *Rag Doll* can be an intensely relaxing beginning exercise.

Rag Doll can also serve as a prelude to *Partner Sculpting* and to *Self-Sculptures.*

OBSERVATION AND CONCENTRATION

Ball Throws

CIRCLE BALL THROW

Circle Ball Throw, one of my most frequently used techniques during the first or second session within a series, immediately establishes a high level of engagement and concentration, as well as responsiveness and interaction between group members. Playful and nonthreatening, *Circle Ball Throw* tends to alleviate initial anxiety in the group.

The group forms a wide circle. Without giving any instructions, I pick up a large ball from the floor, in mime, and throw it to someone in the group. As

I throw the imaginary ball, I say the person's name. I quickly interject that the person is to catch the ball and then toss it to someone else in the circle, calling out that person's name. Before long participants spontaneously change the size and weight of the ball; tennis balls, bowling balls, and balloons are created, and eventually throwing becomes punching and shoving and blowing. Each person pays close attention to the particular ball that is thrown his way and catches it according to its apparent weight, size and shape; the creative modifications and reshaping of the ball occur only after it has been received.

I often follow this exercise with the use of real balls. I toss a very large, light, colorful ball to someone in the group, calling out his name. Then I add a second and third ball. With three or four balls being thrown concurrently, there are no free moments in which to "space out." Everyone has a ball (or sometimes two or three at once!) coming toward him at great frequency. To augment the challenge and fun, especially in a large group, the number of balls can be increased to five or six. It is exciting to witness the high level of concentration and attentiveness this exercise engenders even among easily distracted or disoriented clients.

GET THE BALL

I taunt the group with a ball. Hogging the ball as I run around the room, I suggest that everyone wants it but cannot have it, though they can attempt to usurp it. I finally throw the ball to someone in the group, calling out her name, and stating that the ball is between me and her only. We throw it and pass it between us, all the time moving about, as the group runs with us and dodges us, in an attempt to snatch the ball. Once someone does get the ball, it belongs to that person and another designated member of the group, until it is snatched by someone outside of that pair, and so on.

A variation is to keep the ball tossed between everyone in the group, but away from one designated person. The group runs around, throwing and catching the the ball as the one person attempts to seize it. This variation can bring out feelings of exclusion, whereas the passing of the ball between two people (with the rest of the group trying to get it) promotes a sense of connectedness and relationship (between those two people); for this reason, the earlier version is more appropriate in early sessions.

Get the Ball is very physical and energizing, promoting *Physical Activation* as well as *Observation and Concentration*. *Get the Ball* can be a good follow-up to *Circle Ball Throw,* an effective physical warm-up to the emotional *Line Repetition* (using the lines "I want it," and "You can't have it"), and also as a playful prelude to *Balls Between Backs.*

Guess Where We Are

Guess Where We Are involves imagining oneself in a given place/setting. The group is divided into two subgroups. After being assigned by the leader a given place, the first subgroup nonverbally enacts being in that place. Members of the other group try to identify the place.

A clear progression is recommended, from simple to complex enactments (paving the way for verbal scenework and performance in front of other members) and from structure (giving the members the settings) to freedom (having them come up with their own ideas). The progression can be so gradual and the beginning exercises so nonthreatening that by the end of the series of exercises members hardly realize they are acting and performing.

A typical progression is to first give each subgroup something they will be *watching,* e.g., a tennis match, football game, sad movie, birds. In this initial round, there is neither talking nor moving about. The fact that the members can remain seated, in their row, diminishes anxiety and facilitates concentration. The guessing format further reduces self-consciousness. Once the members reach a state of authentically imagining themselves in the given place, appropriate facial expressions and gestures occur naturally and spontaneously.

The second round involves *waiting* in a given place, e.g., doctor's office or maternity ward or waiting to audition for a play or interview for a job. Again, there is no talking, but at this point members have the option of remaining seated or moving about; they may also interact with one another. In the third round, they are given a setting which naturally entails standing and/or moving, as well as a greater degree of dramatic involvement, e.g., bus stop, airport, laundromat, museum, zoo. This round is also performed nonverbally, but paves the way to verbal dramatic scenes.

An alternate format to *Guess Where We Are* is for the entire group to decide together on a place/setting. As in *Group Mood,* one person in the group (who had stepped outside while the group selected a place) tries to identify the setting. This format, recommended when the objective is not only *Observation and Concentration* but also *Group Collaboration,* can serve as a prelude to *Group Mood* with groups for whom emotional expression is somewhat threatening. *Guess Where We Are* lacks the emotionality of *Group Mood,* but invites more spontaneity and creativity. Groups often come up with wonderful ideas, leading to delightful enactments, and this single game frequently ends up being used throughout the entire session.

A third format is for each member of the group to individually enact being in a given setting, with the rest of the group watching and guessing. This format is effective with clients who are eager to perform. It is most often utilized with children and adolescents.

A variation on *Guess Where We Are* is for participants to imagine *listening* to something, e.g., rock music, classical music, the ocean, which others then try to identify. Given the high level of concentration this variation demands and the subtlety it entails, it should be used only with sophisticated groups.

The nonthreatening, playful, interactive nature of *Guess Where We Are* makes it an excellent technique for very early sessions. *Guess Where We Are* promotes humor and creativity, increases nonverbal expressiveness, and develops the concentration that is necessary for dramatic enactment.

Eating in Mime

The eating of particular foods in pantomime is an effective and nearly failure-proof technique, perhaps because eating is an activity with which everyone is familiar, which often takes place with others, and which has positive associations for most people. *Eating in Mime* can be conducted in any of the formats noted in *Guess Where We Are,* though my preferred format is to have the group divide into several small groups of three or four people.

As in *Guess Where We Are,* the suggestions are often initially given by the leader; after the first round/s, members are asked to come up with their own ideas. Given suggestions are adapted to the level of the group. Some groups require more basic ideas that will not be difficult to portray or to ascertain, e.g., spaghetti, corn-on-the-cob, bananas; others need a greater creative challenge, e.g., artichokes, lobster, grapefruit. After several rounds of foods, beverages can be introduced—ranging from coffee to ice cream soda to margaritas. Sophisticated groups can also be asked to convey feelings associated with given foods or beverages.

Sensory awareness exercises including the smelling of actual foods (see *Touch and Smell,* page 176) are effective antecedents to *Eating in Mime,* as these exercises enhance participants' level of concentration and thereby the believability of the pantomimed activity. *Eating in Mime* can be very naturally followed by *Restaurant Scenes* (see page 200).

Eating in Mime develops the concentration of those eating and the observation of those watching and guessing. Because those watching are often extremely eager to guess, and guessing tends to disrupt the concentration of the actors or actually abort the enactment, I often instruct the audience not to guess until I "cut" the enactment. With groups of children or adolescents who are unable to restrain themselves from spontaneously shouting their guesses, I suggest that guesses are whispered to one's "neighbor" while the enactment is taking place.

A variation on *Eating in Mime* is for the entire group to participate in an imaginary picnic. Each person takes a turn choosing an item from the large (imaginary) bag in the center of the circle and eating this item. Once others in the group identify (silently) what is being eaten, they too begin eating that food (or drinking that beverage). The initiator looks around to determine whether everyone is eating the same thing. This variation can also be effective at the end of the session.

Who Started the Motion

In this Spolin theatre game, one person leaves the room while the others select a leader. When the person returns, he stands in the center of the circle and tries to determine the leader. Everyone in the circle follows the leader's motions and movements as precisely as possible, making it difficult for the person to guess. The leader can change motions as frequently as she wishes, though she must be careful not to be caught making the changes.

Who Started the Motion (also listed under *Mirror Exercises*) requires a great deal of concentration on the part of all players and very keen observation on the part of the person trying to guess.

Three Changes

In this technique described by Spolin, the group stands in two rows facing one another. Each participant observes the person opposite him, noting particulars of what that person is wearing. Both rows then turn their backs, and each person makes three subtle changes to his appearance, e.g., moving a ring to a different finger, unbuttoning a button, etc. Participants then face each other again and try to identify the three changes. A modification is for the subgroups to take turns making the changes and observations, rather than having these be concurrent.

Spolin suggests increasing the challenge by asking participants to make more than three changes. Another way of increasing the challenge is to have several rounds; finding new subtle changes becomes more and more difficult. I have created yet a different variation, heightening group interaction and collaboration: The two rows are seated, and asked to make three changes/ exchanges between them *as a group,* e.g., David's watch is placed on John's wrist, Mary's necklace is given to Kathy, etc. The other group then tries to identify the three group (ex)changes. Sophisticated groups (or those that have already developed some intimacy with one another) use their imagination to augment the challenge. I have witnessed people exchanging belts, earrings, and even socks! When personal boundaries and sense of self are fragile, this variation is obviously not appropriate.

Three Changes (particularly the latter version) can be effectively used as a prelude to *Guess Who's Guilty.*

Guess Who's Guilty

In this theatre warm-up game, the group is divided in half. Each subgroup sits in a row facing the other subgroup. One subgroup is given the role of observer. More specifically, members of this subgroup are told that they are police detectives, whose task it is to observe the other group members. The setting is a waiting area (of a police station) and the detectives have been informed that one of the people is guilty of a crime; the others are innocent. They (the other subgroup) are about to be questioned but are first being observed through a one-way glass mirror. The detectives are given a limited period of time to observe the nonverbal language and facial expressions of the other group before making their guesses as to which person is guilty.

The task of the other subgroup, those being observed, is to fully concentrate. Each must imagine himself in the given situation (made explicit by the group leader, e.g., being detained because smuggled drugs were found on the bus from Mexico to California on which they were all passengers). The guilty person (who has been determined by picking slips of paper, one of which had an x for guilty, or simply by a tap on the back by the leader while the entire group had its eyes closed) must concentrate particularly intently on his situation. For the technique to be effective, it is important that the guilty person be capable of this staid concentration. (For this reason, I often make the selection, rather than having it be random.) It should be made clear that neither he nor any of the others should try to behave in a particular way; rather they should simply imagine themselves in this role and situation.

Once the detectives begin their guessing (or more dramatically, their accusations), the suspects remain silent until all the detectives have reported their guesses. At that point, the guilty person is asked to slowly stand up and turn himself in. Groups will spontaneously capitalize on this suspenseful moment; several suspects may shift or begin to rise, prolonging the tension, until the "real" guilty one is finally standing. Clients delight in this "moment of truth."

The roles are then reversed, with the detectives becoming the suspects, and vice versa. *Guess Who's Guilty* can also be developed by having a round in which the suspects are asked questions. The transition from the nonverbal to the verbal paves the way to improvisational scenes.

Guess Who's Guilty helps groups to comprehend the concept of *imagining* rather than *pretending,* to develop skills in concentration and observation, and to become more attentive to nonverbal language and expression. Adolescents in particular find this game compelling, perhaps because getting into trouble, having feelings of guilt, and being accused are familiar to them. *Guess Who's Guilty* works well with large groups; the ideal size is 10–14 people.

Guess the Topic

Two people are secretly given a topic. The rest of the group listens closely while the two players engage in a conversation about the given subject, without ever naming it explicitly. Their conversation is intentionally oblique, so that the subject is not obvious to the listeners. It may go something like this:
"Have you ever been involved in it?"
"Oh yes, I've tried different kinds for a long time. The first time I did it was when I was a teenager. What about you?"
"No, never."
"Really? Never? Why not?"
"I don't know, maybe I've been afraid."
"My most recent experience has been with my wife. We've been doing it for nearly a year."
"What is that like?"
"It's not necessarily fun, but it's good. It's really helped us to open up. Soon we're going to do it in a group."
As soon as people in the audience *think* they know what is being discussed, they join the players in the conversation. If it becomes clear to the original players that the newcomer/s are not speaking about their topic, they send them back to the audience. (One of the most enjoyable and often hilarious parts of the game is when someone actively takes part in the conversation but gradually realizes that she is talking about something else.) The game can be ended when the entire group has joined the conversation.
As the above example illustrates, the topic can be initially difficult to decipher, especially when the conversers play with innuendos or are deliberately misleading. The conversations are often clever and humorous, and promote a high level of attentiveness and concentration on the part of the listeners. *Guess the Topic* is best used with groups that are verbally sophisticated.
By the way, the topic in the above conversation was psychotherapy.

People Puppets

In pairs, one person is designated as the puppet and the other as the puppeteer. The puppeteer establishes imaginary strings attached to the puppet, which he can manipulate. Beginning with strings that maneuver the puppet's arms, the puppeteer attempts to have his puppet sway or lift his arms in various ways. The puppeteer must be as precise as possible in the way he manipulates the imaginary strings, thereby communicating clearly to the puppet what is intended. The puppet must concentrate fully and observe closely, allowing his body to pick up subtle signals and almost intuit the directions of the puppeteer. (The high level of concentration and responsiveness between the two people in *People Puppets* is very similar to that of *Partner Mirror.*) Once the pair has mastered the basics, more intricate possibilities can be experimented with. The puppeteer may enable his puppet to walk, clap hands, smile, even dance. Each puppeteer may be asked to "show off" his puppet before the rest of the group.

People Puppets is a variation of Spolin's *Puppets and/or Automation,* in which players in a scene act like puppets, or one puppeteer manipulates a large group of people who respond as puppets. *People Puppets* is recommended for sophisticated groups, who do not have difficulty with *Partner Mirror,* and who can sustain intense concentration. It is more demanding and skill-oriented (and indeed develops skills in pantomime), though less intimate, than *Rag Doll* (under *Trust* section). Because *People Puppets* does not particularly promote emotional expression or affect, I use it rarely, preferring instead *Partner Mirror* or *Partner Sculpting.*

Space Substance

This is one of Spolin's theatre games in which the group moves through space as though it were composed of particular evocative substances. The leader calls out these substances, e.g., *fog, mud, molasses.* Spolin suggests having the group imagine new and unknown substances, though given the level of abstractness inherent in the exercise, I find using known substances more effective as a physical warm-up in drama therapy.

Space Substance develops imagination and concentration. I have found it to be most effective with children, and least appropriate with schizophrenic clients who need a greater degree of concreteness as well as interaction. The exercise can be made more concrete with the suggestion of physical environments rather than substances, e.g., *an icy creek, hot sand, a planet devoid of gravity.* It can be made more interactive when participants are given motivation to help one another, e.g., *the rocks are slippery—help one another make it across the creek,* or *one person is sinking in the quicksand—try to help her!*

7

MID-SESSION AND MID-SERIES

The objectives for the middle portion of the session, and the middle phases within the treatment series, are: *expression and communication, character and role development, group collaboration,* and *self-revelation.* The majority of techniques categorized under the first three of these objectives are most appropriate for Phase Two (Scenework) of a treatment series, with the exception of *Telephone,* a primary drama therapy technique that can be adapted to all phases within the series. The techniques categorized under the last objective, *self-revelation,* are geared toward Phases Three (Role Play) and Four (Culminating Enactment). As the nine techniques involving *self-revelation* all hold a paramount place in drama therapy, this final section is the most developed section of the chapter.

EXPRESSION AND COMMUNICATION

Telephone

A telephone is placed in the center of the room. It is disconnected, merely a prop, yet its presence invites calls to be made.

Just as the session is about to begin, a belligerent-appearing adolescent stumbles into the room. It seems he is about to angrily challenge me, but instead his eye catches a glimpse of the phone. Spontaneously, he reaches for it, lifts the receiver, and says: "Hello? (pause). Oh, hi, Dad. How am I doing? How in hell do you think I'm doing? I'm pissed as hell that you put me in this looney bin, man. That's how I am." He slams the receiver. The group is laughing, partly out of anxiety; they are also clearly engaged and intrigued. I ask: "Who can be this Dad, talk on the phone like this Dad would?" Immediately, two boys jump up. "No problem, I know just what he would say." I chose one to play the father, and the other to take over the part of the boy who just instigated the call. Our work for the session has begun.

I first conceived the idea of using a telephone when working with a group of extremely resistant, hostile adolescents. Any verbal instruction was taken as a cue for resistance. I desperately wanted to find a way of beginning the session that would not only bypass all instructions, but would be absolutely irresistible to them. Ideas were discarded as quickly as they formed: I could only envision more responses such as, "This is stupid," "No way will I do that." What was needed was something familiar and relevant, and yet something which would catch them off guard, surprise them into participation. The moment the image of a ringing telephone came to mind, I knew it would work.

For adolescents, the telephone is a cherished object. For any age group, the phone represents communication, at a distance. The fact that this prop is so real prompts clients to come up with realistic scenes; the fact that it is disconnected incites clients to express suppressed feelings. Emotions can be vented safely, without repercussion.

With highly resistant groups, it is effective to have the phone "ring" (by playing on a discreetly placed tape recorder a recording of a phone ringing). The clients spontaneously reach for the receiver, at which point they either begin a conversation or hand the phone to another client, stating that the call is for that person. When less strategy to overcome resistance is required, the following three-step progression is recommended:

1) Clients are asked to think of a call that evokes a particular mood or emotion, and then, one by one, simply dial the number. There is no actual speaking. The audience offers its observations and guesses about the call, e.g., "You're mad at someone," "You can't wait to tell someone great news," "You're getting the courage to ask someone on a date."

2) Progressing from the nonverbal to the verbal, situations elicited in the previous stage are developed. The client dials, again projecting the appropriate mood, and then proceeds to talk, as if there were someone on the other end of the line. New situations and conflicts can also be initiated. Therapeutically, the ensuing monologues are quite revealing to the therapist, as they often reflect the clients' inner concerns. Theatrically, the monologues tend to be compelling in their realism and the truth they bare. Watching the actor listen and respond to an imaginary person is in itself dramatically engaging.

3) The scenes are developed from monologue to dialogue. A second phone is added and another group member assumes the role of the person on the other end of the line. The actors are turned away from each other; as in real-life conversations, there is no eye contact.

Initial calls by adolescents may be attempts to impress their peers. Calls to drug dealers, for example, are not uncommon. These calls can be capitalized on by the therapist by directing follow-up calls which facilitate an in-depth exploration of the initiated issue. But most often teens make calls expressing their yearnings and struggles. Hospitalized youth frequently choose to call home, displaying their homesickness, despite the familial conflicts with which they were inundated. One 14-year-old girl leapt at the opportunity to call home. Her homesickness was intermingled with rage about the way she was admitted into the hospital. Apparently, she was "tricked into it;" her parents did not tell her the "outing" was to a psychiatric hospital. Expression of her anger, pain, and shame was encouraged and gently supported. Much later in the session, after other teens had shared the circumstances of their own hospital admissions, she role played her father, saying, "This is the only way we knew to get you to come here and get help. If we had told you we were sending you to a hospital, you would have run away again, right?" She instructed the girl role playing her to respond, "True." Playing both roles led her not necessarily toward forgiveness, but toward a deeper level of understanding.

In Phase Two (Scenework), *Telephone* tends to elicit humorous and creative ideas. Clients call for pizza, dial a wrong number, call the President to complain about mental health funding. In Phase Three (Role Play), calls dealing with practical situations are typical; clients use *Telephone* to prepare for actual experiences, e.g., asking for (or turning down) a date, setting up a job interview, coping with rejection.

In a group that is entering Phase Four (Culminating Enactment), calls can be emotionally laden. One call evokes another, spiralling the session toward increasing intensity. In one woman's group, a 29-year-old client phoned her mother, with whom she had not spoken in years. Many emotions were apparent. At one point during the conversation, she said softly: "I wanted a mother, not a sister. I needed protection." I asked her to repeat this line, knowing that she and the group could tolerate the deeper feelings and disclosures that would follow.

Affected and primed by this call, the next caller, a 24-year-old woman, confronted her mother on ignoring the sexual abuse by her stepfather she had endured during her teen years. How she had craved protection! Although deep empathy was present among the members in this group, I could sense some rising anxiety among the three women in the group who were themselves mothers. One spoke up. She expressed anger at the responsibilities and pressures of mothering, which are delegated primarily to women in our society, and at the impossibility of being a mother who doesn't make mistakes. Then she let some of her own buried guilt concerning what she perceived as her own failings as a mother spill out.

The room was silent for awhile. On some level, transference within the group was being worked out. Would those who were daughters accept those who were mothers, even with the admission of their small crimes? Would those who were mothers recognize the pain experienced by those who were daughters? The age difference between the women in the group, usually so obscured or irrelevant in our play, was now apparent.

The interpersonal dynamics were finally articulated. As the group examined its feelings and relationships, and as each person's perspective was acknowledged, it was clear that the group was entering yet a deeper level of connection and bonding. One more call was made, this time by a 47-year-old woman to her 21-year-old son, about the years during his childhood in which she regretted leaving him to a babysitter at a time when she began working again and emotionally adjusting to the abandonment by her husband. For many sessions to come, this group referred to the "telephone session" as a turning point in their process.

The calls placed in drama therapy sessions are sometimes of a more symbolic nature than the concrete situations thus far described. Clients may call a part of themselves, a state of mind, an imaginary friend. Sometimes the therapist may direct a concrete call to be followed by a more symbolic one. One client, who had recently been confronted by staff on his tendency to turn anger inward and become depressed, attempted to express anger outwardly in a call to his landlord with whom he was furious. Afterwards, he commented, "What's the use? I'd never do that for real. It'd only get me kicked out of my apartment. It just seems I've been unlucky. I'm fed up with the circumstances of my life." I asked him if he would call Circumstances of Life. He began reluctantly, but as the monologue progressed it became charged with emotion. Charles expressed years of pent-up anger at the "unfair deck" he'd been dealt. Then, responding to my direction, he powerfully stated all he felt he deserved in life. When asked how he felt after the scene he responded, "Healthy, strong. This anger made me feel better without hurting myself or anyone else. Maybe I can use some of the energy I feel now to do something about my situation."

In directing telephone scenes, it is important that the drama therapist know when to initiate a dialogue (with a second person and phone) and when to sustain the scene as a monologue. A dialogue is indicated when one or more of the following applies: 1) The therapeutic emphasis is on the relationship/communication between two people; 2) The given interaction is one that would be fruitful for the client to eventually experience in actuality; 3) The addition of a second person is the only way to amplify the client's involvement or expression.

A monologue is indicated when the client is able to sustain concentration without a partner and: 1) The therapeutic emphasis is on the client's emotional expression; 2) The given situation is one which in reality will never change (because it is marked in the past, the other person is "out-of-the-picture," etc.). For example, when the young sexually abused woman referred to earlier chose in a later session to call her stepfather, only a monologue was utilized. The personification of the stepfather's perspective was unwarranted; the sole task was to give voice to my client's rage, unimpeded. But when an impulsive 14-old girl called her father to express her desire for more freedom, I directed a dialogue to take place, followed by a *role reversal*—in order to facilitate the communication process in this current relationship. The process entailed helping the client to identify and articulate her needs, as well as to gain an understanding of her father's perspective. Through the role play, she experienced the inevitable shift in their dynamic as she expressed her feelings directly, rather than through acting-out behavior.

Monologues and dialogues using a telephone are often so theatrically and emotionally potent that I have included them in performances. In a scene from the play *Inside Out* (discussed in Part III), a woman sitting alone on stage receives a call from her father. The audience hears the father's voice (played by a member of the group) on audiotape, booming through the theatre's sound system. The father, who was physically and emotionally abusive to Karin during her childhood, threatens to disown her if she does not come home "to answer our questions about the direction your life is taking." When she refuses, he assaults her verbally and then slams the receiver. The audience, sensing the authenticity of the scene, is intent on Karin's response. First she reaches for a syringe of heroin, then she considers cutting herself with a razor. But she stops, choosing instead to feel her pain, "to live with it." On stage, in front of many people on many occasions, this 23-year old woman with a history of drug abuse, suicide attempts, and psychiatric hospitalizations speaks her resolution: "I'm going to live now, for me."

It is hard to imagine there was a time before I used the telephone. Now, if I could keep only one prop, this would be the one. Like drama itself, the telephone as prop is *almost real*, treading that thin line between the actual and the imaginary—a line at which such powerful theatre and therapy can take place.

Hand Gestures

One person, seated, places his arms behind his chair. This person is to be a *speaker* in an improvisational scene. Another person crouches behind the chair and juts his arms out (between the *speaker's* arms and ribs), giving the impression that his hands belong to the speaker in the scene. The speaker is then interviewed by the group or by another actor. The person doing the hand gestures gesticulates in accordance with the verbal responses of the speaker. While it is helpful to introduce *Hand Gestures* in this simple manner, there are obviously many variations, including having two people within an improvisational scene both have their respective hand gestures done by others.

It is remarkable how creative the clients playing the hand gestures become, as they respond to nuances of the scene, develop character traits and tics, and both follow and lead their speaking partners. The gesturing is a good role for self-conscious clients who have been timid about performing verbal scenes; they are afforded a chance to shine, without having to be seen or heard. The addition of props that can be manipulated by the hands, e.g., cigarettes, sunglasses, purses, hats, stimulates creativity and magnifies the fun.

Hand Gestures is invariably hilarious. Even more significant than the humor and creativity inherent in *Hand Gestures,* the exercise promotes an empathic connection between the players (the speaker and the person gesturing), who must be acutely sensitive and responsive to each other's cues. *Hand Gestures* also heightens awareness of nonverbal language.

Hand Gestures is so amusing and entertaining to watch that I have incorporated it into performances. In a scene from the play *Episodes* performed by the group *Beyond Analysis,* a psychiatrist and a patient—along with their accompanying hand gestures—improvised a dialogue based on emotions called out by our live audience. Spontaneous puns relating to schizophrenia, which was the subject of the play, kept emerging—from the patient exclaiming she felt disconnected from her body to her responding to her doctor's questioning about her angry gesticulations by insisting, "That wasn't me!"

An effective warm-up to *Hand Gestures* is a game in which each person in the group expresses an emotion or conveys a verbal expression using hand gestures only, while the rest of the group tries to identify the emotion or expression.

Gibberish

This is a technique described by Spolin, in which sounds are substituted for recognizable words. In essence, the players improvise a made-up language. Physical actions, gestures, expressions, and tone of voice help communicate the content. My aim in adapting *Gibberish* to drama therapy has been to facilitate the expression of emotions, in particular anger. The playfulness inherent in *Gibberish* can enable suppressed feelings to be discharged in a nonthreatening manner. Side benefits include a reduction in inhibition and the promotion of humor and spontaneity.

Gibberish can be liberating or intimidating, depending on how and when it is introduced. It should be used only with groups that have manifested spontaneity and confidence, and that are not afraid of appearing silly. The way in which the clients are led into *Gibberish* has a strong bearing on its success. The following is a recommended warm-up and progression: 1) In pairs, clients are asked to speak at the same time, nonstop, without listening to one another. 2) The previous step is repeated, for a limited time period, with the added instruction that everyone speak as loudly as possible, as if engaged in an argument and trying to outscream the other. It should be stressed that the actual words spoken are inconsequential. 3) The previous step is repeated but, in place of English, participants speak in a made-up language, as if they were foreigners in the midst of a heated argument. 4) Each pair is asked to create a situation that involves an argument or display of anger, and then perform it in gibberish. As if witnessing a foreign film without subtitles, the group watches and then guesses what has taken place. The above progression simplifies *Gibberish* by focusing on one type of interaction, an argument, in which tone and affect are clear-cut, transcending language or culture. The progression also immediately places the emphasis of the exercise on emotional expression.

The director can develop the scenes by asking the players to escalate the argument and then to reach a resolution. Or the scenes may serve as preparation for scenes in English that demand the expression of strong feelings. Naturally, the gibberish scenes can be also be less structured; the players can devise their own scenario (without instruction that it be an argument) or can simply engage in an *Impromptu Improvisation.* To add complexity on a dramatic level and to shift the focus from emotional expression to communication, translators can be added to the scene—one for each character. With sophisticated groups, such scenes tend to be riotously entertaining.

Although *Gibberish* is typically viewed as an advanced stage of creative play during Phases One and Two, it can be incorporated as an intervention in the midst of personal and psychodramatic scenes of Phases Three and Four. Such an intervention might be useful when: 1) a trace of laughter is detected in the protagonist as s/he becomes aware of the humor or absurdity in the enacted situation. At that point, the therapist directs the scene to be continued (or replayed) in gibberish, thereby heightening this awareness and exaggerating the new perspective; 2) The protagonist's expression of emotion is blocked, and the therapist feels that switching into a made-up language could release this block; 3) The scene is becoming threatening to the protagonist, and needs to be lightened. *Gibberish* in this case serves as a distancing device.

An adaptation of *Gibberish* is for the entire group to simultaneously speak in gibberish, in the context of either free play or specific scenarios. The leader can, for example, tell the group that they are strangers on a crowded train in a foreign country during rush hour or that they are buddies telling jokes at a bar. Or she may simply call out different emotions, which the group expresses (in gibberish) and develops through spontaneous interactions.

Closely associated to *Gibberish* is a tactic I have used with groups comprised of one or more foreign-speaking individuals. The language barrier can further isolate withdrawn clients. Rather than ignoring the barrier, one can capitalize upon it in a constructive manner. For example, two very withdrawn Chinese adolescents, lost in a group of boisterous, acting-out California teenagers, were asked to enact a scene in Chinese (which was essentially *Gibberish* to the group). The adolescents watching the scene had the challenge of identifying what was taking place. To the surprise and delight of myself and the group, the two actors became quite animated and expressive during their extended scene and were able to clearly communicate the essential content of the scene. After enthusiastic applause and discussion, the American teenagers began asking the Chinese clients how to say various words in Chinese. For the rest of the week, all the teens on the hospital unit were learning Chinese, including some expressions they were forbidden to use in English! For the first time since their admission into the hospital two weeks earlier, the Chinese teenagers were included in their peer group.

Calling Out Emotions

As two actors engage in an improvisational scene, the audience calls out emotions that the actors must immediately "take on" and incorporate into the scene. For example, two actors begin a scene in which they play a husband and wife celebrating their anniversary at a restaurant. An audience member shouts "romantic," and the actors instantly (without any interruption in their scene) interact with one another in a a romantic fashion. Later, another person in the audience calls out "sad," and the actors shift their mood, until some minutes later when "distrustful" is called out, and the mood and dialogue shift again. Generally, the audience responds to nuances within in the scene, calling out an emotion that is either surfacing or underlying an interaction. In some cases, however, the called-out emotion may not be connected to what has been transpiring in the scene, challenging the actors to make a quick shift (and usually resulting in a very humorous moment).

An alternate approach to *Calling Out Emotions* is for one person in the group, rather than the entire audience, to assume the role of director and call out the emotions. Two directors can also be used, one for each actor. With two directors, the two actors can be directed in separate emotions, adding complexity to the scene.

Calling Out Emotions places the emphasis of the improvisational scene on emotional expression. As emotions that the players may not ordinarily express are sometimes called out, repertoire of emotional responses is expanded. After the scene ends, the actors can be asked with which emotions they felt most comfortable and with which they had the most difficulty. *Calling Out Emotions* can also be adapted with the players (or the directors, or the whole group) deciding in advance the emotions they would like to explore; these specific emotions are then incorporated. For example, when asked to select four emotions that are difficult to express, a group of adolescents respond: anger, sadness, love, and fear. In the scene that follows, the two designated directors call out these emotions. Although the emotions are predetermined, the directors still have artistic control in terms of sequence, pace, and frequency, final emotion/moment of the scene, and the way in which they play off the other director and actor. (At times, both directors will have their actors express the same feeling at the same time, at other times they will juxtapose the feelings in interesting ways.) The directors can also monitor intensity, by calling out "more anger" or "more love." The use of directors gives the actors permission to emote, exaggerate, or intensify feeling states. Moreover, it helps the actors to sustain and develop their scene and is therefore particularly useful with clients who need added structure and "backbone" to remain emotionally engaged. *Calling Out Emotions* also provides an opportunity for self-conscious clients (who are still too timid to perform) to take an active and central role via directing the scene.

Calling Out Emotions is based on several of Spolin's techniques: 1) *Changing Emotion,* in which the leader calls out to the actor, who is engaged in a physical activity, various emotions; 2) *Changing Intensity of Inner Action,* in which the leader calls out to the actors in the scene progressively stronger emotions (i.e. suspicion to fear to terror); and 3) *Jump Emotion,* in which each player chooses in advance some radical change of what Spolin calls "inner action" and fits it into the scene (i.e. fear to heroism). In *Calling Out Emotions,* too, the therapist can assume the role of director/coach, although I prefer the above adaptation that engages those watching or particular clients by having them become the directors of the scene. A modification of *Calling Out Emotions* is for attitudes or moods, rather than emotions, to be called out.

With players who have already developed dramatic ease, skill, spontaneity, and emotional range, the results of *Calling Out Emotions* can be enthralling. I have used this technique in many live public performances, with the audience shouting out the emotions. In one scene from the play *Inside Out,* a group therapy scene is enacted. In the midst of the scene, the audience begins calling out emotions, which all the actors (including the group therapist) embody concurrently. Several minutes later, each actor is given a separate emotion. At every performance, this scene was hilariously entertaining, and also contained moments that were poignant and edifying.

I have also used *Calling Out Emotions* at large drama therapy workshops and staff in-service training. One example of its use in staff trainings is for two volunteers to enact a client-therapist session, with the audience calling out emotions for both roles. Mental health workers are thereby given an opportunity to discharge, in a playful, humorous (and typically grossly exaggerated) manner, feelings they have experienced (and kept suppressed) in the counseling situation.

Calling Out Emotions tends to evolve gradually, with the audience experiencing an increasing degree of permission (and power!) as the scene progresses and the actors feeling increasingly "warmed up." And, by the way, I don't think I have ever witnessed a demonstration or performance in which the audience did not call out, at least once, "lust!"

Dubbing and Silent Scene

Dubbing is a technique of Spolin in which the actors physically engage in an interaction and silently mouth dialogue rather than using any actual speech. Translators are added, giving the sense of a foreign language film being dubbed; to heighten this effect, Spolin recommends that the translators use microphones.

Dubbing can be adapted, or preceded, by simply having the physicalized scene, without live translation. In this version, *Silent Scene,* the actors essentially perform in mime (and it is better to discourage the mouthing of dialogue), communicating as clearly as possible within the nonverbal mode what is taking place. When the scene ends, the audience tries to identify what the scene was about. This version is effective with children and young adolescents, and often serves as a nonthreatening prelude to the performance of verbal improvisational scenes. I have made tremendous use of *Silent Scene* when I have had a deaf client within a hearing group. Another variation (see *Storytelling,* p. 233) is for one or two *storytellers* to narrate a story (which is predetermined or devised on the spot), while actors nonverbally enact the story.

Breaking the News

As a means of facilitating the enactment of emotional scenes during Phase Two (Scenework), one actor is instructed to deliver a significant piece of news to the other actor in the scene. The relationship between the two actors is established in advance, but the news is not told in advance to the second actor. The news can be devised by the actor himself, or whispered to him by the therapist, or written on slips of paper. The news may be very dramatic, e.g., the person has just won a lottery, lost a relative, or been betrayed by an unfaithful spouse, or it can be more subtle. In either case, the teller of the news must communicate with care and sensitivity, and the receiver of the news must be prepared for the dramatic and personal challenge of responding with authenticity to a potentially deeply emotional situation. *Breaking the News* should be used only with participants who have achieved some dramatic ease in Phase Two scenes and who have clear internal boundaries between the fictional and the actual.

Video Lip-Syncing

The clients are asked to bring a tape of a song that is especially meaningful to them, one that expresses feelings with which they strongly identify. After the group listens to the various songs, each person has the opportunity of lip-syncing his song as it is played on a stereo. The emphasis is on "singing" the song with feeling and passion, on being as expressive as possible. It is helpful if the song has been memorized. The lip-sync performance is video-taped, intensifying the act and enabling the client to watch himself embodying a new role.

Video Lip-Syncing is recommended for adolescents. In groups of emotionally disturbed adolescents, I have often witnessed withdrawn clients whose verbal communication is minimal and whose emotional affect is flat come alive while lip-syncing, as well as clients whose emotions tend to be volatile discharge feelings with precision and control, as they belt out their songs with passionate intensity. The clients can naturally have the option of actually singing, rather than simply mouthing the words. To diminish performance anxiety, one can involve the entire group by having it become the band backing up the lead singer. Each person chooses his instrument, and—once the video camera is turned on—plays the instrument in mime. Some clients can instead be dancers.

Video Lip-Syncing can be extended into the creation of a rock video (Emunah, 1990). Using both visualization and group discussion, the clients devise images that symbolically convey the feelings of the songs. These images are interspersed on the video with shots of the singer and band. There can also be shots of people moving and dancing, shots of artwork, and excerpts of dramatic scenes that relate to the issues and feelings in the song. The creation of a rock video demands patience and collaboration. There is usually an ensuing sense of accomplishment and pride as clients later view the completed video.

CHARACTER AND ROLE DEVELOPMENT

Family Roles

"You're home late again. Did you stop by at the bar? Huh?" The wife looks angry and accusatory.

"No, I didn't; I had to finish up some work. Now will you please give me some peace and quiet!" responds her husband, as he turns on the television.

Eight-year-old Katie runs in, and begins performing somersaults in front of the television set. "Dad, look what I can do!"

"Honey, show me later, after dinner. I need a little quiet now."

"Typical response. You'll have some other excuse after dinner," mutters the wife. Katie continues to do her somersaults.

"That's pretty neat, Katie," says 12-year-old Lisa, who has just gotten off the phone. "Why, don't you both watch her for a while, and I can help fix dinner," she says to her parents.

The group watches the four players perform this improvisation for five or 10 minutes. When the scene ends, the audience identifies the roles each of the family members portrayed. This is not difficult: the mother was the *blamer,* the father the *avoider,* the younger daughter the *attention-getter,* and the older daughter the *mediator.*

The next scene is more subtle, though the same four roles are incorporated. The players are adult siblings, planning a surprise 60th birthday party for their mother. The characters are multifaceted, and it takes some time before the roles they have probably always played within their fictional family resurface. There is some discussion after the scene as the audience tries to identify the roles and as the players examine the way they felt in the scene and their relationship to their respective roles.

Family Roles begins with dividing the group into subgroups of four people. Each group is to become a family, deciding themselves how they are related and selecting one of four given roles. The above roles—*blamer, avoider, attention-getter,* and *mediator*—are the ones I generally use. (Sophisticated groups can be given a greater selection of roles or asked to come up with their own roles.) Props can be made available to augment the players' development of character and role; a selection of wigs, hats, glasses, fabrics, kitchen and household items, toys, etc., is recommended. Each of these *Planned Improvisations* is then performed before the larger group.

The structured nature of *Family Roles*—the fact that there is a limited choice of roles, that the relationships are decided upon in advance, and that one's objectives within the scene are clear-cut—helps beginning players to sustain the action. The emotional charge inherent in family relationships further supports engagement in and development of the drama; in fact, *Family Roles* often results in the first developed dramatic scenes of the treatment series.

Family Roles is intentionally about a family, rather than one's own family, but the subject of family dynamics naturally provokes reflection and discussion about the dynamics in one's real-life family. *Family Roles* tends to serve as a bridge between imaginary scenes and personal scenes and is therefore best used in Phase Two (Scenework), when the group is at or nearing a point of readiness to make connections between dramatic scenes and real-life experiences.

In the planning stage, clients will typically choose to play the more familiar roles. In psychiatric settings, everyone seems to vie for the role of *avoider.* In workshops for mental health staff, the *mediator* role is immediately snatched. After participants experience success—during the first round of scenes—at being themselves or in a role very similar to their usual behavioral stance, they are usually open to choosing an unfamiliar role. (At this point, the role of the *angry blamer,* which underlies much of the depressive, avoidant stance of many psychiatric clients, becomes very popular.) The new role gives the client permission to experiment with alternative ways of behaving.

An effective warm-up to *Family Roles* is for each subgroup to enact, without using words, the four roles in a generalized way, rather than specifically as a family. The actors move about the room, physicalizing their roles and interacting with the others in accordance with their roles. After the brief nonverbal improvisation, the group identifies each person's role. These simple mini-scenes familiarize participants with the process of playing a given role, feeling the role in their body, interacting with others improvisationally, and performing, thus facilitating the progression to the creation and performance of more complex, verbal scenes.

With the drama therapist's guidance and intervention, the verbal scenes can be extended and developed, both theatrically and therapeutically. The following are several possible directions for scene development: 1) focusing on two people within the scene (and having the others either leave the scene or remain in the background—perhaps engaged in some nonverbal activity); 2) introducing a Double for one of the characters in the scene. The most likely character to be given a Double is the *avoider;* the Double allows the feelings stifled beneath this role to be expressed. (The person who has been playing the role of avoider will often experience relief at the opportunity to become the Double himself.); 3) asking the players to modify their roles, in order to bring about a gradual shift in the pattern of interaction. This often occurs more authentically after the Double has been used, as Doubling facilitates the examination and expression of underlying feelings and motivations.

Family Therapy

A scene is set up in which one or two families are seen by a family therapist. The issues and perspectives of each family member are outlined prior to the onset of the scene via a brief interview by the group leader; the family dynamics and situation are devised collaboratively, as each person's input is built upon. *Family Therapy* scenes need little other preparation. In fact, I often initiate *Family Therapy* at the start of an adolescent group simply by stating: "Whoever wants to be the family therapist, take this chair (the chairs are already arranged in the stage area), whoever wants to be a father, in this chair, a teenager, in that chair," etc. This invitation deflects the attention from the forthcoming performance, emphasizing instead the opportunity to assume particular roles. The chairs are generally immediately filled and the interviews begin.

I devised *Family Therapy,* like *Family Roles,* to meet the needs of groups during the latter half of Phase Two. The scenes are about *a* family, rather than one's own family, but reflections on one's actual family and life roles are likely to be evoked. As the dramatic setting is a therapy session in which issues are exposed and examined, *Family Therapy* scenes tend to be more personally provocative than *Family Roles*. Teenagers, with whom this technique is most relevant because they are so immersed in family conflicts and so eager to enact realistic scenes, often bring up real-life conflicts within the context of the scene. Adolescent client/actors in the role of sons and daughters express pent-up emotions and grievances; those in the role of parents typically embody the affect and stance of their actual parents—initially with some exaggeration and mockery, but as the scene progresses the embodiment becomes more authentic and even empathic.

The most therapeutically significant role is that of the family therapist. The client playing this role has to maintain some objectivity, manifest empathy to all parties, and find ways of intervening. Many adolescents seem eager to play this role, perhaps because of the power they associate with it or because of the chance to gain some mastery over a familiar but intimidating experience—reminiscent of the child's role play of the doctor. Once in role, the adolescent finds the enactment entails more than the assumption of power. It is very moving to witness a teen who is generally emotionally underdistanced manifest emotional detachment at the same time that he is highly engaged in the scene, or a teen who is generally helpless and hopeless find ways of helping the family or instilling hope. Under the guise of the therapist role, I have seen clients display extraordinary perspective and wisdom. The discoveries they make in role lead to important group discussions, as well as to valuable prescriptions for their own lives.

Family Therapy can be developed through role-reversing the characters; in fact, adolescents usually demand the opportunity to switch roles. The therapeutic potency inherent in the embodiment of the role of therapist is often heightened after that client has also played—and felt stuck in—the other family roles.

In residential settings for emotionally disturbed or acting-out adolescents, *Family Therapy* can be followed by the enactment of actual upcoming family therapy or "conjoint" meetings. Adolescents are very anxious about these meetings. When communication in families has disintegrated and feelings have been repressed, practice or preparatory enactment in a safe, contained setting may be the best way of facilitating a productive meeting.

Therapist-Client

Therapist-Client involves the enactment of scenes in which one client assumes the role of client and the other assumes the role of therapist. These scenes are most relevant for people who have extensively experienced the role of client in their lives, such as institutionalized adult psychiatric patients. The long-term assumption of the patient role increases dependency; the shift—albeit in dramatization—to being in the helper position reawakens the stronger and more independent part of oneself. Furthermore, chronic clients not only have been observed by therapists for many years, but have observed therapists for many years; the therapist is one role they know and can play well. Indeed, client portrayals of therapists are usually uncannily astute, not to mention extremely humorous. *Therapist-Client* scenes provide an opportunity for groups of patients to satirize and laugh about experiences they have in common. The fact that therapy, especially inpatient therapy, is stigmatic makes this subject all the more important to enact. Many of the plays I directed within residential psychiatric facilities were composed of *Therapist-Client* scenes, providing comic relief for all members of the community—clients and therapists alike.

Therapist-Client scenes can also be very poignant and therapeutically significant, particularly when the client plays himself as a client (an appropriate role for a client who at a given session does not want to stray from his own identity, feelings, or dilemmas), but can at a point of impasse switch to the therapist role. In this new role, he responds—empathically and supportively— to himself. The responses may also involve confrontation, advice, insights, or wise intimations. In playing one's own therapist, inner resources and healthy reserves are drawn upon and the observing ego is bolstered. In this respect, *Therapist-Client* is similar to the intervention *Developing an Internal Nurturing Parent.*

Restaurant Scenes

After being divided into subgroups of three or four people, participants are asked to plan a scene that takes place in a restaurant. One person is to play the waiter or waitress, the others are customers. During the planning phase, the groups also decide upon a conflict that will emerge during the scene.

Restaurant Scenes are useful *Planned Improvisations* in the early part of Phase Two (Scenework). When introduced at the right point of the treatment series and after appropriate warm-ups, *Restaurant Scenes* invariably build confidence in improvising and performing. The familiarity of the restaurant setting and the clear delineation of roles within the scene lead *Restaurant Scenes* to be relatively easy and nonthreatening for beginning improvisors. The addition of a conflict within the scene facilitates the development of the action. Even clients who are very withdrawn find the waiter role appealing. The waiter has a specific task and need not be present (on stage) the entire time, but can leave and return.

The conflicts in *Restaurant Scenes* are often stereotypical, such as spotting a fly in the soup or some other version of poor service. This sitcom scenario occurs frequently in psychiatric settings. Since the aim is developing the confidence of the players at this point, the scene's simplicity and con- ventionality is not problematic; moreover, given that many psychiatric patients live with a sense of exclusion and alienation from mainstream society, the enactment of the stereotypical can be positive. With sophisticated groups that are comfortable with improvisation, the temptation to enact the stereotypical may be circumvented simply by a statement in the planning phase that the conflict needs to be *between the customers,* rather than between customer/s and waiter. The focus thus shifts to the *relationship* between the customers, leading to a more developed and complex interaction, albeit still typically humorous. The waiter becomes a dramatic foil, who responds to (and impacts upon) the conflict between the customers, e.g., by being nosey, helpful, interruptive, or provocative. The fact that restaurants are public places pro- vides a limitation to potential emotional escalation, thereby increasing the actors' sense of safety in this early stage of the series.

The ideal prelude to *Restaurant Scenes* is *Eating in Mime.* The following is a recommended sequence: 1) *Eating in Mime;* 2) extending *Eating in Mime* to the pantomiming of a full meal. The audience tries to identify the type of food being eaten (e.g., Italian, Chinese), rather than a specific dish; 3) letting each subgroup decide upon some type of eating joint/restaurant, which the audience (following the nonverbal performance) again tries to identify. For groups needing more structure, ideas are provided by the therapist. Examples of settings are an elegant French restaurant, a run-down sleazy diner, a high school cafeteria, a truck stop. Characterization spontaneously emerges in these nonverbal improvisations, paving the way for the forthcoming scenes. 4) now the group is prepared for the fourth step, full *Restaurant Scenes*, in which setting, role/character, and conflict are developed, and verbal language is used.

Newspaper

The group leader sits in the stage area reading a newspaper. She indicates that the setting is a park bench and that the newspaper is a very precious item. Then she challenges the group to try to take the paper away from her. Short of physical force, participants can make any creative attempt to get her to relinquish the coveted paper. Props are laid out to encourage characterization and stimulate imagination.

Gradually, people enter the park scene, generally one at a time. There may be a streetperson who is shaking from the cold and begs for the newspaper as a means of insulation. Or a dogwalker who needs the paper to clean up his puppy's mess. Or a narcissistic criminal who wants to see if his latest crime has been publicized. The leader relinquishes the paper only when a particular interaction dramatically compels her to do so. That person then takes over her role and the next round begins.

Newspaper has a snowball effect: at first there is reluctance, but once people enter, ideas are rapidly generated and the concocted stories and characters become increasingly inventive. The fact that there is a specific challenge and task—to get the paper—stimulates creativity and deflects attention from performance. The format of brief dramatic episodes rather than full scenes further diminishes performance anxiety. Participants can exit shortly after they enter and later reenter as a different character. On the other hand, *Newspaper* does require initiative on the part of individuals in the group and can flounder with a group that requires more structure or that is inhibited by playing imaginary characters. *Newspaper* is best used at the end of Phase One (Dramatic Play) or beginning of Phase Two (Scenework) to augment the playful spirit in a group that has already manifested a degree of spontaneity and creativity, and to stimulate the experimentation with new roles and characters.

TV Interviews

"Welcome to your nightly television interview show, where we interview interesting people and hear stories from all walks of life," the drama therapist begins, adding clauses or creative show titles that seem relevant to the particular group. She continues playing the role of host or places someone from the group in this role. Volunteers then enter the show to be interviewed as particular characters, which may involve the portrayal of known figures or of fictional people—famous or not. A more personalized version of *TV Interviews* is for clients to be interviewed as actual people in their lives, or as themselves, or as themselves projected into the future or as they were in the past (which overlaps with *Yourself at Different Ages*). When characterization is used, props are helpful; when one is portraying oneself, props tend to be distracting.

TV Interviews generally begins with diverse playful characterizations and gradually progresses to more personal interviews. The characterizations often reveal wishes and fantasies, making the transition to the embodiment of a hopeful portrait of oneself in the future quite natural. Even when the entire session entails characterizations rather than personalized interviews, there is typically a progression from stereotypical and superficial character portrayals to more complex and developed portrayals.

A related technique, which can serve as an effective warm-up to *TV Interviews,* is the *Talk-Show Host,* devised by Adam and Allee Blatner (1991). Everyone in the group thinks of an imaginary character. To ease this process, the Blatners frequently suggest a theme, such as an occupation that is intriguing but not immediately familiar. The group forms dyads, with one person taking on the role of interviewer and the other role playing the character he selected. Participants are invited to imagine that they are in front of a television camera and television audience. After about five minutes, they change parts. *Talk Show Host* functions as a basic warm-up for learning role taking.

TV Interviews is especially appropriate for latency-age children and adolescents. Television is usually a big part of their lives, making the technique seem familiar and inviting. The person playing the interviewer has the experience (and the challenge, given these age groups) of bringing out another person. Allowing the interviewer to ask for questions from the live TV audience reduces the pressure and also heightens the engagement of those watching the scene.

TV Interviews can be effectively used when a new member (or several new members) enters an existing group, or when people within a group do not know each other well. The format of interviewing people as themselves provides a structured and playful means of introduction and/or gathering more information about fellow group members.

Hidden Conflict

In this technique described by Spolin, each player decides upon (or is given) an internal conflict. The scene is then played out, but the conflicts are never verbalized. Spolin gives the example of a husband and wife at breakfast. Prior to the onset of the scene, the husband is told that he does not want to go to work today; the wife is told that she wants him to leave soon because she is expecting a secret visitor. As one might imagine, the results of such an improvisational scene are often quite intriguing and entertaining.

I have used *Hidden Conflict* most often with teenagers, as they easily relate to the concept of hiding something and also seem delighted by the format of being given a secret message by me (outside of the room, before the scene begins). Pertinent scenarios are devised. One such example is of a mother and teen daughter; the daughter has just found out that she is pregnant and the mother is anxiously considering explaining the facts of life to her daughter, who she assumes is ignorant. Interrelated conflicts within a scene heighten the dramatic tension and intrigue. *Hidden Conflict* scenes both require and develop improvisational skills; the players need to be able to engage in an interaction on more than one level. *Hidden Conflict* should not be used with groups such as young children or developmentally disabled adults who may have difficulty refraining from spilling out the hidden conflict. *Hidden Conflict* is also inappropriate with those groups of emotionally disturbed clients who are understandably easily distressed by any experience reminiscent of the double messages they were often inundated with in their families of origin.

An ideal follow-up to *Hidden Conflict* is the use of Doubles, who voice the inner thoughts and feelings of the actors. This intervention steers the scene in a more psychological direction. Following these scenes, clients may be asked to reflect on situations in their own lives in which they have kept a conflict or a feeling hidden from another person. The enactment of such situations creates an interesting paradox: the content is about secrecy and yet the fact of enacting the scene before others in the group implies exposure. The experience for the clients is one of being unburdened. Insight into the ways in which one hides, disguises, or lies, and the motivations and fears that underlie this behavior, is also achieved.

Scripted Scenes

Although improvisational scenes are the norm in drama therapy, scenes from existing plays are occasionally used. It is best to introduce *Scripted Scenes* when a group manifests, on its own, interest in working with scripts.

Scenes are then carefully selected by the drama therapist and scripts are brought to the session. The selection is based on relevance to the themes of the group or of particular individuals within the group. The therapist also tries to find roles that particular clients will be able to play easily, to ensure a successful experience, or roles that will promote therapeutic goals for particular clients (e.g., assertion, expression of anger). *Scripted Scenes* can facilitate emotional catharsis and expansion of role repertoire at the same time that it provides clients with a sense of creative achievement, especially when the lines have been memorized.

Groups that are drawn to *Scripted Scenes* tend to be intrigued by acting; they often consist of participants who always wanted a chance to act. The level of engagement in *Scripted Scenes* can be very high; it is not uncommon for clients to want to take the scripts home to practice. On one occasion, two clients in a psychiatric hospital were heard screaming intensely at one another in a relatively private area of the hospital grounds. Suddenly, they were surrounded by hospital staff, who had responded to an emergency signal. It turned out that the two clients were members of my group, rehearsing their scripted scene. The clients later told the story to the other group members with pride: the staff thought their *acting was real!*

Scripted Scenes can be developed by having the actors: 1) be interviewed as their character; 2) revise the ending of the scene; 3) create improvisations based on the scripted scene. The improvisations can include scenarios which take place in the past or future, scenarios that involve fewer or more players than the characters in the scene, or scenarios of therapy sessions with the characters!

GROUP COLLABORATION

Join the Scene

Join the Scene is essentially the same technique as Spolin's *The Where Game.* One person enters the stage area and begins some kind of action. When another person thinks he knows what the first player is doing (or where he is), he enters the scene in any role (and as any character) appropriate to that situation. Other people in the group can join, one at a time, in a similar fashion. The scene becomes verbal with the entrance of the second person.

Join the Scene is a playful and creative way of facilitating group collaboration. Each person's contribution is immediately accepted, supported, and developed. Everyone needs to respond to everyone else, to adapt to the input of others, revising on the spot whatever preconceived notions they may have had about the scene. The complexity of the scene increases gradually. For example, a woman enters the stage area and begins trying on shoes. Another enters with a box of shoes and says, "Here, why don't you try these; I think they may fit you better." The scene between customer and shoe salesperson continues for a few minutes, when suddenly a man enters screeching, "Maggie, where have you been, I've been looking all over the mall for you." The woman quips, "I told you I was going to the shoe place, but as usual you were too preoccupied to hear me." The salesperson watches with curiosity. In the meantime, two other people have entered the store as mother and cranky child. Another enters from a different part of the stage area and, after observing the salesperson for several seconds, says in an authoritarian tone, "Arthur, may I have a word with you?" Typically there is a very spontaneous flow, with intermittent surprises, to the evolution of such scenes. As a means of emphasizing group collaboration and deemphasizing performance, the entire group can be instructed to (eventually) enter the scene; the scene ends when the last person has joined. This works when the group is not larger than six or seven people; with larger groups, the scenes tend to become overly chaotic.

A variation of *Join the Scene* is for the scene to be "frozen" at any given point (by the therapist or a group member), at which time time a new person enters. But rather than adding to the existing scene, the person changes the scene—and those already on stage respond accordingly. This variation works best when the scene is fairly physical, rather than primarily verbal. The point at which the actors are frozen is usually one which is physically evocative. The new scenario thus evolves out of the spontaneous association the person entering the scene had to the actors' physical positions. A great deal of spontaneity is both demanded and developed.

Transformations

Transformations is similar to *Join the Scene*, except that the players themselves initiate the transformation. The "freezing" can be omitted. Thus, one player, in the midst of a scene, can spontaneously transform the scene to an entirely different scene (including a different setting, relationship, etc.), at which point the other actor or actors instantly adapt to the new scenario. This technique, first described by Spolin, was incorporated by experimental improvisational theatre troupes in the 1960s. It has since been developed by drama therapist David Johnson as an advanced form of his developmental approach to drama therapy (Johnson, 1982b, 1986, 1991). Johnson uses *Transformations* almost exclusively in his work with individual clients in drama therapy. Both client and therapist can initiate the transformation at any point in the play, based on associations that are evoked by the material in the scene. In this exciting approach, the process of free association is activated and the person's inner world is accepted and explored within a playful and safely contained space. Johnson states: "As client and therapist become more deeply involved in the material, it often seems like the scene transforms on its own, as if the images arrive from elsewhere, rather than being consciously planned by the participants. Second, images, scenes, and characters that emerge in transformations are often of very primitive and personal content, and reflect the greater in-depth process that is evoked by psychotherapy" (1991, p. 290).

Johnson's *Transformations* is a far more complex process than can be briefly described here and, as it encompasses many therapeutic objectives, could be categorized under various other sections in Part II.

Court Trial

The enactment of a court trial is an excellent way of developing the group's sense of drama and collaboration. The structure of the scene facilitates active engagement. Each person has a clearly defined role and there is a set sequence to the action, as witnesses are called to the stand one at a time. The scene involves the entire group, thus eliminating the often inhibiting actor-audience division. Of particular importance is the inherent sense of suspense and drama in a court trial (consider the term "courtroom drama"). *Court Trial* invariably leads to a highly developed and suspenseful scene, lasting the entire session. The experience of participating in a sustained, realistic, thought-provoking, collectively created drama evokes in members excitement about the possibilities of theatre. The resulting sense of group achievement can be intensified through the use of video playback.

I often begin by asking which roles people would like to play. The role of judge is a very popular choice and it holds particular therapeutic advantages. The fact that it is a central role and yet does not require saying much makes it an excellent part for a passive client who has been in the background of the group. It is also a useful role for a disruptive client (often the instigator of a rowdy adolescent group) who has difficulty maintaining self-control. As judge, the client is put in the position of having to keep order in the court. Given this task, the client exercises power and control *via* the role and thus actually assists the therapist, rather than rebelling against the therapist (Emunah, 1985).

The roles of defense attorney and prosecutor are the most difficult and challenging roles and are best assumed by members who are verbally sophisticated. The defendant is another central role. The roles of witnesses can be both major or minor; the bailiff can be played by someone who would do best with a small, prescribed part, one that does not require verbal or improvisational skills. Any remaining members become the jury, who have the power to decide the verdict. This responsibility tends to help distracted clients remain attentive. (Giving the audience a task always heightens engagement. In the context of a public performance I directed, I once turned the audience into a jury. Audience members had just witnessed a court trial scene; to their surprise, they were instructed to return after the intermission with the verdict.)

Another way of beginning *Court Trial* is to first cast the defendant and decide on the nature of the case. The defendant is then asked to select from other members of the group his own defense attorney and prosecutor. Needless to say, these choices are quite revealing.

The court trial scene is a very verbal one, and in order to heighten its theatrical impact I encourage in my directions nonverbal responses (ranging from subtle glances to angry outbursts), emphatic "objections," and dramatic, emotional summations by the attorneys. Psychological rather than technical arguments are encouraged, including character witnesses and an emphasis on motivation. The committed crime may be symbolic rather than realistic. It may revolve around actual personal, group, or social issues instead of being fabricated. For example, one client in a psychiatric halfway house asked to be tried for "being different." Another time I placed a rebellious, testing client, who had missed several sessions, on trial for absenteeism. He selected his defense attorney and the witnesses who testified in his behalf. Through their roles, group members expressed their feelings, both anger and concern, about his recurrent absences. The defendant became aware of the seriousness of his inconsistency and the effect it had on others. His behavior became a group issue, rather than one between himself and me. The scene led to an exploration not only of the immediate problem of attendance, but of the broader theme of responsibility and commitment, which was relevant to all members of this group of psychiatric clients (Emunah, 1983).

I have had the most success using *Court Trial* with delinquent adolescents who have experienced the court system in real life. They relish the opportunity to replay these often traumatic experiences in safety, especially by assuming a powerful position as judge, attorney, jury. Discussions after the scenes may revolve around actual (or symbolic) crimes and resulting feelings of guilt. On an even more metaphoric level, the discussion and ensuing enactments may involve the exploration of personal relationships in which clients feel prosecuted, defended, or judged.

Court Trial can also be effective in educational settings. The activity offers a creative and enjoyable way of enabling youngsters to reflect not only about the legal system but about fundamental psychological and philosophical questions, such as societal and emotional factors in criminality and the boundaries between innocence and guilt. Students playing attorneys gain practice in articulating points of view. Those playing judge and jury obtain an experience in decision-making and assumption of responsibility.

The court trial scene is a provocative one—mentally, emotionally, and theatrically.

Ideal Therapeutic Community

"I hate this place," 17-year-old Sherry mutters as she enters the drama therapy session on the adolescent unit of a psychiatric hospital. "And don't make me do anything, I've had enough!"

I observe with dismay the immediate effect her entrance has on the other group members, who just minutes earlier had appeared ready for action. Now, sinking into their chairs, they chime in: "Yeah, this place sucks," "I don't want to do anything either, I'm sick of being told what to do."

Sherry is now quietly sulking. Her resistance appears to be emanating from a sense of helplessness and hopelessness. I ask her what she despises most about the hospital. She spurts out a series of criticisms. I then ask her in what kind of place she would rather be. She responds, "It wouldn't be anything like this place." I ask her to describe what it would be like. Before long, Sherry, along with the group, is inventing her ideal version of an adolescent therapeutic community.

It is a natural step to appoint her director of the new facility, marking the shift from discussion to dramatic enactment. She selects her staff from among clients in the group. Some clients and a participating staff member play the roles of newly admitted patients entering from their chaotic worlds—disoriented, hostile, on drugs. The director and her staff, along with the support of teens who have been in the program for some time, skillfully handle each individual. Sherry's affect changes remarkably as she carries out this engaging scene.

When the enactment ends, Sherry is able to speak about the depression and hopelessness she has been experiencing, and the ways in which she might take some charge of her life during her remaining weeks in the hospital as well as after being discharged. A degree of distance and perspective, as well as a sense of hope, is apparent (Emunah, 1985).

The most significant therapeutic aspect to *Ideal Therapeutic Community* is the empowerment it offers. The creation and dramatization enable clients who have lost a sense of control over their environments and their lives to experience being in control, and this control becomes symbolic of internal self-mastery. Secondary gains include an experience of creative achievement and an expanded sense of possibility and hopefulness regarding the future. *Ideal Therapeutic Community* also helps the group to work collaboratively. Like *Court Trial,* there are many subscenes within the larger enactment and the activity typically lasts an entire session. A particular group may want to enact various components of the therapeutic community or trace one client's experience from initial intake to discharge three months later. *Family Therapy* may be also be incorporated into the enactment.

VARIATIONS

Ideal Planet

Like *Ideal Therapeutic Community, Ideal Planet* grew out of a spontaneous occurrence. One day I overheard some members of my adult day treatment group joke about an imaginary planet in which "life was much better." When the session began, I asked them if they were willing to talk about the planet. They agreed. The planet's identity developed gradually, via the interview format. I was moved by their creation: This group of clients, most of whom had been physically and sexually abused as children and many of whom were now self-abusers, devised a planet in which "there is no crime or violence, nor any such thing as hurting others or yourself, nor child abuse—toward others or toward yourself." When I asked whether people on Glockenspiegal (the apparent name of the planet) were ever sad or depressed, I was told that they were, but that there was a sweetness to the sadness, that people let their tears flow freely, that emotion was expressed outwardly rather than turned inward against oneself. The transition from discussion to enactment occurred when I suggested that some earth people could be given a tour of the planet. The resulting tour was elaborate and included taking the visitors through the Glockenspiegalites' special cleansing process, in which one identifies and is rinsed of all negative feelings.

Ideal Therapeutic Community and *Ideal Planet* offer the group temporary respite, albeit in the realm of the imagination, from the trials of the real world. Just as in actual travel to foreign lands, the return home can be difficult. The transition from *Ideal Therapeutic Community* and *Ideal Planet* to the conclusion of the session, at which point clients are again confronted with their real situations, is critical. It is best to end with a discussion that reviews the experience and explores aspects of the invented community/planet that can be taken back to, or incorporated into, one's real life.

Let's Make a Play

The leader begins by simply asking the group, "What would you like to make a play about?" This technique is based on the approach of Dorothy

Heathcote (Wagner, 1976), a British expert in drama-in-education. Heathcote elicits the interests and concerns of the group and then helps them to structure this material dramatically. At times, the content revolves around a particular topic; for example, in a history class, one may have the group devise a play about the Civil War. (The word play here does not imply a performed event in front of an outside audience, though it does imply a developed sequence of scenes which are performed by the group for the group; everyone is involved in the action/acting concurrently.) Heathcote guides the initial discussion about the play by asking probing and thought-provoking questions. The central objectives are to facilitate a deep level of reflection and under- standing with regard to significant issues, to promote empathy and a capacity to relate external events to one's internal experience, and to provide an experience of creativity, mastery, and collaboration. In *Let's Make a Play,* which is geared toward drama therapy rather than drama-in-education, the topics are never prescribed; they are open to whatever social or personal concerns emerge from a particular group.

Unlike most other techniques, *Let's Make a Play* begins without any presuppositions on the part of the leader. It needs no warm-up nor follow-up; it does not rely on a smooth transition from earlier (or to subsequent) tech- niques. It is a full activity in and of itself, involving an entire session. *Let's Make a Play* is most effective with an established group that has developed a positive association to drama/acting, is not overly reliant on the leader for ideas, and is eager to get to the action rather than engage in more structured theatre games. The group is given a great deal of responsibility, with the reward of creating something out of nothing. At first, there is a void (like being confronted by an empty canvas), but gradually an idea emerges, however small, and by the end of the session this idea has blossomed into a mini-play.

Both process and product are significant. The leader facilitates the group's decision-making, choice of roles and development of these roles, and discovery of alternative courses of action within the play. The preliminary discussion can be elaborate, with the plot and characters delineated prior to the enactment, though generally discussion and enactment are interwoven: The discussion leads to enactment, and the ensuing enactment is intermit- tently interrupted (generally by leader) so that the group can step back from the action, reflect on it, and make decisions about it. If a finalized product seems to be important to the group's sense of achievement, video playback can be used. The finalized scenes are recorded (and any discussion or "rehearsal" omitted from the recording), allowing the group at the end of the session to become audience to its own creative work. A great deal of struc- turing and facilitation is generally needed for a group to succeed in all of these tasks within a single session.

Congratulations

I learned this game from Inter-Action, a community arts organization in London. One person leaves the room. The group decides on something (imaginary) that just happened to that person. Often this is something positive that warrants congratulations, such as winning the lottery or receiving an award, though it need not be. When the person returns, the group responds to her in accordance with the contrived situation, but without making the situation explicit. The protagonist plays along (as if in a scene in which she is aware of what happened), all the while trying (inwardly) to determine what has happened. Examples of situations drawn from one group of hospitalized teenage girls are: being pregnant, being suspended from the drama therapy group, getting a part in a play in the community, separating from a boyfriend. Comments in the first round dealing with pregnancy included, "So, how do you feel," "What are you going to do about it" and "Have you told your parents?" Some added personal notes, as "It happened to me too, I was really shocked." It is uncanny how fitting the responses of the protagonists in *Congratulations* generally are, long before they have any clear notion about what is being discussed.

Congratulations requires the protagonist to let go of preconceptions, to tolerate ambiguity and uncertainty, and to be responsive to the comments and tone of the group. The group needs to be somewhat sophisticated verbally, or at least to have the capacity for subtlety and nuance. It is important, too, that the group make choices sensitively; the leader ensures that situations that protagonists may find offensive or distressing are not used. In some groups, the choices are always positive (winning a contest, getting a job, receiving word that one will soon be discharged from the hospital, etc.), though still often related in some way to the protagonist's real life. Group members that have clear boundaries between role and self usually enjoy playing out all kinds of possibilities, even ones that are "unpleasant." *Congratulations* affords people the opportunity to live out, in the imaginary realm, a specific life event. Many people sustain the game even after they are clearly aware of the decided-upon situation as a way of prolonging the experience of *being in* this situation.

SELF-REVELATION

Sculpting and Self-Sculptures

Sculpting involves having a client set up a tableau by placing other members of the group in particular positions. A typical usage of *Sculpting* is the representation of one's family of origin.* Attention is paid not only to the positioning of each person, but to the positioning of each person in relationship to every other person in the tableau. The sculpture of one adolescent girl, for example, included a father who was placed in the far corner of the stage area, with his back turned away from the others. Her brother was curled up in the other corner with one hand holding a bottle and the other covering his eyes. Her mother was placed standing on a chair, towering over her daughter (my client)—with one arm reaching over to hold the daughter and the other hand poking her in a punitive fashion. The daughter was placed cowering just beneath the mother, but with her arms reaching outward, as if grasping for freedom. Such telling and evocative sculptures are not uncommon. In family therapy, each member of the family can create a sculpture, thereby identifying and communicating his or her perception of the family dynamics.

An adaptation of the familiar technique of *Sculpting* is *Self-Sculptures,* one of my most frequently used self-revelatory techniques. One person is asked to sculpt or mold others to represent various aspects of herself. The technique has a number of developmental stages, though each one stands on its own, and the therapist can stop at any point:

1) The protagonist selects three others in the group to represent significant parts of herself. (The number of selected others can also be open-ended.) She physically maneuvers each one, placing the person in a particular posture and position. A further level of complexity is added when the protagonist places the three parts in relation to each other, e.g., a psychically dominant part may be placed in front of, or blocking, the others.

2) Once the sculpture is complete, the protagonist is asked to stand behind each part and to verbally articulate something about that part, in first person. She begins with, "I'm the part of (name of person) that . . ." e.g., "I'm the part of Diane that is very vulnerable and easily gets hurt."

3) The sculpture "comes alive," meaning that each person embodies— in movement or gesture, sound or word—the part of the protagonist s/he represents. The protagonist can also orchestrate the enactment, directing each part in turn, as a conductor. After a few minutes, the mini-scene is frozen in action, becoming a sculpture once again. The direction to come alive and then freeze is given by the protagonist; in this way she has control over the duration of the scene. If the scene is too painful or overwhelming to witness, she can quickly freeze it. The freezing of the scene can also be used as a

---

*Virginia Satir uses this technique with families, calling it *Family Sculpture* (1988). The technique has also been referred to as *Statue Building* (Seabourne, 1963), and in psychodrama as *Action Sociogram* (Blatner, 1988b).

"pause," at which time the protagonist reflects on what she has created and modifies or redirects the actors as a way of refining the representation of her internal self-image. Sometimes there are several such rounds of refinement, until the protagonist/director exclaims, "That's exactly how I feel!"

4) The protagonist is asked to take over one of the roles. After some time, she may be asked to take over a different role, until she has embodied each part. The last role is usually the most emotionally challenging and intense; this is the role the protagonist intentionally avoided playing earlier.

At this point, the drama therapist may intervene in various ways, according to the issues that are evoked. Possible interventions include directing the protagonist to: 1) step outside of the scene and make revisions that symbolize her hopes for inner change or psychic integration (sometimes entailing the addition of a new part); 2) address each of the parts (from the vantage point of her self-observing ego—the part of her that can witness and direct her internal self)—towards the goal of self-acceptance; 3) focus on two parts only, thereby facilitating the examination of the dynamics between these parts.

Whether or not all of the above stages are incorporated depends partly on the depth and complexity of the sculpture that is presented. A sculpture depicting more surface aspects to the self might be best left at that. There is usually an increasing degree of self-revelation in the sculptures as the session progresses. The therapist should consider waiting until an emotionally evocative sculpture (that clearly touches many group members) is presented before developing a single person's scene. This also gives more members of the group the opportunity to create a sculpture. The depictions of the self, however simple and brief, are always interesting to witness and members of cohesive groups are usually fascinated to see the artistic, dramatic manifestation of aspects of their peers, not only aspects with which they are familiar but also aspects which come as a surprise. An emphasis on group members' perceptions of each other could lead to a game in which the group tries to identify which person (and which aspect of that person) is being represented by a given sculpture. Generally, however, the session spirals toward developed, individualized, psychodramatic scenework, rather than accentuating group interaction.

Self-Sculptures is best preceded by an exercise that familiarizes clients with people-sculpting and with the format of sculpting three people who then "come alive." As with all self-revelatory techniques, clients can more easily enter emotional territory if they are not distracted by complicated instructions. A recommended warm-up to *Self-Sculptures* is *Partner Sculpting,* followed by *Sculpting a Scene* (see p. 157). Progressing from *Sculpting a Scene* to the more personal domain, one person is asked to mold three people as three emotions that are particularly relevant to her at this time in her life. From this point, the group will be fully prepared to engage in *Self-Sculptures.*

Self-Sculpture scenes are typically poetic, poignant, and emotional, with touches of humor. An aesthetic quality emerges as the scenes are developed, paving the way to *Self-Revelatory Performance* (see p. 224); indeed, *Self-Sculptures* is an excellent technique to use during the session/s preceding *Self-Revelatory Performance. Self-Sculptures* facilitates the transition from Phases Three (Role Play) to Four (Culminating Enactment) by encouraging symbolic as opposed to concrete enactment and prompting dramatizations that deal with internal struggles and the relationship one has with oneself. *Self-Sculptures* should be used only at a time when group members know one another well, not only because of the self-revelation it entails, but because the auxiliaries' role playing requires a keen understanding of the protagonist's psychological dynamics and dilemmas.

The therapist's creativity in directing *Self-Sculpture* leads to new variations of the technique. The final sculpture in one session contained three easily identifiable parts. After the protagonist played each of the parts herself, I asked everyone in the group to join the scene, becoming any one of the three parts they wished. The individually focused session thus culminated in a very lively and energetic group scene. In another session, a sculptress who presented surface aspects of herself (though the session had moved to a deeper level) was asked to add a "part beneath each part." The initial representations became the protectors of the more vulnerable parts that lay underneath. Collectively and intuitively, the six actors physically and vocally improvised the complex internal interactions. In yet another session (which is discussed at the end of Chapter 4), a client molded *everyone* in the group, giving tangible form to the multitude of complex and intense feelings that were evoked by the news of a neighbor's diagnosis with AIDS. *Self-Sculptures* have also led to verbal scenes in which various parts of oneself convene for a meeting to discuss the dynamics of their interrelationship.

Self-Masks

Blank masks are distributed. Simple paper or cardboard cut into the shape of a face, with holes for the eyes and string on the sides (so that the mask can be worn), can be used. The clients are asked to fill in the mask with their own self-portrait. The portraits can be abstract and expressionistic, revealing self-image rather than attempting to replicate external features. Various media are made available to encourage free artistic rein; clients may draw, paint, make collages, adorn the mask with objects, etc. This use of masks facilitates self-revelation, as opposed to the emotional expression facilitated by the use of pre-existing masks (see *Masks and Mime*, p. 156).

The completed masks are set in a row on display. A volunteer walks up to the row of masks, selecting one mask that particularly intrigues him. He addresses that mask, asking it questions or making comments. The person to whom the mask belongs responds, in first person, as the mask. It is important that the interviewer continue to look at (and relate to) the mask rather than face the person; this distance frees the creator of the mask to disclose more, under the protective guise of the mask-role, and enables the mask to come alive as a kind of independent character.

Self-Masks bridges the gap between art therapy and drama therapy. The artistic creations are usually fascinating to behold. Certain similarities often exist between the masks within a particular group. The masks of numerous clients with psychotic diagnoses have contained third eyes and question marks. Many masks of survivors of abuse have had fiery red, thickly painted streaks, disclosing their rage. The dialogue between group member and mask often leads the creator of the mask to new insights. This verbally oriented activity can be followed by a physical one, in which clients wear their masks and move or dance accordingly, bringing into the session yet another creative arts therapy modality—dance therapy. One or several clients can perform a simple improvisation using movement and sound. As masks are inherently theatrical, little structure is needed. Alternatively, an interactive game can be played in which a mask is placed on one person in the group, without that person seeing which mask it is. He then has to guess which mask he is wearing, based on the way the group relates and responds to him.

Self-Masks can be modified in many different ways. The following are several examples of modifications: 1) Clients create two masks—one representing their social mask and the other representing a part of them that others rarely see. The latter can be made on the reverse side of the former, rather than using a separate blank mask. 2) Clients create several masks, representing various aspects to themselves. This variation can be nicely integrated with *Self-Sculptures.* 3) Instead of a self-portrait, clients create a mask of a hero, goddess, or powerful being (often of a mythical or spiritual nature), which they honor and hope to internalize. 4) Rather than using paper or cardboard, a gauze mask of the person's actual face is made. Gauze is cut into strips, moistened with warm water, and layered on the person's face (which has been coated with petroleum jelly). The layers are added one at a time, once the previous layer has dried. Space is left for nostrils, mouth, and, if the person wishes, eyes. This process, usually conducted in pairs, requires trust and a tolerance for touch. The final imprints of the persons' faces are then painted or decorated.

Establish the Relationship

In this technique developed by Spolin (as *Who Game*), player A is seated in the stage area. Player B enters with a predetermined role and a clearly defined relationship to A. By the way B interacts, both verbally and nonverbally, A must ascertain his role, all the while playing along in the scene as though he knows.

In adapting the *Who Game* to drama therapy, the leader begins by assigning the role to B (often by whispering it or taking the person out of the room for a moment to secretly tell her). Familiar relationships are emphasized: Adolescents, for example, may be told that the person in the chair (A) is their teenage son, or parent, or counselor. Suggestions that lead to very entertaining scenes may be given: For example, in a group of adults, B is told that A is a blind date whose personal ad she responded to and whom she is now meeting at a cafe. Therapy scenes (usually with B entering as the therapist) are invariably funny and telling. After some time, the leader stops assigning roles and members devise their own ideas.

Establish the Relationship facilitates active listening. The A player is challenged to respond to all the minute cues he receives, to use his intuition but to be wary of any preconceptions and projections that might steer him in the wrong direction. *Establish the Relationship* works best with people who are able to tolerate ambiguity and uncertainty (as A needs to play along even before he has any idea of the situation he is in) and are easily capable of subtlety and nuance (as it is important that B not make her role immediately obvious)—the same qualities referred to under *Congratulations*. *Establish the Relationship* is placed under the *Self-Revelation* category because it invites reflection about the dynamics in relationships and because it is an effective warm-up to a more explicitly personal technique, *Person in Your Life*.

Person in Your Life

Person in Your Life is a therapeutically-geared adaptation of the more dramatically oriented Spolin technique, *Establish the Relationship* or *Who Game*. Following the same format as *Establish the Relationship*, B enters the scene with a particular role in mind, except in this technique the role is based on a particular relationship in his real life. The person seated in room, A, assumes the role of the person who enters, though still waiting for cues regarding the relationship that is being played out. For example, John sits in the stage area. Anthony enters snarling, "You know I really can't understand you. There you are, as usual just sitting, accomplishing nothing." John knows that he is playing Anthony, though he is not yet aware of who Anthony is playing. He responds quietly, "I'm not just sitting, I'm thinking. And you know, I wish you could understand me." Gradually, it becomes evident that Anthony is playing his father, berating his son (Anthony, played by John) for not being more professionally successful.

Person in Your Life usually entails a role reversal, so that the person who entered the scene has the opportunity of responding as himself to the relationship that he initiated. In the above example, Anthony switches to playing himself, revealing his reactions to his father's disapproval. By now John has a clear idea as to how the role of father should be played. The resulting psychodramatic scene may be developed through the use of various therapeutic interventions (see Chapter 5).

Establish the Relationship is a good warm-up to *Person in Your Life* because it enables clients to become familiar with the format of the game, thereby reducing the confusion that is otherwise common at the onset of *Person in Your Life*. The degree of emotionality and self-disclosure in *Person in Your Life* is up to the person initiating his role; someone can choose to enter as someone as innocuous as his hair stylist. The activity will often begin with less personal scenarios (especially when it follows the more playful *Establish the Relationship*) but will spiral toward increasingly personal and emotional scenarios, with clients eventually revealing the primary relationship dynamics with which they are currently grappling.

A simplified offshoot of *Person in Your Life*, which can serve as a warm-up or follow-up, is to have the group form pairs. One takes on the role of someone in his life; the other listens or asks questions. The focus is on having the person taking on the role speak about himself. That is, Mark plays his younger brother, Charles, talking about his feelings toward (and perception of) Mark. His partner, Sarah, simply listens as herself or she, too, may be in role (playing, for example, her husband, Ira, talking about Sarah). The roles are explicit from the onset and the conversation takes place with everyone seated. As a warm-up to *Person in Your Life*, this variation provides non-threatening practice in assuming the role of someone in one's life. As a follow-up, it offers clients an arena for further exploration of the relationships they enacted earlier and/or exploration of relationships that were evoked by scenes played out by others in the group.

Yourself at Different Ages

The client plays herself at different ages, past or future. For example, two clients in their late 20s both play themselves as they remember being at age 13. In an improvisational fashion, they meet for the first time, perhaps at a resort or summer camp, and engage in a conversation about their lives. Or a teenage client is interviewed, by the therapist or another group member, as himself at age six, at which time his parents got divorced. Or this same client is interviewed as himself five years from now, at age 21. The client projects an image of himself at this future date and from this vantage point reflects on his life five years ago, at which time he was struggling with adolescent issues. Future projection in *Yourself at Different Ages* is similar to *Reunion,* described in Chapter 8.

When projection into the future is used, the picture clients present of themselves can be very revealing, particularly of their level of motivation and hopefulness regarding change. I have found, most strikingly in work with emotionally disturbed or acting-out adolescents, that the clients who embody positive roles as their future self (five years in the future, when they are young adults, is a good time period to use with adolescents) are usually those who are beginning to make significant strides in treatment and are willing to continue to work hard to further their emotional growth. Clients who portray themselves as being in the same place or in worse shape (seemingly as a kind of joke within the scene) are often those who are most overtly resistant to therapy and/or are hopeless about their situation. Those who create positive but very unrealistic portrayals, usually of a grandiose nature unconnected to their emotional selves (e.g., "I'm now a millionaire"), are covertly resistant to change. These parallels are not formulas or diagnostic categories, but rather observations; in interpreting any role, the therapist is guided by many different factors, as discussed in Part One.

When regression into the past is used, it is important that clients be properly prepared, as age regression is not easy to achieve dramatically. As a warm-up, the entire group can be asked to simultaneously play themselves at a particular age. Or in pairs, each person can have a turn being interviewed as himself at a given age. A more theatrically oriented warm-up is Spolin's *How Old Am I,* in which participants are given slips of paper indicating a particular age (or choose the age themselves), and then nonverbally convey this age as they improvise waiting at a bus-stop.

Yourself at Different Ages revives memories of the past and enables emotions and sensations that one experienced at particular times in one's life to be relived. It can easily be incorporated into individual verbal therapy. When the client refers to herself at a certain time in the past, the therapist simply asks her to speak as herself at that age; when she refers to the future, the therapist suggests she speak as herself at that future time, thereby making the projection more vivid. *Yourself at Different Ages* is similar to *Playing with Time,* an intervention (described in Chapter 5) that may be incorporated in the direction and development of any improvisational scene.

A more complex and psychodramatic variation of *Yourself at Different*

Ages is for someone in the group to take over the role that was being played (of a fellow group member at a particular age), while the original person returns to herself in the present, addressing this earlier (or future) self. An example can be found in Chapter 3, in the story of Ivan.

Becoming Your Own Therapist

"I feel I can't go on any longer." These words are spoken by Ariana, a severely depressed 20-year-old woman. "Life is just too unfair, too painful. And I'm tired of feeling pain."

I gently ask her to pick someone in the group to whom she can speak these feelings directly. She motions to Michelle, a person with whom she feels affinity. Michelle sits next to her and listens. "I feel my past is just too full of ugliness. And I can't wipe it out. And there's nothing good enough in my life now to make up for all I've been through. Plus today I found out my halfway house is going to close down. It's too much to have to deal with. I'm having feelings again of wanting to just end it all."

Michelle continues to listen empathically. I invite members of the group to stand at Ariana's side and Double for her, as a way of offering support and acknowledgment, as well as encouraging further expression. Two people enter the scene and soon a third joins. Ariana now seems less self-conscious and her words are spoken with greater intensity and affect. After some time, the scene reaches an impasse. I ask Ariana and Michelle to switch roles.

I quietly indicate to Ariana that she is now in the role of her ideal (version of a) therapist. She looks anxious for a moment, but Michelle's words immediately grab her full attention. "I've been through about all I can take. The pain I feel is too overwhelming," Michelle says, astutely replicating Ariana's tone and affect, at the same time bringing to the words her own lived experience. Ariana listens. She has no response, but is clearly moved to witness her state of mind played back to her. The playback implies that she has been heard and understood. Perhaps Michelle has even been in this place herself, for real.

Increasingly moved by the mirror-image of herself and engaged by the task inherent in her role, Ariana eventually finds words. "I know how hard it is. It isn't fair. And it may never be easy. But all you have been through has also made you strong. You've made it this far. And if you stop now you may miss out on what could turn out to be the better half of your life." Michelle listens intently, introjecting comments that further challenge Ariana. I end the scene just after Ariana says, "Don't give up now. I'm with you. Come to me, and I will help you, always, to go on."

Becoming Your Own Therapist enables the client to reach within herself for reserves of strength and self-nurturance. In the role of therapist, the client often discovers her own answers and manifests perspective, hopefulness, or wisdom that previously seemed beyond her domain. Finding these resources within herself and hearing her own voice deliver the words of encouragement or advice have far more impact than hearing another person tell her the same thing. Ownership of the therapist role (as a part of oneself) generally occurs implicitly, though at times this ownership is fairly explicit, as evidenced by Ariana's last lines above.

Becoming Your Own Therapist is often used as an intervention in the scenes of Phases Three (Role Play) and Four (Culminating Enactment), and overlaps with the therapeutic objective of *Introducing an Internal Nurturing Parent,* described in Chapter 5. It is best used with clients who are capable of expressing and tolerating complexity and ambiguity; otherwise, the therapist role risks being played in a superficial manner, involving advice-giving and forced positivism.

The role of a best friend, wise older person, or spiritual guide can be used in place of the role of therapist, depending on which image will be most facilitative to a particular client. In the culminating scene of Christine's therapy, described in Chapter 3, the client is asked simply to become "an adult trying to help." In some cases, following a psychodramatic scene about a childhood experience, the client is asked to become himself in the present day and to tend to the child he was with the adult strengths he now possesses, as described in the story of Harold in Chapter 5.

Magic Shop

Magic Shop is a well-known and very useful psychodramatic technique. The group members are invited to come, one at a time, to a magic shop in which they can purchase human qualities. The shopkeeper is often played by the therapist, at least initially, though the role can also be assumed by a member of the group. The shopkeeper has an important function: She engages each customer in a dialogue about the desired quality, in an attempt to help the customer achieve clarity and insight. As money is unacceptable, the customer and shopkeeper must find the appropriate remuneration for the purchase. Remuneration is usually in the form of qualities (or facets of the self) that need to be relinquished in order for the purchased item to be truly effective, or positive qualities that the store wishes to stock, and with which the customer is sufficiently endowed that he can afford to surrender some of that quality.

The shopkeeper may need to first help the customer become more specific regarding his purchase. The following dialogue is an example of the first part of a negotiation:

Customer: Well, finally I made it to this magic shop. I've heard so much about it. What I want is love.

Shopkeeper: Love! Well, that's a very popular request in our store. But we've got hundreds of kinds of love. What sort are you looking for?

Customer: I want to feel like people really care for me.

Shopkeeper: You don't feel that people care for you?

Customer: I don't really believe them if they say they do. I don't feel I deserve to be cared for.

Shopkeeper: What would help you to feel deserving?

Customer: I guess to feel I'm worth it. That I'm a worthwhile person. Maybe what I really need is that, worth.

Shopkeeper: Well, we carry just that, self-worth.

Customer: Oh good. That's what I want. Give me a lot.

Shopkeeper: I can make you a special blend of self-worth. What ingredients should I sprinkle in? *(begins pantomiming the preparation)*

Customer: Can you put in a little self-esteem? I'm a little low on that. I guess I really don't love myself very much . . . do you, carry, uh, self-love?

Shopkeeper: Ah, I can certainly blend in some self-love and sprinkle in for you some self-esteem. This will be a first step to feeling the care and love other people have for you.

Customer: Thank you. When can I start using it? *(reaches for package)*

Shopkeeper: Hold it! First, we have to make a deal. What are you going to give up for it?

Negotiations between shopkeeper and customer can be brief or extended. Although there is a range in magic shop barters from the mundane to the profound, it is important that some degree of poetic justice be achieved (Blatner, 1988b). I usually make the distinction between surrendering aspects of the self that "get in the way" of the desired quality and making a "donation" to the store of sought-after qualities; both are asked for. The first part of the barter is more insight-oriented; the latter part, the donation, helps the client identify within himself positive qualities. As the bartering can be a kind of mini-session of individual psychotherapy, I usually play the shopkeeper (especially when working with lower functioning groups), but call upon group members to become assistant shopkeepers as a way of actively involving them and creating a more collaborative process.

Magic Shop is most effective with groups that are capable of abstract thinking and that can remain engaged in an individually oriented activity. The tendency for *Magic Shop* to be very verbal and cognitive can be balanced by the inclusion of more dramatic elements, such as having the customer visualize and physicalize the surrendering of given qualities or aspects of himself, rather than simply verbally naming what is being surrendered. The establishment of a playful ambiance from the beginning enlivens the activity and stimulates the imagination. The shopkeeper can be an eccentric character, the store can be hidden deep within a forest necessitating an arduous trek on the part of the curious customer, and the store's stock of qualities can come in many different forms, such as lotions, powders, liquids, etc. Some psychodramatists emphasize the imaginative component of *Magic Shop*; Eva Leveton (1991), for example, has each person in the group create his own setting for the shop and has both shopkeeper and customer assume roles of mystical or nonhuman creatures, heightening the playful and symbolic nature of the activity.

I usually follow *Magic Shop* with the enactment of scenes in which the client must make use of his purchase (not necessarily in the same session). The client refers to the purchase in the enactment. For example, a client who purchased assertiveness is placed in a dramatic situation that requires assertive action. He begins by taking out his purchased potion and rubbing it on. Fortified, he confronts the situation at hand. The audience gets to see whether or not his purchase has worked! This enactment helps bridge the gap from the abstract to the concrete, from the envisioning of inner change to the actualization of that change, albeit in the fictional mode.

Identifying the Conflict

"Move out," a chorus of people lined up in the right side of the room shout. "It's time. I'm 24. I gotta do it."

"Not yet, not now. At least living at home is familiar. I can't deal with any big change, I'm not strong enough," the group lined up on the other side of the room retorts, with equal conviction.

Gina, the depressed young woman (mentioned in Chapter 5, p. 113) whose personal dilemma is being enacted, sits in the center of the room. At first she wheels her chair toward the right, but then, equally affected by the second chorus, she moves to the left.

"I'm stronger than I think," someone on the right side says. Gina doesn't budge, but when someone else adds, "And I have lots of support now, I can get help dealing with the change," Gina inches in that direction.

"Help isn't good enough. I know I'm too scared." "It's too soon, it'd be like leaving childhood behind. I can't do that. There's too much I still need." Gina spontaneously wheels halfway across the room toward the people whose words have mirrored her feelings.

"The opportunity is now, with Sandy needing a roommate. I've been dealing with this issue of moving out for a long time. Now it's time to act." "To move on." "To take a risk." Many people in this group are speaking enthusiastically at once. Then someone interjects, "Besides, what I still need emotionally I may wait for forever in my mother's home and never get." Almost as though propelled on its own, Gina's chair moves straight to the person who has spoken these last words.

In *Identifying the Conflict,* a person sits in a chair (preferably one with wheels) in the center of room and presents a conflict with which she is currently grappling. Once the two basic sides of the conflict are identified, all members of the group join, choosing the side they wish to play out (usually the one they most relate to). The two groups stand on either side of the protagonist at equal distance from her. The protagonist talks about the dilemma in some more detail, giving clues to the two groups about their forthcoming tactics.

Identifying the Conflict is set up as a kind of competition, with each group trying to seduce the protagonist to its side of the room. The means of seduction is the voicing of thoughts and feelings that reflect those of the protagonist. (The leader may need to orchestrate the vocalizations, so that each group speaks, chorus-style, in turn.) The protagonist physically moves in the direction of each group, to a small or large degree, in accordance with how true the words ring. The exercise ends when the protagonist is completely on one side or the other.

The protagonist gains clarity throughout this process, via the resounding of the many aspects to, and ramifications of, her conflict, as well as the witnessing of her own spontaneous responses. The way in which she moves her chair is often reflective of her way of dealing with the conflict: Some protagonists remain in the center for a long time, with little movement toward either side; some make great strides in both directions, swayed by each argument, and bringing about suspense with regard to which side she will end up on; others inch gradually but steadily toward one side. The bombardment of input can be intense, but it is this intensity that helps the protagonist make the transition from a cognitive analysis of her conflict to a heightened awareness of her emotional and intuitive responses. When the round has ended, the group can review the process by having the protagonist reflect on the remarks that were particularly significant.

Identifying the Conflict can be preceded by a physical game that represents being torn in two directions: One person is literally tugged by two people who stand on either side. After experiencing this tugging, the person in the center identifies a conflict and offers some lines to both sides. The pulling begins again, this time with words added. Each party struggles to get the protagonist to her side.

Identifying the Conflict is best followed by scenes revolving around the decision that was made within the exercise. In the example above, the client,

Gina, ended up on the side of moving out of her mother's home. She was then directed to enact a scene in which she tells a friend of her decision. Stating after this scene that, "It felt good," she was asked to play another scene, taking place four months in the future, in which she and her roommate, Sandy, are cooking dinner together. These enactments afforded Gina the opportunity of *previewing* the reactions she may have after making a given choice. Sometimes clients will enact both decisions as a way of "living them out," in the hope of gaining clarity about their inner desires. Much of the difficulty in decision-making stems from the fear of the unknown. Dramatic enactment cannot help predict the future, but it can provide a rare opportunity to preview, in action, potential responses to our life decisions.

Self-Revelatory Performance

In what I refer to as *Self-Revelatory Performance*, members of the group transform personal material into theatrical creations. The aesthetic component is primary rather than secondary and the final scenes (which are, in a sense, *products,* compared to the process-oriented improvisations that typically occur in the drama therapy session) are performed within a clearly established *theatrical space*. The performance may be simply in front of the group or to an outside audience, as will be described in Part III.

Self-Revelatory Performance is distinguished from autobiographical theatre in that in addition to being based on one's real life, it presents issues whose exposure demands a high level of risk-taking, partly because they are current issues, rather than past issues which have already been resolved. Autobiographical theatre, for example, can involve storytelling about past adventures (à la Spalding Gray) without being intensely intimate or emotionally on-the-line, whereas *Self-Revelatory Performance* is always on the emotional edge.

The issues dealt with in *Self-Revelatory Performance* generally emerge from the drama therapy process the client has been through thus far; the performed scene may be an outgrowth or extension of a technique, improvisational scene, or *culminating scene* that has taken place in the group. *Self-Revelatory Performance* takes the subject matter further, exploring it in greater depth via the creative process and product.

The process of creation is an evolutionary one; the work develops gradually, over a period of time. This process generally involves working on one's own, outside of the group. The dramatic/therapeutic material is experimented with, molded, edited and refined. Although the final scene may be improvisational rather than scripted, it is structured, rehearsed, and timed, with the final line or moment set in advance. The client confronts many choices during the process of creation, in terms of how best to articulate the issues and to respond to them. The increased emphasis on aesthetics intensifies the therapeutic process: The process of creating the piece entails discovering and drawing from inner resources, giving form to feeling, communicating nuance and complexity, crystallizing and clarifying issues, and achieving a powerful sense of self-mastery and achievement.

Even when the performance is simply in front of one's own group, which is the most common use of *Self-Revelatory Performance*, a heightened sense of theatricality exists. Theatrical lighting is set up and a formalized *sacred space* is created. Each person's scene is performed, one after the other, interrupted only by applause after each scene. The scenes are diverse, but a sense of collective creation invariably emerges. The performance of all group members' scenes in the same (extended) session fosters the intimate ambiance in which inner lives are shared.

New self-disclosures in the context of the scenes are common. As in ritual purging ceremonies of ancient cultures, clients often have a powerfully cathartic experience. Many experience forgiveness, a deeper level of acceptance, and relief—as though freed of a heavy burden. There is a special intensity to the applause that follows each scene; it is an acknowledgement of both the product and the person.

It is important that the scene contain an element of movement or transition or transformation, rather than being a static replication of reality. The audience not only sees the actor's world, which is communicated theatrically, but watches the actor struggle with, or come to grips with, this world. The transition or transformation may involve new forms of expression, coping mechanisms, insights, or perspectives. The issue must be current so that there is an immediacy to this transformation; this immediacy is theatrically compelling and at times riveting. The creation of the scene itself and the transition contained within it imply a kind of transcendence, which the audience witnesses and applauds. The scene is often a step ahead of the client/actor's real life—that is, the transcendence may not have been experienced yet in reality, but the creation and performance of the scene bring the person in closer contact with the actualization of this transcendence in real life.

Theatrical styles and forms vary greatly in *Self-Revelatory Performance*. Ideally, the selected form reflects not only the person's affinity and skill but the particular issue. Some clients confront the audience with stark monologue, others use the distance of masks or puppets; some reenact realistic scenes (with group members playing auxiliary roles), others tell their story via metaphor. A student in a drama therapy course I teach performed a dream-like sequence of free-association images that were repeatedly transformed, giving the audience a peek into his inner world. Another student played the roles of both contestant and host on a television game show, "The Game of Life." In the process of answering the host's questions, which were asked in a lighthearted, commercial fashion, she revealed startling and harsh facts about her background. Environmental pieces, in which the audience is taken to a specific site that relates symbolically to the content of the scene or evokes a particular mood, have been used. One student's performance, dealing with her fluctuating "up and down" states of mind, took place in an elevator, with the audience watching from the hall stairway. The closing of the elevator doors provided a perfect ending to the scene. Another student, grappling with body-image issues, utilized the ladies' bathroom as her stage set. Much of the performance was viewed through mirrors (Emunah, 1989).

A modified version of *Self-Revelatory Performance* is for participants to create their scenes during the session, rather than developing and rehearsing the scenes over a period of time on their own. This modification is effective in brief, intensive workshops. Various props, instruments, music tapes, fabrics, masks, etc., are made available, and participants are asked to spend about 45 minutes—either individually or in small groups—developing a dramatic piece about an issue that surfaced during the course of the workshop. The scenes are then all performed in front of the group. Obviously, the resulting scenes are much simpler than scenes developed over time, but the heightening of the aesthetic component and the formation of a ritualistic theatrical space can nonetheless be experienced.

Paving the way to *Self-Revelatory Performance* is critical, as the process of performing intensely personal scenes involves a great deal of risk-taking and courage. *Self-Revelatory Performance* should never be introduced prematurely. On the day of the performances, warm-up exercises are also very important. These warm-ups can entail trust exercises (such as *Nurturing Falls*), vocal exercises (such as *Voice Games*), and *Group Mirrors* in which feelings regarding the upcoming event are playfully acknowledged and expressed.

Self-Revelatory Performance is best followed by a simple ritual bringing the group together in celebration of its work and validation of the intensity and intimacy that have been experienced. Verbal discussion is rarely appropriate; a great deal has already been conveyed through the medium of theatre. The poetry, potency, and richness of this medium are often awesome, evoking a sense of the sacred and bringing the group to a kind of altered state of consciousness. It is best to sustain the magical power in the room rather than to diffuse it via "translation" into verbal language. At the following session, after everyone has had time to absorb and digest the experience, verbal discussion and processing are important. If the performances have been videotaped (which is recommended), subsequent sessions may involve the viewing of the tape in conjunction with further discussion; the integration of the multileveled experience of *Self-Revelatory Performance* occurs gradually, over a period of time.

Confronting Yourself on Video

A client sits in front of a TV monitor and confronts her own image.

"Look at you. You look so pathetic. Looking at you makes me feel like doing it again, cutting you and starving you."

Seven months later, the same client faces her image again on the TV monitor. "Your eyes look so vulnerable. I feel like holding this vulnerability. Looking at you and thinking of the things I've done to you makes me feel sad. But I'm not going to hurt you or abandon you again. *(long pause)* I know it's hard for you to believe me. But we're in this together now. And your face, my face, I see a kind of beauty I never noticed before."

Confronting Yourself on Video involves an intense and intimate encounter with oneself. The client is usually alone in the room. The video camera faces the client, allowing her to view her image on the TV monitor as she speaks. Feelings about oneself and issues of self-esteem generally surface. I devised this technique partly as a way of examining and documenting clients' changing images of themselves as treatment progressed. An example of *Confronting Yourself on Video* used in this context can found in Chapter 3, in the story of Christine. This technique should be used sparingly and cautiously; many clients will find it too disturbing or difficult.

A variation of *Confronting Yourself on Video* is to have the image recorded and then played back to the client.* As the client watches the playback, she responds to it, creating a kind of live dialogue with herself. The recorded section can be a particular aspect of herself. An example, drawn from a student's *Self-Revelatory Performance,* is a woman standing at the side of the TV. On the screen, the audience witnesses the highly negative and self-critical part of herself; at the same time the audience watches her, live, attempting to respond to the image rather than being "sucked up" by it. This variation can also be used with audiotape (the client makes a recording of an aspect of herself, and then responds to it live), as exemplified by Jamie's scene in Part III (p. 275). The interaction between video image (or audiotape recording) and live person is theatrically compelling and ideally suited to *Self-Revelatory Performance.*

---

*Drama therapists who have explored various usages of video in drama therapy include Landy (1986), Petitti (1989), and Dequine & Pearson-Davis (1983).

8

CLOSURE OF THE SESSION AND SERIES

The objectives for the techniques of the final portion of the session and the last phase of the treatment series revolve around: *giving and receiving, collective creativity, intergroup perceptions,* and *review and celebration.* Most of the techniques categorized under *giving and receiving* and *collective creativity* are geared toward the closure of sessions during all phases within the treatment series; many are particularly useful during Phases One (Dramatic Play) and Two (Scenework). *Collective creativity* is similar to *group collaboration,* a category in Chapter 7, in that the entire group is involved in play together. However, it is dissimilar in that the techniques listed under *group collaboration* are extended activities, most of which last an entire session (with the exception of *Congratulations*), whereas those under *collective creativity* are brief exercises (with the exception of *Theatre Ritual*), designed for a small portion of the session, generally the closure. The techniques categorized under *intergroup perceptions* are best used during the latter phases of the treatment series, when members know one another well. Most of the techniques under *review and celebration* are geared toward Phase Five (Dramatic Ritual) (at any point during the sessions of Phase Five).

GIVING AND RECEIVING

Hand-Squeeze

Of all the techniques in this book, *Hand-Squeeze* is probably the one I use the most often. It is simple and unifying, with a perfect balance of intimacy and playfulness. I find it an extremely effective way of ending the session, and in some series I incorporate it in ritualistic fashion at the closing of every session.

The group is seated in a circle on the floor, holding hands, eyes closed. The leader begins by passing a gentle hand-squeeze to the person next to her. As soon as this squeeze is felt, that person squeezes the next person's hand, and so on. After a couple of rounds, the leader softly says, "faster," challenging the group to pass the squeeze as quickly as possible. The rapid transmission of the squeeze through the circle brings about (and expresses) a sense of interconnectedness and life energy within the group. Many clients have described experiencing the passing of the hand-squeeze as a heartbeat or pulse of the group. To add a playful touch, the leader may send a hand-squeeze in the opposite direction, at the same time reminding people to keep the original squeeze going. With two squeezes simultaneously passed around the circle, concentration is heightened. The silence is usually broken by laughter, especially when someone gets two squeezes at once.

There are countless variations to *Hand-Squeeze*. In series in which *Hand-Squeeze* is used as a closing ritual to each session, variations to the theme can be introduced on a regular basis, or clients can be asked to invent new versions. For example, the squeeze can be passed by placing one's hand on the next person's far shoulder, thus transmitting a *Shoulder-Squeeze* rather than a *Hand-Squeeze*. More playful varieties include placing feet in the center and passing a foot tap, or placing hand to knee and passing a knee squeeze. Angela, a client whose scene is described in Chapter 5, devised the passing of a nudge: Participants sit closely, with the sides of their bodies in contact and, one at a time, each gently bumps her body against the next person. The challenge is to avoid falling over!

A variation that I initiated in recent years is for the original *Hand-Squeeze* to be followed by having the group inch closer together, still seated, forming a kind of huddle. Everyone grabs someone else's hand in the circle, but not the hand of the person next to her. There is a lot of reaching and stretching, sometimes straining; the close physical contact intensifies the feeling of intimacy and interconnection. Again with eyes closed, I begin by squeezing the hand I am holding. That person squeezes the hand she is holding, and so on. After a minute, the leader needs to check that everyone has received at least one squeeze because sometimes there is a closed circuit, neces-sitating starting over. This variation is best used with groups that have achieved a fairly high level of emotional closeness; it is important that the exercise reflect, at the same time that it heightens, a feeling already existent within the group.

To add a verbal component to *Hand-Squeeze*, participants may be asked to utter a word as they pass the squeeze to the next person. The word (or phrase or image) can be an expression of a feeling, or wish, or something about the session they particularly want to hold on to or take with them. It can also be a blessing they offer to the group.

Transforming the Object

This technique described by Spolin involves creating an object in pantomime and passing it to the next person in the circle, who handles the object and then transforms it into a different object, passing it on to the next person, and so on. (Drama therapist Bernie Warren [1984] uses the image of "magic clay" with which one molds objects, and then kneads the clay back into a ball.) *Transforming the Object* stimulates imagination and affords participants the experience of creating something out of nothing, which is the basis of all creative work.

VARIATIONS

The following are three variations of *Transforming the Object*. I find them most applicable in work with schizophrenics who have difficulty distinguishing between fantasy and reality, and for whom an exercise involving passing something that does not actually exist is at times disturbing. These variations are also effective in almost any group.

Transforming the real object

Rather than creating an object in pantomime, a real object is brought in and transformed. Each person uses the object in a different way. For example, a stick is passed around the circle. One person turns it into a stick shift in a car he is driving, the next turns it into a baton, the next turns it into a back-scratcher. Simple objects (e.g., balls, hats, and wigs), which are easily reminiscent of many different articles, help stimulate the imagination. The handling of a tangible object facilitates the creative process for clients who might have difficulty passing a totally imaginary object. *Transforming the real object* is empowering because it symbolizes that with imagination there are countless ways of perceiving (the world).

Transforming the newspaper

A newspaper is passed around the room. Each person uses or changes the newspaper in some fashion. Objects can be created, as in the above technique, though generally this variation is more free-associative and less concrete. Each person follows his impulse upon receiving the paper. For example, one person may tear out holes, the next may crumple the newspaper, the next rip it up. In one "high-functioning" group, someone burned the newspaper, but the next person made use of the ashes to paint her face, symbolizing the countering of destruction with transformation.

Passing the substance

This version is similar to the original *Transforming the Object* in that what is passed is totally imaginary, but some structure and concreteness is added.

A type of substance is identified and passed around the circle. For example, I may begin by saying (and showing) that *IT* is extremely hot. Each person passes the hot substance quickly to the next. After about one round, it is transformed by me or someone else in the group, perhaps to something freezing or heavy or sticky. This variation is the one I utilize the most because it engenders a greater level of sharing and interaction among the group (the substance is received and passed for some time rather than constantly being transformed) and because expression is heightened in response to the substances that are passed. Clients who manifest minimal affect will often become highly expressive and engaged, especially as they mime passing sticky or slimy substances (a favorite in groups). This version can easily be used as a warm-up to the original *Transforming the Object.*

Pass the Facial Expression

One person in the circle covers his face with his hands and emerges with a mask created out of his own face. The mask can be of a particular facial expression. He turns his head to the person next to him and pantomimes removing the mask and placing it on that person. That person immediately duplicates the facial expression and then passes the same expression/mask to the next person, and so on. A variation is for the person taking on the facial expression to do so via a brief process of *Mirroring;* both people maintain eye contact for a few moments, and once the person has accurately assumed the expression, the original person lets go of it. (With this variation, the panto-miming of the passing of a mask is not used.) The round is completed when the last person in the circle takes on the original facial expression. The next person then initiates the passing of a different facial expression, and so begins another round.

A warm-up to *Pass the Facial Expression* is for everyone to relax and exercise facial muscles for a few minutes. Then one person assumes a facial expression which the entire group instantly mirrors. This helps the group practice taking on another person's facial expression. It is best to emphasize capturing the tone and feeling of the expression, rather than focusing on mimicking the precise structure of the facial muscles.

Gifts in Mime

Sitting in a circle, each person in the group, one at a time, gives a gift to another member of the group. Names can be drawn from a hat or each person can select the person to whom she is making an offering. The gift is created and given in pantomime; money and practicality are of no concern!

The gifts may be material items that the person likes or needs (e.g., a scarf, skis, a car), metaphorical (e.g., a shawl to represent warmth and comfort, a bird to represent freedom), or a human quality (e.g., love, assertion, hope). Many gifts make references to particular scenes or themes from the group's journey together.

The person to whom the gift is given receives it in mime, demonstrating by her handling of the gift that she understands what has been proffered.

COLLECTIVE CREATIVITY

Magic Box

The use of *Magic Box,* a technique developed by Johnson (1986), is a means of symbolically *containing* what has taken place in the session. An imaginary box is brought to the center of the circle (often brought down from the ceiling or from some other designated part of the room where it is kept between sessions). Clients place in the box (or, earlier in the session, take out) emotions, experiences, sensations, insights, fears or wishes related to the session. These items are then stored, in safety, inside the magic box until the next session, at which time the box can be reopened.

Theatre Ritual

Theatre Ritual is not a technique but a process, in which there are innumerable possibilities. Particular rituals are devised to meet particular occasions or symbolically reflect relevant themes during the course of the series. The rituals are especially significant at the end of the series, when issues of separation and termination must be faced. *Theatre Ritual* helps clients to contain and express complex feelings by embodying these feelings in shared metaphor. The group may enact a burial, resurrection, bonfire, journey from entrapment to freedom, journey toward intimacy. Movement and sound, music and image are often incorporated. Typically, *Theatre Ritual* is collectively and improvisationally created by the group, though it can also be designed by the therapist or consciously preplanned by the client/s.

Because *Theatre Ritual* is so personalized and generally "free-flowing" (and involving images stemming from the unconscious), it cannot be delineated in greater specificity; leaders should use their imagination and creativity in facilitating this process.

Story-Building and Storytelling

In Spolin's *Story-Building* technique, the group leader orchestrates the telling of the story by pointing to different people in the group, who immediately pick up from where the last person left off. This requires participants to be quick-witted and spontaneous; when one person is stopped mid-sentence, the next person called upon must keep the story "flowing," continuing without missing a beat and without repeating the last word that was spoken. *Story-Building* is particularly entertaining when the players are also attentive to intonation, tonality, and expression. Many improvisational theatre companies utilize this technique in performances. It is recommended that *Story-Building* be conducted with the group standing in a cluster, as in *Emotional Orchestra*.

In *Storytelling*, one person begins to tell an original story. Whenever he decides to stop speaking, the next person in the circle takes over, continuing the story from where the first person left off. The last person in the circle ends the story. *Storytelling* is less pressured than *Story-Building*; each person decides for himself how long he wishes to speak and at what point he wants to stop. The content of the story can be totally open-ended or some initial direction can be given, such as a theme or type of story to be told (e.g., fairytale).

An alternate format to being seated in a circle is for the group to lie down in a circle, with heads in the center. Eyes can be closed; when the speaker wants to stop, he nudges or taps the person next to him, who immediately takes over.

Story-Building and Storytelling could also be categorized under Observation and Concentration (Beginning of the Session and Series) and under Group Collaboration (Mid-Session and Mid-Series). They are placed here because of their frequent use at the closure of sessions (during early phases of the series); like children's bedtime stories, these techniques can be utilized to promote relaxation and intimacy.

VARIATIONS

One-word-at-a-time

The group is asked to create a story or simply to carry on a conversation, with each person uttering only one word. For example: the first person says "We," the next says "are," the third says "a," and so forth. There is a kind of suspense to the development of the story, along with a great deal of amusement, especially when many adjectives are interjected. Groups sometimes need to be reminded to bring sentences to a close; closure of sentences helps sustain logical content. I often use this technique at the end of a session by asking the group to attempt to talk about itself (feelings, dynamics, hopes, etc.) in this fashion. This version of *Storytelling* should not be used with groups that have difficulty with sentence syntax or with careful listening. With all other groups, it is very effective.

A variation of *One-Word-at-a-Time* is *Dr. Know-It-All*. Three people assume the role of one character, a Dr. Know-It-All. The group asks the doctor questions (usually of a psychological or philosophical nature), to which he/they respond in the fashion of *One-Word-at-a-Time*. I have incorporated *Dr. Know-It-All* into live improvisational performances in which the audience asked the renowned doctor (comprised of three psychiatric patients) questions about mental health and about life!

Narrating and enacting a story

This variation is a technique designed by Spolin (which she calls *Story-Telling*), in which one person tells a story—either an existing story or an invented one. As he narrates, others in the group dramatize the story, primarily in mime but occasionally using dialogue. This version works well with children. As Spolin points out, it is best if the narrator allows the players some flexibility and spontaneity so that they are not merely parroting the story.

Although this technique is most applicable to early phases, I have also used it during Phases Three (Role Play) and Four (Culminating Enactment), with the narrator coming forth with a personal monologue about a significant life experience or event. The dramatists usually enact the story abstractly rather than literally, symbolizing, for example, underlying feelings or mood through movement. This variation is similar to *Playback.*

Playback

One person tells a real-life story, which several others then enact. The enactment may not be a literal translation; rather, the players attempt to capture the emotional essence of the person's story. This is a complex process called *Playback Theatre*—a powerful blend of psychodrama, drama therapy, and theatre developed by Jonathan Fox (in Schattner & Courtney, 1981). In live performances, Fox invites the audience to tell stories revolving around personal or social issues; these stories are then "played back" by his company of specially trained actors and musicians.*

Playback can be creatively applied to organizational development; an organization, institution, or community group can have its issues playfully dramatized and transformed!

---

*A number of Playback Theatre companies based on Fox's approach have been formed internationally.

Mutual storytelling

In *mutual storytelling,* a technique developed by psychiatrist Richard Gardner (1981) for work with children, the client invents a story, guided by the therapist's interviewing and questioning. At the conclusion of the child's story, the therapist tells a similar or parallel story, but one that incorporates a therapeutically oriented resolution and presents constructive alternatives.

Personal storytelling

A person tells a real-life story, but uses third person instead of first person. The increased distance (Landy, 1986) facilitates the process of disclosure and the capacity to achieve a kind of metalevel consciousness of life events and scripts.

Speaking of storytelling, Keen & Valley-Fox (1989) propose interrogating one's own life, as a way of creating a conscious autobiography rather than following an unconscious script. We don't really know our story until we tell it, they say, and it is through the telling that we begin to perceive our previously unconscious mythology and to take an active part in the shaping of our story from here on. In autobiographical storytelling, the narrator can be asked at a certain point to shift from third to first person as a means of decreasing the distance and experiencing a heightened emotional connectedness to the content of the story.

Storymaking

Much of the work of British drama therapist Alida Gersie (1991; Gersie & King, 1990) has focused on using existing myths and stories from around the world to help people deal with universal themes and struggles, such as death and loss, love, and hope. Sometimes Gersie tells a group a story and then has subgroups dramatize parts of the story that touched them. Or the initial story will be used to instigate the creation and enactment of personal stories. Gersie's work is not really a technique, but rather a complex series of drama therapy processes that she has thoughtfully developed over many years.

Fortunately/Unfortunately

In this technique of Butler and Allison (1978), a story is told around the circle, with each person beginning a new sentence alternating with the word "fortunately" and "unfortunately." Instead of a story, the group can be asked to simply carry on a conversation, perhaps about relevant group issues! *Fortunately/Unfortunately* is amusing and facilitates inventiveness and spontaneity. It can also have a cathartic effect, as it tends to reflect, in an exaggerated form, the constant ups and downs in life and the potential to view the same events from positive and negative perspectives.

Part of a Whole (*or* Machine)

In this technique described by Spolin, one person initiates the activity by becoming part of a large animate or inanimate moving object. As soon as someone else in the group is able to identify the object, he joins, becoming another part of the whole object. This continues until the entire group has joined. Players can begin by using movement only and later add sounds.

Part of a Whole is essentially the same as Spolin's well-known *Machine* exercise, in which one person starts a simple mechanical and repetitive movement. Others join, one at a time, adding parts to the machine in a complementary way. Movement and sound are incorporated in rhythmic fashion. Once the whole group is involved, the leader can increase the tempo of the machine, and then slow it down until it comes gradually to a halt; the halt can become the ending to the session.

A variation of *Part of a Whole* and *Machine* is to divide the group in half. Each subgroup creates a specific kind of machine or other inanimate object and then performs it for the other subgroup, which tries to identify it. Another variation, related to *Join the Scene,* is for participants to join a given scene, becoming either players in the interaction or *inanimate objects.* The inanimate objects can be collectively created; for example, two or three people may form one piece of furniture in the living room in which the scene takes place. These variations are less likely to be used at the end of a session than the original *Part of a Whole* or *Machine.*

To add an emotional component to these playful exercises, I have introduced an *Emotional Machine,* in which the machine manufactures given emotions.

Group Statue

Like *Part of a Whole, Group Statue* involves having everyone in the group join, one at a time, to collectively form one whole. In *Group Statue,* the whole is of a statue. Interesting abstract configurations can be constructed out of the many bodies. It is best to suggest that some parts be physically linked to other parts. To give the group feedback, the final statue can be photographed with an instamatic camera.

One variation is to begin in a circle. One person enters the center of the circle, putting herself into a frozen position. The next person can make one change to the center statue (i.e. to the person in the center), such as placing an arm in a different position. The following person can make another change. The third person joins the statue, putting herself in some position that relates to or complements the original person. This continues through the circle, with every third person becoming part of the statue.

Another variation is for the statue to come alive, making movements (and possibly sounds) for a brief moment, before freezing once again, into a slightly altered shape. The group leader can call out *move* and *freeze* a number of times in rhythmic fashion. Emotions or themes can also be called out to stimulate the formation and reformation of particular kinds of statues.

Group Poem

One person writes an opening line of an original poem on a piece of paper. She then folds the paper, so that the next person does not see what she has written. Each person in the group adds a line, folds the paper, and passes it to the next person in the circle. When everyone has contributed a line, the poem is read out loud and, collectively, the group decides upon a title. As a way of avoiding long waiting for one's turn, everyone in the group can begin a poem and then pass it along, so that at the end there are as many poems as people.

Group Poem works best when a particular theme is given or the first words of each line (except possibly the last line) are set. For example, the group leader states that the poem is to be about the emotional depth and growth that suffering engenders, or she asks everyone to begin the line with "When I look back. . ." When a group manifests pride in its creation, the leader can bring bring typed copies of the final poem to the following session.

Poetry therapists use numerous variations on *Group Poem,* as well as many related techniques.

INTERGROUP PERCEPTIONS

Poetic Associations

One person thinks of someone in the group. Everyone tries to guess who that person is by asking a question in this form: "If this person were a _____ , what would he/she be?" The blank can be any category, e.g., a fruit, an animal, a color, a season, a type of music, a car model, etc. The person answering the questions visualizes the individual she has selected, and responds according to her associations to and perceptions of that individual. After one or more rounds of questions, everyone makes her guess and the person who has been responding to the questions tells who it is.

Poetic Associations works best with a group of eight to 12 people who know each other well. Participants must be intuitive and capable of abstraction. Responses should reflect intangible perceptions rather than facts. For example, the response to "What kind of car would this person be?" may be "VW Bug" even though the person actually drives a Cadillac. It is fascinating to discover how people are perceived by others and how they perceive themselves. Sometimes it is obvious to the group who the person is; other times everyone has a different guess.

A creative challenge exists not only for the person responding to the questions but for the questioners. New categories are constantly invented, e.g., "If this person were a natural landscape...," "a fabric," "furniture," "a kind of shoe," "a facial feature," "a punctuation mark." Both questions and answers utilize the imagination and the results are often quite poetic. The responses can be recorded, abridged, and read aloud (e.g., river, turquoise, deer, dusk, semicolon...), serving as a gift to the person described. The game can easily be followed by the writing of poems using imagery and metaphor to further express perceptions members have of one another.

The idea for this game stems from my early childhood. My mother and I would "make up" foods or objects that particular relatives and friends reminded us of; we eventually had attributions for virtually everyone we knew. We never rationalized our responses (in fact any literal translation polluted the image); we just *sensed* that my aunt was fresh strawberries, my uncle a brown leather wallet, my cousin cornflakes. If we disagreed, we would reflect harder until we found an image that "clicked" for both of us. We played this game for years. I guess I never stopped.

True and False Statements

"I have two sisters, one older and one younger; all three of us work in professions connected in some way to healing."

"I have one brother, two years older than me, who is a brilliant plasma-physicist."

I speak these two statements with equal conviction. However, one of the statements is in reality true and the other is false. The listener attempts to guess which statement is true. (In the above example, the second one is true.) In a group setting, each person takes a turn presenting the two statements. The group members make their guesses based on either the content of the statements or the process—that is, the nonverbal language of the speaker. Some people, for example, may unwittingly avoid eye contact when telling the lie.

As participants choose their own statements, the game may evolve in a light and playful fashion or may become very intimate; major self-disclosures are sometimes made in the context of *True and False Statements.* The content of the statements may revolve around experiences in one's past, facts about one's family, or simply personal preferences. The two statements need not be related. Groups sometimes begin with light material (such as hobbies or favorite foods) and gradually progress to the more personal realm. Regardless of the level of disclosure, *True and False Statements* invariably leads participants to learn more about one another.

Most adolescent groups thoroughly enjoy *True and False Statements,* perhaps because the process of lying is often as familiar to them as that of truth-telling, and having this lying sanctioned brings relief. The structure of the game facilitates the sharing of secrets that teenagers may have yearned to disclose but either had not had the opportunity to or had been afraid of others' reactions. On the other hand, *True and False Statements* is not recommended for use with schizophrenic clients who have difficulty distinguishing between fantasy and reality (or lies and truth), as they may find the false statements disturbing and threatening.

Of all the techniques in this book, *True and False Statements* is the one I have most used outside of the professional setting for my own personal enjoyment! I find it a fascinating way of getting to know someone, especially at an early stage, when both parties know few facts about the other's life. The game affords the rare opportunity of testing initial impressions and examining perceptions, projections, and intuition. While this is most exciting at an early interaction with another, in group work it is best to play *True and False Statements* after the members have achieved some degree of familiarity with one another.

The process of speaking the false statement as though it were true gives participants a taste of the experience of *acting,* which involves, in Stanislavski's (1936) terms, the *magic if.* As one speaks the statement, one permits oneself to fully *imagine* (as opposed to *pretending*) that the statement is true, the same process that is used in playing a role or putting oneself in a fictional improvisational situation. When I speak the first statement above, I envision having the two sisters I never had in reality; I picture being a middle child. In this sense, *True and False Statements* is similar to *Introducing Yourself as Another* (p. 162). In both situations, the false statements (or fantasies) are often as revealing as the true ones.

Answer as Someone Else

The group sits in a circle, with one person in the center. The person in the center asks individuals in the group particular questions. However, the person being addressed does not respond; rather, the person to his right answers for him, saying what he thinks that person would say. It is important that the questioner maintain eye contact with the person he is addressing, not with the person who is verbally responding. The therapist is usually the first person in the center, as a way of establishing the game and setting the tone of the questions.

Answer as Someone Else is a fascinating technique for exploring group perceptions, examining the degree to which members know one another, facilitating disclosure and confrontation, diffusing antagonism, and promoting identification and empathy. I first devised *Answer as Someone Else* for a special intensive session with a group of four adult siblings and two spouses, all in their 20s, who had in the past been very close but were currently undergoing interpersonal difficulties and felt themselves to be at a prolonged impasse. No one was willing to talk and everyone seemed to feel misunderstood, frustrated, and distrustful. They were, however, willing to speak for (or as) each other. We ended up carrying out *Answer as Someone Else* for the full three hours; each person eventually had the opportunity to answer as each other person as well as to become the questioner. Each round was followed by a lengthy discussion, in which feedback was given regarding the accuracy of the responses. This process resulted in a progressive unleashing of suppressed feelings, harbored resentments, misunderstandings, and conflicts stemming from the past, and an examination of issues related to long-standing family dynamics. The conflicts were by no means all resolved by the end of the session, but communication was opened and the six participants left feeling confident about their capacity to continue to work through the issues and hopeful about the prospects for change in their interrelationships.

Answer as Someone Else is ideally suited for work with families. It is also very useful in work with groups of people who know one another well and can tolerate confrontation and disclosure. It is particularly effective at helping groups deal with interpersonal conflict and blocked communication. Some of the best experiences I have had using *Answer as Someone Else* have been with groups of staff who work closely together. Alongside the sharing of feelings and perceptions, the game easily promotes playfulness and humor as participants take on each other's role. After a few rounds, participants often intentionally switch seats in order to have the opportunity of answering as a particular other person in the group (or having a particular other answer as them).

An extension of *Answer as Someone Else* is for everyone to take on the role of someone else in the group, not only verbally but in the context of a dramatic interaction. An example of this variation can be found in the story of Christine in Chapter 3. A more structured variation, which involves less dramatic role-taking, is to place the name of someone in the group on each person's back. Everyone tries to figure out who he is playing (that is, whose name is on his own back) by the way in which others relate to him.

Sculpt the Group

The basis of this technique is the same as *Sculpting,* in which one person creates a still-life tableau by molding or placing other people in the group in particular positions. In *Sculpt the Group* (akin to the psychodramatic technique of *Action Sociogram*), a volunteer creates a sculpture that represents her image of the group dynamic. This can be a rather complex task in which certain people are physically linked or in close proximity to certain others in the group, placed in the center or on the outskirts, etc. After sculpting the entire group, the sculptor also places herself in the picture.

Sculpt the Group frequently leads groups to confront interpersonal issues that have been avoided. Because of the very direct feedback regarding how one is seen by others, this technique should be used only at a point at which all members of the group will be able to tolerate and discuss whatever emerges. It is also best to allow time for several people, or even for everyone in the group, to create a sculpture so that diverse perspectives are represented.

A variation, which entails less specific feedback regarding the way in which individuals are perceived, is to create sculptures representing the "essence of the group." The group in this case is presented as one entity; particular interrelationships and roles are not depicted. The sculpture can be completely abstract, expressing perhaps a feeling tone or an image which the sculptor associates with the group at this point in time.

Secrets

Secrets is designed for groups that have become intimate and trusting. Everyone writes down a secret that he has not yet shared with the group but is prepared to disclose. The slips of paper are placed in a hat. Everyone then draws one slip, reads it silently, and tries to imagine that that secret belongs to him. One at a time, each person discloses the secret to the group, *as if* it were his secret. The group can be asked to respond with support and empathy to each disclosure, or to identify whose secret it actually is, or simply to listen until all the disclosures have been made. The round of disclosures, along with whichever structure the leader chooses to incorporate, is always followed by a discussion in which real ownership is established and "processing" of reactions occurs. This processing revolves around how participants felt disclosing their secret, hearing it spoken by another, and embodying another's secret.

In my years of practice I have used this technique only three or four times because, generally, I find it best for self-disclosures to be made directly by the individual (albeit sometimes through the context of a dramatic scene or game such as *True and False Statements*). The relinquishing of the disclosure to another person in the group may be experienced as a relinquishment of a sense of personal control, making this process potentially countertherapeutic. Another pitfall is that the revealed secrets may end up being extremely intimate for some and more peripheral to others. The pacing of self-disclosure in groups and the discussion that ensues are very delicate and critical processes (Yalom, 1985).

On the rare occasions that I did choose to use *Secrets*, the group responded positively. The level of empathy was heightened as members fully experienced and embodied carrying another's secret. A sense of universality about that which we hide and feel shame was very present. The level of intrigue was also great, but even greater was a quality of sharing; the secrets in a sense belonged to, and certainly were contained by, all of us.

A lighter and safer variation of *Secrets* is for everyone to write down an unusual experience (or other category of information) that others are unaware they have had. As the secrets are read out loud, everyone tries to guess to whom each one belongs. This variation can be used as an icebreaker at recreational and social gatherings with large groups of people who do not know each other well.

REVIEW AND CELEBRATION

Guess that Scene

Searching for a playful means of helping a group to review the treatment series and recall the multitude and diversity of scenes that were created, I devised *Guess that Scene*. Everyone picks a slip of paper on which a past scene is briefly synopsized (in one to two sentences, including the names of the group members who played roles in that scene). One at a time, clients perform a single line or moment from that scene, preferably one that captures the essence of the scene. The line is drawn from any of the roles within the scene and is spoken as the person who had played that role spoke it. The physical position and place in the room that the person remembers that character to have been in is also assumed. The line should be very brief; at times, even a single word suffices. The person freezes after the one line/ moment, at which point the group tries to identify the scene and the group members who played roles in it.

Scenes representing all phases within the series are included. *Guess that Scene* brings back the imaginative scenes in the early phases as well as the more personal scenework in later phases. The group is reminded of the scope of its work. This reminder occurs on an emotional as well as cognitive level: the *dramatic* recapturing awakens the full memory of the scene, along with the feelings one had while watching the scene or playing a role in it. The scene is revived, on stage, if only for a moment. Clients have described experiencing *Guess that Scene* as a fast-speed replay of the series. Groups typically manifest delight at the entertaining way in which they are reminded of these scenes and surprise at the quantity and range of scenes that took place over the course of the series.

To help the group express the evoked feeling of appreciation for its work, *Guess that Scene* can be followed by having everyone walk around and, at a prescribed moment, stop before another person. Each person is asked to tell her partner a scene that she particularly appreciated (that the partner was in), perhaps one that had personal meaning for her as she watched it. The group then walks around again and forms new pairs. The categories can be modified: "Tell your partner something that you particularly appreciated about her presence in the group," "Describe a quality of hers you admire," or "Tell about a change you noticed in her as the series progressed."

I have found *Guess that Scene* to be so effective that I incorporate it at the end of nearly every series. In classes on drama therapy, I follow the scene review with a review of the techniques and processes we used by having each person enact in about 20 seconds the technique/process that is described on her slip of paper.

Reunion

Two participants improvise meeting one another at some designated point in the future. The setting and time are specific, i.e., at a bus stop or airport five years from now. The actors respond to the fabricated surprise encounter spontaneously; for some, the recognition is instant, for others it is gradual or hesitant. Following the recognition and greeting, they talk about how and what they are doing now and reminisce about the drama therapy group they were once in together. The focus of *Reunion,* when it is used at the end of the treatment series, is on this reminiscence. The drama therapist often needs to give directions during the scene that remind the players of this focus.

I devised *Reunion* as a means of helping the group at the conclusion of the series to review various stages, scenes, feelings, or relationships. The fact that the review takes place from the vantage point of the future (albeit imaginary future) increases distance and perspective, facilitating the capacity to view the experience of the treatment series in conjunction with this period in the person's life in its totality, and to assign it meaning. The distance also helps many people to perceive and acknowledge the inner changes they underwent and the progress they made, as well as to express and examine particular difficulties they encountered during the process. Feelings regarding others in the group, including the therapist, commonly come up in the conversation (e.g., "I remember feeling really uncomfortable around Kate at the beginning, but then I grew to love her," "Remember Renée? She was so. . . ."). An example of *Reunion* can be found in the story of Christine (Chapter 3).

When *Reunion* is incorporated at earlier points in the series, the emphasis can be placed on the projection of oneself into the future rather than on reminiscence; utilized in this way, *Reunion* overlaps with (or can be developed by using) *Yourself at Different Ages.*

Parachute

The gradual billowing of a parachute, surrounded by a group of people who have worked closely together, creates an aesthetically delightful image and an exhilarating sensation. The impression of physical expansiveness and openness as the parachute rises to increasing heights parallels and enhances the uplifting, celebratory, and often exuberant feeling in the group at the culmination of the treatment series.

Parachute games are described in *The New Games Book* (Fluegelman, 1976). The parachute is set in the center of the room and everyone is asked to quickly grab hold of it. With the group spread out equidistantly and with everyone shaking his end of the parachute up and down rhythmically and synchronistically, the parachute will begin to rise and billow.

Once it is fully billowing, the leader of a drama therapy group can call out various categories, and those people who meet the criteria for that category run into the center, under the parachute, for just a moment, and then return to their places. If *Categorical Groupings* (see p. 160) was used at the onset of the series, some of the same categories can be called out once again, reviving the memory of that first session and fostering the sense of having come full circle. Categories that relate to group members' participation and accomplishments in the series are then called out, e.g., "All the people who created a *Self-Sculpture,*" "All the people who didn't miss a single session," "All the people who volunteered to use the *Telephone,*" "All the people who played a Double in someone else's scene," or "All the people who used masks in their *Self-Revelatory Performances.*" This provides a playful and ritualized way of reviewing the series and acknowledging individuals for their work. The calling out of categories occurs at set intervals, e.g., at every third rise of the parachute, so that each round is punctuated and framed by the rise and fall of the parachute.

To familiarize the group with the rhythmic pattern and format of running into the center and returning to one's spot, the following variation is a helpful prelude to the calling out of categories: At every third rise of the parachute, the names of two people in the group are called out. These two people must immediately switch places with one another—before the parachute buries them!

The calling out of categories can be followed by having everyone in the group run under the parachute at once. This should obviously occur at a point at which the parachute is very high so that the group can experience the magical feeling of being enveloped together, if only for a moment.

Another possibility, recommended as the culmination of the play with the parachute, is for participants to return to their places on the periphery of the parachute and to bring the parachute back to a full billow. At a prescribed moment, all simultaneously and rapidly pull the parachute underneath them and sit down. A womb-like tent is formed, held up by the bodies sitting inside it, in a circle. The initial expansiveness and exhilaration of the activity transforms into a quiet and contained intimacy, reflecting the other dimension of the treatment process: the deep closeness that has evolved and the safe, contained, and sacred space that has been created. Clients are usually content to simply sit this way for a few minutes, looking at one another in silence and basking in the peaceful and nurturing ambiance pervading the space they share.

Toasts

This is a very simple process in which participants toast one another on their accomplishments and successes, hopes and dreams. Comments about values the group shares or feelings that have developed within the group can also be phrased in the form of a toast. The physical gesture of toasting glasses may first be conducted in pantomime and then followed by *real* toasting, using actual glasses and nonalcoholic champagne. Whether toasting in mime or for real, the clicking and sipping at each round is important. The clicking—each person with each other person—symbolizes the sense of comraderie and the significance of every relationship within the group; the sipping punctuates each toast. *Toasts* provides a structured, ritualized, and spirited way of acknowledging and expressing feelings—including pride and gratitude—and of celebrating the closure of the series. However, *Toasts* is not appropriate for substance-abusing groups.

Diplomas

Diplomas or certificates are distributed to everyone in the group. Each diploma has printed on it the person's name (in bold letters, in official style, calligraphy, or more playful, colorful form). In addition, there are words such as: "The above member has completed a 30-session series of drama therapy. Aside from his attendance and participation, he has. . . :" The rest is blank; each person fills out his own diploma, identifying his particular successes or accomplishments in treatment.

Diplomas facilitates the process of reviewing and identifying one's areas of growth and progress, along with validating oneself for these—an important life skill. *Diplomas* also provides tangible acknowledgment of the successful completion of the series. This concretism is especially appropriate in work with children; it is also well suited to emotionally disturbed clients, many of whom have had few experiences of success and completion in their lives. The risk in using *Diplomas* is that it can seem infantilizing. Therefore, it is best used when a group has naturally joked about the fact that they should receive diplomas for all their hard work, a comment which in my experience is not uncommon.

When the diplomas are filled in, the group comes into its familiar circle. Each person has the option of reading his diploma out loud. As a way of developing the activity, other group members can suggest additions, which the person may choose to include on his diploma. As a way of augmenting the ceremonial quality, everyone in the group can sign each diploma after it is read.

Group Photo

Closure of the treatment series entails helping clients to *carry within* themselves the experience they underwent and the changes they manifested. Tangible reminders, given to group members at the end of the series, can facilitate this process. This is especially true in work with children, particularly those who have endured many separations in their lives and for whom termination can be very difficult. Photographs are a good example of tangible reminders that clients can take with them. This *transitional object* eases the pain of separation. It may also bolster the person during a difficult period at some future point, when the memory of the treatment experience has dimmed. In *Group Photo,* the group positions itself into various shapes, intermittently freezing like a statue, which the therapist photographs. Many of the ideas described under *Group Statues* can be incorporated. Emotional expressions can also be suggested to educe dramatic pictures. Individual photographs or photo collages are given to each person in the group.

Re-Fortuned Cookies

The element of fun and surprise inherent in Chinese fortune cookies has always appealed to me, along with the interaction the process of opening and reading aloud the fortunes tends to provoke. The particular sayings, however, do not always match the excitement of the process. Therefore, I devised *Re-Fortuned Cookies,* in which the fortunes are removed (a tweezer works best), and new ones, written by the therapist, are inserted. The therapist uses her creativity in devising fortunes or sayings that relate to the themes and/or goals of the particular group.

More personally, I have used *Re-Fortuned Cookies* as a very special gift to loved ones. Each cookie in the carton contains a typed saying beginning with "You are. . . ." It is important to note that many of the techniques in Part II can be incorporated, with minor adaptations, into our personal lives.

Part III

PERFORMANCE
The Story of Seven People and the Play They Created About Their Lives

9

DEVELOPMENT OF A
GROUP AND A PLAY

THEATRE AND THERAPY

Traditionally, in theatre, the people seen on stage are actors, and these actors play characters. But an entirely different paradigm exists: *theatrical productions in which real people tell real-life stories.*

Often, the people in such theatrical productions have never appeared on stage before. Nor have they have been visible offstage. Their lives have been hidden from public domain and their stories have been kept secret, at times even from themselves. On stage, they *come out* with their private identities and histories.

The performers may be prison inmates, recovering drug abusers, physically or developmentally disabled people, war veterans, survivors of sexual abuse, the homeless. They may be immigrants or refugees, ethnic minorities, adolescents, senior citizens. My own work has been with people who have been in and out of psychiatric hospitals.

Parts I and II of *Acting for Real,* comprising the process and techniques of drama therapy, do not sufficiently convey the scope of the field; the other important dimension to drama therapy is public performance. Performance transforms notions about theatre and about therapy. The setting of the therapy scene changes from closed room to public stage; the cast changes from client and therapist to client/*actor,* therapist/*director,* and outside *audience.* The therapeutic impact of performance is different from, and often greater than, process-oriented drama therapy. The ramifications of performance extend from groups to communities, from therapy to education, from the personal to the universal.

My most intense reflections on the marriage between theatre and therapy occurred with members of *Beyond Analysis,* a theatre company of ex-psychiatric patients which I founded in 1979. Together, we explored the relationship between process and product, between life and art. With some of them, most notably Stacey and Alex, I appeared on television and radio interview shows, and from our respective positions of client/actor and therapist/director, our perspectives from the inside and the outside, we attempted to communicate the dynamic power inherent in this marriage.

My hope is that the story of *Beyond Analysis* and the play *Inside Out* will inspire drama therapists to produce performances by special populations, as well as to create theatre pieces drawn from their own life experience.

Drama therapists who have already been conducting such work include (but are not limited to): David Johnson (1975, 1980), who has produced plays with psychiatric patients and, along with his colleague Miller James, with Vietnam veterans; David Morgan Lovis and Warren McCommons, founding members of Theatre Unlimited, a company of developmentally disabled (as well as non-disabled) actors, John Bergman (Director of Geese Theatre) and Raymond Gordon (Director of now defunct Cell Block Theatre) (Ryan, 1976), who have produced plays with prisoners; Lynn Johnson (1990) as well as Louis Moffett and Liliano Bruto (1990), who have produced plays with recovering substance abusers.*

"We gain the full dignity and power of our persons only when we create a narrative account of our lives, dramatize our existence. . . ." (Keen & Valley-Fox, 1989, p. xiv). The discovery of our life stories, and the communication of these stories via performance—in which personal, social, or cultural truths are revealed—propel us toward wholeness.

I tell the story here of one group, over one year, and the production of one play in the hope that the microscopic illuminates—emotionally as well as conceptually—the macroscopic, that the personal illuminates the universal. I tell the story of seven unique people, each grappling with issues that reflect and inform our shared human struggles. Their lives profoundly touched my own, and their courage and creativity have been for me a compelling source of learning and inspiration.

The rate of recidivism among psychiatric patients is frighteningly high. Over and over in my work in psychiatric institutions I saw patients who had made tremendous progress return to the institution. At first the constant relapses stunned me. But as I became habituated to this phenomenon, I also began wondering whether there were ways in which the needs ex-patients

---

*A number of alumni from the Drama Therapy Program at the California Institute of Integral Studies have created performances (some as part of their thesis project) about their own life struggles or about their work as therapists, including Amy Elliot, Jill Silverman, Armand Volkas, Barbara Roush, and Hillary Hurst.

face upon reentry into the community could be constructively addressed.

Reinstitutionalization is precipitated largely by social isolation and an inability (or lack of motivation) to deal with the stress and frustration of everyday life. Participation in a theatre company, I thought, could impact on these issues. A theatre company facilitates a high level of social interaction and provides a sense of belonging, connectedness, and intimacy—ingredients essential to the well-being of all people. A theatre company provides an ongoing creative outlet for the expression of emotions. The confidence and self-worth that are developed in any effective drama therapy process are magnified by successful performance before outside audiences. Perhaps long-term participation in a theatre company could modify the insidiously low self-esteem so pervasive among this population.

The idea of starting a theatre company was based not solely on addressing the needs of psychiatric patients, but also on my own desires: to work with people over a longer period of time, outside of the institutional environment, and to produce theatre, based on real-life stories. In process-oriented drama therapy sessions, I had witnessed innumerable powerful dramas, dramas enacted by non-actors about core themes in their lives. I knew that with some direction these scenes could be transformed into aesthetic creations worthy of stage performance. I also felt that these dramas *had to be seen on the outside,* as a healing force for the larger community. Barriers between those who have been institutionalized and the community needed to be broken. Taboo subjects needed to be publicly addressed, stigmas and projections needed to be shattered. People who had lost their voices needed to find they had something to say and a way to say it, and the rest of us needed to listen. In listening, we would find not only our compassion but our common humanity.

With a grant from the California Arts Council and meeting space donated by Intersection, a theatre arts center in San Francisco, I selected seven people with whom I had worked in various psychiatric institutions. All had been recently discharged; most had a history of multiple hospitalizations and suicide attempts. The work would be challenging for them and for me, but if it could provide a means of using the darkness constructively, of "turning pain into art," as one member later phrased it, then our efforts would be worth it.

The following story begins after Beyond Analysis had already been meeting for a full year and produced one original play. The group members during this second year of the company's life consisted of both new and continuing members. By this stage, the project was funded by multiple grants (California Arts Council, San Francisco Foundation, Zellerbach Family Fund), covering all aspects of the work: twice weekly workshop sessions, extra rehearsals preceding performances, monthly individual and group sessions, plus costs related to theatre production. The effort devoted to this project may appear to reach surprising proportions and some facets of the work may seem unorthodox. The challenges presented by producing public theatre perform- ances with severely depressed and unstable participants can be enormous. The overall effort, nonetheless, is equalled by the overall reward.

BEYOND ANALYSIS: THE EARLY GROUP PROCESS

First Two Phases

There is no demarcation between the stage and audience area; the entire theatre is bare—one huge windowless space. The walls are black, but the room is dramatically lit by colorful theatre lights. I walk through the open space, joining it in some way, finding my relationship to it, just as I will soon join the players, finding my way towards them.

The four group members whom I know well—they have been in the com- pany since its inception one year ago—make the first entrance. They seem excited to be back after the month interim. Alex, a youthful 40-year-old African- American man, greets me with a hug. Latisha, a beautiful, 27-year-old African- American woman, is less demonstrative, but smiles graciously and accepts my hug. Stacey, a Latina, and Susan, who is Caucasian, are both 30. Stacey is dark and Susan fair, but both have the same cropped haircuts, petite body frames, and similar projection of something between sprightliness and ner- vous energy. Soon, the new members, whom I know only from our brief work in institutions, enter. All three appear anxious and withdrawn. Jamie is the youngest of the group: a tall, thin, 22-year-old gay man who had just relocated from New York; his flaming red hair seems to contradict his shy, discreet demeanor. Karin, a 23-year-old Asian-American woman, and Larry, a 46-year- old Caucasian British man, are both noticeably attractive. His posture is stiff, hers is hesitant, watchful. The three stand at a distance from one another, in the vicinity of the theater's entrance.

I am conscious of wanting to acknowledge the skills of the old members, to respect and nurture their interrelationships, and to devise new challenges for them. At the same time, I need to help the new members feel comfortable and connected enough to the process that they will continue to come. Before long, a new identity, based on the dynamics between these seven players, will have to be created. For several months, our work will revolve around forming a cohesive group and building skills, with little attention given to the eventual performance.

The first session and all subsequent early sessions focus on playful interaction. The central goal at this stage is the development of a cohesive group; the development of a performance piece will come much later. Warm-up exercises break through the isolation with which participants enter sessions. Given the old members' desire for newness, rather than a feeling of starting over, I devise new techniques. The lighthearted spirit manifested by the four of them makes possible the use of processes that would feel too silly with a group of all new members. One warm-up involves simply milling around and saying others' names as they are encountered, but gradually speaking louder and louder, as though everyone were hard-of-hearing. Another warm-up combines *Fast-Speed Handshake* and *Hand Gestures:* Everyone is asked to mingle at a party, shaking hands with others, but not with their actual hands— rather, each person has someone standing behind him embodying the hand gestures. The early sessions are successful in promoting a high level of interaction and transforming the initial atmosphere from one of passivity and awkwardness to one of activity and aliveness.

The year-long experience of half of the group rapidly propels us into Phase Two (Scenework), in which dramatic scenes are enacted. The group responds especially well to *Planned Improvisations.* In one session, *Gibberish* arguments are followed by scenes in which an argument gradually escalates. Alex and Latisha play husband and wife, a relationship that recurs in their improvisations, indicative of their bond which is based on having been in the last series together and on being the only two African-Americans in the group. Latisha is especially expressive as she angrily confronts her husband on inviting guests without telling her beforehand. The two fight in the kitchen, all the while impressively imagining their guests are in the adjacent room. I introduce *Calling Out Emotions,* in which the group calls out a multitude of emotions, which the actors incorporate in their interaction. Then I add a new element: As the actors engage in the scene, another person expresses through movement and gesture the emotions that are being expressed (or suppressed). The movement occurs behind a lit sheet, so that the audience sees only the person's shadow. In this way, everyone gets a chance both to perform and to witness a multidimensional theatrical piece.

Despite the high level of engagement in the warm-ups and scenes of the early sessions, the commitment to attend regularly is tested. At the third session, only four people show up. Several people are again absent at the fifth session. Clearly, my consistent reminders about the importance of regular attendance (as well as my suggestion that a motto for our group be "no excuse is a good excuse") has not sufficed.

As a way of regularly addressing group issues, the last session of each month is devoted entirely to group discussion. At our eighth session and first "monthly," we sit around a large table. I begin by acknowledging the difficulty of coming when one is in a depressed or withdrawn state and invite the group to share feelings evoked by the absence of fellow group members as well as feelings related to the group process thus far. Some speak about feeling inadequate in comparison to (the perceived skills of) other group members. Others speak about having little positive experience with commitment—both in terms of maintaining a commitment themselves and of being able to rely on others in their lives to keep one. Fears of letting others down or being let down are shared. We end the session with a surprise cake in honor of Larry's birthday; all important events and holidays in this series will be acknowledged and ritualized.

Everyone not only shows up at the next few sessions, but comes early. To my further delight, the group—on its own—soon begins a tradition of meeting a half-hour prior to the session at a neighboring coffeehouse.

But just as I conclude that the initial testing and inconsistency is over, I am reminded instead that this journey is to be a very delicate if not rocky one, with no certainties. I also learn how greatly my presence is relied upon at this stage. I miss one session in order to give a presentation at an out-of-town conference. When I return, everyone is withdrawn. I find out that Stacey has been hospitalized and Karin has decided to drop out of the group. Partly to meet the challenge of the group's regressed level and partly to compensate for my own disappointment, I lead an unusually dynamic session, using expansive movement and provoking fervent interaction in the open theatre space, followed by an extended and emotive process of *Circle-Mirror-Transformation,* in which our excitement and fears are nonverbally played out.

Karin's Fear

As cautious and sensitive as Karin has been, I am nonetheless surprised by her departure and by the fact that she did not speak to me directly of her decision, but rather left a message for me with Alex. In the preceding weeks, she appeared to be more connected to the group and almost always reveled in the acting processes. I appreciated her presence and her giftedness; it seemed she had a great deal to offer the group and that she herself would benefit in significant ways from being in the group.

Whether or not her decision is unchangeable, I want to understand her reactions and, if necessary, offer her some closure. The morning after her absence, I phone her.

A quiet hesitant voice answers. "Oh, hi. I hope you got the message that I decided to drop out."

"Yes, I did. I'd like to meet with you so that we can talk about it."

Her voice becomes tense. "I've already made up my mind. I've given it a lot of thought, and I already talked to my doctor about it. There's no chance I'll change my mind."

"I understand that. But I'd still like to talk with you in person to hear your thoughts and feelings about the decision you've made."

I hear a faint and tentative "ok."

We meet early that evening. Karin enters a few minutes late, wearing a long skirt, sandals, and a black felt hat. She sits down across from me. We begin with a long silent pause during which time she looks at me, into my eyes, as if trying to find the person she trusted a week ago. I know when she has. Then I ask her a question. With Karin it is best to do this without words.

"I liked the group. I'm glad I was in it till now. It was even much better, easier, than I'd expected. More fun, something I usually don't think about having. But now I need to stop."

I ask again, silently.

"I'm never going to get up on any stage. There's no way I can perform in front of an audience full of strangers. You might say we have plenty of time before the performance, but I've already calculated how much time is left. There's no way I can be ready in just five months." She fixes her eyes on me as she speaks. Her expression is both intense and fragile. "I figured it's better to leave now. If I quit just before the performance, or even after we begin creating the play, it wouldn't be fair. It's better for the group that I quit now."

She speaks so earnestly and convincingly that a part of me believes she is right; she won't make it to the end, so it is best that she leave now. But I also know there is more to the story and more ways of interpreting the story thus far. There is a complex web of feelings to unravel, a mystery to unfold.

"Tell me your fears about performing," I say gently.

"I just want to be anonymous. I don't want to be seen. Anywhere, even on the streets, I feel like hiding." There is a sense of urgency in her tone now. "I could never be seen on a stage in front of a lot of people. A performance means exposing myself. That's precisely what I don't want to do."

"Tell me more, about wanting to be anonymous."

And now I get the clues I have been waiting for. "If I were thin, it'd be different. But I can't show myself the way I am now. I would need to lose at least 40 pounds before the performance. Actually, at least three weeks before the performance, so everyone could be sure I'd go through with it." She pauses, reflecting. "At first I thought I'd gradually lose the weight. I figured out there were about 23 weeks till we perform, which means I had 20 weeks and that meant losing just two pounds a week. I thought I could do that. But now I realize there's no way I'm going to lose that much."

I listen with not only my ears but my eyes, and wait.

"Instead of losing, I've been gaining. Going on binges. Especially after our drama sessions. I come home and gorge myself with food. Or do drugs." She watches my expression, as if to check the impact of her disclosure. I have the distinct impression that she at once desires and fears surprising or disturbing me. Yet, on a deeper level, I sense she craves a response that is calm and unaffected, but still empathic. And this is what she gets.

"I think I do it because I'm so anxious about the performance. And I told myself before joining this group that my main priority is losing weight. If the group is causing me to gain, I can't continue with it."

There is an obvious obsessiveness to both the content of her words and to the process by which she focuses the discussion on this sole issue. I wonder what issues lurk underneath.

"Are there other aspects of the group that have been bothering you? That make you anxious, aside from the idea of performing?"

She looks at me cautiously, as if to make sure I am safe ground. I sense her concern not only for her own safety, but for mine. She wants to be sure the ground she treads on will not crumble. I reassure her, again without words.

"It seems everyone else in the group can play a part in a scene and then snap right back into themselves again when the scene ends," she begins in a steady tone. "I can't do that. It hurt last week, when everyone laughed at the scene where I played a little girl and then told me what a good actress I was. Because I didn't feel I was being funny or acting. I felt I just became the girl. And afterwards I panicked, because I was still the girl."

I feel as though my eyes are able to hold her hands.

"It can be very frightening to act if you lose sense of who you are while playing the part."

She nods. "It's as if when the part's over, I'm supposed to become Karin again, but I don't know who Karin is, and there's no one to come back to."

It is my turn to nod. My heart is opening to her, empathizing with the myriad feelings with which she is flooded, the complex challenges with which this process has presented her. And I feel for the exquisitely intense and lovely person she has—through it all—become.

She is increasingly assuaged by our conversation, or rather by her disclosures. I have simply listened to her and understood, not analyzed. But now I sense her need also for some verbal response.

"It would take time to help you find Karin, to feel that there is a self to come back to. You have a lot of talent in acting, though I know this thought is also scary to you. Some of this skill comes from your perceptiveness. You can identify and empathize so well, leading you to be able to play many parts well. What you'd need to work on is having some distance from the parts you play."

"In a way it's flattering to think maybe I'm a good actress. But I feel more like a freak. I just turn into the part I play."

"You may identify with certain characteristics in the girl, or the teacher you played last week, or any role you play, but these roles just touch on aspects of you, not all of you. Professional actors find a piece of themselves that corresponds to each role or emotion they are to play."

She is listening intently.

"It may be that over time you could feel enlarged by being capable of playing so many roles so fully, rather than sucked empty when the scene ends. That you find out a lot about who Karin is from the roles, that playing many roles will eventually help you build a self. So that gradually you, Karin, could embody the role without being consumed by it."

I am losing her. These projections are too hypothetical; they don't match her experience at this time. And any reference to the future may appear to be negating her decision to drop out.

There are so many issues at hand: first, her weak ego-boundaries and poorly defined sense of self. When there is little sense of self, acting can be very threatening. Each theatrical role is larger than the person. Once the self becomes a more clearly differentiated whole, this is reversed; the self is larger than the role and can therefore encompass it. A related issue is that of transition, not only out of roles, but out of the structured, interactive environment of our group sessions to the isolation of her apartment.

But the issues that I feel are most paramount to address at this time are her fear of performing and her use of food and drugs. It is the latter that, according to her logic, necessitates quitting the group, thereby allowing her to avoid facing the fears. I am also conscious of my own investment in the goal of helping people sustain a commitment to a project that I believe will ultimately benefit them.

"If our group was set up differently," I venture, "so that it was just a workshop, without any performance or production, would that change things for you?"

"It still would've been very hard, but I probably could have done it."

"You're really terrified of performing."

"If I were thin now, I wouldn't be. When I'm thin, I can do anything. I get manic actually. And I keep losing weight. I was anorexic for years. I was even much thinner than you." She checks for my reaction, but, not getting one, continues. "I weighed under 90 pounds. And I felt great. But when I'm fat, like now, it's the opposite. I feel grotesque. I know I look horrible and I don't want to be seen."

Her language makes me flash on the Elephant Man. But across from me I see a beautiful woman. Her slightly superfluous weight is negligible next to the perfectly chiseled features and dark flawless complexion, the large expressive hazel eyes, and the long jet black hair that frames a strikingly pretty face. I know the worst thing I could say is, "But you're lovely, Karin."

"My parents were both thin and perfect-looking. My mother was blond and used to be a model. She wanted slender, graceful children, little white ballet dancers. But both me and my sister were chubby and looked very Asian. My mother didn't know what to do with us. She was embarrassed by us.

"I don't talk about this to anyone, I mean nobody knows that I feel so grotesque. If I told anyone, they would just think it's a question of wanting to lose weight, like everyone else, and they wouldn't realize I feel like a freak. They would just say, 'But you're pretty, Karin,' which makes me want to scream. It means I'd have to keep my hair long or stay thin or I wouldn't be pretty anymore. People don't really know me or see me."

I feel stuck in a no-win situation. If I say, "Well, if you feel it's crucial to lose weight in order to be in the group, then why not try to accomplish this," she'll think I agree with her self-assessment. If I say, "Karin, your feelings about weight should be dealt with separately, and not affect your commitment to *Beyond Analysis*," she'll feel I have misunderstood everything. Her compulsive and impossible set-up—no loss of weight meaning no possibility of performance, and performance meaning no possibility of losing weight—creates a bind that keeps her from taking risks and from having potentially positive experiences. I search for a way to circumvent this bind.

"What if you didn't worry about the performance yet and just concentrated on the process for now?" I ask, checking first to see if there has been any modification in the stance with which she had entered this meeting.

"No, I won't ever be seen on any stage."

"How about if you're not seen?"

She looks at me questioningly.

"What if you were cloaked and covered and no one could tell it was you? Or if we just heard your voice and didn't actually see you?"

She looks surprised and disarmed.

"Would that count as performing?"

"I have no preconceived notions as to what performance entails. Our play can be anything—we have no playwright to please, it's entirely up to us. Maybe it'll be full of voices or shadows or echoes or masks, I don't know." I speak sincerely, yet am struck by my own words. Clearly the process of expanding my own limited conceptions—to accommodate the realities of the seven people with whom I work—is underway.

"I could play the Elephant Man."

We're getting somewhere.

"Like in the movie, or a different version?"

"I saw the movie twice. I identified so much with the Elephant Man that for days I lost track of who I was. That's a part I could play."

"That could be a very powerful scene."

"It's just that I don't want anyone I know to see me performing."

I detect traces of what will later become very evident and problematic: her terror at being seen not only in a negative light, but also in a positive successful light.

"If you were disguised, no one would recognize you."

"I could do that. I didn't know that was possible."

"Karin, I like you and I like working with you." I speak slowly, as if the timing of my words might affect her absorption of them. "And you contribute a lot to the group. Also it seems that much of the time you've actually been really enjoying yourself. What's most important to me is the process, our process, us, not the performance. There will be a performance, but that comes later, and it will be adapted to who we each are, what each person's needs are, and what each of us can or cannot do. We can work together, all the way, all through this process, even during the hard periods."

She is listening carefully. Her face has softened. And she looks relieved.

"You'll take me back?"

"Of course." For the first time she is smiling.

"If I have other problems or get very anxious, I can talk with you about it?" Her tone is partly serious and partly impish.

I nod. "It's important that you do. We can try to understand and work through the hard periods together, rather than you deciding to quit when something seems insurmountable. That's what a commitment means, sticking with it, even during the roughest periods."

"I'll try. I really will."

She is quiet for a moment.

"I already told my therapist that I'm quitting, though. She didn't say anything, but she didn't look surprised. I've dropped out of everything I ever began."

"Maybe this time will be different," I say softly.

"I don't understand why you took all this time and effort to talk with me. It would've been easier to just forget about me."

"I didn't want to forget about you."

She is quiet again.

"I feel like you believe in me. And I can't understand why."

My meeting with Karin confirms the critical function of the individual meetings which I hold monthly. The struggles and conflicts shared by all the group members can be handled to a large extent in our group process (and group "monthlies"), but there are numerous other issues, particular to each person, that would be both impossible and emotionally overwhelming for the participants to tackle during the group sessions. If I want to see each person through this journey, attentiveness and time alloted to each person, individually, is going to have to be part of my job.

THE CHALLENGE OF COMMITMENT AND WELLNESS

The Group's Entrance into Phase Three

The group is noticeably relieved to see Karin and Stacey, who has just been discharged from the hospital. Stacey describes the stress that triggered her hospitalization and her commitment now "not to fake it." They all seem to immediately understand when she says, "Even if I'm not sure who I am, I'm not going to pretend to be someone I'm not." Karin is especially taken by Stacey; I can see she is treading that thin line between empathy and mergence.

As a way of augmenting the group's interest in theatre and increasing their connectedness to each other and to the community, we periodically go to performances. At our first theatre outing, Karin appears delighted. She is struck by the fact that one of the actresses is heavy. "She was good," she exclaims after the show, "and her size wasn't even an issue within the play—it didn't even come up."

At the following session, I initiate *Planned Improvisations* based on the show we had seen, which had revolved around a wacky agoraphobic couple. Each group is to portray an eccentric couple, with one person playing a social worker who visits them in their home. Alex and Susan play a poverty-stricken couple living on cat food. Larry plays a straight social worker, trying to determine whether welfare is warranted, and shocked by what he sees—a role that has emerged repeatedly in his improvisations. Alex and Susan are wonderfully entertaining as people at the edge of insanity, who over the years have taken on cat qualities and mannerisms. They paw, lick, and meow at each other, alternating between playfulness and aggression, while their dog— played with striking precision by Karin—chases them around the apartment.

When the group compliments the four of them on their acting, Karin says she still feels like the dog. The group laughs, but after the session I talk with her. We examine how she relates to the dog, what parts of her are expressed via the dog, and how she felt prior to taking on the role. Finally I feel she has been sufficiently *de-roled,* though I realize that in future sessions I may need to curtail her role playing by inhibiting the full development of her scenes. Before she leaves, we consider nurturing activities she can engage in upon returning to her apartment.

The warm-ups continue to emphasize playful interaction, in ever-changing variations. During one game, group members are given a batch of colorful crepe paper necklaces, which they are to place on as many other people in the group as possible, all the while trying to avoid being "necklaced" themselves. Aggression is indirectly expressed via sword fights with feather dusters. The party setting is used frequently to invite the informal mingling which is still awkward to the group in real life. In one party interaction, everyone is given a restriction—

one thing they are not allowed to do (e.g., can't smile, can't make eye contact, etc.)—but instructed to appear as natural as possible. At the end of another party interaction, I distribute plastic cups filled with juice. Everyone is asked to bring the cup back the next session, filled with some kind of simple gift for the person whose name is written on the bottom of the cup.

Just as the group is beginning to feel like an entity and attendance by all has become regular, Stacey is hospitalized again. Her rehospitalizations are a sore reminder to the group of the ever-present possibility of slipping back; relapse is a reality they have all experienced. Jamie and Larry are the most visibly shaken. Suddenly, Larry, who had been unusually quiet, makes an announcement:

"I want to let you all know that I just got suspended from my halfway house for not getting out of bed in the morning. I broke my commitment to go regularly to my volunteer job. Since everything is now up in the air, I'm not sure I can keep coming to this group."

All members recognize this dynamic: when one thing falls apart, might as well let the rest go. But they are not about to let this happen to one of their peers.

"Larry, you made a commitment to us and it's important to us that you keep it."

"Just because you screwed up in one part of your life doesn't mean you have to screw everything up."

"Let's do some scenes about this."

Karin plays the counselor who tries to convince Larry to get out of bed, and then they reverse roles. After playing counselor, Larry comes back to playing himself, in the form of a *Double*—voicing his inner thoughts as he refuses to face the day. Via *Taking Over the Role,* group members express their identification with Larry's dilemma, acknowledge his feelings, and offer alternatives. This entrance into Phase Three is appropriate not only to the stage of our group process but to the fact that before long we will need to begin developing a play based on real-life experience.

Stacey's Truth

I visit Stacey in the hospital. She is panicked that I may kick her out of the group. But once reassured that I will let her back, she appears to be in good spirits. She has been actively participating in all the activities on the unit. Stacey thrives on structure and collapses without it. The lack of structure in her life apart from *Beyond Analysis,* combined with the stress of having to move out of her apartment and a recent visit to her family, had precipitated this hospitalization. The crisis unit has become a kind of second home (or more precisely, unfortunately, a first home) for her.

She is discharged after only a few days. But she does not show up at the next session. A day later I get a garbled phone call from her. By her extensive use of metaphor, I can tell she is still in crisis. She says something about a baby crying, about dying, about leaving the planet. It is hard to sort out reality from fantasy and symbol. From what I can gather, she went to stay with her foster parents rather than following through on her discharge plans — to go for pre-scheduled interviews at a halfway house and an employment program. Knowing how conscientious and responsible Stacey is when not in crisis only heightens my concern.

Given her emotional state and the fact that she has no car, I pick her up at the foster parents and take her to a nearby coffeehouse. Once again, I am struck by the enormous commitment this project entails — given the fragility of the group members and my goal of producing a play with them outside of an institutional setting. I listen to Stacey's ramblings about how babies need care, about oblivion calling, about having too much responsibility, knowing that during this time she is slowly finding her way back to me and to our relationship. From the muddle, a few pieces of information emerge in the form of two troubling facts. The first fact is that Stacey has taken a real baby home with her. Apparently she had befriended a young woman in the hospital. The woman had left her baby in the care of her parents while she was hospitalized. Stacey promised the woman that if she (Stacey) was discharged first, she would care for the baby until her friend's discharge. I am at once moved by Stacey's compassion and aware of the transferential aspect to her act; in her own infancy, she was often left to the inadequate and abusive care of her grandparents.

The other fact is that she has been shooting up speed.

As I silently consider bringing her back to the hospital, she says, "When I told the truth in the past, they always put me back into the hospital." The theme of truth, of sorting reality from fantasy or disguise, is a central one for Stacey. The imagery in her language both reveals and belies her own truths. As the layers unravel and she gets closer to communicating to herself and to another what is real, she experiences a sense of impending danger. And sure enough, this is what her self-revelatory performance was to be about.

The potential benefits for Stacey of getting through this crisis without re-hospitalization outweigh the risks. Together, we come up with a plan for her to return the baby to its grandparents and then tackle the issue of drugs. In a dark corner of the parking lot, she ritualistically destroys her needles in front of me.

She agrees to keep the commitments she made at the time of her discharge from the hospital. I write down these agreements in the form of a medical prescription she promises to fill. Then, as a way of drawing her back to the present, I speak about the group. For a brief moment, her eyes sparkle and I catch a glimpse of the playful, spirited young woman with whom I had worked throughout the previous year. But the calmer and clearer state she has reached is a tenuous one. Given the brink on which she stands, I ask her to phone me daily over the next few days.

She sticks to our plan. "But nothing seems real," she reports, "I'm just going through the motions." On the third day, just after our group session, there is a shift. "Seeing my family is my downfall," she declares, "I'm getting divorced from them." This valiant resolution has been made before but never upheld, despite the recommendations of her many therapists. Always there was one more return home in the futile attempt to obtain some of what she never got. "I had a dream about you last night," she continues. "You were sitting next to me in my hospital bed. I was in a feverish half-asleep state, and you were warding off my negative thoughts. Every now and then I asked you if you were still awake and you said yes."

The element of transference in my relationship to Stacey and other members of the group is undeniable. It is as though the group members are climbing a steep and precarious cliff, and I am the rope to which they cling. Playing such a pivotal role evokes many clinical and ethical considerations. It is important for me to foster independence rather than dependency, to be a facilitator not a rescuer. The responsibility for wellness ultimately lies with the clients themselves. Yet, given my belief that not only must unmet needs of childhood be addressed, but the client should have some reparative experience,* in conjunction with my belief in the clients' healthful drives and capacities once past crisis points, I feel that helping them to avoid slipping backwards is warranted. I discuss these issues in an ongoing fashion with a consultant; testing and analyzing my intuitive choices in the context of clinical supervison is a critical component to the backstage process of my own journey with the group.

HOSPITALIZATIONS—FICTIONAL AND ACTUAL

Hospital and Therapy Scenes

The rapid approach of the Christmas season is taking its toll on the group. Jamie's depression, in particular, becomes more acute. Feeling suicidal after a rejection by a new lover, he checks into the hospital. The group members

---

*Winnicott (1958), among others, views therapy as an arena for reversing the client's experience of early environmental failures. Meeting the client's regressive demands (at least in early stages of treatment) is a way of constructively addressing and repairing developmental deficits incurred as a result of inadequate parenting during infancy.

are once again confronted with fears about rehospitalization. I suggest a scene taking place in a hospital. Better to face the fear and gain creative mastery over it than to avoid it.

"Let's make it a really hip hospital," Karin says playfully.

"A place to mellow out," Susan chimes in.

"Marin Mellow Memorial Hospital." Stacey loves satire.

"Check me in, I need it!" Latisha volunteers, and they all laugh, partly in relief at Latisha's acknowledgment of the withdrawn and anxious state she has manifested in recent sessions.

Responding to Latisha's willingness to joke about such a serious subject, Larry joins in the fun. "Ok, I'll admit you. I'm Dr. Hip."

Dr. Hip ushers in the new patient, inducing her into a relaxed trance state. "Getting into it, sweetheart?" he says lackadaisically. "Please don't call me sweetheart," she retorts, in role. "That's good, tell me your feelings, baby. Now follow me into group therapy."

"Which takes place in the hot tub," shouts Stacey from offstage.

Immediately four people rush on stage and into an imagined hot tub. All appear extremely relaxed, especially Karin, who idly claims, "I've been in the hospital for two years. I wouldn't want to be anywhere else."

Alex enters as a masseur, ready to "work on" the new patient after group therapy.

"Medication time," cries Susan from off stage. All the patients rush to get their daily dose of the only medication offered at Marin Mellow Hospital: valium.

The group is completely engaged in this satire, delighting in each other's humor and wit. Their obvious enjoyment comes from dealing with a subject with which they all are intimately familiar and yet normally shield from discussion. Joking about and enacting hospitalization is liberating: the emotional charge and stigma associated with institutionalization is diffused, along with the secrecy and shame.

We enact another hospital scene, this time a realistic one. The group seems eager to portray "what it is really like." Alex volunteers to be the newly admitted patient, and the rest of the group immediately sets up an initial intake scene in which Alex's mental status is assessed by the entire clinical staff.

"Doctor, where is this patient's chart?" Latisha asks over Alex's head.

"Alex, this isn't a test, so please relax." Stacey begins the questioning. "Do you know where you are?" Barely waiting for a response, she continues: "Who is the President of the United States?"

Satisfied that the new patient is "oriented to time and place," Karin continues the interview. "Now, Alex, I want you to tell us what the following expressions mean to you, quickly, without thinking first," she speaks with authority. "A rolling stone gathers no moss. People in glass houses shouldn't throw stones."

The staff appear mildly bored; some comment that it is nearly lunchtime and make suggestions where to go for lunch.

"I think I can wrap this up," Larry takes command, developing the satirical underpinnings of the scene. "I would like to try my well-known hypotenuse theory on this patient. Now, Mr. Allen, these questions concern geometrical figures. Which of these three figures—the circle, the triangle or the square— remind you of home?" He stands and pauses, as though basking in the brilliance of the question. "Now, which remind you of yourself?" "Well I'm no square!" Alex responds. But he is the only one who laughs.

I am impressed by the group's capacity to interweave realism with satire, and by their skills at working collaboratively within the improvisational mode. For the first time, I catch a glimpse of our performance-to-be.

At the following session, Larry plays a psychiatrist and three people play his patient—as though they are one person. The format is an outgrowth of Storytelling techniques the group is familiar with, in which one person imme- diately continues a story from the precise point at which the previous person left off. In this doctor-patient scene, three people play one character, each proceeding from (and expanding upon) the content and tone of the previous actor. Everyone in the group takes a turn playing (part of) the patient, a role that demands keen listening and responsiveness to both the verbal and nonverbal language of fellow players.

Latisha: "It's really hard for me to trust. I don't know if I can trust you, or the T.V. . . . "

Karin: "or God, or my own perceptions. And I have all these feelings. . ."

Susan (with escalating emotional affect): "that are so hard for me to express but I feel like I'm going to explode if I keep them inside any longer."

Latisha: "So I'm going to try to tell you everything I'm feeling. . ."

Karin (with increasing resolve): "right now, I'm going to tell you everything I'm feeling right now."

Susan: "Finally, I feel ready to open up, to talk to you."

Larry (looking at his watch, then speaking calmly): "Well, our time is up for this week. Try to remember how you're feeling so that when you come back next week we can continue from this point."

In watching these scenes, I am struck by the group's insight into mental health and the mental health system, insight based on extensive personal experience that leads to biting humor, subtle interaction, and intense emo- tionality. I am excited at the thought of creating a performance that revolves around this topic. But I also apprehend that our play cannot be only about what it is like on the inside; for the group members' personal growth, it needs to also be about *the outside,* about what happens once the institution is left behind. That is, not only about where group members have been but about where they are headed.

At the following session, Jamie is back from the hospital and the group is in better spirits. Larry, who had strongly identified with Jamie's depression, is energized by Jamie's return. In a noteworthy change from his more typical improvisational roles of controlled authority figures, Larry plays a roguish, defiant six-year-old boy, protesting his mother's attempts to buy him a suit. The behavior displayed in the role is reminiscent of the puerile rebelliousness manifested toward the counselor in his scene about refusing to get out of bed.

In the discussion following this scene, group members share childhood memories in which they felt "stuffed in a suit," or expected to behave in a way that felt unnatural. The related enactments are striking, especially Karin's memory-scene. From her early childhood, Karin was an animal lover; her father was a hunter. In the scene, she is forced at dinner to eat the meat he'd killed that day—which, she says, "is like eating Bambi." I note the group's emergent capacity to deal with not only socially pertinent issues, but personal ones, involving the present and the past.

Jamie's Pain

Four days before Christmas, Jamie is back in the hospital. He reports that after "a bad experience" with a man he'd picked up in a bar (who had dropped him as soon as they arrived at a party), he overdosed on pills; he "didn't want to feel this pain again." The attempt was not life-threatening, but it landed him back in the mental hospital and led him to be kicked out of his halfway house for breaking the no-suicide rule. He is informed that the next step (should there be yet another suicide attempt) is long-term institutionalization at the state hospital.

I wonder what deeper level of pain and rejection underlies the current rejection, what primal experience has led Jamie to have such a low tolerance for rejection by lovers, even by strangers. I also wonder whether my expectations have been unrealistic: Perhaps it is not feasible to create a public performance with this population. How can such an event be planned when I cannot count on the cast members being out of institutions or even commited to staying alive?

Asserting that attendance at his theatre group is critical, Jamie manages to be granted a pass by the hospital. He doesn't want to be kicked out of the group and he doesn't want to let the group down. When he tells the group the news, there is a long silence. I can almost feel the thoughts swimming through the dark theatre space: "Can we trust Jamie? Will he eventually die on us? Can we trust anyone in the group? Can I myself be trusted? If Jamie O.D.ed because he had a rough weekend, what about me? Mine was rough, too, and the next one may be worse." We get into a circle, the familiar circle that invokes a sense of boundaries and containment.

Larry breaks the silence. He speaks with authority and impatience, in a dogmatic tone. "Jamie, you're just going to have to stop and look at your problems. And eventually you're going to have to start dealing with them." In taking on this teacher-like role, Larry maintains a protective distance.

But at least Larry has initiated the discussion. "Well, I'm really glad that you're OK and that you came tonight," Latisha offers. Others chime in with support. The fact that Jamie will not be allowed back to his halfway house, a place that had over the past year become a home, elicits a great deal of concern.

While others are focusing on Jamie's practical predicament, Karin is looking at him piercingly, as though trying to reach inside him, to the wounded part. "Jamie," she finally says softly and deliberately, "please call me next time. Even if it's three or four in the morning, call me."

"Yeah, Jamie," Alex jumps in. "You can call me anytime, I be there to talk to you. You got friends, man."

Silence again. In this moment I perceive the group to be on a critical brink: To ingest Jamie's depression, take on its weight, means sinking; to remain separate from him and yet contain him means staying afloat, above surface.

The force of ingestion is powerful. Jamie's state is familiar territory; they have all been there. It is a frightening place, but also an inviting one. To desire life and to stay alive is a struggle, and to release that struggle, tipping the balance toward numbness, toward death, is an ever-present temptation. Maintaining boundaries between self and others, being separate and whole, is also a constant struggle.

They all turn toward me when I speak. "It can be very hard to hear about someone else who is going through something you've been through, or who has painful feelings that you can truly relate to and understand. It's scary to both understand profoundly and yet to help, and I'm moved by how all of you are managing this — managing to help each other, while still taking care of yourselves."

Perhaps relieved by the notion that one can both identify and remain separate, the tone and content of the discussion shifts to another level. During the dialogue that follows, I am audience, privileged and humbled, as I listen to a group of people, all of whom have known utter darkness, give to each other in a way that I, or any other professional, could not give. I had known suffering, and was to know it yet more fully in later years, but had never descended to the pit of despair, to the point of wanting to end life. This is their turn to help each other.

"Jamie," Karin begins, "I tried to do it, too, put myself to sleep forever. I even succeeded, but they brought me back. And I'm glad they did. Some-times I think of all I would've missed if I had died. The pain—yes, but also the joy. The simple, precious things, like nature, like sights of beauty. It takes courage to live, but it's worth it."

"I feel like you a lot Jamie." It is Stacey, who has been silent until now, speaking. "I've tried to end it all, too, lots of times. But I go on because I hope our efforts will be rewarded in the end, that it will all be worth it. And I know there are surprise gifts along the way, like new friends. It's just hard to always remember they exist when you don't see them around for a while. I know there's a purpose and meaning to everything, even if we still have to find it."

"I tried to do away with myself, too. Once with pills, once by slashing my wrists, once by running in front of a car. I know what it's like," Susan says. "But I want to try to remember at these times that it's not always that way, that things change."

One person after the other discloses his own experience with suicide. Jamie gazes intently at each person as he or she speaks.

"My father committed suicide, Jamie," Larry divulges, his tone tense but unusually gentle. "I've been there myself, but I'm trying to do things differently now, and I think I'm slowly getting stronger. It's a challenge not to give up. And mostly I feel like, damn it, I'm not going to do the same thing he did."

"I think we can help each other not to give up," Latisha says, and they all nod.

It is time to move.

I unroll a large sheet of butcher paper which spreads halfway across the room, and lay out colored crayons and magic markers. I instruct everyone to gather around the paper, each person claiming a section of it. The statements I make are written down and then completed, in stream-of-consciousness fashion: This group is _____; *Name of person in group* is _____; I hope I can _____; Our performance will _____. I present statements that elicit reflection and, in a nonthreatening way, broach a subject that has barely been mentioned (since the individual meetings held before the series began): that of The Perfor-mance. But the process of the activity is more important than the content. "Now take up more space, write bigger!" I exclaim. "Expand your section. You're greedy; you want more space to write in."

With the addition of the magic ingredient—interaction—comes laughter and animation. Everyone relishes the permission to become assertive, if not aggressive. I find myself improvising; this part of the exercise wasn't planned. "Now walk around the entire sheet, reading it as if it's graffiti on a bathroom wall, and respond to parts, give your own comments." Everyone strolls, stretches, scribbles. The image of graffiti seems to be stimulating and freeing; responses, after all, are anonymous. My eye catches phrases rich with poetry, humor, and wit. But most of what I decipher is praise for fellow members of the group: Jamie is *a deeply fine human being*; Karin is *talented*; Stacey is *being born*. Soon there are responses to responses, whole dialogues, and the sheet grows dense with color and conversation and imbued with feeling and spirit.

We set off to Stacey's new apartment for the prearranged holiday potluck celebration. It is two days before Christmas. Despite the energy with which we leave the theatre, once at Stacey's home the group withdraws. Larry is isolated in a corner; Karin sets herself apart from the group by refusing to eat or to take part in the group photographs. Latisha chain-smokes and appears very tense. Perhaps she is thinking again about Jamie. Perhaps she fears that now that someone in the group is back in the hospital the status of the group is changed: We can no longer claim to be a group of *ex*-psychiatric patients.

Dinner is over. It seems there is someone in every corner of the living room, but the center is empty. Alex has brought champagne and I suggest we offer toasts, necessitating our gathering close together. "To seven wonderful people," I propose. Each glass clicks with every other, and soon eyes meet, too. It strikes me that this is a marking point, a time to remind the group of its accomplishments during the past 12 weeks. I propose another toast: "Congratulations to each one of you—for completing the first half of our process, meeting a major part of your commitment already, and doing so superbly!" This phrasing is a new twist for the group; each had been wondering, "Will I make it to the end?" instead of thinking, "So far I *have* made it."

The tone in the room has shifted, and others join in with toasts of their own. A playful, game-like ambiance is established as each person proposes a toast, followed by the clicking of every glass with every other.

As "The Performance" can now be tolerated as a concept, albeit a mysterious and abstract one, I offer one more toast: "To the most exciting, original, emotionally moving, stirring, funny, powerful. . ." (laughter as I add adjective upon adjective) ". . .upcoming performance of Beyond Analysis!" Spontaneously, the group applauds.

After a conversation about fears, hopes, and ideas regarding the performance, Stacey tells us that she is a closet songwriter and offers to sing a song she recently wrote. With trembling hands, she reaches for her guitar. And then come these words, in the form of a most lovely melody:

I come to you my friend
And you say we're going to have a party
But does your party invite this feeling
I called to you my friend

But once again I found I've only been dreamin'
Seems I'm forever dreamin'

It is getting late. As a way of ending, I motion to the group to gather in a small circle, with Jamie lying on the floor between us. Slowly, we lift him *(People Lifts).* In the holding and rocking that follows, the compassionate and intimate tone of today's sesssion is revived.

I drive Jamie back to the hospital. He is quiet. We arrive moments before his curfew. Just before getting out of the car, he gives me a hug and says, "This is the first Christmas in my life that I've had a family."

Shared Experiences

Knowing how vulnerable the group can be during the holiday season, I provide added structure. There are extra individual meetings, an outing to an improvisational theatre performance, and assignments—including working on a script from a published play (necessitating getting together with others), and writing a monologue based on a train of inner thoughts.

Susan announces that she has written a monologue conveying her inner thoughts as she rides the bus. Converting the monologue into a dramatic scene, the group becomes passengers on the bus, each silently absorbed in his or her own world. Susan, too, is a silent passenger, but her inner thoughts are heard on audiotape. The sharp contrast between her tumultuous internal state and her calm external appearance (and the placidity surrounding her) creates dramatic tension.

"Am I one of these people or can I appear to be one of them? Everyone is so separate. I feel so alone. No one is talking to me. I don't belong here. I'm an alien. Oh no, everyone is noticing me. That I'm different. They don't like me."

"Relax. Just wait till my stop. Ignore the people. I'll read the ads. (she looks up) One - out - of - every - seven - people - will - be - hospitalized - this - year. Oh, God, relax."

The monologue continues, reflecting the intensity, insecurity, and paranoia with which Susan is inundated. The scene is a relevant one; the group has often referred to bus rides as traumatic episodes, and to feeling alien in public places.

The group continues to discuss and enact common experiences, eliciting relief and humor, a kind of joking about one's own culture. In a spoof of group therapy, Susan once again takes center stage by playing the therapist, struggling to lead a group of very disturbed people. Introjecting the technique of *Calling Out Emotions,* everyone—therapist included—instantaneously exhibits whatever emotion I call out. As always, the group members draw on their own emotions and neuroses in playing the scene.

When the final emotion, "fear," is called out, everyone delights in the exaggerated portrayal of a familiar feeling. But the most humorous part of the scene is hearing Susan respond to the chaos by saying in a panic-stricken voice, "I have all these people depending on me. . . . to lead a group. . . . and I don't know how to do it. . . ."

As I enter one session, I find everyone recounting stories about his or her hospital admissions. Stacey's story has particular theatrical potential. Perceiving a light pole to be at an angle and falling, she struggled to hold it up, for hours, until police arrived. Unable to convince her that the pole wasn't falling, the friendly cops finally helped her to hold it up. When she was adequately reassured that it was back in place, they carted her to the hospital.

The segue from storytelling to dramatization has become natural to the group, and we enact the scene. The moment in which the cops, played by Alex and Jamie, *act as though* the light pole is falling is comical and touching. An intimacy and rapport (between them and Stacey) develop as they enter her reality.

I try to evaluate which scenes will work in a performance, which scenes are interrelated, themes that are surfacing, and how to direct the group into a deeper exploration of these themes. Although the shared recollections of experiences in psychiatric institutions provide a cathartic experience for the group (and a potentially educational one for outside audiences), the past must not be overemphasized; from both therapeutic and theatrical perspectives, engagement in present-day issues is critical. In one session, the group (divided into two subgroups) is asked to discuss and then create a scene revolving around challenges faced upon *leaving* institutions.

Alex portrays running into old friends (played by Susan and Latisha) who do not know he had had a nervous breakdown and had been hospitalized. For a long time, he avoids responding to their questions about where he has been, circumventing the questions in clever and humorous ways, until finally he tells them the truth despite his fears about how they will react.

Stacey portrays returning home to relatives (played by Karin and Larry) who treat her as though she may fall apart again at any moment. In the scene, she withdraws. When I suggest that she replay the scene, showing us how she copes with their treatment, she is at a loss. The group offers suggestions, representing new options for Stacey, options not yet incorporated into her real life. With some effort, she reenacts the scene, this time taking a more active stance. First, she explains to her family that they don't need to treat her so delicately. Then, alone in her room, she reminds herself—out loud—that even though they may worry that she may "crack up" again at any moment, she is not the same fragile person who entered the hospital three months ago. Even if others do not recognize the changes she has made, these changes still exist, and she does not need to "live down" to the expectations and perceptions of others.

Guest artists from the Black Repertory Theatre company (at which we will soon be seeing a production) are invited to conduct a mask-making session with the group. For the first time, the group responds enthusiastically to instruction by "outsiders." This is partly due to the sensitivity and warmth of the instructors, but also a manifestation of the group members' increased readiness to reach outward, toward the community, as well as their increased interest in developing theatrical skills. The other dimension to this acceptance is cultural; the exposure to leaders and role models of different races is critical.

These instructors are periodically invited back, and other theatre artists representing diverse cultures and approaches to theatre are brought in, not only to teach the group new skills but to critique some of the scenes we have been reworking. It is time to have our material, which deals so much with inside culture, be witnessed by people from the community.

I am grateful for the respite from turmoil and crisis and for the positive reports I hear during this period. Larry and Stacey have obtained part-time jobs. Alex has begun volunteering at the Black Repertory Theatre. Like Stacey, he has begun to manifest excitement about our performance. I am deeply appreciative of his presence in the group; in most respects, he has been the most stable and reliable member. Karin's panic after playing roles has eased and, given her sense of being accepted "as is" by me and the group, she now feels ready to "go through with" the performance.

I begin to shift my energy toward the construction of the play. But before long the players draw my attention back to themselves. Latisha is depressed and withdrawn. Susan is exceedingly jealous of the growing relationship between Stacey and Karin, and has begun to act out by frightening them with bizarre phone calls and by engaging in self-destructive behavior. A mediation session is held between the three of them, and extra individual meetings with Susan are arranged. Jamie is hearing voices again. Resisting discouragement, I try to look at the positive side: Everyone is coming to every session regardless of mood or crisis. Everyone is getting by without rehospitalization. There seems to be a momentum toward the performance, a tacit sense that no matter what happens, the show must go on.

TURNING PAIN INTO ART: CULMINATING SCENES

Jamie's Challenge

Jamie refers to the voices he hears as "Rocky," and says that Rocky instructs him to commit suicide. The personification of the voices leads me to try a little experiment. I bring a tape recorder to the next individual session with Jamie and suggest that we record Rocky's messages.

Playing Rocky, Jamie begins: "C'mon, go ahead and do it, it'll be all over. No more pain. See that sprinkler up there? All you have to do is tie a sheet around it and hang yourself from it. C'mon and end it all. I'll help you. You won't be alone, I'll be there with you."

After just a few minutes, Jamie wants to play the tape back. As we listen together to what he has just recorded, his mood becomes sullen and withdrawn, as though "sucked up" by Rocky.

I suggest he respond to Rocky rather than just passively listen.

We record a little more of Rocky's insidious monologue and then play it back. As Jamie struggles to find a response to Rocky, he becomes slightly more animated, but remains at a loss for words. He is too lured by Rocky's words to have a counter reply.

A week later Jamie hands me a script. "It's for the play," he says. Apparently Rocky had visited that night, at which point Jamie recorded what Rocky told him, along with tentative replies.

Before beginning work on Jamie's scene at the next session, I offer the group some precautionary words: "We're about to work on an intense scene, about something difficult to confront directly, but very important to deal with — suicidal thoughts."

"Oh, that stuff, suicide, voices, no big deal," they immediately respond with humor and irony. "We can handle that everyday stuff," "Quotidian!" The group has by now developed a facility at confronting the hidden, darker side of life.

I ask Jamie to think about circumstances that precipitate Rocky's appearance. He selects Latisha to play a nurse at the hospital who informs him that he has been kicked out of his halfway house.

"Jamie," Latisha improvises, "I'm sorry but the halfway house just called to say they're not going to take you back because of your last suicide attempt."

Dejected, Jamie reaches for the phone and dials a long-distance number.

"Hello, Ma?"

Long pause.

"Ma?"

No response.

"Ma, are you there? This is Jamie."

Shaken, he slowly puts down the receiver. "She hung up on me," he mutters to himself. "Seems like everyone is hanging up on me."

I begin playing the tape of the voices.

"C'mon and end it all. See that sprinkler up there? All you have to do is tie a sheet around it and hang yourself from it . . ."

Jamie is silent. His voice on tape, playing Rocky, continues.

"You won't be alone anymore."

"How about plugging in the razor in the water. You done pills before and you know that won't work. So do what I say and join me."

Struck by the words "join me" and "you won't be alone anymore," I recall that Jamie's twin brother died in a car accident eight years ago.

"C'mon and end it all. Just once and it'll be all over. No more worries, no cares."

Jamie listens intently, but the only response he offers is an occasional meek "No," or "Leave me alone." I ask him to speak more and to speak louder, to fight back a little harder.

As I watch Jamie, I also observe from the corners of my eyes the rest of the group watching Jamie. The turn inward has begun, cueing me to intervene before the state of withdrawal settles. I stop the scene and ask for responses. Everyone is silent. It is crucial for the group members to surmount their feelings of powerlessness and mergence, and crucial for Jamie to feel their support. Instead, there is both too much distance (between Jamie and the group) and not enough distance. Then I remember the discussion we had a few weeks ago. I direct the group to enter the stage.

I remind them of the day Jamie came to the session from the hospital and ask them to reach out to him again, as they had then, with one or two lines, beginning with the word "I".

Huddled together on one side of the bare stage, all the group members find within themselves the strength to go back to that discussion and to the time in their own lives when they were on the brink of suicide. In chorus style, the lines—born out of suffering and despair, but manifesting resilience and faith—are not so much spoken as cast toward Jamie in the hope that he will take hold of them. Jamie listens intently, as though absorbing each word. The magic and potency of the discussion have been brought back to life, or rather brought to theatre.

If Jamie does not need to rely on Rocky, on death, in order not to feel alone, perhaps he will be able to fight back.

With the group still standing in its huddle, now silent and waiting, I begin playing the tape again.

"Shut up," shouts Jamie. "I don't want to do it." And then a line that surpasses anything that could have been scripted emerges: "You're a part of me, and only a part, a small part." The line indicates, for the first time, ownership of the voice as a part of him rather than an external phenomenon. A part he can rise above, answer back, with other parts of himself.

More lines come forth; finally, there is a dialogue with Rocky. I instruct Latisha to call Jamie in for group therapy. Rocky's coaxing continues, pulling Jamie in two directions. I tell Jamie to gradually end the scene, in any way he wishes.

"Don't go out there," booms Rocky. "Stay with me and end it all."

"No!" Jamie shouts with a voice I haven't heard before, a voice that possesses strength and conviction, albeit packed into only one word. "I will survive, I will make it."

"Louder, stronger, Jamie," I call out from offstage.

"I will make it. I will survive," he roars. "I want to live. Nurse . . . I'm coming!"

Work on Jamie's scene highlights the point at which theatre and therapy intersect. The theatrical goals for this *culminating scene* (see Chapter 2) are identical to the therapeutic goals: Jamie needs to find responses to the voices and to deliver these responses with conviction and forcefulness. The scene both befits Jamie's personal journey at this time and belongs in our play; it reflects not only the immediate struggle faced by one cast member but the ongoing struggles of everyone in the group. Even more importantly, it represents a universal struggle—whether to give up or to go on.

If this scene is part of our play, I wonder, then why not have other *culminating scenes* about the struggles of individual cast members? Act One could be about how cast members were admitted into mental hospitals, what it is like inside these institutions, and issues they face upon being discharged from hospitals. Act Two could explore personal issues in greater depth.

In the individual meetings, I begin to help group members view their life struggles as potential material for our play. I do this not only as director, concerned with the development of a performance piece, but as therapist, believing that to take hold of one's pain and then to shape and transform it into a communicative art form is healing.

Abuse and Denial of Reality: The Devastating Duo

Karin speaks with me about a recent crisis with her father. He requested that she return home to "answer questions about the direction your life is taking." When she refused, he ragingly disowned her.

With little guidance, Karin is able to translate this life scene into a drama. She writes a script, drawn from the real-life phone conversation. She directs Larry to play her father and records his voice on audiotape. In the scene, the audience will hear both sides of the conversation.

Then she decides to add the phone call received from her mother soon after the father's call. The mother makes no mention of what just took place. A script demonstrating the mother's denial of reality is written and recorded.

In the scene, we first hear the conversation between Karin and her father.

"Your mother and I have been sitting all day thinking about you. We were looking at the course offerings at U.C. Berkeley. Why didn't you enroll in the science class? We told you we would be glad to pay your tuition."

"It just didn't interest me. It's not something I want to do with my life right now."

"Well, what are you doing with your life? You have no career, no plans. We want you to come home to Texas for a while and answer our questions. We will pay your airfare and the cost of putting your dogs in a kennel."

"No, that's not something I want to do right now. It would not be in my best interest."

"Well, with an attititude like that you will never receive any financial support from us again."

"O.K., Father, if that's how you want it, that's fine."

Suddenly, without warning, the father begins raging. "Then you are no longer my daughter, I do not consider myself your father. As far as I am concerned, you are dead. I never want to hear from you again."

Not getting a response from her, he adds, "And every day I will regret having brought a creature like you on to the face of this earth!" Then he slams the receiver.

Karin is left frozen on stage. The enactment has revived real feelings. I ask her to try to voice these feelings out loud.

"Daddy . . . why? Oh God, I'm going to get the razor," she says in a tremulous tone. "No, I'll shoot up. I'm going to go crazy. I'll go into the hospital. Damn it, I don't want to do that either." She is holding herself and rocking, as if to soften the pain. "It really hurts. I feel like I've been aborted."

Clearly, work on this scene will be similar to work on Jamie's scene — helping Karin find the strength to stay with the pain, and then to master and transcend it.

The challenge increases; the phone rings again and we hear the conversation with her mother. When the mother says goodbye, not wanting "to run up the phone bill," Karin is left alone to face the onslaught of self-destructive urges.

"They're crazy," she says spontaneously.

Then the wailing starts. "Damn it, why can't they love me? Can't I ever be good enough?" She kicks the the chair furiously and flails her arms. "Damn, damn, damn," she screams.

The group is tense and still.

The flailing ceases and the holding and rocking resume.

I stand near her but wait, trusting that she knows how to proceed — for the scene and for herself.

"It isn't them, it isn't me, it's us. But I'm not going to play out their fantasy. I'm not going to go crazy, go to the hospital." At this she stands up and begins pacing.

"I'm going to be strong. I'm not going to play out their fantasy. It's my life now."

Through the improvisational mode, with the group as witness, Karin begins to separate herself from her parents, to tear herself away from the family enmeshment and choose something new:

"I'm going to be strong. I'm going to sit with the pain. I'm not going to numb it out or lose control. I'm going to feel it. And live with it. I'm going to live now." Her tone is quiet and tentative.

I ask her to repeat this line.

"I'm going to live now. For me." Her tone is becoming stronger, surer. "I'm going to live, for me."

The group applauds.

At the end of the session, Karin asks to take the tape recording home, to practice the timing of her responses. Concerned about her listening repeatedly in the solitude of her apartment to her father's booming rejection, I hesitate. When I explain the reason for my hesitation, she says, "Actually, it becomes less *lethal* as I work on it. Like building up an immunity to my own pain." I am struck by this manifestation of *aesthetic distance.* In taking control of the scene, Karin is no longer the powerless victim. The creative process impels mastery. I give her the tape.

Highlighting the abuse and the denial of reality with which Karin has had to contend, another scene is generated, this time based on a childhood memory.

"Mommy, can we go now," says Karin tremulously, playing herself as a child. "You said if Daddy hurt you again we'd go to a motel."

"Karin, get ready for school," her mother, played by Latisha, mechanically responds.

"School, I can't go to school," she cries, now panic-stricken. "He shot my doggy! And he keeps getting drunk and hurting us. Please, Mommy, let's go to a motel. You said . . ."

"Your father says he's sorry, and he'll be a good Daddy from now on," interrupts her mother. "So get ready for school. Remember, Karin, we're a happy family."

Stacey identifies strongly with Karin's scenes; she, too, has a family history of abuse, alcoholism, and denial of reality. The latter was most injurious, leading to a constant doubting of her perceptions. Inspired by Karin's courage, Stacey conceives scenes about her own life. Following the format of Karin's scenes, the present-day drama is preceded by a childhood trauma.

"A nice family outing that turned out to be! You got drunk again and dangled the damn kid over the alligator pit," says Karin, playing Stacey's mother. "You did it to embarrass me."

"Will you shut your mouth," retorts Larry, "I was playing with my kid."

"You call that playing with your kid?" Karin says accusingly.

The argument escalates, until Stacey, running toward her mother for comfort, gets thrown to the ground by her father, who promptly storms out.

"Now you know your daddy didn't mean to hurt you," the mother says, kneeling beside Stacey to check her bruise. "It's bleeding and we're going to have to go to the doctor and get this stitched. Now I need you to learn a little story about how you got hurt."

Stacey lies on the floor crying.

"Now you were playing with your sister. . ."

"My sister's not here," Stacey whimpers.

"It doesn't matter. It's a story, like I tell you before bedtime. Now you were playing with your sister at the top of the stairs. . ."

"We don't have any stairs."

"And you fell all the way down. And if you tell the story good like Mommy wants you to, Mommy will really love you."

"You will?"

"Yes, I will. Now let's practice the story. . ."

A few minutes later they are at the doctor's office. Alex, as the doctor, asks little Stacey how she got hurt.

Under her mother's scrutinizing gaze, Stacey attempts to speak. But no words come out. "Well. . .uh, uh. . ."

"Tell me, what happened?" the doctor asks again.

"Uh, uh. . ."

The doctor looks toward the mother, perplexed. "Can't she speak?"

I end the scene on that line.

In real life, Stacey had been electively mute throughout much of her childhood.

In the present-day scene, Stacey is serving coffee to two of her mother's friends. When they ask her how she is doing, her mother immediately answers for her. After several times of being interrupted, Stacey finally gives up trying to converse.

"What are you doing now, Stacey?" the guests ask again. Stacey is stunned to hear her mother reply, "Oh, she's working as an occupational therapist."

When the guests leave (ironically telling Stacey on their way out how nice it was to talk with her), Stacey confronts her mother:

"Why did you tell those lies, that I'm an occupational therapist?"

"Well, Stacey," her mother retorts, "you've been a patient in occupational therapy for so long, I figured it was the only thing you could talk about!"

THE PERFORMANCE PROCESS

Anticipating the Performance

It is nearing the end of our fourth month of working together. The mounting emotional intensity of the scenes gives rise to a growing anticipation of the performance. Sensing the group's eagerness for structure, I devise "scripts." Outlines of the prospective structure of the play, the scripts are intended to lend tangibility to the performance and to stimulate the group's own ideas.

Rather than formally distributing the scripts, I instigate a game in which everyone attempts to grab as many scripts as possible, finally obtaining the script that bears his or her name. This playful, interactive warm-up circumvents anxiety and adds levity to a potentially charged moment. The *Back Pushes* that follow further ease apprehension. But when we sit down to review the scripts, Larry and Latisha grow visibly tense, and Karin suddenly exclaims that she is about "to have an anxiety attack." Before I can respond, she runs out of the room. I proclaim a 15-minute break.

"Let's come into a circle, standing," I say, after the break, motioning the group into a small huddle. Karin appears more relaxed as a result of the support she received from Jamie and Susan. "Do what I do, as I do it," I add, initiating the familiar *Group Mirror*.

"I'm scared," I shout, as I begin running. My words and movements are immediately echoed by seven people. Our expressions of fear turn into terror, until we run wildly away from one another.

"Let's call off the show!" Everyone joins in, adding variations to this line and clearly delighting in the process. "The show's cancelled." "Couldn't go through with it." "No show!"

The relief turns to disappointment and regret, so we resurrect the show. "OK, let's do it!" "We're gonna do it!" Anxiety has given way to excitement.

Following the *Group Mirror* exercise, I ask Latisha and Larry to sit in the audience rows and pretend to be people watching the performance by *Beyond Analysis.*

Playing a conservative man with a mid-Western accent, Larry mumbles to Latisha, "I hear the people in this show are crazy, is that right?"

"The cast has all experienced emotional distress and been hospitalized," Latisha explains calmly, "but now they're on the outside, getting well. They shouldn't be viewed as freaks."

"Once a nut, always a nut, that's what I say."

"Well, I'm here to see my sister," Latisha replies politely.

Larry's expression is one of amazement. "You mean you know someone in the show? Your sister's crazy?"

"Not anymore," responds Latisha as her sister. "She's doing great. Anyway, the show's starting. Watch, you may learn something!"

The improvisation continues, with others in the group taking over the role of audience members, until everyone has had a chance. Some play people they know; others play strangers.

Three parts of this session are so effective in dealing with the anxiety associated with the performance that they become staples during the forthcoming two-month rehearsal period: 1) the format of having a break (which the group begins referring to as "anxiety attack period!"); 2) *Mirror* exercises in which fears are expressed; 3) the improvisation in which the actors become the audience. The latter technique not only fosters exploration of cast members' concerns about being seen (by particular people and by general audiences) but heightens awareness of aesthetics and communication.

In the following sessions, scenes indicated on the scripts are reenacted, and group members give one another astute critiques. The capacity to examine scenework from an aesthetic perspective and to tolerate critical feedback has noticably increased.

In the process of developing and refining the scenes from a theatrical perspective, and particularly of formulating final lines, therapeutic issues are crystallized. Stacey and Karin become more conscious of the impact of the double messages they were inundated with as children, Jamie connects his suicidal ideation with feelings of abandonment and rejection, Larry sees how fearful he is of fully engaging in life. I continue to be struck by the natural intertwining of theatrical and therapeutic goals.

The Rehearsal Process

As the sessions progress into a rehearsal mode, Latisha becomes increasingly withdrawn and resistant, to the point of shutting her eyes during our discussions or reading a book during another member's scene. My efforts to involve her are met with hostility.

At our next "monthly," Karin begins by stating that she misses Latisha. Concerned that Latisha will not be able to tolerate direct confrontation, I say something about the inevitability of anxiety in a performance group, thereby normalizing the experience, and ask each person to think about his or her own ways of manifesting anxiety. We then examine factors precipitating anxiety and how to deal with the anxiety. Everyone shares how s/he would like to *be responded to* at these times. The tension in Latisha's face eases during this group discussion, and finally she speaks. "I'm freaked out about the performance. I need a lot of space when I get anxious. It's best not to invade it. Just let me know it's OK, that I'm OK."

Latisha is ready at the next session to explore possibilities for her own scene. The group reminds her of the fact that her nervous breakdowns are precipitated by going back to work. She admits that just *hearing* the word "work" makes her jump. "Pressure is what makes me crack," she says, which makes me think of her extreme difficulty in coping with the pressure of the performance. "And yet, having a job is considered to be a sign that you're better, proving after you've been out of a hospital that you're now normal."

The group forms a line, facing Latisha. I ask them to shout—in the format of *Storytelling: One-Word-at-a-Time:* "Latisha - you - really - ought - to - think - about - going - out - and - getting - a - job!"

Her smile only half shields a look of panic. We begin a scene in which she faces a new job. An office is set up, with Latisha sitting at the reception desk. As she is bombarded with phone calls, new tasks—copying, typing, filing—are incessantly brought to her desk. The pressure mounts when three co-workers simultaneously insist that their work needs to get done before lunch. Without warning, Latisha throws the phone on the floor and storms out.

"I know I didn't do it right. Maybe next time it'll be different," she says quietly, somewhat relieving the group of the fear that Latisha's loss of control was *real.* I suggest a scene in which this "next time" is depicted.

We replay the scene. When the three people barrage her with work, she stands up and faces them. Calmly and assertively, she says, "Sorry, but it'll have to get done when I come back. It's noon, and that's my lunchtime." And off she walks, in a dignified fashion, as the group cheers and applauds.

Interactive games continue to predominate the early parts of each session, even during the rehearsal phase. On Valentine's day everyone is asked to sneak a present to someone else in the group during the session—without being seen. In another session, intergroup tension and aggression are released via a *Bubble-War.* Visits by guest artists and outings to local theatre productions also continue.

The outings expose the group to wide ranges of theatrical experiences and also provide a forum for unstructured interaction. One Sunday, after seeing an autobiographical performance, we walk over to a nearby park. The group is energized and feisty. Watching their playful mingling, I marvel at the ease in their interactions, at the close-knit friendships that have developed, and at the distinct sense of group identity.

"Our play is going to be really powerful. The stuff we're dealing with isn't seen in other theatre performances," Susan says excitedly.

"No, they're in for a real surprise," Stacey grins. "The Beyond Analysis Horror Picture Show." Everyone laughs.

"I can just picture it. Renée calmly tells the audience the show will start a few minutes late. Then she speeds over to fetch us on the Golden Gate Bridge," Jamie jokes, checking to see that I'm smiling. (The Golden Gate is a notorious spot for suicides.)

"Well, on the way to the theatre today," Karin adds to the teasing (of the group and of me), making reference now to my continued insistence on commitment, "Stacey and I were rushing, so we wouldn't be late. In the car we thought, what if we get into an accident? We pictured Renée saying to the group, 'Now Karin and Stacey got into an accident. We will excuse their absence, but I don't want the rest of you to think this will always be a good excuse, that you can all get into car accidents. They're in a coma, but I've arranged with the hospital to have them here for our rehearsal on Tuesday.' "

After some more banter and teasing, the discussion becomes serious. The pros and cons of *coming out* as former psychiatric patients are considered. We talk about what we want the performance to convey—regarding mental health and illness, the mental health system, the lives of the people in the group, and human struggles. "The performance should show what it's really like, inside the system," Alex says. "And what it's like to leave . . .," "to enter the outside world," interject Stacey and Latisha. "It should also portray," Susan says, "what it's like inside oneself." "And what it's like to move from the internal outward, toward others," Karin articulates, "by revealing ourselves."

The discussion leads us to a title for the play: *Inside Out*.

Karin arrives at the next session with a poem. Not wanting our play to give the impression that blame and responsibility are being placed entirely on the past, specifically onto parents, she writes a poem addressed to her parents. In strikingly beautiful and powerful language, she intimates the way abuse is passed on generation to generation.

> *. . . For so long I have carried the burden of love's absence . . .*
> *Was this our inheritance then?*
> *These tangled strands of an endless double helix*
> *Draped round us in a long glistening chain*
> *Linking us always together*
> *Like a necklace*
> *Like a noose?*
> *I know you never knew your parents either*
> *Nor they their own. . . .*

Aside from Karin's poem, all scenes will be improvised, allowing for new lines to emerge at all performances—creating an immediacy on stage that can be theatrically riveting and a therapeutic process that is continuously unfolding. The structure and the final lines of each scene, however, will be set.

The structure for the play as a whole is becoming clear. Act One begins with admission into a psychiatric hospital. In the first scene, the entire group plays a team of therapists, evaluating the new patient, Alex. In the second scene, Stacey is brought to the hospital by the police who helped her hold up the light pole. The following scenes depict what it is like on the inside— inside the hospital and inside the mind of the patient. Scene Three is a group therapy session, in which Susan plays the therapist. The audience calls out emotions, which all the actors incorporate. Scene Four shows Susan as herself, on the bus, coping with an onslaught of emotions and perceptions as she heads toward her session with her psychiatrist. This leads to the doctor-patient scene, Scene Five, in which Larry plays the psychiatrist and Susan, Latisha, and Karin the patient. Act One culminates with issues faced upon leaving the hospital: In Scene Six, Alex confronts friends who want to know where he has been; in Scene Seven, Stacey confronts the awkwardness of her family as she returns home.

Act Two explores individual struggles. Each scene is prefaced by the central protagonist. Stacey, who is last seen on stage as Act One ends, begins Act Two with scenes about the double messages she has been subjected to: the childhood scene in which she is asked to lie about how she got hurt, followed by the present-day scene in which her mother answers for her. In the next scene, Karin shares her struggle to cope with double messages and abuse, via her childhood scene in which her mother denies the severe abuse that has just taken place, followed by the adult scene in which she receives rejecting and disturbing telephone calls from her parents. Progressing to a deeper level of emotional intensity, Jamie's confrontation with his suicidal voices follows. Karin then reads her poem. As she reads it, huge slides of her as a young child, and then of her in the present day are projected behind her. These are followed by brief slide images of each person in the group, as a child and as an adult. Larry's scene, in which he resists the counselor who tells him to get out of bed, interjects humor until the depth of his struggle— to face life—gradually becomes clear. So, too, with Latisha's scene, as it builds from the difficulty of facing a new job to the struggle of coping with the pressures of life.

In each of the scenes in Act Two, the actors not only *portray* their struggles, but *grapple with* these struggles on stage. The pain and the self-destructive response to the pain are confronted and then responded to in new, healthful ways. These new responses become previews, if not blueprints, of the next stages in the actors' real lives.

For the finale of *Inside Out,* the cast members enter the stage, one at a time, repeating a powerful line from their scene (in most cases the last line), a line that reflects their will to prevail. The other actors on stage join in, repeating this same line in unison, along with gestures and expressions initiated by the entering actor. Latisha enters last, declaring, "Next time will be different!" The entire cast repeats this line with her, in ever-increasing volume and intensity. As they do so, they move toward one another, ending up arm in arm, facing the audience, until they shout the line for the final time and take their bows.

Each scene in Act Two is rehearsed not only in the group sessions but in individual sessions. During the individual sessions, nuances are examined and emergent emotions or insights are developed. Significant lines are under-scored and the spontaneous utterance of new lines is encouraged.

Prominent directors from the theatre community are invited to observe rehearsals. Their participation not only affords expert critique, but helps the group get used to being seen by outsiders.

Outside of the sessions, on my own, I work on finding ways of strength-ening the dramatic connection between scenes, making transitions more smooth, and augmenting the theatrical potency of the play via music, lighting, and slides. Along with Stacey, who becomes actively involved in all areas of the production, I select relevant and powerful musical scores to also be played as the audience enters, during intermission, and as a segue between scenes.

I photograph each person in the group. *Inside Out* begins with the pro-jection of life-size close-ups of each cast member, as Jimmy Cliff and Guilly Bright-Plummer's song *Sitting Here in Limbo** plays.

Sitting here in limbo
Waiting for the dice to roll
Sitting here in limbo
Knowing that I have to go
Well they're putting up resistance
But I know that my faith will lead me on.
I don't know where life will lead me
But I know where I've been
I can't say what life will show me
But I know what I've seen
This little boy is moving on . . .

The final slide, just before the first scene begins, shows the whole group together.

Three weeks before the production, I hire one of the instructors from the Black Repertory Theatre, to whom the group had responded well, as stage

---

manager. I also hire lighting and sound technicians. We begin rehearsing three to five days a week, and sessions are extended to three-hour blocks. The excitement and tension mount. I solicit the group's assistance in dealing with the many production tasks at hand, including printing programs, organizing tickets and refreshments, and obtaining props. The added tasks help to constructively channel some of the anxiety.

My role of theatrical director is highlighted at this point; I have come to care deeply about the production. But my other role, that of therapist, is also fully engaged during this pre-performance period, a period that brings the group to a critical emotional brink. It is a prime time for sabatoge, for inciting failure, a potential dynamic within the group that must be understood and circumvented. The fear of rejection by the audience—the outside world—is tremendous. At the same time, there is a will to failure, a compulsion to repeat one's history, to stay with what is familiar. The product hinges on the process: Lack of scrupulous attention to the process puts the performance at risk. I know this from experience. Last year, at the final rehearsal for the play *Episodes,* one of the members of *Beyond Analysis* who had very significant roles throughout the play suddenly walked out. This year, even as I devote as much time as possible to refining the product, I make no sacrifices of the process.

The greater fear—albeit less conscious—is of success. Through the group sessions and the added individual sessions with each person, I begin to comprehend the associations with success: If the performance is a success, will others' expectations of me be different? Will I let people down eventually, since they will expect too much from me? Will I be abandoned by my support systems if they think I have made it? What if I am successful on the outside but still feel inadequate and miserable on the inside?

All fears are examined, validated, and enacted, thereby reducing their potency and making them more manageable. Acting out the fears in the group sessions reduces the risk of acting out on one's own. We not only rehearse the play, we rehearse the feelings associated with performing the play, preparing for the emotions that may surface on the day of the performance. We play with time, enacting (and coping with) the onslaught of feelings that may occur in the wake of the performance. The performance is put into perspective, as one part of the process—a process that is to continue well after the performances are over. The performance is a climactic point in the group's process, to be followed by a period of intimate sharing, reviewing, and celebrating.

The Performance Day

Finally the day arrives. During the intense group warm-up before the show, we express—via voice, movement, and words—a feeling of readiness.

Trust exercises both heighten and reflect the sense of closeness and support within the group. I congratulate the group before the show begins, stating that the real achievement has already occurred. They have made it this far, to the point of experiencing this level of intimacy as a group and this degree of readiness to perform before an outside audience. We sit together for a few moments in silence and then form a *group hug.* Their faces are vibrant. I note that they are far more prepared for success than for failure.

The stage manager, Norman, stays backstage with the group throughout the show, while I help coordinate the sound and light technicians in the light booth. This is the point at which I must *let go;* the show is now in the hands of the group. I trust that they will be able to perform without my presence backstage; I also trust that they can feel my support across the distance. I watch the audience arriving, packing the house. The ushers inform me that we have sold out. The lights go down, the theatre is silenced, and *Sitting Here in Limbo* begins. The life-size slides of the cast members flood the blackened stage, one at a time. Then the photograph of the cast together, looking straight out to the audience, appears. Suddenly, I hear my heart pounding, sense my own anxiety. But as the lights go up, there they all are—the seven people I have come to care so deeply about—live on stage, beginning the first scene.

I listen with relief not only to what takes place on stage, but to the sounds of laughter and tears coming from the audience. The applause after each scene is intense. By the end it is riveting, and when the actors shout for the final time, *Next time it will be different!* and give a tentative bow, there is a standing ovation.

The audience continues standing as *Sitting Here in Limbo* once again resounds throughout the theatre.

The applause is not only for the play, but for the real people who have shared on stage their life struggles and victories.

10

SELF-REVELATORY PERFORMANCE

At the end of theatrical productions, the actors come onto the stage and are applauded for their creative achievement. This direct an acknowledgment is limited to the performance arts; in nonperformance arts, the artist is not necessarily present at the time the viewer/audience witnesses the art work. One usually experiences a painting, photograph, or poem independently of the person who created it. In the performing arts, however, the artist and the art product are witnessed concurrently, diminishing any potential dissociation between the two. The intertwining of product and person is intensified in dramatic art by the fact that the instrument used in creating the product is the artist's own body.

During the live applause, the actors shed their roles, taking their bows *as themselves.* In self-revelatory or autobiographical performances,* there are no roles to shed; the actors have been *coming out* as themselves throughout the performance. The applause is thus all the more direct, the line between artist and person all the more thin. Moreover, there is no playwright behind the scenes: The actors are not only the actualizers but the innovators of the production. They are applauded not only for their creative achievement, but for the process they have been through in creating it, for their courage to reveal themselves, and for who they are as people.

The response of the audience fills the actors with a deep sense not only of accomplishment but of acceptance. This potent experience of acceptance is intensified when the actors are people who have experienced social stigmatization (e.g., mental patients, the disabled, elderly, homosexuals) and when their identity has been made explicit to the audience. The actors' past roles (on which the stigmatization was based) and current successful roles are simultaneously

---

*For a distinction between self-revelatory performance and autobiographical theatre, see Chapter 7.

beheld by the audience. The actors' reaction to this recognition by the audience is one of exhilaration, pride, and affirmation of identity. This reaction is heightened by the sharing of the experience with one's group of fellow actors (Emunah & Johnson, 1983).

It is imperative that the production not only represent a personal achievement for the actors but that it be successful in theatrical terms. "Successful" does not necessarily imply a polished or flawless product, nor does it imply meeting standards of *traditional* theatre. But it does mean attaining excellence according to generally held aesthetic notions—that works of art should be communicative, evocative, and engaging. "Communication is a key word here," writes Arthur Robbins (1988), "for a completed work of any medium becomes art only when it touches us as a living truth...When symbolic form includes multiple levels of communication and transcends its individual parts to communicate a larger meaning, it approaches the level of aesthetic communication" (p. 95).

The production must be worthy of plaudit by outside critics, rather than only by friends of the actors who understand the challenge the process has posed. Without this achievement on an aesthetic level, the praise by the audience is merely a reflection of support for the people on stage, rather than an authentic response to the actors for the gift they have bestowed. Applause aimed at the people only (and excluding the product they have created) risks being condescending, if not infantilizing. Moreover, the limited expectations that the audience had (of the special population on stage) are reinforced; the audience's preconceptions are unchanged by such a production. Of greater consequence is the fact that the actors' pleasure in a polite response by an audience is short-lived. The longer-term effect of such an experience is often countertherapeutic, in contrast to the profoundly positive impact on self-esteem and self-image engendered by a theatrically successful performance.

The very essence of self-revelatory performance, in which traditional boundaries—between actor and self, actor and audience, theatre and real life—are dissolved, begets an authenticity and immediacy that can be theatrically riveting. There is a palpable tension in the theatre, as real people express their pain and grapple with their real-life struggles. The usual distance in theatre, in which actors play *characters* and audiences empathize and identify with these characters, leading to catharsis and insight, is drastically decreased in self-revelatory theatre. The empathy and identification with the *real people* on stage result in a more direct catharsis and a deeper level of self-analysis on the part of the audience.

This mutual probing and purging is reminiscent of Grotowski's *holy theatre,* in which the actors' exposure of their "innermost core" invites the audience on a similar journey of psychological and spiritual examination.

Though not referring to autobiographical theatre, Grotowski (1968) states that the actor must "undertake an act of self-penetration," unraveling exterior masks and discarding social roles until arriving at the essence of truthfulness. "It is a question of giving oneself," Grotowski says. "One must give oneself totally in one's deepest intimacy, with confidence, as when one gives oneself in love" (p. 38). The actor's work is an offering, in Grotowski's terms even a *sacrifice,* aimed at transformation.

Self-revelatory performance is not only a new kind of therapy, but a new genre of theatre. It builds upon the works of Grotowski, Artaud, The Living Theatre, and other experimental theatre directors and companies who explored boundaries, the actor's own process, and the relationship between actor and audience. In their view, the function of theatre was not to provide entertainment but to address the emotional and spiritual needs of the audience and to enrich the quality of life. At the end of his book, *Experimental Theatre,* Roose-Evans (1970) predicted that "it is not improbable that yet one more barrier will be broken down—that between the professional and the amateur. . . . Theatre will no longer be an entertainment for a minority relaxing at the end of a day's work, but a meaningful activity for thousands of leisured people. . . . I think it probable that we shall see the drama, the dance, taken out of the hands of the professional and restored to the people" (p.153).

Self-revelatory performance by amateur actors can be compared to neo-realist films in which "real people" are used rather than professional actors. In a review of *Beyond Analysis'* production of *Inside Out,* critic Michael Gallantz (1981) wrote: "The most provocative question raised by *Inside Out* may be one raised only indirectly: when does real life turn into art? It's a question we might not even think about because the show does have much theatrical skill and ingenuity—in the fast-moving, well-timed production; in the integration of tapes, slides, prepared pieces and improvisation, and in the avoidance (most of the time) of pat resolutions. At times even the acting shines, especially. . . (examples cited). . . *But the production gains intensity from the knowledge that the people on stage are for the most part telling their real-life stories. As in neo-realist films, there's a trade-off of smooth edges for immediacy . . . The incontrovertible genuineness of* Inside Out *is part of its vitality"* (p. 28).

In the world of theatre, there has been a proliferation during the past 10 years of autobiographical plays, storytelling based on real-life experience, and performance art based upon the actor's experience in-the-moment. There is a heightened consciousness of the artistic and the healing potentiality (for both actor and audience) in the use of real-life material, a consciousness that has likely been influenced by the synchronous development of the field of drama therapy.

The greatest potential pitfall in self-revelatory theatre—whether in the context of theatre or drama therapy—is that of self-indulgence. The personal must translate into the universal, the experience of the particular actor must elucidate the broader human experience. The play cannot be only "for the actor's good," but must edify, move, and inspire the audience on multiple levels. A production that seems to serve the actor only is likely to also be limited in terms of therapeutic benefit. It is through the process of elevating the aesthetic level of the production—including excavating inner material, expanding and then chiseling and editing, discovering original and potent modes of communication and then refining these—that one achieves clarity and mastery. The aesthetic and therapeutic strands are thus intertwined.

A related pitfall is stagnation, a kind of stage repetition of one's life script, in which theatre mirrors—without *illuminating*—real life. Self-revelatory performance is theatrically and therapeutically powerful when there is a sense of movement and transition, of striving toward new territory or understanding, and when experience is viewed from a wide angle as well as a telephoto lens, from multifarious perspectives and realms of consciousness. The actor must examine himself both from the inside out and from the outside in.

Humor is one way of manifesting perspective and of reaching for universality. Emotional stories achieve an aesthetic balance when laced with humor. The introjection of humor increases the tolerance on the part of both actor and audience for intense self-revelation. Humor in performance serves not just as a respite from emotionality; the poignancy of the actor's struggle is heightened when the audience sees that the actor can pull back enough from his pain to laugh at himself or at the way his situation relates to that of others. (This use of humor to heighten poignancy works only when the actor's sense of humor is a demonstration of strength, rather than of defensiveness.) In *Healing Fiction,* James Hillman (1983) writes: "The best entry into imperfection is humor, self-irony, dissolving into laughter, the acceptable humiliation that requires no compensation upwards. The sense of imperfection may be one way into communal feeling: another surer one is the all-too-human bond of the sense of humor" (p. 109).

A combination of structure and improvisation is most conducive to self-revelatory performance. The structure is a necessary part of the aesthetic organization and refinement of the piece. The retainment of an improvisational component heightens the sense of immediacy on stage. Witnessing a person on stage not only communicating but struggling, *live,* with a real issue, is theatrically suspenseful. Improvisation helps the actor to stay *in the present moment,* a state that is important in any performance but particularly critical in self-revelatory performance.

Improvisation also facilitates a dynamic process between the actor and the performance piece: The performance continuously affects and informs the person's life, and the changes in the person's life affect and inform the performance. In essence, the performance and the performer's personal process evolve concomitantly. In Jamie's scene (described in Chapter 9), new lines were frequently spoken during performances. In one performance, Jamie suddenly shouted at his suicidal voices, "So what if I'm gay!" For the first time, he connected the personal rejection by his mother and the larger rejection by society to his homosexuality. More strikingly, this new line reflected Jamie's increased acceptance of himself and his sexuality, a sexuality that until then he had kept secret. Once ready to *come out,* Jamie found the ultimate form in which to do so: on stage, in front of many people, forever marking the moment in which he publicly affirmed his sexual identity.

Though a public event, theatre is highly intimate. In each performance, there is a unique interaction between actor/s and audience. "The performance is a happening. It is the intrinsically poetic moment; the moment when, with the spectator's presence contributing the final drop, the chemical precipitate appears. The performance is an act of love . . ." claims Jean-Louis Barrault (in Aaron, 1986, p. 104). In self-revelatory performance, the subtle actor-audience interaction expands into a sense of communion. Following performances by *Beyond Analysis,* audiences were invited to mingle with the actors in the theatre's gallery. The most common comments were expressions of kinship with the actors and a feeling of unexpected identification with the actors' struggles. Most people came to see a play about foreigners—people whose experiences they knew little about—and found instead a way back to their own inner pain and joy.

Despite explicit indications in self-revelatory theatre that the material is drawn from real life, audiences still frequently ask whether what they have witnessed on stage was true. This surprising question comes from the long-term association between theatre and fiction. When there is no fiction, the emotional catharsis that the theatre has always sanctioned is intensified. In the darkened, communal, sacred theatrical space, the audience can cry together for the pain of the people on stage, for their own pain, for the human condition. *Inside Out* was attended by many psychiatrists who claimed that after years of building a kind of immunization to the pain of their patients (a professional safeguard in long-term work with people's problems), the play enabled them to see the actor/patients' reality with fresh eyes and, for the first time in many years, to cry.

For the actors, the sense of kinship and shared emotionality with the audience brings about a sense of connectedness with the outside world. This connectedness is especially significant for people who have experienced themselves as different or alien, who have been institutionalized or segregated. The combination of the feelings of connectedness, accomplishment, and acceptance, in conjunction with the ensuing rush of love for one's fellow actors and director with whom one has shared the entire journey, is awesome. As the actors walk off the stage, with the applause of the audience still flooding their ears, they experience a rare and sacred sensation: glory.

But this glory is short-lived. As the actors exit the theatrical stage, they unknowingly enter a new therapeutic stage, a stage that is to present the greatest challenge yet: dealing with post-performance depression and the integration of success.

11

POST-PERFORMANCE DEPRESSION AND THE INTEGRATION OF SUCCESS

The theatrical performance is a climactic event, bringing forth a tremendous sense of release, exhilaration, and fulfillment. But treading on the heels of this intense rush of excitement is a feeling of emptiness. The months of exhaustive preparation preceding the culmination have filled, if not taken over, the actors' lives. In some ways similar to postpartum depression, the letdown following the completion of a work of art is familiar to artists of all disciplines. Once the finished art product is *set free,* the artist is left depleted and must again face the "blank slate," without knowing when or whether the creative impulse or opportunity will reappear. The transitory nature of performance accentuates the feeling of emptiness; when a performance ends, the product ceases to exist, etherealizing the actor's sense of accomplishment. Moreover, the collaborative process inherent in theatre, fostering intimacy and emotional bonding with one's fellow actors, makes the loss at the conclusion of the performance all the more formidable.

In self-revelatory performance, there is yet another component, compounding the post-performance experience. The sharing of aspects of one's real life via the theatrical mode impels mastery and empowerment. One not only creatively communicates pain and struggle, but manifests the transitions one is currently undergoing or pursuing. The theatrical act helps to concretize and integrate the transitions, resulting in a modification in self-image. With special populations, the on-stage manifestations of life transitions combined with the victory of performing in a successful play beget not a subtle modification but a dramatic alteration in self-image. This alteration is especially profound with people who have a negative self-image and a long history of failures.

The alteration in self-image is also influenced by the sense of power that comes from evoking strong feelings in an audience. One is an actor, not a spectator, an activator, not a victim. One is capable of eliciting laughter, tears, and reflection (Emunah & Johnson, 1983). For people who have felt power-less, who have been the *recipients* of care rather than the givers, the role of actor is extremely potent.

Once the performance ends, however, the new positive self-image is threatened. In fact, "taking apart the stage set, clearing away props and cos-tumes, and witnessing the now empty performance space devoid of audience or life becomes associated in the patient's mind with disintegration or de-struction of the new self-image" (Emunah & Johnson, 1983, p. 237). Post-performance depression in conjunction with the fear of losing the new self-image can lead to social withdrawal, substance abuse, or acting-out behavior. In work with people with a psychiatric history, brief rehospitalizations and even suicide attempts are not uncommon (Johnson, 1980; Emunah & Johnson, 1983). The realization that the performance—however potent—has not altered one's external situation (family, finances, housing, etc.) further contributes to the post-performance letdown.

The extreme stress revolves not only around the prospective dissolution of the new self-image but, more complexly, the feared annihilation of the previous negative self-image. Success is unfamiliar territory, contradictory to one's prior experience. Success is also experienced, usually on an uncon-scious level, as burdensome; the person dreads the higher expectations that will now be placed on her. It is as though the victory of the performance is too much to have to continue to live up to. An internal battle with success ensues. This battle occurs in its most dramatic and potentially deleterious form both in the weeks prior to the performance—as one approaches the possibility of success (and may attempt to sabotage this possibility)—and in the weeks following the performance. After the performance, when the success is real rather than imagined, the old self may attempt to reassert itself, as a way of dealing with the confusion between the two self-images.

The struggle with post-performance depression and the integration of the new self-image yields fertile therapeutic ground, requiring the drama thera-pist's utmost attentiveness. The performance must be viewed as one part of the overall process—a climax, not a finale. The experience of the cast mem-bers after the performance period needs to be validated and assimilated. The provision of a high level of support and structure diminishes the likelihood of self-destructive behavior. An intensive schedule of sessions is recommended, to parallel the intensity of the pre-performance rehearsal stage. The emphases in these post-performance sessions are on sharing feelings and concerns and on celebrating the collective accomplishment. The sharing of feelings occurs through both verbal and dramatic processes. The celebration involves special outings and rewards, along with dramatic rituals, marking the climactic event. Given the transitory nature of performance, tangible reminders of achievement are important. These typically include videotapes and photographs of the performance, reviews and articles about the production, and dramatic reenactments related to the performance event. Finally, the continued experience of intimacy and bondedness with one's cohort is a critical component of the post-performance stage.

The post-performance period, with its foci on closure and celebration, corresponds to Phase Five of a drama therapy treatment series. The process the group has undergone is reviewed and encapsulated in its entirety. The recognition by the drama therapist of the challenges and growth the whole experience has entailed for the client/actor, along with her recognition of both new and old self-images, help foster the integrative process. Past self and newly evolving self are witnessed concurrently, reducing the client/actor's need to disown either one.

The post-performance period may involve a gradual tapering off of performances. The run of public performances by *Beyond Analysis* was followed by intermittent smaller performances at institutions, festivals, and conferences. A slow transition—from an intense performance schedule to a cessation of all performances—tends to ease the process of dealing with post-performance depression and the integration of success. On the other hand, the opportunity to extend a run or "take the show on the road," when this entails an increased level of responsibility and commitment rather than a progressive decrease, can be countertherapeutic. Such opportunities reflect the success of the production, but often generate a conflict for the client/actors, and hence a conflict for the drama therapist between the roles of director and therapist. To a director, the opportunity of expanding and refining the production and having it be seen by more people is appealing. To a therapist, the psychological implications inherent in such an opportunity warrant careful consideration. Increased demands can exacerbate the client/actors' anxieties regarding the expectations that accompany success. The client/actors fear that others will perceive them now as having "made it," and will no longer see how vulnerable they still feel inwardly. They also fear that their tenuous hold on success may be jeopardized; with ongoing performances, ultimate failure continues to lurk as a possibility. Only after the final performance can they definitively say, "I did it!"

This definitive statement of success and closure—"I did it!"—is a necessary precursor to the capacity to embark on new projects. Eventually the success experienced in this endeavor provides the confidence and impetus to start other ventures outside of the group. Many members of *Beyond*

Analysis auditioned for plays in community theatres or obtained part-time jobs during the months following the public performances. Though the performance itself does not alter one's external reality, an integrative post-performance period can lead one to make positive life changes.

In sum, the success that has been experienced by the first round of performances needs to be assimilated before the cast can be asked to go further with this same project. The group members need time to catch up with the success of the product they created. They need to catch up with the victory of accomplishment, the victory of being part of a close-knit group, and the victories displayed within their particular scenes. The onstage manifestations of life changes need to be lived offstage, incorporated into real-life experience. In a scene from *Inside Out,* described in Chapter 9, Jamie fights voices—which he refers to as Rocky—urging him to commit suicide. One evening, about two months after the final public performance, Jamie was rejected by a new lover and the voices returned. He came to the following session with a look of triumph on his face. "Rocky came back last night," he reported, "but I pretended I was in my scene, and Rocky ran away, scared shitless!"

"I can play scenes in drama better than I can play scenes in my life," says Jamie, the client quoted in the first sentence of *Acting for Real.* And six months later, he states: "The way I'm acting in my life now is catching up with the way I act in drama." Like Stacey and Karin, Christine and Shawn, and so many other clients whose words have elucidated the nature of drama therapy, Jamie's stage acts eventually translated into life acts. And it was the person he had become through dramatic performance that carried him forth into the next stage of his life.

Epilogue

The focus of this book has been on the fundamental concepts, processes, and techniques of drama therapy, with an emphasis on work with groups in psychiatric treatment. However, the applications and impact of drama therapy span a much wider spectrum, from the individual to the community, and from the clinical setting to the real world.

Drama Therapy with Individuals

Though drama therapy is most commonly conducted in groups (due to the collective nature of drama as an art form and to the tradition within creative arts therapies of group work), there is an increasing interest in its use in in-depth individual and family treatment. The use of drama therapy with individuals provides an active, creative, and playful approach to psychotherapy, in which the client's emotional and physical engagement in the healing process is as nurtured as his mental engagement. Role play and dramatic processes can be seamlessly integrated into traditional verbal therapy; enactments stimulate discussion and discussion prompts enactment. Each mode amplifies the other, helping the client enter deeper realms of feeling and awareness.

The movement from one mode to another need not be abrasive. For example, a client begins to describe a disturbing phone conversation he had the previous evening with his father and is handed a telephone by the therapist, who suggests he show rather than tell what transpired. The dramatic mode puts the client into the present and facilitates a connectedness to his *emotional* experience. The phone call may be hypothetical rather than a replay of a real event; the client expresses to his father feelings he otherwise would have verbally communicated to the therapist. In either case, the dramatic process brings real life, or real-life feelings — with all their nuances — more fully into the session. A significant by-product is that the therapist, who becomes audience to or player in the client's life drama, is likely to experience a heightened degree of empathy.

Drama therapy with individuals is not limited to the clinical arena. The instincts and wisdom of children, who spontaneously integrate dramatic play into their lives, can remind us all of the value of this accessible art form. Throughout the life cycle, we should have the freedom to try on new roles; to put ourselves in someone else's shoes; to actively express feelings; to revive dormant parts of ourselves; to play and to dream; to preview, review, and rehearse life.

Actors know the healing effect their craft has on their lives. Actress Geraldine Page, interviewed by psychologist Brian Bates (1987), states that "acting is a release; it is a way of taking anguish and making something beautiful out of it." Bates adds: "Actors recover and use those experiences which most of us never confront. . . . inevitably actors allow more of themselves into their conscious lives—negative as well as positive aspects" (p. 66). Articulating the significance of acting for personal growth, Bates says: "Simply walking as someone else makes the world look and feel different. But to interact with others as a changed person—a character transformed—is an enlightening experience. . . . A change in persona can change your life" (p. 94).

Drama Therapy with Families

The use of drama therapy with families is in some ways an extension of what many family therapists have already discovered—that an active approach to treatment, in which dramatic techniques and role play are incorporated, elicits important information and enlivens the therapy session. Moreover, nonverbal and creative processes help bridge the age gaps beween members of the family.

The roles we play in life stem from the roles cultivated within our family of origin. Recognition of these roles—as we are playing them in our families—may have a profound effect on our development. The examination by all family members of their roles and unconsciously collaborative scripts, along with ongoing revision of these, could be a way of growing up healthy. Awareness, expressiveness, and flexibility—key ingredients in mental health—can be developed and nurtured outside of the clinical context, in the home. What if couples reversed roles in the middle of heated arguments? Reenacted the first time they met? Improvised future scenarios? What if children played parents for a day and parents became their children? Or if all family members periodically molded each other (as in Sculpting) according to their perspectives on the family dynamics? What if dinners were followed by charades, and instead of acting out movies each member pantomimed the most significant feelings or experiences of the day? Or enacted significant world events? What if dramatic rituals and rites of passage, as the Blatners recommend in The Art of Play (1988), were thoughtfully constructed and woven into the family's fabric of life?

Drama Therapy in the Community

Drama therapy can be applied not only to individuals, families, and groups, but to communities. Contemporary communities are often factionalized; fears, hostilities, and prejudices abound. A sense of alienation pervades urban cities. Gang wars and drug wars are killing minority youth. With the decline of the extended family, the gaps between the generations have widened. Older people are stigmatized and isolated. Drama therapy provides a means of breaking barriers, promoting understanding and respect, exploring differences, and celebrating commonalities.

Drama therapy draws upon and expands the field of sociodrama. Groups in the community come together not only to psychodramatically tackle specific social issues but simply to interact in new ways and to find artistic means of expressing their concerns. The interaction and sharing first occur within the group itself and then extend to the public, via performance. In the San Francisco Bay area, drama therapist Armand Volkas brings together Jewish children of holocaust survivors and Germans of the post-war generation; "Teens Kick Off" performs plays by teenagers about substance abuse; Stagebridge Theatre Company produces plays that dispel stereotypes about aging—the cast is composed of people over 70.

During a time in which countless children are being sexually abused, growing numbers of people are dying of AIDS, and millions are left homeless and penniless, the need to face ourselves, expose our secrets, and find compassion if not solutions is paramount. In the shared communal space of the theatre, communities can bear witness to themselves and become empowered to make changes.

Drama Therapy in Society—A Dream

The applications and impact of drama therapy extend beyond communities. One of the greatest challenges facing the world today is achieving peace. Imagine dissonant factions within a country (or between countries) participating in joint drama therapy groups—from early childhood through adolescence. Group members comprised, for example, of Arabs and Israelis would regularly reverse roles, express their own pain and that of others in the group, share wishes and dreams, try out solutions, develop close and caring relationships with one another, and collaboratively create theatrical performances based on real-life matters.

Aggressive drives can sometimes be dramatically acted out rather than literally acted upon. Landy (1986) relates the story of a man who tried to plan a global drama, in which a nuclear war was to be enacted as a creative way of preventing the real event. Landy says: "If a gun fires and a bullet is discharged, destruction can follow. If a gun fires and a flag appears that says "Bang!" the violent impulse is discharged in laughter. If we were all to enact our personal and political wars in play, perhaps we, too, could circumvent the actual consequences of destructive action" (p. 235).

Drama therapists may never be invited to facilitate role reversals between diplomats or to shout "Freeze!" in the midst of arms negotiation talks, but their skills and tools may nonetheless one day be incorporated into the political arena. While drama therapists are not specialists in international affairs, they are specialists in helping people to see each other's perspective, identify patterns, explore history and project into the future, find alternative ways of responding, move from intellectualization to emotional connection or from emotionality to objective reflectivity. I believe that these areas of expertise are applicable both to the individual and to society. Drama therapy involves not only personal healing but collective transformation.

There are people who have solidified into a single role and others whose roles are forever unfolding and expanding. Vibrant, ageless people are ones who change throughout their lives, allowing roles to dissolve and be reshaped, experiences to be deeply affecting, and perceptions to be altered. "The important thing," says Marat in the play *Marat/Sade* (Weiss,1970), ". . . is to turn yourself inside out, and see the world with fresh eyes" (p. 46).

Whether applied to individuals, families, groups, communities, or societies, drama therapy implies loosening the ties that bind us and limit our evolution. At the heart of drama therapy is the experience of liberation, expansion, and perspective. The essence of drama therapy is uncovering and integrating dormant aspects of ourselves, enlarging our conception of who we are, and finding our intrinsic connection with others.

Acting for real is not acting to entertain, escape, or mislead; it is acting for release, discovery, and renewal. Acting for real means acting fully, acting feelingly, and acting knowingly—drawing from our depths and stretching to our heights, beginning in the safe, contained drama therapy session and extending into the wide open stage of real life.

References

Aaron, S. (1986). *Stage fright: Its role in acting*. Chicago: University of Chicago Press.

Adler, A. (1924). Progress in individual psychology. *British Journal of Medical Psychology*, 4: 22–31.

Adler, A. (1939). *Social interest: A challenge to mankind*. New York: Putnam.

Adler, A. (1963). *The practice and theory of individual psychology*. Paterson, New Jersey: Littlefield, Adams.

Adler, J. (1969). *Looking for me*. 16mm film. Distributer: Berkeley Extension Media Center, University of California, Berkeley, CA.

Alexander, F. & French, T. M. (1946). *Psychoanalytic therapy: Principles and applications*. New York: The Rothald Press.

Artaud, A. (1958). *The theatre and its double*. (M. C. Richards, Trans.). New York: Grove Press.

Barker, C. (1977). *Theatre games*. London: Methuen.

Barnett, M. (1973). *People not psychiatry*. London: Allen and Unwin.

Bates, B. (1987). *The Way of the actor: A path to knowledge and power*. Boston: Shambhala.

Beck, A. (1976). *Cognitive therapy and the emotional disorders*. New York: International Universities Press.

Blatner, A. (1988a). *Acting in: Practical applications of psychodramatic methods* (2nd ed.). New York: Springer Publishing.

Blatner, A. (1988b). *Foundations of psychodrama: History, theory, and practice* (with A. Blatner) (3rd ed.). New York: Springer Publishing.

Blatner, A. (1991). Role dynamics: A comprehensive theory of psychology. *Journal of Group Psychotherapy, Psychodrama, and Sociometry*, 44: 33–40.

Blatner, A. & Blatner, A. (1988). *The art of play: An adult's guide to reclaiming imagination and spontaneity*. New York: Human Sciences.

Blatner, A. & Blatner, A. (1991). Imaginative interviews: A psychodramatic warm-up for developing role-playing skills. *Journal of Group Psychotherapy, Psychodrama, and Sociometry*. 44: 115–120.

Bradshaw, J. (1988). *Bradshaw on the family: A revolutionary way of self-discovery*. Pompano Beach, FL: Health Communications.

Brook, P. (1968). *The empty space*. London: MacGibbor and Kee.

Buhler, C. (1962). *Values in psychotherapy*. New York: Free Press of Glencoe.

Butler, L. & Allison, L. (1978). PlaySpace. Unpublished pamphlet. (Available from PlaySpace, Polytechnic of Central London, 309 Regent St., London W1R 8AL, England).

Campbell, J. (1988). *The power of myth* (with B. Moyers). New York: Doubleday.

Chaikin, J. (1984). *The presence of the actor*. New York: Antheum.

Cole, D. (1975). *The theatrical event: A mythos, a vocabulary, a perspective*. Middletown, CT: Wesleyan University Press.

Collomb, H. (1977). Psychosis in an African society. In C. Chailand (Ed.), *Long-term treatments of psychotic states*. New York: Human Sciences.

Corey, G. (1986) *Theory and practice of counseling and psychotherapy*. Monterey, CA: Brooks/Cole Pub. Co.

Corsini, R. & Wedding, D. (1989). *Current psychotherapies* (4th ed.). Itasca, IL: F. E. Peacock.

303

Courtney, R. (1964). *Drama for youth: A handbook for young people in youth clubs and schools*. London: Pitman.

Courtney, R. (1967). *The Drama studio: Architecture and equipment for dramatic education*. London: Pitman.

Courtney, R. (1968). *Play, drama, and thought: The intellectual background to drama in education*. London: Cassell.

Dass, R. (1989). *The listening heart*. Paper presented at the California School of Professional Psychology Colloquium Series, Alameda, CA.

Dayton, T. (1990). *Drama games: Techniques for self-development*. Deerfield Beach, Fl.: Health Communications, Inc.

Deikman, A. (1982). *The observing self: Mysticism and psychotherapy*. Boston: Beacon.

Dequine, E. & Pearson-Davis, S. (1983). Videotaped improvisational drama with emotionally disturbed adolescents. *The Arts in Psychotherapy*, 10: 15–21.

Ellmann, R. (1969). *The artist as critic: Critical writings of Oscar Wilde*. New York: Random House.

Emunah, R. (1983). Drama therapy with adult psychiatric patients. *The Arts in Psychotherapy*, 10: 77–84.

Emunah, R. (1985). Drama therapy and adolescent resistance. *The Arts in Psychotherapy*, 12: 71–80.

Emunah, R. (1989). The use of dramatic enactment in the training of drama therapists. *The Arts in Psychotherapy*, 16: 29–36.

Emunah, R. (1990). Expression and expansion in adolescence: The significance of creative arts therapy. *The Arts in Psychotherapy*, 17: 101–107.

Emunah, R. & Johnson, D. R. (1983). The impact of theatrical performance on the self images of psychiatric patients. *The Arts in Psychotherapy*, 10: 233–239.

Erikson, E. (1950). *Childhood and society*. New York: Norton.

Erikson, E. (1958). The nature of clinical evidence. In D. Lerner (Ed.), *Evidence and inference*. Glencoe, Ill.: The Free Press.

Fluegelman, A. (1976). *The new games book*. Garden Way, NY: Dolphin Book.

Ford, D. & Urban, H. (1963). *Systems of psychotherapy: A comparative study*. New York: Wiley.

Fox, J. (1981). Playback theatre: The community sees itself. In G. Schattner & R. Courtney (Eds.), *Drama in therapy, Vol. 2* (pp. 295–306). New York: Drama Book Specialists.

Fox, J. (Ed.). (1987). *The essential Moreno: Writings on psychodrama, group method, and spontaneity*. New York: Springer Publishing.

Freud, A. (1928). *Introduction to the technique of child analysis*. New York: Nervous and Mental Disease.

Gadon, E. (1989) *The once and future goddess: A symbol for our time*. New York: Harper & Row.

Gallantz, M. (1981, May–June). *ArtBeat Magazine*, p. 28.

Gardner, R. (1981). Dramatized storytelling in child psychotherapy. In G. Schattner & R. Courtney (Eds.), *Drama in Therapy, Vol. 1*. New York: Drama Book Specialists.

Gersie, A. (1991). *Storymaking in bereavement: Dragons fight in the meadow*. London: Jessica Kingsley.

Gersie, A. & King, N. (1990). *Storymaking in education and therapy*. London: Jessica Kingsley.

Goffman, E. (1959). *The presentation of self in everyday life*. Garden City, NY: Doubleday.

Goffman, E. (1961). *Encounters: Two studies in the sociology of interaction*. Indianapolis: Bobbs-Merrill.

Goffman, E. (1967). *Interaction ritual: Essays on face-to-face behavior*. Garden City, NY: Anchor Books.

Goldman, E. & Morrison, D. (1984). *Psychodrama: Experience and process*. Phoenix, AR: Eldemar Corp.

Grotowski, J. (1968). *Towards a poor theatre*. New York: Simon and Schuster.

Haley, J. (1973). *Uncommon therapy: The psychiatric techniques of Milton H. Erickson, M.D.* (1st ed.). New York: Norton.

Haley, J. (1980). *Leaving Home: The therapy of disturbed young people.* New York: McGraw-Hill.

Halifax, J. (1982). *Shaman, the wounded healer.* New York: Crossroad.

Hillman, J. (1983). *Healing fiction.* Barrytown, NY: Station Hill Press.

Hodgson, J. & Richards, E. (1967). *Improvisation.* London: Methuen.

Horney, K. (1939). *New ways in psychoanalysis.* New York: Norton.

Irwin, E. (1981). Play, fantasy, and symbols: Drama with emotionally disturbed children. In G. Schattner & R. Courtney (Eds.), *Drama in therapy, Vol. 1.* New York: Drama Book Specialists.

Irwin, E. (1983). The diagnostic and therapeutic use of pretend-play. In Schaefer, Charles, & K. O'Conner (Eds.), *Handbook of play therapy.* New York: Wiley.

Irwin, E. & Shapiro, M. (1975). Puppetry as a diagnostic and therapeutic technique. In I. Jakob (Ed.), *Transcultural aspects of psychiatric art,* Vol. 4. Basel, Kargero.

Jennings, S. (1983). Models of practice in dramatherapy. *Dramatherapy,* 7: #1: 3–8.

Jennings, S. (Ed.). (1987). *Dramatherapy: Theory and practice for teachers and clinicians.* Cambridge: Brookline Books.

Jennings, S. (1990). *Dramatherapy with families, groups, and individuals: Waiting in the wings.* London: Jessica Kingsley

Johnson, D. R. (1980). Effects of a theatre experience on hospitalized psychiatric patients. *The Arts in Psychotherapy,* 7: 265–272.

Johnson, D. R. (1981). Some diagnostic implications of drama therapy. In G. Schattner & R. Courtney (Eds.), *Drama in therapy: Vol. 2.* New York: Drama Book Specialists.

Johnson, D. R. (1982a). Principles and techniques of drama therapy. *The Arts in Psychotherapy,* 9: 83–90.

Johnson, D. R. (1982b). Developmental approaches to drama therapy. *The Arts in Psychotherapy,* 9: 183–189.

Johnson, D. R. (1984). Representation of the internal world in catatonic schizophrenia. *Psychiatry,* 47: 299–314.

Johnson, D. R. (1986). The developmental method in drama therapy: Group treatment with the elderly. *The Arts in Psychotherapy,* 13: 17–33.

Johnson, D. R. (1991). The theory and technique of transformations in drama therapy. *The Arts in Psychotherapy,* 18: 285–300.

Johnson, D. R. (1992). Drama therapy in role. In S. Jennings (Ed.), *Drama therapy: Theory and practice. Vol. 2.* London: Routledge.

Johnson, D. R. & Munich, R. (1975). Increasing hospital-community contact through a theater program in a psychiatric hospital. *Hospital and Community Psychiatry,* 26: 435–438.

Johnson, L. (1990). Perspective: Creative arts therapies in the treatment of addictions: The art of transforming shame. *The Arts in Psychotherapy,* 17: 299–308.

Johnstone, K. (1989). *Impro.* London: Routledge.

Jung, C. (1964). *Man and his symbols.* Garden City, NY: Doubleday.

Kahn, M. (1991). *Between therapist and client: The new relationship.* New York: W. H. Freeman.

Keen, S. & Valley-Fox, A. (1989). *Your mythic journey: Finding meaning in your life through writing and storytelling.* Los Angeles: Jeremy P. Tarcher.

King, N. (1975). *Giving form to feeling.* New York: Drama Book Specialists.

Kipper, D. A. (1986). *Psychotherapy through clinical role playing.* New York: Brunner/Mazel.

Klein, M. (1932). *The psycho-analysis of children* (A. Strachey, Trans.). London: Hogarth Press.

Kohut, H. (1971). *The analysis of the self: A systematic approach to the psychoanalytic treatment of narcissistic personality disorders.* New York: International Universities Press.

Kohut, H. (1984). *How does analysis cure?* (A. Goldberg, Ed.). Chicago: University of Chicago Press.

Laplanche, J. & Pontalis, J. (1973). *The language of psychoanalysis.* New York: Norton.
LaBerge, S. (1985). *Lucid dreaming.* New York: Ballantine Books.
Landy, R. (1986). *Drama therapy: Concepts and practices.* Springfield, IL: C.C. Thomas.
Landy, R. (1990). The concept of role in drama therapy. *The Arts in Psychotherapy,* 17: 223–230.
Landy, R. (1993). *Persona and performance: The meaning of role in theatre, therapy, and everyday life.* New York: Guilford.
Langley, D. (1983). *Dramatherapy and psychiatry.* London: Croom Helm.
Leveton, E. (1991). *A clinician's guide to psychodrama* (2nd ed.). New York: Springer Publishing.
Lowenfeld, M. (1935). *Play in childhood.* London: V. Gollancz.
Mahler, M. (1975). *The psychological birth of the human infant: Symbiosis and individuation.* New York: Basic Books.
Mangham, I. (1978). *Interactions and interventions in organizations.* New York: Wiley.
Maslow, A. (1967). The creative attitude. In R. Mooney & T. Razik (Eds.), *Explorations in creativity.* New York: Harper and Row.
Maslow, A. (1968). *Toward a psychology of being* (2nd ed.). Princeton, NJ: Van Nostrand Reinhold.
Maslow, A. (1971). *The farther reaches of human nature.* New York: Viking Press.
May, R. (1961). *Existential psychology.* New York: Random House.
May, R. (1975). *The courage to create.* New York: Norton.
McCall, G. J. & Simmons, J. L. (1978). *Identities and interactions: An examination of human associations in everyday life.* (Rev. ed.). New York: Free Press.
McNiff, S. (1988). The shaman within. *The Arts in Psychotherapy,* 15: 285–291.
Mead, G. H. (1934). *Mind, self and society from the standpoint of a social science behaviorist.* Chicago, IL: University of Chicago Press.
Miller, A. (1983) *For your own good: Hidden creativity in child-rearing and the roots of violence* (H. Hannum & H. Hannum, Trans.). New York: Farrer, Straus, Giroux.
Miller, A. (1986). *Thou shalt not be aware: Society's betrayal of the child.* New York: Meridian Books.
Minuchin, S. (1974). *Families and family therapy.* Cambridge, MA: Harvard University Press.
Moffett, L. & Bruto, L. (1990). Therapeutic theatre with personality-disordered substance abusers: Characters in search of different characters. *The Arts in Psychotherapy,* 17: 339–348.
Moreno, J. (1941). *The words of the father.* Beacon, NY: Beacon House.
Moreno, J. (Ed.) (1945). *Group psychotherapy: A symposium.* Beacon, NY: Beacon House.
Moreno, J. (1946). *Psychodrama: Vol. 1.* Beacon, NY: Beacon House.
Moreno, J. (1953). *Who shall survive? Foundations of sociometry, group psychotherapy and sociodrama* (2nd ed.). Beacon, NY: Beacon House.
Moreno, J. (1959). *Psychodrama: Vol. 2.* Beacon, NY: Beacon House.
Moreno, J. (1969). *Psychodrama: Vol. 3* (with Z. Moreno). Beacon, NY: Beacon House.
Moreno, J. (1972). In J. Hodgson (Ed.), *The uses of drama: Sources giving a background to acting as a social and educational force.* London: Methuen.
Moustakas, (1966). *The authentic teacher: Sensitivity and awareness in the classroom.* Cambridge, MA: Doyle.
Moustakas, (1967). *Creativity and conformity.* Princeton, NJ: Van Nostrand.
Petitti, G. (1989). Video as an externalizing object in drama therapy. *The Arts in Psychotherapy,* 16: 121–126.
Piaget, J. (1962). *Play, dreams and imitation in childhood.* London: Routledge and Kegan Paul.
Pitzele, P. (1991). Adolescents inside out: Intrapsychic psychodrama. In P. Holmes & M. Karp (Eds.), *Psychodrama: Inspiration and technique.* London: Tavistock/Routledge.
Robbins, A. (1988). A psychoaesthetic perspective on creative arts therapy and training. *The Arts in Psychotherapy,* 15: 95–100.

Rogers, C. (1951). *Client-centered therapy: Its current practice, implications and theory.* Boston: Houghton Mifflin.

Rogers, C. (1961). *On becoming a person: A therapist's view of psychotherapy.* Boston: Houghton Mifflin.

Roose-Evans, J. (1970). *Experimental theatre from Stanislavski to today.* New York: Universe Books.

Rossi, E. (1985). *Dreams and the growth of personality: Expanding awareness in psychotherapy* (2nd ed). New York: Brunner/Mazel.

Russell, J. (1975). Personal growth through structured group exercises. In R. Suinn & R. Weigel (Eds.), *The innovative psychological therapies: Critical and creative contributions.* New York: Harper and Row.

Ryan, P. (1976). Theatre as prison therapy. *The Drama Review.* 20: 31–42.

Sarbin, T. (Ed.). (1986). *Narrative psychology.* New York: Praeger.

Sarbin, T. & Allen, V. (1968). Role theory. In G. Lindzey & E. Aronson (Eds.), *The handbook of social psychology* (2nd ed.). Reading, Mass: Addison-Wesley.

Satir, V. (1988). *The new peoplemaking.* Mountain View, CA: Science and Behavior Books.

Schattner, G. & Courtney, R. (1981). *Drama in therapy, Vols. 1 & 2.* New York: Drama Book Specialists.

Schechner, R. (1973). *Environmental theater.* New York: Hawthorn.

Scheff, T. (1981). The distancing of emotion in psychotherapy. *Psychotherapy: Theory, Research and Practice,* 18: 46–53.

Schön, D. (1983). *The reflective practitioner: How professionals think in action.* New York: Basic Books.

Schutz, W. (1967). *Joy: Expanding human awareness.* New York: Grove Press.

Seabourne, B. (1963). The action sociogram. *Group Psychotherapy,* 16: 145–155.

Slade, P. (1954). *Child drama.* London: University of London Press.

Spolin, V. (1982). *Theatre game file.* Evanston, IL: Northwestern University Press.

Spolin, V. (1983). *Improvisation for the theatre: A handbook of teaching and directing techniques.* Evanston, IL: Northwestern University Press.

Spolin, V. (1985). *Theatre games for rehearsal: A director's handbook.* Evanston, IL: Northwestern University Press.

Spolin, V. (1986). *Theatre games for the classroom: A teacher's handbook.* Evanston, IL: Northwestern University Press.

Stanislavski, C. (1924). *My life in art.* Boston: Little, Brown.

Stanislavski, C. (1936). *An actor prepares.* New York: Theatre Arts.

Sternberg, P. & Garcia, A. (1989). *Sociodrama: Who's in your shoes.* New York: Praeger.

Strauss, P. & Goldfischer, M. (1988). *Why me? Coping with grief, loss, and change.* New York: Bantam.

Wagner, B. (1976). *Dorothy Heathcote: Drama as a learning medium.* Washington, DC: National Education Association.

Ward, W. (1957). *Playmaking with children from kindergarten through junior high school* (2nd ed.). Englewood Cliffs, NJ: Prentice Hall.

Warren, B. (1984). Drama: Using imagination as a stepping-stone for personal growth. In B. Warren (Ed.), *Using the creative arts in therapy.* Cambridge, Mass.: Brookline Books.

Way, B. (1967). *Development through drama.* London: Longmans.

Weathers, L., Bedell, J., Marlowe, H., Gordon, R., Adams, J., Reed, V., Palmer, J., Gordon, K. (1981). Using psychotherapeutic games to train patients' skills. In R. Gordon & K. Gordon (Eds.), *Systems of treatment for the mentally ill.* New York: Grune and Stratton.

Weiss, P. (1970). *The persecution and assassination of Jean-Paul Marat as performed by the inmates of the asylum of Charenton under the direction of the Marquis de Sade.* (6th ed.). New York: Pocket Books.

Wethered, A. (1973). *Drama and movement in therapy: The therapeutic use of movement, drama and music.* London: McDonald and Evans.

Willet, J. (Ed.). (1964). *Brecht on theatre.* New York: Hill and Wang.

Winnicott, D. W. (1958). *Collected papers, through paediatrics to psycho-analysis.* New York: Basic Books.

Winnicott, D. W. (1960). The theory of the parent-infant relationship. *Maturational Processes,* 37–55.

Yablonski, L. (1975). *Psychodrama: Resolving emotional problems through role-playing.* New York: Basic Books.

Yalom, I. (1985). *The theory and practice of group psychotherapy* (3rd ed.). New York: Basic Books.

Zweben, J. & Hammann, K. (1970). Prescribed games: A theoretical perspective on the use of group techniques. *Psychotherapy: Theory, Research, and Practice,* 7 (1), 22–27.

Index